Studies in the History of Law and Justice

Volume 13

urpose of this book series is to publish high quality volumes on the history of nd justice.

gal history can be a deeply provocative and influential field, as illustrated by the th of the European universities and the *ius commune*, the French Revolution, American Revolution, and indeed all the great movements for national liberation ugh law. The study of history gives scholars and reformers the models and rage to question entrenched injustices, by demonstrating the contingency of law and er social arrangements.

Yet legal history today finds itself diminished in the universities and legal ademy. Too often scholarship betrays no knowledge of what went before, or why gal institutions took the shape they did. This series seeks to remedy that eficiency.

Studies in the History of Law and Justice will be theoretical and reflective. Volumes will address the history of law and justice from a critical and comparative viewpoint. The studies in this series will be strong bold narratives of the development of law and justice. Some will be suitable for a very broad readership.

Contributions to this series will come from scholars on every continent and in every legal system. Volumes will promote international comparisons and dialogue. The purpose will be to provide the next generation of lawyers with the models and narratives needed to understand and improve the law and justice of their own era.

The series includes monographs focusing on a specific topic, as well as collections of articles covering a theme or collections of article by one author.

More information about this series at http://www.springer.com/series/11794

Stefan Huygebaert · Angela Condello
Sarah Marusek · Mark Antaki
Editors

Sensing the Nation's Law

Historical Inquiries into the Aesthetics of Democratic Legitimacy

Springer

Editors
Stefan Huygebaert
Department of Art History, Musicology and Theater Studies
Ghent Legal History Institute, Ghent University
Ghent
Belgium

and

Research Foundation—Flanders (FWO)
Flanders
Belgium

Angela Condello
Department of Law
University of Roma Tre
Rome
Italy

and

Department of Philosophy
University of Torino
Turin
Italy

Sarah Marusek
Department of Political Science
University of Hawai'i
Hilo, HI
USA

Mark Antaki
Faculty of Law
McGill University
Montreal, QC
Canada

ISSN 2198-9842 ISSN 2198-9850 (electronic)
Studies in the History of Law and Justice
ISBN 978-3-030-09246-7 ISBN 978-3-319-75497-0 (eBook)
https://doi.org/10.1007/978-3-319-75497-0

Softcover re-print of the Hardcover 1st edition 2018

Printed on acid-free paper

This Springer imprint is published by the registered company Springer International Publishing AG part of Springer Nature
The registered company address is: Gewerbestrasse 11, 6330 Cham, Switzerland

Acknowledgements

We would like to sing the praises of Desmond Manderson, who initially hosted the venue for this volume's inspiration, the Interpellations conference of the Law and Humanities Association of Australasia convened in Canberra at Australian National University in December 2013. As conference participants, we were inspired to further collaborate in order to continue the conference's intellectual creativity in this collection of work. We would also like to express our appreciation for the Springer team, the reviewers, editors for Studies in the History of Law and Justice, and all those involved in helping us to see this collection to completion.

Stefan Huygebaert
Angela Condello
Sarah Marusek
Mark Antaki

Contents

Editors and Contributors

About the Editors

Stefan Huygebaert is a Research Foundation Flanders (FWO) Ph.D. Fellow at the Ghent Legal History Institute and Department of Art History, Musicology and Theatre Studies (Ghent University). His dissertation, entitled *Visual Ideals of Law and Justice*, is an iconological study of legal imagery in nineteenth-century Belgium. In 2014–2015, and again in 2016–2017, he was a Ph.D. fellow (Stipendiat) within the Minerva Research Group *The Nomos of Images: Manifestation and Iconology of Law* at the Kunsthistorisches Insitut in Florenz (Max-Planck-Institut). He publishes and teaches on legal iconography and nineteenth-century art, and recently co-edited the catalogue for the exhibition *The Art of Law: Three Centuries of Justice Depicted* (Groeningemuseum, Bruges).

Angela Condello is Temporary Lecturer at the University of Roma Tre and Fellow Researcher at the University of Torino where she also directs LabOnt Law. She cooperates with the Human Rights Committee of the Italian Senate of the Republic. In 2015, she was Fernand Braudel Fellow (EHESS, CENJ) and in 2014 she was a Fellow at the Käte Hamburger Kolleg "Law as Culture". Until 2016, she was Guest Professor at the Law School of the University of Ghent. She teaches Law and Humanities at Roma Tre. She organizes the International Roundtables for the Semiotics of Law and is in the boards of Law Text Culture, Law and Literature. She is Associate Editor of *Brill Research Perspectives in Art and Law*. She recently received a *Jean Monnet* award.

Sarah Marusek, Ph.D. (University of Massachusetts Amherst 2008), is an Associate Professor of Public Law in the Department of Political Science at the University of Hawai'i at Hilo. Her research interests focus on sites of constitutive law, legal geography and legal semiotics that engage legal pluralist frameworks of everyday jurisprudence. She teaches courses in U.S. Constitutional law, legal studies and legal geography.

Mark Antaki, Ph.D. (University of California, Berkeley 2005), is an Associate Professor in the Faculty of Law at McGill University. His research interests focus on law and the humanities, law and language, as well as the history of ideas. He teaches courses in public and private law as well as legal theory. Some of his publications include: "Declining Accusation" in George Pavlich and Matthew P. Unger, eds., *Accusation: Creating Criminals* (Vancouver, UBC Press, 2016); "Un-stating Law" in Shauna Van Praagh, Lionel Smith and Helge Dedek, eds., *Stateless Law: Evolving Boundaries of a Discipline* (Burlington, VT: Ashgate, 2015); "'No Foundations'? " (2014) 11 No Foundations: Interdisciplinary Journal of Law and Justice 61–77; "Genre, Critique, and Human Rights" (2013) 82 University of Toronto Quarterly 974–996 (special issue on law and literature).

Contributors

Mark Antaki Faculty of Law, McGill University, Montreal, Canada

Angela Condello Department of Law, Roma Tre University and Department of Philosophy, University of Torino, Rome and Torino, Italy

Stefania Gialdroni Department of Law, Roma Tre University, Rome, Italy

Catherine Le Guerrier Faculty of Law, McGill University, Montreal, Canada

Nadirsyah Hosen Faculty of Law, Monash University, Clayton, VIC, Australia

Stefan Huygebaert Ghent Legal History Institute and Department of Art History, Musicology and Theater Studies, Ghent University and Research Foundation—Flanders (FWO), Ghent, Belgium

Desmond Manderson ANU College of Law, Australian National University, Canberra, Australia

Sarah Marusek Department of Political Science, University of Hawai'i, Hilo, USA

Richard Mohr Social Research Policy & Planning, Sydney, NSW, Australia

Paolo Napoli EHESS, CENJ, Paris, France

Anne Wagner Centre Droits et Perspectives du Droit, équipe René Demogue, Université Lille—Nord de France, Lille, France

Oliver Watts Sydney College of the Arts, Sydney, NSW, Australia

Chapter 1
Introduction

Mark Antaki, Angela Condello, Stefan Huygebaert and Sarah Marusek

Abstract We are said to live in an age of democratic legitimacy. The rightfulness of a political and legal order is meant to reside in a widespread belief in the rightfulness of democracy. Contemporary democratic legitimacy is tied, among other things, to consent, to representation, to the identity of ruler and ruled, and, of course, to legality and the legal forms through which democracy is structured. The nation, its unity, and whatever democratic legitimacy its form of rule enjoys, become tangible and emerge as much in shared taste, in the pre-supposition and generation of aesthetic *con-sensus*, as in the formation or execution of a common will or the inculcation or reasoning of a common reason. This introduction presents the ten chapters of the edited volume, each of which engages with the intersection of aesthetics and law, and, more specifically with the question of how the nation—and its (fundamental) law—are 'sensed' by way of various aesthetic forms.

M. Antaki
Faculty of Law, McGill University, Montreal, Canada
e-mail: mark.antaki@mcgill.ca

A. Condello
Department of Law, Roma Tre University, Rome, Italy
e-mail: angela.condello@uniroma3.it

and

Department of Philosophy, University of Torino, Torino, Italy

S. Huygebaert (✉)
Ghent Legal History Institute and Department of Art History, Musicology and Theater Studies, Ghent University and Research Foundation—Flanders (FWO), Ghent, Belgium
e-mail: stefan.huygebaert@ugent.be

S. Marusek
Department of Political Science, University of Hawai'i, Hawai'i, USA
e-mail: marusek@hawaii.edu

S. Huygebaert et al. (eds.), *Sensing the Nation's Law*, Studies in the History of Law and Justice 13, https://doi.org/10.1007/978-3-319-75497-0_1

We are said to live in an age of democratic legitimacy. The rightfulness of a political and legal order is meant to reside in a widespread belief in the rightfulness of democracy.[1] Contemporary democratic legitimacy is tied, among other things, to consent, to representation, to the identity of ruler and ruled, and, of course, to legality and the legal forms through which democracy is structured.[2] While this kind of conventional wisdom may be questioned, e.g. we may be seeing rescue displace democracy as what legitimates rule,[3] our goal here is not to upend this conventional wisdom but to challenge and expand the ways in which we can understand and appreciate democratic legitimacy. If (democratic) communities are "imagined",[4] we argue that their "rightfulness" must be "sensed"—analogously to the need for justice not only to be done, but to be seen to be done.

Democracy and democratic legitimacy are not simply conceptual or rational achievements. As participants—subjects, citizens—of political and legal orders, we are not interpellated merely conceptually or rationally but also sensually and aesthetically. In this volume, we seek to draw attention to the aesthetics of democratic legitimacy and to the way democracy and law are sensed, felt, embodied, experienced.[5] Chapters primarily focus on the sense of sight rather than engage with the full spectrum of the human sensorium.[6] However, using the "visual" as an entry-point into the "sensorial" and "sensual" more broadly leads us to discover the *con-sentirer* or *feeling together* at work in consent and consensus. It encourages us to interpret political and legal representations[7] as always already aesthetic and bound up with modes of making present that are historically and culturally located and contingent. Likewise, it moves us to look into the practices of sensual identification that come along with the identity of ruler and ruled.

---

[1]On legitimacy generally, see Weber, Max. 1946. Politics as a Vocation. In *From Max Weber: Essays in Sociology*, eds. Hans Gerth, and Charles Wright Mills. New York: Oxford University Press.

[2]Schmitt, Carl. 1992 (1923). *The Crisis of Parliamentary Democracy*. Trans. Ellen Kennedy. Studies in contemporary German social thought. Cambridge, MA: MIT press.

[3]Meister, Robert. 2011. *After Evil: A Politics of Human Rights*. New York: Columbia University Press.

[4]Anderson, Benedict R. 1991 1983. *Imagined Communities: Reflections on the Origin and Spread of Nationalism*. London/New York Verso.

[5]On (the culturally constructed nature of) sensing, see Howes, David, and Constance Classen. 2014. *Ways of Sensing: Understanding the Senses in Society*. London/New York: Routledge, in particular the chapters 'The politics of perception: sensory and social ordering' and 'The feel of justice. Law and regulation of sensation'.

[6]For a more general bibliography on the human sensorium, see Porcello, Thomas, Louise Meintjes, Ana Maria Ochoa, and David W. Samuels. 2010. The Reorganization of the Sensory World. *Annual Review of Anthropology* 39:51–66. For a recent compendium on law and the visual, see Wagner, Anne, and Richard K. Sherwin. 2014. *Law, Culture and Visual Studies*. London: Springer.

[7]On representation, see generally Pitkin, Hanna Fenichel. 1972. *The Concept of Representation*. Berkeley: University of California Press.

The nation, its unity, and whatever democratic legitimacy its form of rule enjoys, become tangible and emerge as much in shared taste,[8] in the pre-supposition and generation of aesthetic *con-sensus*, as in the formation or execution of a common will or the inculcation or reasoning of a common reason. In a like manner, representation answers the challenge of actualizing, making present (and therefore tangible) this *con-sensus*, and not simply such things as pre-existing "preferences" or "interests". History provides us with diverse forms of national representation, themselves often tied to focal moments in which the nation is conceptualized, embodied, enlivened and forged through sensory means. These moments, as they involve understandings and enactments of order, power, and control, are properly understood as key *legal* moments, as matters of concern for legal historians and scholars.

This edited volume brings together ten essays, each of which engages with the intersection of aesthetics and law, and, more specifically with the question of how the nation—and its (fundamental) law—are 'sensed' by way of various aesthetic forms. They are written by scholars in law, political science, history, art history and philosophy, each of whom works in an inter-disciplinary fashion or with an inter-disciplinary sensibility. The main chronological focus is on the post-revolutionary period spanning from the late eighteenth and early nineteenth century's age of revolution until our own age of contested democratic legitimacy, although several authors demonstrate how specific aesthetic forms feature much older roots, going back as far as early Christianity. The chapters engage with different parts of the so-called Western world, namely Europe, North America, and Australia and explore the rich contextualizations of law that happen in these places.

Part I, *Revolution, Constitution, Republic*, gathers three chapters, each of which grapples with the question of (republican) foundation and the sensing of the *res publica*. Within each chapter, the authors engage with the transition from revolution to constitution and the resulting republic and/or nation-state, as reflected in art works from the long nineteenth century and—more particularly—from the *age of revolution* as defined by Eric Hobsbawm.[9]

Mark Antaki and Catherine Le Guerrier treat Jacques-Louis David's unfinished *Tennis Court Oath* as an attempt to capture the moment in which the new republican sovereign is presaged or emerges. Taking David's "corporeal aesthetic" as their entry-point, Antaki and Le Guerrier present and examine three inter-related modes of engagement with or appreciation of the *Oath*. They consider the *Oath* in turn as Monument, as Portrait, and as Tableau in order to engage with some of the layers of sense and sensibility at work in the *Oath*. For instance, considering the *Oath* as Monument raises such questions as the liberties David took to immortalize liberty. Considering it as Portrait leads one to ask whether and how it participates in

[8]See, e.g., Arendt, Hannah. 1982. *Lectures on Kant's Political Philosophy*, ed. Ronald Beiner. Chicago: University of Chicago Press.

[9]Hobsbawm, Eric. 1962. *The Age of Revolution: Europe 1789–1848*. London: Weidenfeld and Nicolson.

the political theological logic of incarnation that animates the King's Portrait. Considering it as Tableau leads one to ask about its ties to theatre and Diderot's aesthetics and to wonder whether it does away with representation as incarnation.

Stefan Huygebaert examines events and moments from constitutional history, their depiction and their relevance within the history of the nation and its fundamental law, the constitution, by way of the artistic device that he calls the Decisive Constitutional Moment. The meaning of this device lies in the interplay between monument and memory, between commemoration and communication, and between the moment of depiction and the depicted moment. Huygebaert treats different artistic media (painted, engraved, sculpted) and ends his chapter with an analysis of the competition entries for the Belgian constitutional monument known as the Congress Column, following the pan-European 1848 revolution.

Like Antaki and Le Guerrier's, Oliver Watts' chapter concerns a painting in France, a country with a long tradition of kings' portraits. Like Huygebaert's case study, it concerns the 1848 revolution and its aftermath. More specifically, it looks at the 1848 appropriation of the revolution of 1789. Watts extends Hélène Toussaint's iconological analysis of Gustave Courbet's famous *Allegory* (Paris, Louvre). In his chapter, Watts interprets the nude woman in the painting as an effigy of the republican Marianne, "the body of democratic France", a portrait rather than an allegory. Using Lacanian theory, Watts explores the sovereignty within the painting and calls for attention to the notions of natural law and social contract. In the case of Courbet's *Allegory* as well, the moment of creation and the specific historical context of France in the aftermath of the 1848 revolution and imperial take-over prove vital for an understanding of the sensation of the nation. As opposed to the official visual rhetoric, which Huygebaert deals with for the Belgian case, Watts provides the reader with the means to grasp the subversive quality of a non-official work of art, and traces the representation of the French nation therein.

Part II, *The Aesthetic Constitution of Office*, continues one of the themes introduced in part one, namely the embodiment of the nation and its law (e.g. Watts writes about the "body of democratic France" during the Second Empire). The focus of part II, however, is on the embodiment of the nation and its law in "office" and in "official" representations or constructions thereof.[10]

Stefania Gialdroni writes about the Italian Supreme Court building as both a functional Palace of justice or an "office", and a national symbol of the Italian nation. Just like Stefan Huygebaert, she situates her specific focus within a broader pan-European discussion of the legal-national architecture of palaces of justice. Her treatment of the architecture of palaces of justice is tied to the seeing and sensing of justice, but it is also tied just as much to questions of national and legal unity and unification. Indeed, her chapter invites us to situate traditional moments of what we might call "legal nationalism", such as codification, within a much broader sensorial context.

---

[10]On the notion of office see, e.g., McVeigh, Shaun. 2015. Afterword: Office and the Conduct of the Minor Jurisprudent. *UC Irvine Law Review* 5 (2):499–512.

Just as the portrayal of the king's body in his portrait is meant to say something about and even constitute kingship itself, so too does the photograph of a president both comment and establish the office he occupies. Anne Wagner focuses on official presidential photographs of the Fifth Republic (1958–2012). She looks at presidents as office-holders, and scrutinizes how their representation leads us to understand the office itself and, at the very same time, national identity and unity. She interprets the (representation of the) body as a code, and deconstructs the mechanism of coding (encoding; decoding). In so doing, she focuses on "visual elements" in terms of a "consensual symbolism" that contributes to the rhetorical power of images.

Whereas all chapters in the book obviously deal with time and temporality, Part III, *Untimely Reflections on the Nation's Law* invite us to consider more radically when and where we are—and do so in very different ways. Desmond Manderson turns to a key thinker on time, Walter Benjamin, and seeks to refine his thinking on the "here and now of the work of art" in such a work as *The Work of Art in the Age of its Mechanical Reproducibility* (1936). He locates this work in relation to the Mexican mural movement (1935) and the Paris Universal Exhibition (1937). In so doing, he wishes to better call into question the "ideological alliance between art and law", an alliance we have seen explored in other chapters, so as to draw attention to art's capacity not simply "to embody and unify the nation, but to disturb and critique it".

In his chapter, Paolo Napoli proposes a hypothesis regarding the genealogy of the American national motto "In God We Trust", found among other places, on American coinage and banknotes since 1864. Genealogies too involve a reconsideration of when and where, and therefore who, we are. Napoli's efforts to understand "common identity through common trust" lead him to focus on the "deposit (of faith)" and its centrality to the "emergence of the Church as an institution". He explores the relation and intersection of theological and legal rationalities. In so doing, he sheds light on the notions of office and institution, encouraging us to enrich our thinking about the institution of the nation-state as exemplified by the institution of the Church.

Part IV, *Out of Many, One* engages with the theme of national unity introduced in earlier chapters but with a particular focus on the transformation of plurality into unity, including the perpetual failure and violence of this transformation. In this way, the two chapters invite us to consider the dissensus in consensus. Both chapters treat what we might call the "everyday" and allow us to consider how ostensibly ordinary objects and actions are ripe for interpretation as sources of democratic legitimacy. Law may well need ordinary objects and actions to enliven it as commonsensical. As aesthetics of law, the examples of the coin and regional cuisine are two sources of ontological fodder that sustain or counter the legitimacy of a democracy.

Sarah Marusek's chapter on American quarters examines the coin as a cultural text of law, an aesthetic which includes legal "statements" about pluralism (i.e. the literal flip side of the coin) as well as, and conversely, the ignoring of realities of conquest, obliteration and slavery (i.e. the figurative flip side: that which is *not* shown on the quarter, what is not part of the consensus). The design of this cultural text reminds the viewer of what is vital to the public memory. However, the design, as well as the final product (the coin), is a state-sponsored construction of national identity that is paradoxically rich with (un)intended perspectives and conflicted realities.

Richard Mohr and Nadirsyah Hosen examine food as symbolic and regulated, casting food choices as part of our self-definition. Food and the choice of what to eat offer views on citizenship and justice that exist between "authenticity" and "fusion". "Our identity is negotiated in the terms of the norms we apply to the food we ingest" and in ways that reveal and reflect the internormative spectrum of gastronomically-determined democratic legitimacy. The heart, as well as the stomach, are keys to national identities that are themselves expanding in ways that generate new tastes.

Lastly, in Part V, *Consensus*, Angela Condello offers a tentative conclusion. Whereas all of the chapters refer to different aesthetic means of the representation of national identity producing democratic legitimacy, in this concluding chapter, Condello focuses on the interconnection between representation and the consensus on which legitimacy is based. This interconnection, she argues, originated with the birth of the modern state and with the creation of a fictional entity whose legitimacy and power are based on a consensus. Such a fictional entity, be it symbolically represented through a Biblical animal-monster or a Parliament, gains epistemic and ontological validity through different levels of agreement, among which the one constructed on the sensible perception of the rightfulness or validity of the institution plays a central role.

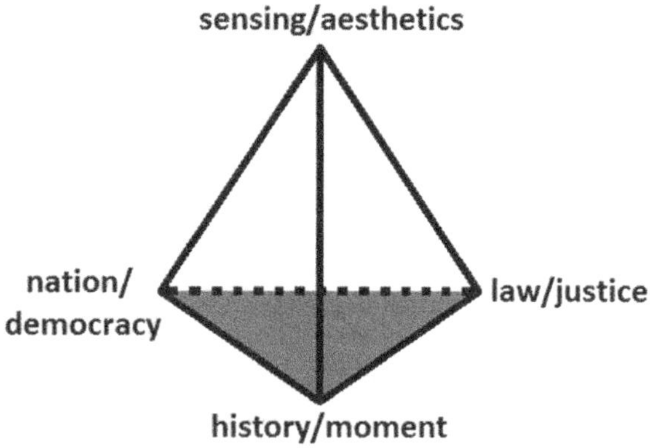

Fig. 1.1 Schematic representation of the interdisciplinarity of *Sensing the Nation's Law*

This collected volume can be situated within a triangular pyramid (Fig. 1.1) with sensing, nation, history and law at its four corners. Part of what we aim to demonstrate in collecting these essays, is that the sensory or sensual is not only the tip of the pyramid or iceberg, but also part of the foundation of the edifice: democracy and the nation's law need sensory "expression" but, and in addition, sensory experience grounds or makes possible democracy and the nation's law.

References

Anderson, Benedict R. 1991 (1983). *Imagined Communities: Reflections on the Origin and Spread of Nationalism*. London: Verso.

Arendt, Hannah. 1982. *Lectures on Kant's Political Philosophy*, ed. Ronald Beiner. Chicago: University of Chicago press.

Hobsbawm, Eric. 1962. *The Age of Revolution: Europe 1789–1848*. London: Weidenfeld and Nicolson.

Howes, David., and Constance Classen. 2014. *Ways of Sensing: Understanding the Senses in Society*. Oxon, New York: Routledge.

McVeigh, Shaun. 2015. Afterword: Office and the Conduct of the Minor Jurisprudent. *UC Irvine Law Review* 5(2):499–512.

Meister, Robert. 2011. *After Evil: A Politics of Human Rights*. New York: Columbia University Press.

Pitkin, Hanna Fenichel. 1972. *The Concept of Representation*. Berkeley: University of California Press.

Porcello, Thomas, Louise Meintjes, Ana Maria Ochoa, and David W. Samuels. 2010. The Reorganization of the Sensory World. *Annual Review of Anthropology* 39:51–66.

Schmitt, Carl. 1992 (1923). *The Crisis of Parliamentary Democracy*. Trans. Ellen Kennedy. *Studies in Contemporary German Social Thought*. Cambridge (Mass): MIT press.

Wagner, Anne, and Richard K. Sherwin. 2014. *Law, Culture and Visual Studies*. London: Springer.

Weber Max. 1946. Politics as a Vocation. In: *From Max Weber: Essays in Sociology*, ed. Hans Gerth, and Charles Wright Mills. New York: Oxford University Press.

Mark Antaki, Ph.D. (University of California, Berkeley 2005), is an Associate Professor in the Faculty of Law at McGill University. His research interests focus on law and the humanities, law and language, as well as the history of ideas. He teaches courses in public and private law as well as legal theory. Some of his publications include: "Declining Accusation" in George Pavlich and Matthew P. Unger, eds., *Accusation: Creating Criminals* (Vancouver, UBC Press, 2016); "Un-stating Law" in Shauna Van Praagh, Lionel Smith and Helge Dedek, eds., *Stateless Law: Evolving Boundaries of a Discipline* (Burlington, VT: Ashgate, 2015); "'No Foundations'? " (2014) 11 No Foundations: Interdisciplinary Journal of Law and Justice 61–77; "Genre, Critique, and Human Rights" (2013) 82 University of Toronto Quarterly 974–996 (special issue on law and literature).

Angela Condello is Temporary Lecturer at the University of Roma Tre and Fellow Researcher at the University of Torino where she also directs LabOnt Law. She cooperates with the Human Rights Committee of the Italian Senate of the Republic. In 2015, she was Fernand Braudel Fellow (EHESS, CENJ) and in 2014 she was a Fellow at the Käte Hamburger Kolleg "Law as Culture".

Until 2016, she was Guest Professor at the Law School of the University of Ghent. She teaches Law and Humanities at Roma Tre. She organizes the International Roundtables for the Semiotics of Law and is in the boards of Law Text Culture, Law and Literature. She is Associate Editor of *Brill Research Perspectives in Art and Law*. She recently received a *Jean Monnet* award.

Stefan Huygebaert is a Research Foundation Flanders (FWO) Ph.D. Fellow at the Ghent Legal History Institute and Department of Art History, Musicology and Theatre Studies (Ghent University). His dissertation, entitled *Visual Ideals of Law and Justice*, is an iconological study of legal imagery in nineteenth-century Belgium. In 2014–2015, and again in 2016–2017, he was a Ph.D. fellow (Stipendiat) within the Minerva Research Group *The Nomos of Images: Manifestation and Iconology of Law* at the Kunsthistorisches Insitut in Florenz (Max-Planck-Institut). He publishes and teaches on legal iconography and nineteenth-century art, and recently co-edited the catalogue for the exhibition *The Art of Law: Three Centuries of Justice Depicted* (Groeningemuseum, Bruges).

Sarah Marusek, Ph.D. (University of Massachusetts Amherst 2008), is an Associate Professor of Public Law in the Department of Political Science at the University of Hawai‘i at Hilo. Her research interests focus on sites of constitutive law, legal geography and legal semiotics that engage legal pluralist frameworks of everyday jurisprudence. She teaches courses in U.S. Constitutional law, legal studies and legal geography.

Part I
Revolution, Constitution, Republic

Chapter 2
Monument, Portrait, Tableau: Making Sense of and with Jacques-Louis David's Tennis Court Oath

Mark Antaki and Catherine Le Guerrier

Abstract On 20 June 1789, the members of the newly-established National Assembly swore the famous Tennis Court Oath: not to separate until they had given the polity a new constitution. This chapter examines Jacques-Louis David's ambitious—and never finished—attempt to capture this revolutionary moment. It inquires into how his *Tennis Court Oath* allows and invites one to sense the nation and its sovereignty. It does so by considering the *Oath* as, in turn, Monument, Portrait, and Tableau.

2.1 Introduction: The Revolutionary Moment?

This chapter examines some of the ways in which Jacques-Louis David's unfinished *Tennis Court Oath* allows one to sense the nation and its sovereignty. To adopt and adapt a phrase from Marie-José Mondzain: no new power without a new image.[1] Political power and sovereignty—whether royal, republican or other—are not simply brute facts, doctrinal categories, or even discursive ones. They must be sensed to make sense. To borrow Claude Lefort's language: their *mise en sens* goes along with a *mise en scène*.[2] David's projected painting is part of a whole wealth of practices and images that belong to and signal a shift from monarchical to republican

[1]She writes: "No power without an image." Mondzain, Marie-José. 2005. *Image, Icon, Economy: The Byzantine Origins of the Contemporary Imaginary*. Stanford, CA: Stanford University Press, 158.
[2]Lefort, Claude. 1988. The Permanence of the Theologico-Political? In *Democracy and Political Theory*. Trans. D. Macey. Minneapolis: University of Minnesota Press, 219.

M. Antaki (✉) · C. Le Guerrier
Faculty of Law, McGill University, Montreal, Canada
e-mail: mark.antaki@mcgill.ca

C. Le Guerrier
e-mail: catherine.leguerrier@mail.mcgill.ca

S. Huygebaert et al. (eds.), *Sensing the Nation's Law*, Studies in the History of Law and Justice 13, https://doi.org/10.1007/978-3-319-75497-0_2

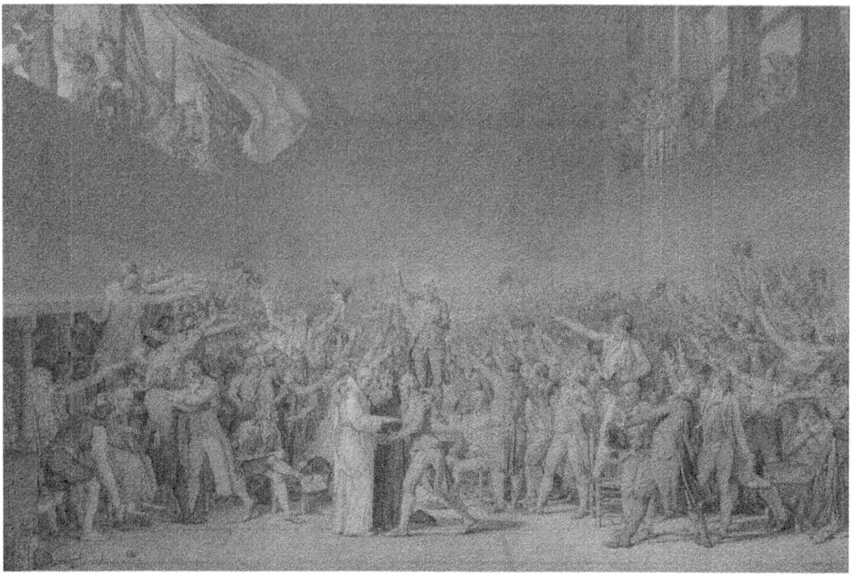

Fig. 2.1 David, Jacques Louis (1748–1825). *The Oath of the Tennis Court (Jeu de Paume), June 20th 1789*. 1791. Pen and wash with brown ink, heightened with white, on paper, 66 × 101 cm, MV8409; INVDessins736. *Photo* Gérard Blot. © RMN-Grand Palais/Art Resource, NY

practices and images. The *Tennis Court Oath* both reflects and imparts a revolutionary sensibility, thereby conjugating power and representation anew. (Fig. 2.1)[3]

David's never completed painting is of no ordinary scene. As we shall see, David dedicates his efforts to immortalizing the moment and to showing its extraordinariness. The moment in question is, of course, the famous Tennis Court Oath[4] of 20 June 1789, when the members of the newly self-established National Assembly,[5] locked out of their meeting room by royal order, re-assembled in the royal tennis court and swore an oath not to disband until they had established a new constitution for the kingdom. This moment, if not "the revolutionary moment"[6]

[3]On the conjugation of power and representation, see, e.g., Marin, Louis. 1988. *Portrait of the King*. Trans. M. Houle. Minneapolis: University of Minnesota Press. Marin, Louis. 1981. *Le portrait du roi*. Paris: Les éditions de minuit.

[4]We use italics when writing of David's work and no italics when writing of the event itself. In both cases, we capitalize "Oath".

[5]The Assembly had only been in existence for three days; it was composed mostly of the representatives of the Third Estate of France, assembled in Versailles for an Estates General called by the King to consult his subjects on the question of the kingdom's finances—the first Estates General since 1614.

[6]Tackett, Timothy. 1996. *Becoming a Revolutionary: The Deputies of the French National Assembly and the Emergence of a Revolutionary Culture (1789–1790)*. Princeton: Princeton University Press, 146, but in reference to the oath of 17 June. See also Stefan Huygebaert's chapter in this volume.

was part of the "remarkably rapid radicalization of the Third Estate."[7] Only three days prior, the members of the Third Estate and some of the clergy assembled in Versailles for the Estates General had repudiated their former division into Estates and re-constituted themselves into a new body, swearing a first momentous oath "in the name of God, the king, and the nation" to fulfill their functions "faithfully and zealously".[8] On 23 June Mirabeau would reject the King's demands that they disband by claiming that the men are present by the will of the people. On 27 June, the three orders would become one as the nobility joined the National Assembly. On 9 July, the Assembly would "adopt the designation of Constituent Assembly".[9] 14 July, of course, would see the storming of the Bastille. And the next day, Jean-Sylvain Bailly, the famous astrologist who had presided over the Tennis Court Oath, would become the first mayor of Paris.

The Tennis Court Oath of 20 June is thus one of several important moments in which "the French nation," by virtue of "its" "representatives", comes into existence, demonstrates a resolve to exist, and acquires what is perhaps the ultimate political potency and responsibility: that of (re-)founding or (re-)constituting the polity, of giving it a new fundamental law. To be sure, at the time of the Oath, the members of the National Assembly had not yet repudiated monarchy. As Timothy Tackett writes: "Although in constitutional terms the National Assembly had effectively claimed ultimate sovereignty—through its decrees of 17 June and 20 June—most deputies preferred not to consider the full implications of their actions as they concerned monarchy".[10] Indeed, Bailly recounts how he spoke the Oath so loudly and clearly that his words made their way to the crowd outside the building—which in turn cried "Vive le roi" ("Live the King").[11] As the quote from Tackett shows, there was an important difference between what the National Assembly "effectively" did and the "implications" the deputies considered.

At the time David began thinking of painting the Oath, probably in spring 1790, he was already famous for his paintings of episodes from Antiquity—but not particularly involved in politics. In October 1790, the recently-established *Société des Amis de la Constitution* (re-named the *Societé des Jacobins* in 1792) asked him to produce a painting of the Oath (along with which a set of engravings was also to be produced).[12] David's preliminary sketch was first exhibited briefly in David's workshop in May 1791 and then in September of the same year, at the Salon.[13] On 28 September, the National Assembly decreed that the completion of the painting

[7]Tackett, 1996. 120.

[8]As found in Tackett, 1996. 147.

[9]Tackett, 1996. 211.

[10]Tackett, 1996. 153.

[11]Bordes, Philippe. 1983. *Le Serment du Jeu de Paume de Jacques-Louis David. Le peintre, son milieu et son temps de 1789 à 1792.* Paris: Ministère de la culture. Éditions de la Réunion des musées nationaux, 15.

[12]Bordes, 1983. 48.

[13]Bordes, 1983. 44.

was to be financed by the Treasury and that the painting would be placed in the future meeting place of the National Assembly.[14]

David subsequently became a member of the Convention in 1792,[15] of the Committees of General Security and General Instruction, and of the Revolutionary Tribunal.[16] As "Pageant Master" of the Revolution,[17] he was responsible for the organization of festivals, the erection and transformation of monuments, the creation of a new museum and support for the arts.[18] In this capacity, he worked to make the Revolution felt, to give a sensory and sensual presence to the nation and its ideals in France, its buildings, its streets.

David eventually and definitively abandoned the *Tennis Court Oath*, although it is difficult to know exactly when. He first set aside the *Oath* sometime in 1792.[19] But he maintained an interest in the project throughout the Terror[20] and, in 1795, even asked for a space to finish it.[21] In December 1801, he became first painter of the Empire, announcing to the press that he had given up painting the *Oath.*[22] The huge canvas—projected to be six meters tall and ten meters wide[23]—would remain mostly blank. Commentators ascribe its incompletion both to the ambition of the work and, as we shall see, to David's inability to keep up, so to speak, with the Revolution.[24] In any case, the work and its incompletion are both fascinating and instructive.

The present chapter is divided into three parts. Each part aims to better articulate what the work achieved or could have achieved (and what it never fully became). Each also addresses what it is fruitful to think about in order to attend to what the work achieved or could have achieved. Our emphasis is on the *Oath* as an entry point and not an endpoint; we are more interested in the questions the *Oath* raises than the answers it provides. Our chapter invites one to approach, experience, and contextualize David's work as, in turn, Monument, Portrait, and Tableau. Each part draws out—and draws on—the significance of the *Tennis Court Oath*'s

[14]Bordes, 1983. 53–54.

[15]Loty, Laurent. 2009. L'inachèvement emblématique du serment de jeu de paume. *Dix-huitième siècle* 41:1, 35.

[16]Roberts, Warren. 2000. *Jacques-Louis David and Jean-Louis Prieur: Revolutionary Artists, The Public, The Populace, and Images of the French Revolution.* Albany: State University of New York Press, 258.

[17]Dowd, David Lloyd. 1948. *Pageant-master of the Republic: Jacques-Louis David and the French Revolution.* Lincoln: University of Nebraska Press. & Roberts, as n. 16, 258.

[18]Johnson, Dorothy. 1993. *Jacques-Louis David: Art in Metamorphosis.* Princeton: Princeton University Press, 73.

[19]Bordes, 1983. 30.

[20]Bordes, 1983. 86.

[21]Bordes, 1983. 85.

[22]Loty, 2009. 38.

[23]Bordes, 1983. 54.

[24]See, e.g., Loty, 2009. 35.

"corporeal aesthetic" by inviting the reader—and thus the viewer—to different but complementary literatures. The aim of each part is to attend to the significance of the work by way of these keywords[25] and not to replace the viewer's own encounter with the work and its richness. Their succession ought to deepen one's appreciation of the work, thereby allowing one to better experience some of the different, albeit inseparable, layers of sense and sensibility to be found in it. Together, the three parts aim to draw attention to the richness and complexity of David's attempt to capture "the revolutionary moment" of national sovereignty by attending to the *Oath's* conjugation of power and representation, to the ways in which it shows the reciprocal belonging of the power of representation and the representation of power.[26]

Our consideration of this new image of power begins with an attempt to understand better how David wished to monumentalize the Tennis Court Oath. He wished to capture it as an event worthy of memory and repetition, even eternally. In order to do so, we introduce the work and address some of its aspects that contributed to monumentalize the nation's sovereignty, i.e. to liberty's event and advent (B). We then consider the *Oath* as a successor to the portrait of the king, as a "visualization of the regenerated body politic"[27] (C). This brings us to consider the *Tennis Court Oath* both in political theological terms and in relation to Abbé Emmanuel Joseph Sieyès's understanding of the National Assembly. We subsequently turn to the theatrical quality of the work and in so doing, move from Sieyès to Denis Diderot and from the "portrait" to the "tableau" (D). In so doing, we see how the "tableau" implies a turn away from "incarnation", a necessary keyword in any political theological appreciation of the *Tennis Court Oath*. The last two sections focus less on the work itself and more on what it invites us to consider when we approach it as portrait and as tableau.

As may already be apparent, much is packed into each of these keywords: Monument, Portrait, Tableau. Unpacking them can contribute greatly to appreciating the work, its ambition, and the significance of its incompletion. Read one way, the sequence of these keywords moves us from the most obvious or accessible—monument—to the least obvious or accessible—tableau—a technical term or term of art tied to Diderot's aesthetics and probably less familiar to today's reader. Read another way, however, the sequence moves from the more general to the more specific. And, in so doing, it brings us closer and closer to ourselves, to our own present aesthetic and political sensibilities and to their inter-belonging and intertwining.

---

[25]Williams, Raymond. 1995. *Keywords: A Vocabulary of Culture and Society*. Oxford: Oxford University Press.

[26]Marin, 1988.

[27]De Baecque, Antoine. 1993. *The Body Politic: Corporeal Metaphor in Revolutionary France, 1770-1800*. Stanford: Stanford University Press, 194.

2.2 Monument

To treat a contemporary event as a legitimate subject for high art, as one would a scene from classical history, was unusual. David's sketch, presented at the 1791 Salon, was among the very few paintings at the Salon that did not borrow their subject from the past.[28] By depicting the Tennis Court Oath, David, a history painter, shone a light on this revolutionary moment, vouching for its great significance and its certainty to be (come) history. In a letter to the president of the National Assembly dated 5 February 1792, he wrote, "Oh my fatherland! Oh my dear fatherland! We will therefore no longer be obliged to go looking in the history of the ancient peoples, for something to paint… No, the history of no people offers me something so grand, so sublime as this Tennis Court Oath… French Nation! It is your glory that I wish to propagate".[29]

If the Oath was the most sublime moment in history, both the building and David's projected painting were to be the most monumental of monuments. So grand and sublime was the moment that David wanted to preserve the building itself as a "temple of patriotism".[30] These words are drawn from the draft of the 28 October 1790 motion presented to the *Société des Amis de la Constitution* by Dubois-Crancé, which David himself drafted. This temple would offer "the greatest lesson ever offered by a monument".[31] Indeed, David wished that the members of the National Assembly return to the Tennis Court every year to "repeat the oath that saved France".[32] As for the painting of the Oath, it would be "the most useful monument of courage and patriotism that any century ever produced".[33] As Édouard Pommier underlines, the Revolutionary patrimony—eternal and unchanging—to be bequeathed to the future was, at once, the Oath and the building.[34] Moreover, as he emphasizes, their monumentalization was part and parcel of an act of erasure: that of, as in the draft Dubois-Crancé speech, "centuries of error".[35] Precisely as a *monument*, the *Tennis Court Oath* takes part in the work of inheriting, of remembering and forgetting, and of bequeathing.

---

[28]Reichardt, Rolf and Hubertus Kohle. 2008. *Visualizing the Revolution: Politics and the Pictorial Arts in Late Eighteenth-century France*. London: Reaktion Books, 92.

[29]Bordes, 1983. 165: "O ma patrie! O ma chère patrie! nous ne serons donc plus obligés d'aller chercher dans l'histoire des peuples anciens, de quoi exercer nos pinceaux… Non, l'histoire d'aucun peuple ne m'offre rien de si grand, de si sublime que ce serment du Jeu de Paume… Nation française! C'est ta gloire que je veux propager…"

[30]Bordes, 1983. 149: "le temple du patriotisme".

[31]Bordes, 1983. 149: "la plus grande leçon que jamais ait offert aucun monument".

[32]Bordes, 1983. 149: "répéter le serment qui a sauvé la France".

[33]Bordes, 1983. 150: "le plus utile monument de courage et de patriotisme qu'aucun siècle ait jamais produit".

[34]Pommier, Édouard. 1991. *L'art de la liberté: Doctrines et débats de la Révolution française*. Paris: Gallimard, 39–41.

[35]Bordes, 1983. 149. and Pommier, 1991. 39: "tant de siècles d'erreur".

As Angela Condello does in this volume, we wish to draw attention to the etymology of "monument." Condello writes:

> The very word "monument" derives from "*monère*" (to remember, to let someone know) and the termination "*mèntum*" indicates the means through which we remember. Therefore, the monument fixes an instant in its most exemplary form, be it a gesture or a collective action of a group of people (in the Tennis Court, or in the Parliament).[36]

In addition, "*monère*" in Latin can also mean "to warn" (as in the English "admonition"). As a monument, perhaps David's *Tennis Court Oath* attempts simultaneously to erase a past and, at one and the same time, to admonish Frenchmen—to exhort them—to keep and repeat this oath, lest they return to "centuries of error". Perhaps every monument, as a monument, points to the fragility of the memory to be instilled and the commitment or practice necessary to do so. In the case of the *Tennis Court Oath*, the monument itself points to and represents what is needed for the memory to remain. David's challenge, then, was to make the oath eternally present, i.e. both eternally urgent and eternally possible.

So, David saw both the building and his painting as monuments meant to teach and commemorate "courage and patriotism". Moreover, the painting itself is composed, one might say, monumentally. Dorothy Johnson notes that "[w]hat is most striking visually about the compositional structure of the *Oath of the Tennis Court*, in fact, is its similarity to the structure of a sculpted pediment",[37] of which president Bailly appears at the apex. The pediment, she explains, "serves an extremely important didactic and ideological function; it communicates in a direct and perpetual manner to the 'people' since it is typically placed on public view at an important civic site".[38] Indeed, the structure of David's composition was so similar to that of a sculpted pediment that David d'Angers—a student of David who among other things was responsible for the pediment relief of the Pantheon—"chose to transpose it to an actual pediment he planned for the Chamber of Deputies".[39]

While David did not borrow the subject from the past, he saw his past work as preparing him for the task of being liberty's artist, of commemorating the Revolution's key men, moments, and virtues.[40] In the draft Dubois-Crancé speech, David wrote that we ought to tell the "true friends of the constitution" that we have chosen "the author of Brutus and the Horati, this French patriot, the genius of whom preceded the Revolution"[41] to produce this monument. With *The Lictors Bring to Brutus the Bodies of his Sons* (Paris, Musée du Louvre), David painted a father's willingness to sacrifice his own sons for the republic. (Brutus's sons having

---

[36]See Angela Condello's chapter in this volume (Chap. 11, p. 263).

[37]Johnson, 1993. 77.

[38]Johnson, 1993. 77.

[39]Johnson, 1993. 77. It is worth comparing d'Angers's pediment relief to Léopold Morice's high relief at the place de la République.

[40]See, e.g., Bordes, 1983. 42.

[41]Bordes, 1983. 150: "vrais amis de la constitution" and "l'auteur de Brutus et des Horaces, ce Français patriote, dont le génie a devancé la Révolution".

treasonously tried to restore the monarchy Brutus had worked to replace with the republic). With the *Oath of the Horatii*, David painted heroic patriotism, readiness to die, and an oath taken to that effect. The oath, however, was a wholesale addition of David's to the original tale found in Livy. Thematically, then, David was perhaps the perfect candidate to represent the event in all of its patriotic charge (Fig. 2.2).[42]

David's "genius" resided in the manner in which he addressed these patriotic themes: in "a style that would give birth to a new age both in painting and sculpture".[43] Indeed, perhaps of as great or even greater significance than the themes it addressed, the *Oath of the Horatii* anticipated the *Tennis Court Oath* aesthetically. At the Salon of 1791, David would exhibit his sketch of the *Tennis Court Oath* right below that of the *Oath of the Horatii*,[44] his earlier and famously "sculpturesque" work.[45] This positioning is telling. The *Oath of the Horatii* signaled a "revolutionary, corporal aesthetic" in which the body itself is "eloquent".[46] Johnson recounts how "[a]fter the appearance of the Oath of the Horati at the Salon, critics … suddenly began to focus their attention on the pantomime of figures in painting, an aspect they had ignored or considered subordinate to physiognomy until David's daring reforms".[47] And with the *Tennis Court Oath*, as Antoine de Baecque puts it, "[f]or the first time, David meets a contemporary subject that he deems worthy of his "expressive bodies".[48] With the *Oath*, David transforms the bodies of antique heroes into those of contemporary "grands hommes",[49] for instance by showing muscles bulging under the men's coats, *culottes* and *haut-de-chausses*; one preparatory study even showing Robespierre as an "antique warrior".[50]

By way of its corporeal aesthetic, the *Oath of the Horatii* anticipates the *Tennis Court Oath* as capturing a moment of the regeneration of individual bodies and of French society as a whole. As Johnson writes, of the *Oath of the Horatii*, "…*The Oath* does literally *embody* pre-Revolutionary radicalism. In *The Oath* David countered prevailing fears of the physical and moral degeneracy that seemed to threaten the very structure of French society, with emblematic images of regenerate man".[51] The revolutionary aesthetic, the regenerate man, also accompanied a new public, a new society. Of the *Oath of the Horatii*, Thomas Crow notes "[t]he alarm,

---

[42]Also fraternal and hence masculine charge. On gender in the *Oath*, see, e.g., Roberts, 2000. 231. See generally Landes, Joan B. 2001. *Visualizing the Nation: Gender. Representation, and Revolution in Eighteenth-Century France*. Ithaca: Cornell University Press.

[43]Johnson, 1993. 60.

[44]And besides his *Brutus* and *Death of Socrates*. Trey, Juliette and de Baecque, Antoine. 2008. *Le Serment du Jeu de paume: quand David réécrit l'histoire*. Versailles: Éditions Artyis, 18.

[45]Johnson, 1993. 8.

[46]Johnson, 1993. 14.

[47]Johnson, 1993. 69.

[48]De Baecque, 1993. 186.

[49]On David's representation of "grand hommes", see, e.g., Johnson, 1993. 74.

[50]Roberts, 2000. 245.

[51]Johnson, 1993. 66.

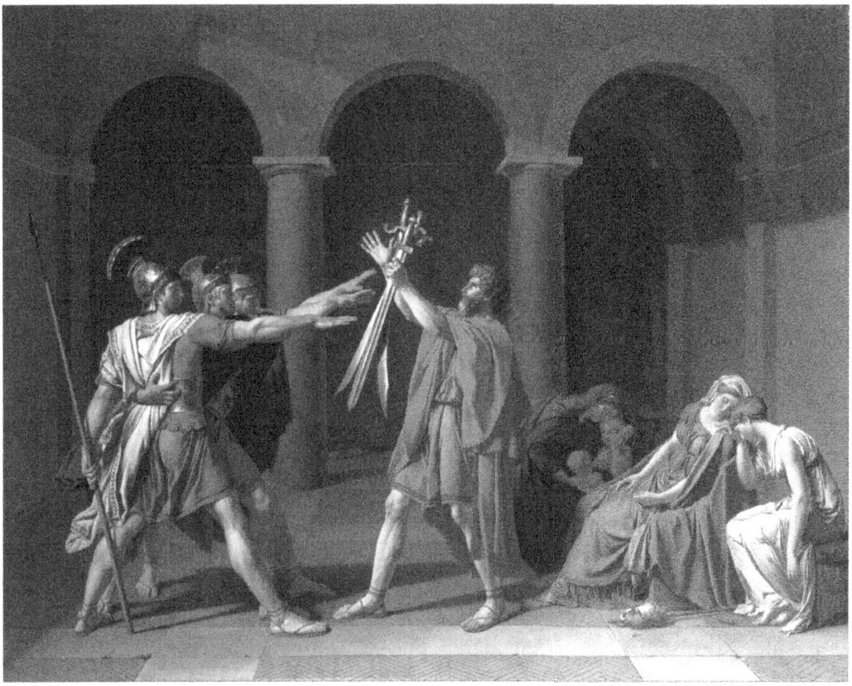

Fig. 2.2 David, Jacques Louis (1748–1825). *The Oath of the Horatii.* Ca. 1784. Oil on canvas, 330 × 425 cm. Inv. 3692. *Photo credit* Scala/Art Resource, NY

anxiety and fear expressed by the conservative critics are accompanied by a perception that David has made an unholy alliance with a public whose desires and interests are alien to their own. They sense that this new and imperfectly known public is being appealed to by the violation of those artistic values they most prize".[52] This corporeal aesthetic of David's belonged to "the special language of truth and virtue".[53] Crow goes on: David's artistic language is Jean-Louis Carra's—a radical pamphleteer—"langage de la vérité: strained, stiff, awkward, obvious".[54] David's artistic language is analogous to a political language that attacks and undermines aristocratic pretense and pretension. Political tracts such as Carra's "read like a particularly fierce variety of anti-Rococo art criticism applied to persons instead of pictures. The insistent emphasis of this literature is on the action of unmasking…"[55]

[52]Crow, Thomas. 1985. *Painters and Public Life in Eighteenth-Century Paris.* New Haven: Yale University Press, 220.

[53]Crow, 1985. 227.

[54]Crow, 1985. 227.

[55]Crow, 1985. 221.

If David aimed to depict a contemporary event in all of its greatness, he also took the liberty[56] of depicting it only so much as it was worthy of memory and greatness. His concern was with what we might call the truth of the event as much as with the event itself. Put differently, he was concerned as much, if not more, with what should have happened as with what in fact happened. For instance, he staged the coming together of the three clergymen (at the front) who symbolically make visible the unification of French society at play in the Oath. One of them, Dom Gerle, moreover, was not even a deputy at the time of the Oath.[57]

Indeed, David had many decisions to make regarding who to include, to exclude, to make recognizable, to place in a position of prominence. Some, including a representative who was not present at the Oath, asked from the moment the painting was being discussed, to please be included in the work of art.[58] And, as time went on, the inclusion of certain men - such as Mounier and Bergasse who "did not hide their regret for having taken the oath"[59]—in the work became problematic given the course of the Revolution as these men abandoned (or were deemed to have abandoned) the truth of the event. By 1791, Bailly had been shunned and guillotined for his implication in the Champ de Mars shootings, involving Lafayette, him and a group of armed men, and a crowd of protesters demanding the King's deposition;[60] Barnave was criticized for having developed ties with the royal family as he escorted them to Paris following their failed escape from the city.[61] Barnave, alongside Mirabeau, had been pantheonized after his death, but both were de-pantheonized later on.[62] The epithet of "grands hommes"[63] was being given away and taken back at a rapid pace, and David had, at least at first, attempted to follow this (r)evolution and only give place to "grands hommes". Indeed, it is fruitful to think about David's sketch as analogous to the Pantheon,[64] as testifying to the difficulty of constituting a common sense of greatness and a shared—and stable—"realm of memory".[65]

We get a further sense of the liberties David took in order to monumentalize "courage and patriotism", to immortalize liberty, by comparing his depiction of the Oath with the choices of others who tackled the subject, such as Jean-Louis Prieur

---

[56]Here as well as two paragraphs below, we borrow and adapt the phrase from Roberts who writes of how "David took liberties". Roberts, 2000. 227.

[57]Roberts, 2000. 242.

[58]Loty, 2009. 29.

[59]Bordes, 1983. 49: "qui ne cachaient pas leur regret d'avoir prêté le serment".

[60]Presenting a petition David himself had signed. Loty, 2009. 32.

[61]Loty, 2009. 34.

[62]Loty, 2009. 34.

[63]The Pantheon's *frontispice* reads: "Aux grands hommes, la patrie reconnaissante".

[64]See Ozouf, Mona. 1998. The Pantheon: The École Normale of the Dead. In *Realms of Memory: The Construction of the French Past*, vol. 3, ed. Pierre Nora, 325–346. Trans. A. Goldhammer. New York: Columbia University Press.

[65]Nora, 1988.

and Charles Monnet (Fig. 2.3) in drawings-turned-engravings.[66] As we have already seen on a smaller scale with regard to the clergymen, David chose to capture the truth of the event not simply with regard to who was there but also *how* they were there. As opposed to Prieur and Monnet, who depict the action along the whole length of the tennis court, as is more likely to have happened, David pushes, so to speak, all the deputies onto one half of the tennis court. Doing so allows him to adopt the view from the other side of the median line,[67] thereby "making" room for the viewer at eye-level, if not that of the participants then of Bailly.[68] Locating the viewer in the room closer to the ground rather than in the air also allows David to capture the individuality of the participants to the oath, to represent bodies with great detail, and represent faces in the likeness of some of the most prominent oath-takers. It also allows him to make the men bigger, more present and imposing. Paradoxically, the aerial view adopted by Prieur and Monnet allows more space between the men, puts forward a less packed scene, but shows the men as a non-descript and almost unimportant mass. While Prieur and Monnet's pieces present a loose(r) gathering, David's presents a tense, compact group of men.

Relative to Prieur and Monnet, David's choices generate a heightened effect of both individuality and unity. It allows him both to attend to the bodies of these individual "grands hommes" and to graphically capture their uniting "into one body" and, in so doing, their "manifest[ing] qualities of a collective 'grand homme'".[69] Together with the elegant proportions and symmetry of the room, the gust of wind, the lightning[70] and the mystical, perhaps divine, quality of the light falling from the sky, David puts forward an overabundance of feeling and presence, showing a scene of enthusiasm, almost too pregnant with spirit. David depicts a moment of fraternal communion, showing the covenantal, sacramental character of the oath,[71] the will to unity of individuals (though not all of them, Martin Dauch, deputy of Castelnaudary, depicted at the far right with crossed arms, opposed the motion).[72]

Several commentators draw attention, as well, to a liberty David did not take. While one can spot the use of allegory, such as the gust of wind or the lightning, David does not make use of an obvious allegorical figure. Rolf Reichardt and Hubertus Kohle point to Monnet's insertion of a "figure personifying Liberty" among "a number of personifications on a cloud bank, somewhat resembling a holy

[66]See generally Bordes, 1983. 41ff.; Reichardt and Kohle, 2008. 94, 96 and Roberts, 2000. 227ff.

[67]Reichardt and Kohle, 2008. 41.

[68]Of course, what is eye-level for a viewer depends also on the location and height at which the huge work was to be fixed.

[69]Johnson, 1993. 84.

[70]See, e.g., Fuhrmeister, Christian. 2009. 'Eripuit caelo fulmen sceptrumque tyrannis': The Political Iconography of Lightning in Europe and North America, 1750-1800. *Transactions of the American Philosophical Society* 99, 144–163.

[71]See, e.g., Agamben, Giorgio. 2010. *The Sacrament of Language: An Archeology of the Oath.* Stanford: Stanford University Press.

[72]Bordes, 1983. 15.

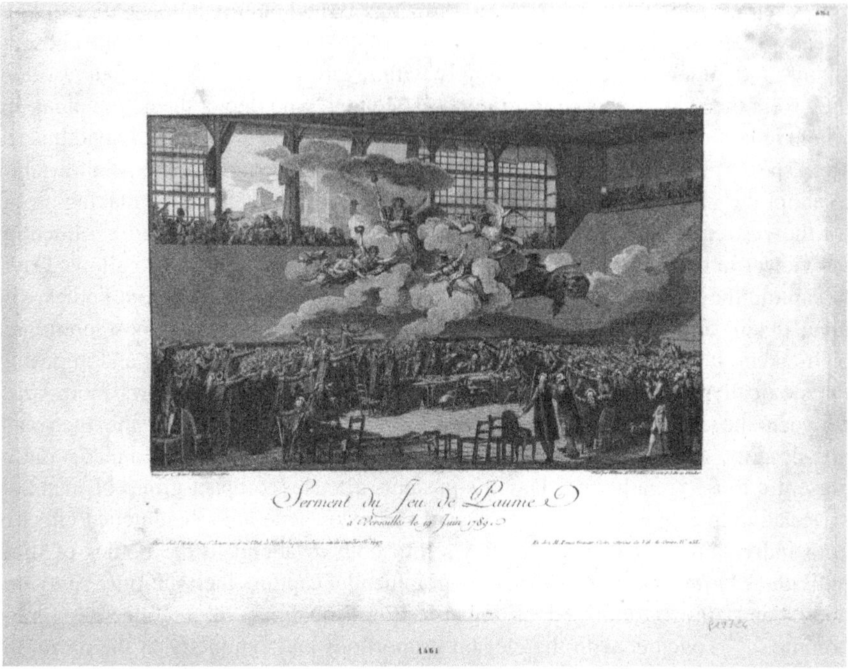

Fig. 2.3 I.S. Helman after Ch. Monnet, *Oath of the Tennis Court in Versaille 19 [i.e. 20] June 1789*, 1792. Europeana/Bibliothèque nationale de France

aura".[73] They suggest that "[a]llegories were a means of imparting universal significance to events" but that "David appears to have believed that the events of his time had universal significance in and of themselves".[74] It is perhaps significant that David did not shy away from allegory in some of his other work as pageant-master of the Revolution. Yet, as Johnson reminds us, his paintings of great Revolutionary men and events almost never included such figures.[75] In any case, David's use of an obvious allegorical figure would have likely filled the large empty space in the *Oath* above the men. His non-use draws attention to the space, allows it to be constitutive of the work, perhaps as much as the men themselves.

Bailly's position facing us, the viewers, rather than the men is perhaps the most obvious and striking liberty David took with the original scene. We can surmise that Bailly would not have stood in such a way, facing the empty half of the room! Prieur and Monnet confirm this doubt. Both show Bailly facing the length of the room; Monnet's Bailly stands by a table with a text in his right hand, while Prieur's Bailly is probably the figure standing on a table, and in both cases the majority of

[73]Reichardt and Kohle, 2008. 96.
[74]Reichardt and Kohle, 2008. 96.
[75]Johnson, 1993. 117.

the oath-takers are either facing him or standing to his left and right. David, on the other hand, places "his" Bailly at the center of all structural lines of his painting—or rather, he so places his Bailly's eyes.[76] The vanishing lines eventually guide the eyes of the viewers back to Bailly's eyes, the very eyes that confront the viewer by looking straight *at* him (and then him or her).

If many of the liberties David took aimed to immortalize the scene, Bailly's facing the viewers may point to David's general efforts to "take" them "in". In a published review of David's sketch presented at the Salon of 1791, a contemporary of David's wrote that "In Mr. David's composition… one feels oneself carried away before having been able to reflect on the nature of the illusion one experiences. One believes oneself to assist and take part in this immortal scene that prepared the triumph of French liberty…"[77] Bailly's turning to the viewer suggests a demand that the viewer not simply "assist" the scene but take part in it. The illusion referred to in the review is thus not the immortality of the scene but the viewer's own presence and involvement in it. Indeed, as we mentioned, the *Oath* was meant to be housed in the National Assembly and the representatives were, in the words of Bordes, to be "called to take part physically and spiritually in the oath".[78]

In other words, Bailly's turning, together with the fraternal energy of the *Oath*, means that perhaps the viewer is meant not only to experience the covenantal, sacramental quality of the Oath but also to take part in it.[79] We might speak of this not only as the viewer's interpellation, his (or her) being called or hailed[80] *as* present or future, actual or potential oath-taker, but also as his (or her) incorporation into the *National* Assembly or the Nation it was meant to "represent." Like the portrait of the king, to which we now turn, we see here a work of sovereign *self*-recognition, a point Marin emphasizes in his work on the king's portrait.[81] It may even be that the "success" of David's *Oath* as a "monument" depends on its success as such a "portrait" (Fig. 2.4).

---

[76]Kemp, Wolfgang. 1994. The Theatre of Revolution: A New Interpretation of Jacques-Louis David's *Tennis Court Oath*. In *Visual Culture: Images and Interpretations*, ed. Norman Bryson, 202–227. Middletown: Wesleyan University Press, 207.

[77]As found in Bordes, 1983. 163: "Dans la composition de M. David …on se sent entraîné avant d'avoir pu réfléchir sur la nature de l'illusion que l'on éprouve. On croit assister et prendre part à cette scène immortelle qui a préparé le triomphe de la liberté française…"

[78]Bordes, 1983. 59: "appelés à prendre part physiquement et spirituellement au serment".

[79]See, e.g., Agamben, 2010.

[80]Althusser, Louis. 1972. Ideology and Ideological State Apparatuses. In *Lenin and Philosophy and Other Essays*. New York: Monthly Review Press.

[81]Marin, 1988, 7–8 and 212–213. See also "The Portrait of the King's Glorious Body" in Marin, Louis. 1997. *Food for Thought*. Trans. Mette Hjort. Baltimore: Johns Hopkins University Press. 189–217.

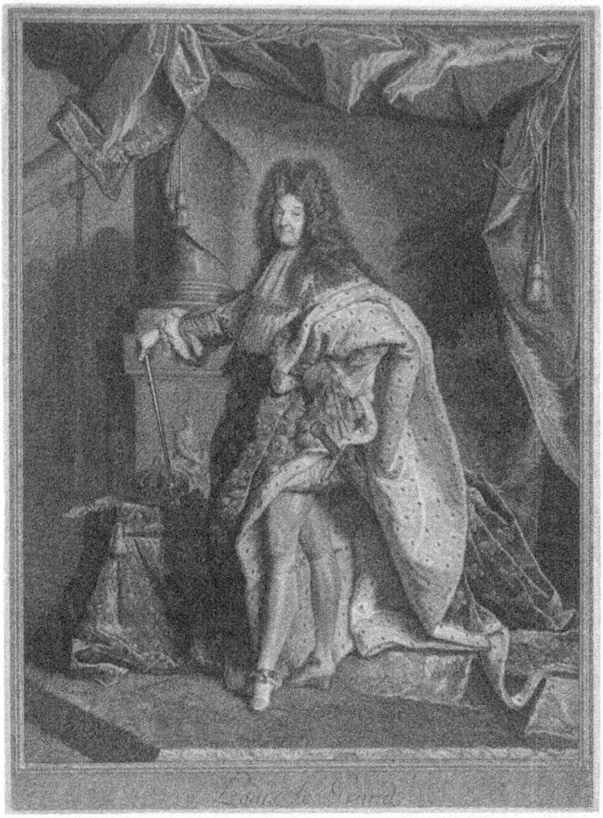

Fig. 2.4 P. Drevet after H. Rigaud, *Portrait of Louis XIV standing in front of his throne*, ca. 1701, print, Rijksmuseum, Amsterdam

2.3 Portrait

As we mentioned above, September 1791 saw the exposition of David's completed sketch of the Tennis Court Oath at the Salon. This was the first "free" Salon;[82] under David's influence, the Assembly had decreed that the Salon would be open to all artists. This decree was not only about taking the "Royal" out of the "Salon;" it was also part of a reaction against intermediate corporate bodies standing between

[82]Chaudonneret, Marie-Claude. 2010. Les artistes vivant au Louvre (1791–1848): du musée au bazar. In *'Ce salon à quoi tout se ramène': Le Salon de peinture et de sculpture, 1791–1890*, ed. James Kearns and Pierre Vaisse, 7–22. Bern: Peter Lang. 7.

the individual and the Nation.[83] September 1791 also saw the King accepting the new Constitution (on 20 September[84]). Two weeks later, the National Assembly asked—required—the King to donate a portrait representing him accepting the Constitution and showing his son this acceptance.[85] As we now know, the 1791 Constitution was short-lived. It was so, in part, because it reflected the ambivalence relative to the monarchy that characterized the men who took the Tennis Court Oath. Indeed, the Constitution identified two representatives of the nation: the legislative body and the king. The trial and execution of Louis XVI in 1793 ostensibly did away with one representative body in favour of the other.

In its request to the king for his portrait, the National Assembly did not impose a specific artist on the king. Surprisingly, it turns out that the King asked David to undertake his portrait and that David even worked to this end.[86] The only traces of this work are, interestingly enough, in the same sketchbook David used for sketches of the spectators in his *Tennis Court Oath*.[87] The preparatory sketches for the portrait reveal more of a "hommage" to the Constitution than to the king.[88] The proposed portrait, it might be said, does not show a sovereign. What is more, the preparatory sketches for the king's portrait lead David beyond the envisaged portrait to a sketch of the French people offering the Constitution, crown, and scepter to the king, "illustrating the idea," in the words of Bordes, that "monarchical authority is *granted* by the revolutionary constitution".[89] In a key moment in the sequence of sketches, David finds himself moving from "a metaphor of the king as Hercules to a metaphor of the national power as Hercules", rejecting the former in favour of the latter. A "new man" takes the place of the king.[90] Thus, David's preparatory sketches for the king's portrait showed, even flaunted, the concretization of the task the men taking the Oath had assigned themselves. Nevertheless, the proposed portrait preserved the king's body, allowing it to co-exist with the Assembly's. Even if David's sketches reveal more of a "hommage" to the Constitution than to the king, we see here the same artist at work on the two potentially rival representative bodies of the nation, and doing so at a time of hostility towards other "bodies".

The *Tennis Court Oath*, just like the portrait of Louis XVI, can and should be seen as a "representation of the new sovereign body regenerated by the

[83]Caubisen-Lasfargues, Colette. 1961. Le salon de peinture pendant la révolution. In Annales historiques de la révolution française. 164: 193–214. 195ff.

[84]Bordes, 1983. 78.

[85]Bordes, 1983. 78.

[86]Bordes, 1983. 79.

[87]See generally Propeck, Lina. 1993. David et le portrait du roi. In *David contre David: Actes du colloque organisé au musée du Louvre par le service culturel du 6 au 10 décembre 1989*, vol. 1. Ed. Régis Michel, 293–318.

[88]Bordes, 1983. 79: "hommage."

[89]Bordes, 1983. 79: "l'autorité monarchique est *concedée* par la constitution révolutionnaire".

[90]Propeck, 1993. 309: "métaphore du roi en Hercule, devient métaphore du pouvoir national en Hercule" and "homme nouveau".

Revolution".[91] Both the *Oath* and the portrait answer the question: in which body is the nation to be found? Previously, the absolutist pretension was that only the portrait of the king could re-present the sovereign body. More than simply the "head" of the realm, as he was in pre-absolutist times, the king *was*—or had taken in—the whole of the realm. As Louis XIV said "L'État c'est moi" (we leave this famous phrase untranslated) and "[t]he nation does not make a body in France, it resides entirely in the person of the King".[92]

The Revolution saw the nation "dare" make a body separate from that of the king.[93] Emancipated from the king, however, this body was not to be found just anywhere. As Sièyes said "[t]he People in its political activity is but in national representation; it makes a body only there".[94] One all-incorporating body (and absolutism) appears to have replaced another. David's *Tennis Court Oath*, then, ought not simply to be related to a tradition of collective portraits,[95] but also depicts the representatives united into *one* body in which—and only in which—the nation *is*.

It is important, then, to consider David's *Tennis Court Oath* as part of a shift from "the sovereignty of the body from the king to the nation",[96] as Antoine de Baecque has insightfully done. According to de Baecque, the Revolution certainly accomplished "the defeat of the body of the king": it rendered the king's body "impotent" by way of such things as satire and often graphic obscenity, thereby confronting its "procreative function, the primary function in a hereditary monarchy".[97] (The *Tennis Court Oath* must not be appreciated in abstract from more "popular" "art.") The defeat of the body of the king is an important part of what Roger Chartier calls the "symbolic and affective disinvestment that transformed relations with authority when it was deprived of all transcendence".[98]

---

[91]Propeck, 1993. 299. Writing of the proposed portrait of Louis XVI: "la représentation du nouveau corps souverain regénéré par la Révolution".

[92]Our translation. As found in Berns, Thomas and Frydman, Benoît. 2005. L'esprit de corps pensé: Généologie de l'esprit de corps. In *L'esprit de corps, démocratie et espace public*, ed. Gilles J. Guglielmi, 159–181. Paris: Presses universitaires de France, 172. They cite to Apostolidès, Jean-Marie. 1981. *Le Roi-Machine. Spectacle et politique au temps de Louis XIV*. Paris: Editions de Minuit, 13: "La nation ne fait pas corps en France, elle réside tout entière dans la personne du Roi".

[93]Berns and Frydman, 2005. 173 cite to Apolostidès, 1981 for the following words pronounced by Louis XV before the Parlement of Paris on 3 March 1766: "Les droits et intérêts de la nation, dit le Roi, dont on ose faire *corps séparé* du monarque, sont nécessairement unis avec les miens et ne reposent qu'en mes mains" (emphasis is that of Berns and Frydman).

[94]As found in Berns and Frydman, 2005. 176. They find these words in Marcel Gauchet, *La Révolution des droits de l'homme*. 1989. Paris: Gallimard, XVIII: "Le Peuple dans son activité politique n'est que dans la représentation nationale. *Il ne fait corps que là*".

[95]Bordes, 1983. 33–35.

[96]De Baecque, 1993. 8. See also, e.g., Melzer, Sara E. and Norberg, Kathryn, eds. 1988. *From the Royal to the Republican Body: Incoporating the Political in Seventeenth- and Eighteenth-Century France*. Berkeley: University of California Press.

[97]De Baecque, 1993. 30.

[98]Chartier, Roger. 1997. *On the Edge of the Cliff: History, Languages, and Practices*. Trans. Lydia G. Cochrane. Baltimore: Johns Hopkins University Press. 75.

De Baecque, however, disagrees with those Revolutionaries for whom the "weight of royal symbolism spoils the register of discourse of the body".[99] He charts the persistence of the register of discourse of the body in the Revolution, even pointing to "the elaboration of a fresh corporeal metaphor"[100] to be found in the thinking and writing of Sièyes and in David's *Tennis Court Oath*. Locating the *Oath* in the persistence of the register of the body makes even more central the corporeal aesthetic we pointed to above and allows one more readily to appreciate the *Oath* as a successor and rival to the portrait of the king, as participating in a symbolic and affective (re)investment in an ostensibly new and perhaps non-transcendent authority (to return to Chartier's words).

Strikingly, de Baecque goes so far as to say that "David represented the Tennis Court Oath literally".[101] One might even say that, as opposed to Monnet and Prieur, the liberties David took in departing from what likely happened allowed him to represent the Oath *literally*! De Baecque explains: David "offers us a vision of the embodiment of the nation according to Sieyès",[102] the author of the oath, the "doctor of the body politic".[103] "[I]n place of the three orders, sometimes divided, sometimes united, but always ready to dissolve", Sieyès substituted "the indivisible body of the nation".[104]

David "drew the corporeal projection of a political text itself constructed around organicist metaphor: here is a body politic made precisely from human bodies".[105] David's regenerated body politic can be understood not only metaphorically, but anatomically,[106] as a figure taking the form of one great organism made up of a multitude of little corporeal fragments.[107] For example, this body has a head in the person of Bailly, a heart in the persons of the three clergymen embracing each other.[108] Moreover, this body combines and exhibits certain "qualities" drawn from individual men, such as "the 'ecstacy' of Barnave, the 'strength' of Dubois-Crancé, the 'speech' of Mirabeau, the 'wisdom' of Sieyès, the 'fraternity' of the clerics, and the 'calm determination' of Bailly".[109]

---

[99]De Baecque, 1993. 77.

[100]De Baecque, 1993. 77.

[101]De Baecque, 1993. 192.

[102]De Baecque, 1993. 195–196.

[103]De Baecque, 1993. 76.

[104]De Baecque, 1993. 96.

[105]De Baecque, 1993. 192.

[106]De Baecque, 1993. 192 and 195.

[107]De Baecque, 1993. 195.

[108]De Baecque, 1993. 193: "The composition of the *Oath* is clearly established according to two axes linked by a certain number of lines of convergence, sometimes broken: 1. A frieze of people in the foreground that represents the expression of the body of the Assembly. 2. The vertical axis drawn from the group of the three religious men and extending up to the head of President Bailly: the *heart* and *face* of the body. 3. Finally, the lines of convergence bearing the series of multiple heads and hands: the *skeleton* of the body."

[109]De Baecque, 1993. 197.

The *Oath*'s corporeal aesthetic, however, reveals more. De Baecque draws attention to David's ambivalent relation to Johann Joachim Winckelmann specifically and more generally to "the canons of propriety and the codes of beauty of the norm, that of the classical revival".[110] "David's bodies are charged," he writes, in a way "that carries them well beyond ideal beauty".[111] In many cases (but not all), "grace" gives way to "agitation".[112] According to de Baecque, David's departure from ideal beauty is tied, among other things, to his will to capture a *revolutionary* event of *regeneration*. This leads him to push some of his bodies towards the "'grimace', toward what is taboo in noble art".[113] The "rupture," the "decisive instant", David seeks to capture is also "an initiatic rite".[114] Accordingly, David *multiplies* his enthusiastic bodies and *crams* them together in order to show not only the re-birth of individual men but the birth of a "great sovereign organism" like the "Hobbesian figure of the Leviathan".[115]

This collective body of the representatives is "majestic and calm in places, but convulsive, electrified, 'mesmerized' in others". This, writes de Baecque, "suggests an integration of evil within the body of the Assembly".[116] David's distance from Winckelmann is tied to David's painting, at one and the same time, the "body of deputies" and "its counterpart," the hydra, the mythical multi-headed beast whose heads grow back when they are cut off, a "monster" closely associated with the "old world" and its "despotism".[117] De Baecque thus ties the corporeal aesthetic of David's *Oath* to the problem of the unity of the Assembly. In "monumental" terms, the potential presence of traitors in the Assembly means the *Oath* is the impossible representation of an event outstripped by what it engendered or participated in. When thinking of the *Oath* as portrait, that same presence, manifest, for example, in the agitation of bodies, points to the fragility, perhaps impossibility, of the Assembly as a body that can rival the king's in its unity and majesty.

Indeed, to experience and to understand the *Tennis Court Oath* as a version of, or successor to, the portrait of the king is to inquire into whether and how the bodies of the representatives and the collective body which they together form could somehow take the place of, and do the psychic and affective work of, the body of the king. Could the Assembly form one perpetual body in which all citizens "could recognize themselves and in which everyone recognized their sovereign"?[118] In the words of Lefort: could the "members" of society be "so captivated by the image" of the body of representatives "that they project on to it their own union, that their

[110]De Baecque, 1993. 186.
[111]De Baecque, 1993. 191–192.
[112]De Baecque, 1993. 196.
[113]De Baecque, 1993. 198.
[114]De Baecque, 1993. 195.
[115]De Baecque, 1993. 196. The words in italics are variations of words de Baecque uses.
[116]De Baecque, 1993. 201.
[117]De Baecque, 1993. 200.
[118]De Baecque, 1993. 8. But writing about the body of the king.

affects are precipitated in an amorous identification with that body"?[119] Seeing the *Tennis Court Oath* as a portrait of the new sovereign body allows one to pursue the questions of the interpellation and incorporation of the viewer raised at the end of our treatment of the *Oath* as Monument.

In thinking along these lines, de Baecque and Lefort follow in the footsteps of Ernst H. Kantorowicz's *The King's Two Bodies: A Study in Medieval Political Theology*, the famous study tracing and articulating the doctrine or idea of the king's two bodies—natural and political, mortal and immortal—one of the "essentials" of which was "[t]he migration of … the immortal part of kingship, from one incarnation to another as expressed by the concept of the king's demise".[120] In his work on corporeal metaphor in the French Revolution, de Baecque acknowledges a debt to Marcel Gauchet's reading of Sieyès's translation or transformation of the king's two bodies into the nation's two bodies. As Gauchet says, "[r]epresentatives [have] become the visible, fallible, mortal body of the invisible, perpetual body of the Nation".[121]

De Baecque, however, despite noting Sieyès' "theologico-political vocabulary" and that Sieyès' "bodily metaphors are haunted by his religious education",[122] believes Gauchet does not sufficiently attend to Sieyès's secularization, even demystification, of this political theological doctrine. It is significant that Kantorowicz chose "mysticism" as the first word in his introduction to *The King's Two Bodies*. The king's immortal body was a, if not *the*, key part of, the *corpus mysticum* of the realm,[123] itself modeled on or akin to "the totality of Christian society in its organological aspects".[124] (Previously, however, the term *corpus mysticum* referred to the Eucharist, "the consecrated host".[125]) Could the nation have two bodies without participating in mysticism? If not a *corpus mysticum*, what could this second body be?

When writing principally about the *Tennis Court Oath*, and referencing its apocalyptic, baptismal, even resurrection-ary character,[126] de Baecque says that David "sees in this 'wonderful regeneration' the result of the process of incarnation of the body politic of the new National Assembly".[127] "Incarnation" is an important word here, hearkening back to the doctrine of the king's two bodies and to the Christian mystery of a God made flesh. To the extent that the *Tennis Court Oath*

---

[119]Lefort, 1988. 242–243, writing of Michelet on monarchical incarnation.

[120]Kantorowicz, Ernst H. 1957. *The King's Two Bodies: A Study in Medieval Political Theology*. Princeton: Princeton University Press, 13.

[121]De Baecque, 1993. 101 citing Gauchet, 1989. 26.

[122]De Baecque, 1993. 97. One such word is "adunation" used until the sixteenth century "in order to designate the grouping together of the apostles around Christ".

[123]Kantorowicz, 1957. 220.

[124]Kantorowicz, 1957. 119, 209.

[125]Kantorowicz, 1957. 195.

[126]De Baecque, 1993. 195.

[127]De Baecque, 1993. 195.

invokes or performs *incarnation*, one might say that it remains in, participates in, or adapts the political theological doctrine of the king's two bodies.

When writing principally about Sieyès, however, de Baecque claims that Sieyès' thinking "turns mystical reincarnation into a permanent elective renewal".[128] After all, Sieyès had proposed the replacement of deputies in thirds such that the body of the National Assembly would always remain in being.[129] As de Baecque explains, Sieyès' plans for the Assembly's "permanent regeneration"[130] would grant it a "durability that places it in direct rivalry with the body of the king: a body that has become perpetually political".[131] With such an Assembly, there would be no need for the equivalent to the cries of "The King is dead. Long live the King". There would be no competition, or shadow or echo thereof, between the dead body of the king and the king's effigy during funerary rites.[132] While Sieyès would retain bodies politic and incorporation, there would presumably be no more problems that come along with the fleshly character of sovereignty (recall the difference between the carnal and the corporeal). Nevertheless, de Baecque recognizes that "Gauchet comments on what history did indeed decide to preserve: the fallible body of the National Assembly".[133]

Raising the question of the *Tennis Court Oath* as a successor or rival to the portrait of the king involves not only thinking about the transformation of the king's two bodies into the nation's two bodies but also about the work of David's *Oath* itself with regard to republican power. Recall that Lefort writes of the "captivation" of the "members" of society by the "*image*" (our emphasis) of a body. As one scholar puts it, echoing Louis Marin, "like state power itself, the 'body' in which it is located is no mere pre-social lump of flesh but an instituted body, one instituted in part by being represented".[134] Does, can, David's *Oath* institute a national, republican body, by representing it?

On this point, de Baecque is close not only to Kantorowicz but to Marin,[135] for whom the portrait of the king operates as "the sacramental body of the monarch", just as the consecrated host.[136] Marin writes that he is "in all modesty" expanding Kantorowicz's work: "for 'classical' absolutism: the king has only one body left, but this sole body, in truth, unifies three, a physical historical body, a juridico-political body, and a semiotic sacramental body",[137] There are no 'two

[128]De Baecque, 1993. 100.

[129]De Baecque, 1993. 99.

[130]De Baecque, 1993. 101.

[131]De Baecque, 1993. 102.

[132]Kantorowicz, 1957. 423.

[133]De Baecque, 1993. 102.

[134]Schmitter, Amy M. 2002. Representation and the Body of Power in French Academic Painting. 63: Journal of the History of Ideas, 399–424, 400.

[135]De Baecque, 1993. 8.

[136]Marin, 1988, 12.

[137]Marin, 1988, 14.

bodies' of the king without this third semiotic sacramental one. The portrait makes possible the incarnation of the immortal body of the king into his mortal one. In its "sacramental mystery", the king's portrait "makes one conceive of the union of subjects in a same collective body whose head is the king, the body of the kingdom whose subjugated [assujettis] members find an identity in the king's name that the portrait inscribes".[138]

So, to think about the *Oath* in relation to the portrait of the king of absolutism, which it ostensibly displaces and replaces, is perhaps also to think of it as doing the semiotic, sacramental work of incorporation by performing or participating in the mystery of incarnation. We have already mentioned how, in monumental terms, the *Oath*'s almost necessary incompletion is tied to aspiring to the impossible representation of an event outstripped by what it engendered or participated in. However, perhaps the necessary incompletion of the *Oath* also bespeaks an impossible incorporation, or more precisely an impossible incarnation. As Berns and Frydman points out, "the figure of *incarnation…* offers the perfect model (and the measure) of incorporation, as total fusion of multiplicity".[139]

Perhaps the incompletion of the *Oath* reflects not simply that David could not "keep up" with the Revolution but also, and relatedly, that his aesthetic—to which, as we have seen, de Baecque points—bespeaks a fleshly disruption of a body politic at a time when thinkers such as Sieyès were reaching for a way of thinking incorporation without mystical incarnation. While these thoughts are all tentative, we can at least affirm the fruitfulness of asking whether and how the *Oath* points to, in the words of Berns and Frydman, "the necessity of approaching the figure of incorporation independently of the model of incarnation".[140] In this way, it could be both a successor to, and a departure from, the king's portrait.

In our next part, we turn to a model—and measure—of representation that ostensibly departs from incarnation, that of the tableau. Such a model and measure allows us to pursue the idea of the interpellation and incorporation of the viewer. It also allows us to pursue a theme implicit in treating the *Oath* in relation to that of the king's portrait: the theme of the sovereign's own self-recognition in his image. With the move from portrait of the king to portrait of the nation, the subject's recognition of the sovereign and the sovereign's own self-recognition ostensibly become, or collapse into, one. Perhaps too, then, the success of the *Oath* as a portrait of a (republican) sovereign is itself dependent on its success as a tableau (Fig. 2.5).

---

[138]Marin, 1988, 209. Marin, Louis. 1981. *Le portrait du roi*. Paris: Les Éditions de Minuit. 255.

[139]Berns & Frydman, 2005, 165: "la figure de l'*incarnation* qui offre le modèle parfait (et la mesure) de l'incorporation, comme fusion totale de la multiplicité."

[140]Berns & Frydman, 2005, 166: "la nécessité d'aborder la figure de l'incorporation indépendamment du modèle de l'incarnation".

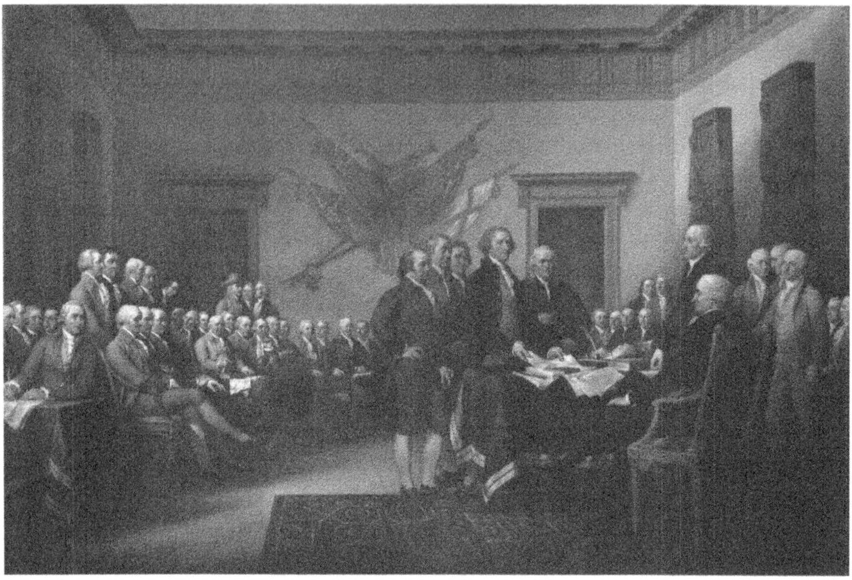

Fig. 2.5 John Trumbull, *Declaration of Independence*, 1818 (placed 1826), oil on canvas, Rotunda. U.S. Capitol. Architect of the Capital

2.4 Tableau

Étienne-Jean Delécluze, David's student and future biographer, noted that the men in David's *Tennis Court Oath* appeared in stark contrast with those in John Trumbull's *The Declaration of Independence*: "In the act passed by the Americans, all is calm, and one would think there were wise and upright merchants making a deal [qui contractent un marché]. In the *Tennis Court* of Versailles, everyone is in convulsion, and some even have the attitude of actors. Is it the fault of the men, is it the fault of the painter, is it everyone's fault? It's a curious and good question to deepen".[141] Delécluze's remarks about convulsion anticipate de Baecque's analysis of David's departure from grace in his painting of agitated bodies.[142] Delécluze's remark about some men having the attitude of actors says something more. Indeed,

[141]Bordes 1983. 38 and 103, note 117: "Dans l'acte passé par les Américains, tout est calme, et l'on dirait des marchands sages et probes qui contractent un marché. Dans le *Jeu de paume* de Versailles, tout le monde est en convulsion, et quelques-uns même ont l'attitude de comédiens. Est-ce la faute des acteurs, est-ce la faute du peintre, est-ce la faute de tous? C'est une question curieuse et bonne à approfondir".

[142]Bordes writes that Delécluze, in ascribing convulsion to all the men, misses that Bailly and Sieyès, right at the center, are just as calm as the American men. Bordes, 1983, 38.

why would David's *Oath* resemble a "theatre scene", even a "dramatic finale"[143] and what might be the significance of this resemblance? Delécluze raises the question of what we might call the theatrical or dramatic (to use the terms loosely and interchangeably for the moment) character of David's *Oath* and of the Oath itself. A question, as we shall see, not unrelated to our appreciation of the *Oath* as a successor to the king's portrait.

Delécluze raises the possibility that David attempted to capture a moment that was lived, even performed, theatrically or dramatically. Tied to this possibility are the questions of whether and how the representatives were, self-consciously or not, playing parts on a political 'stage' and of whether and how they were living out, in Marie-Hélène Huet's words, "the Revolution's constant concern with making the people into a public".[144] Recent scholarly work, following Huet's, has inquired into the relation of Revolutionary politics and theatre, from the "remarkable number of actors and dramatists" rising to power, to the "political culture" of the Revolution borrowing "from dramatic and theatrical convention"[145] to "the general merging of the theatrical and political stages".[146] The projected National Assembly meeting place in which the *Oath* was to be placed was itself inspired by a (semicircular) design of theaters which had only recently been elaborated.[147] Moreover, it has been noted that "even before the National Assembly had officially come into existence, the deputies of the third estate had distinguished themselves from the deputies of the first two estates by breaking with tradition and allowing the audience to witness their debates".[148] It has also been suggested that the men taking the Tennis Court Oath "consciously or not, modeled their performance on David's *Oath of the Horatii*, precisely in the manner of a living tableau".[149]

Delécluze also raises the question of David's responsibility not merely for capturing the theatrical or dramatic quality of the moment but also for rendering the moment theatrically or dramatically. Monumentally, one might say that David "rewrites" history.[150] In terms of portrait, one might say David "re-incorporates" or

[143]Bordes 1983. 59 turning to Dowd, David L. 1960. Art and Theater During the French Revolution: The Role of Louis David. Art Quarterly 23:1, 3–20.

[144]Huet, Marie-Hélène. 1982. *Rehearsing the Revolution: The Staging of Marat's Death* 1793–1797. Berkeley: University of California Press, 35.

[145]Buckley, Matthew S. 2006. *Tragedy Walks the Streets: The French Revolution in the Making of Modern Drama.* Baltimore: Johns Hopkins University Press, 3.

[146]Friedland, Paul. 2002. *Political Actors: Representative Bodies & Theatricality in the Age of the French Revolution.* Ithaca: Cornell University Press, 2.

[147]Kemp, Wolfgang. 1994. "The Theatre of Revolution: A New Interpretation of Jacques-Louis David's *Tennis Court Oath*" in *Visual Culture: Images and Interpretation*, eds. Norman Bryson, Michael Ann Holly, and Keith Moxey. 209.

[148]Friedland, 2002. 180.

[149]Thévoz, Michel. 1989. *Le théâtre du crime: essai sur la peinture de David.* Paris: Les éditions de minuit, 15: "les députés ont, consciemment ou non, calqué leur prestation sur le Serment des Horaces, à la manière d'un tableau vivant, précisément". See also Cecilia Feilla. 2013. *The Sentimental Theatre of the French Revolution.* Farnham: Ashgate, 65.

[150]Drawn from the title of Trey and de Baecque, 2008.

"re-incarnates" the body politic. For the purposes of this section, we might speak of a "(re-) staging" of the event, of a new mise-en-scène, to go along with a new mise-en-sens (to return to Lefort's words from our introduction). David's re-staging of the event raises not simply the question of the relation of theatre to politics but also the question of the relation of painting, of David's painting, and of the *Oath* in particular, to theatre. Matthew Buckley writes of an "early political appropriation of bourgeois theatricality, immensely powerful in 1789" that "reached its highpoint in Jacques-Louis David's attempt to commemorate the Tennis Court Oath".[151] Cecilia Feilla notes the general interpenetration and mutual influence of painting and theatre, including the performance of paintings on stage and paintings inspired by plays. Of David, more specifically, she writes, "his monumental paintings reflect the dramaturgy of the stage"[152] and identifies him as "perhaps the figure who best exemplifies the interpenetration of visual, dramatic, and political culture during the years 1789–1799".[153] And, perhaps most tellingly, Michel Thévoz writes that the "referential code" of David's painting, "is theatre".[154]

Just as Sieyès becomes crucial when thinking of David's *Oath* as a potential successor to the king's portrait, so too does Denis Diderot become crucial when thinking of its theatrical quality. Indeed, Feilla notes that "the formal strategies of Diderot's sentimental aesthetics are deployed by David for a political message and end".[155] David's expressive or eloquent bodies, to which we have already pointed, resonate greatly with Diderot's "intense readings of the corporal signs in paintings exhibited at the Salons" in prior decades.[156] These readings are themselves tied to Diderot's elaboration of the drame or "drame bourgeois" (a dramatic form aspiring to the representation of "the ordinary life of familiar people"[157]) in which elaboration gesture and pantomime figured prominently.[158] We pointed out Bailly's turning to face the viewer of the painting. Scholars debate whether Bailly's turning to face the viewer is—or is not—the kind of *coup de théâtre* (or plot twist relying on an unforeseen incident)[159] Diderot so decried.[160] If it were, it would undermine David's *Oath* as a *tableau* which Diderot describes—in theatre—by turning to painting: "A disposition of characters on the stage, so natural and true, that if

[151]Buckley, 2006. 38.

[152]Feilla, 2013. 87.

[153]Feilla 2013. 86.

[154]Thévoz, 1989. 8: "Le code de référence de sa peinture, c'est le théâtre."

[155]Feilla, 2013. 87.

[156]Johnson, 1993. 23.

[157]Jack Undank, 1986. "Diderot and the Phenomenology of the Ordinary" Diderot Studies 22: 143-170, 152.

[158]Johnson, 1993. 19.

[159]Diderot, Denis. 1757. *Entretiens sur le fils naturel* in Oeuvres Esthétiques, ed. P. Vernière. Paris: Garnier, 1966. 88: "Un incident imprévu qui se passe en action, et qui change subitement l'état des personnages, est un coup de théâtre".

[160]Bordes, 1983. 59.

faithfully rendered by a painter, it would please me on canvas, is a tableau".[161] Bailly's turning could potentially make the scene appear unnatural and false as the actors would no longer be "absorbed" in their own activities.

Michael Fried has seized on the idea of absorption to describe a mid-eighteenth century "anti-theatrical" tradition of painting in France—in which Diderot and David both feature significantly—which "treated the beholder as if he were not there".[162] In so doing, he insists on anti-theatricality as a kind of sensibility that informed the appreciation and production of works of art—and not as an inherent quality of certain works.[163] Seen in this light, the "grimace" to which de Baecque draws attention might be judged—or not—as akin to a *coup de théâtre*, as undermining the naturalness of the scene. Indeed, the entry for "grimace" (with respect to painting) in Diderot and d'Alembert's *Encyclopédie* opposes grimace to grace, associating the former with a kind of charge (another word de Baecque uses) or fakeness.[164] Both in terms of the theatrical or dramatic quality of the scene and David's potentially theatrical or dramatic rendering, one might say that the *Oath* invites one to consider, or ought not to be appreciated without considering, the "revolutionary anxiety about theatricality".[165]

As we have hinted at, the tradition Fried draws attention to is tied to a change in genre from "theatre", and all the conventions to which Diderot was averse, to "drama".[166] Feilla writes of a "representational shift from portrait to tableau in theatre"[167] and associates the "*tableau* in art" generally with the rejection of "the theatricality of court painting".[168] With this shift, theatre (and art more generally)

[161]Diderot, 1757. 88: "Une disposition de ces personnages sur la scène, si naturelle et si vraie, que, rendue fidèlement par un peintre, elle me plairait sur la toile, est un tableau".

[162]Fried, Michael. 1988. *Absorption and Theatricality: Painting and Beholder in the Age of Diderot*. Chicago: University of Chicago Press, 5. See also Fried, Michel. 1993. David et l'antithéatralité. In *David contre David: Actes du colloque organisé au musée du Louvre par le service culturel du 6 au 10 décembre 1989*, vol. 1, ed. Régis Michel, 199–227; as well as Fried, Michael. 2015. *Another Light: Jacques-Louis David to Thomas Demand*. New Haven: Yale University Press.

[163]See, e.g., Fried 1993. 214. See also Fried, 2015. 12.

[164]Watelet, *Encyclopédie, Dictionnaire raisonné des sciences, des arts et des métiers, par une Société de Gens de lettres. Tome 7.* [1757] Le Breton 1757. 948: "Je sais que vous pouvez m'objecter que presque toutes les expressions que vous envisagez autour de vous sont ou chargées ou feintes, que presque tout ce qu'on appelle grâce est affectation et grimace… Refléchissez, pénétrez-vous des sujets que vous traitez, descendez en vous-mêmes, et cherchez-y cette naïveté des grâces, cette franchise des passions, que l'intérêt que vous avez à les saisir, vous fera trouver".

[165]Maslan, Susan. 2005. *Revolutionary Acts: Theater, Democracy, and the French Revolution*. Baltimore: Johns Hopkins University Press, 75.

[166]Fried 1993. 202. He writes: "Dans les textes que Dideroit écrivit dans les années 1750 et 1760, théâtre et art dramatique deviennent des concepts antithétiques. Le vrai drame exclut le théatre tandis que le moindre soupçon de théâtre tue le drame".

[167]Feilla, 2013. 73.

[168]Feilla, 2013. 75–76.

no longer concerns itself with the "portrait of an isolated hero".[169] Along with the shift from the extraordinary to the ordinary comes, in Diderot's terms, an emphasis on "conditions" rather than "characters".[170] This emphasis is tied to the possibility of spectatorial self–recognition: the focus on conditions rather than characters, Diderot says, makes it harder for the spectator to say something like "that's not me!"[171]

Relating Diderot's views on tableaux to "tabular forms" as "procedures of knowledge" more generally,[172] Feilla suggests the tableau dramatizes "the diverse positions of individuals in society and their relations" so as to best "convey a moral lesson".[173] Buckley describes the Oath itself as resonant with Diderot's aesthetics and with the tableau specifically: "no other event during the Revolution so satisfied Diderot's demands for a moment of harmonious inevitability that revealed true social relations, a moment that clarified the connections between virtuous action and favourable circumstance and, in so doing, conveyed the promise of a reformed society".[174] If de Baecque emphasizes David's *literal* representation of the Oath with regard to the *body* of the National Assembly, the *Oath* as tableau is also key to David's allowing the truth of the event to interpellate the viewers of his work. For Diderot, the self-absorption of those rendered in a tableau is meant to enable the viewer both to understand the set of relations presented and, as importantly, "to be moved by its emotion".[175]

The shift in genre from portrait to tableau corresponds to a political shift from king to nation, from monarchy to republic. It might even be useful to think of the tableau as the portrait's "anti-genre", as emerging as the portrait's antithesis,[176] just as, politically, republicanism ostensibly emerges as monarchy's, or at least the *ancien régime*'s antithesis. In this way, the very form of the tableau is Revolutionary, just as are David's expressive bodies. (Paradoxically, and as we mentioned above, because the king's portrait is tied to sovereign *self*-recognition,

---

[169]Feilla, 2013. 72.

[170]Diderot 1757. 153: "Que ce ne sont plus, à proprement parler, les caractères qu'il faut mettre sur la scène, mais les conditions. Jusqu'à present, dans la comédie, le caractère a été l'objet principal, et la condition n'a été que l'accessoire; il faut que la condition devienne aujourd'hui l'objet principal, et que le caractère ne soit que l'accessoire".

[171]Diderot 1757. 153: "Pour peu que le caractère fût chargé, un spectateur pouvait se dire à lui-même, ce n'est pas moi. Mais il ne peut se cacher que l'état qu'on joue devant lui, ne soit le sien".

[172]Feilla, 2013. 70, turning to Foucault, Michel. 1973. *The Order of Things: An Archeology of the Human Sciences*. New York: Vintage.

[173]Feilla, 2013. 71.

[174]Buckley, 2006. 39–40.

[175]Feilla, 2013. 74.

[176]Fowler, Alastair. 1982. *Kinds of Literature: An Introduction to the Theory of Genres and Modes*. Cambridge, MA: Harvard University Press 1982, 175.

it may well be that the *Oath*'s success as a portrait requires its success as a tableau as well.) More generally, it may well be that shifts in political sensibility go along with what we may call shifts in aesthetic sensibility and even that all political shifts and critiques of any significance necessarily undermine, upset, re-appropriate existing genres.[177] For instance, Diderot's related defence of the novel and its invitation to "identification" or "empathy" figures prominently in Lynn Hunt's account of the rise of human rights.[178] And, she even writes of novelists inviting their readers to "daily life as a kind of substitute religious experience".[179]

It should not come as a surprise, then, that the decline of "incarnation" may be an important feature of the shift from portrait (of the king) to tableau (of representatives). Paul Friedland is perhaps the scholar who most engages with the decline of the logic of incarnation with regard to theatrical representation, political representation, and their relation. He even sees a "conceptual identity" between these two forms of representation and argues that "a radical and simultaneous revolution … struck both in the second half of the eighteenth century".[180]

Prior to 1750, Friedland writes, the widely-held conception of the work of theatrical actors was that "[b]y lending their bodies to the words of the author and giving flesh to the spirit of the character, actors performed a profane version of Christ's Incarnation".[181] He writes that the *ancien régime* "ostracized" actors (as well as Jews and executioners) because their own performances (or views) of incarnation "toyed with or negated the sanctity of the corpus mysticum".[182] Friedland traces the revolution in theatre to François Riccoboni's mid-century tract, *L'art du théatre*—as well as to Diderot's very similar work twenty or so years later. With regard to the passions actors presented, verisimilitude would replace truth and "imitation" would replace "transubstantiation" and "metamorphosis".[183] Indeed, "this new, artificial system depended, not on the actor's belief (it actually precluded

[177]See, e.g., Victoria Kahn on how Hobbes' *Leviathan* as political critique going along with a critique of romance. Kahn, Victoria. 2004. Wayward Contracts: The Crisis of Political Obligation in England, 1640–1674. Princeton: Princeton University Press.

[178]Lynn, Hunt. 2008. *Inventing Human Rights: A History*. New York: W.W. Norton & Co. 55. On the themes of this paragraph and for an engagement with Hunt, see Antaki, Mark. 2013. "Genre, Critique, and Human Rights" University of Toronto Quarterly 82:4, 974–996.

[179]Hunt, 2008. 58.

[180]Friedland, 2002. 3.

[181]Friedland, 2002. 19.

[182]Friedland, 2002. 4, 5.

[183]Friedland, 2002. 21. At 22: "Diderot maintained that acting had nothing to do with the presentation of true passions but rather with the abstract or figurative representation of those passions in outward mannerisms". Buckley, however, writes that "rather than marking a move away from models of metamorphosis to models of imitation, the shift in theatrical aesthetics that took place during the pre-Revolutionary period marked a shift away from a frankly theatrical stage—one that traditionally acknowledged and foregrounded the explicitly fictive quality of theater—to a stage devoted to the effective creation of a realist-illusionist theatre, in which fiction became (or was to become) indistinguishable from life". Buckley, 2006. 36–37.

the actor's belief), but rather (echoing Fried) on the *spectator's* belief".[184] Friedland actually goes further: "the new theater set about *inventing* the modern spectator, to whom it then transferred the burden of belief".[185] Indeed, the new system was tied to, and called for, changes in theatre design and in the actual conditions of theatrical representation (such as "the fourth wall"). As he writes, the "passive and silent individual, seated in the darkness, obsessed with the action on the lighted stage" had not exited prior to the theatrical revolution.[186] This is a key point because of the intertwining of aesthetic interpellation (e.g. as theater-goer, as novel-reader) and political interpellation (e.g. as citizen).

With regard to *political* representation, then, Friedland makes a parallel claim. He argues that there was a shift from "[a] politics of embodiment" to "[a] politics of vraissemblance". Paradoxically, he ties this shift to the *séance de flagellation* of March 1766, a "royal denunciation of parlementary arrogance" during which Louis XV stated that some would "dare make a body separated from the monarch".[187] Friedland notes that around this time royal propaganda meant to influence "public opinion" began to grow. He writes: "for the political actor of the king, whose legitimacy had always been a self-evident consequence of re-presentational embodiment, to turn to the political audience for legitimacy signals a turning point in the history of political representation".[188]

Even prior to the turn to "public opinion," the rise of absolutism had challenged existing notions and practices of representation and had, as Marin suggests, effectively turned the king's two bodies into one. Following Kantorowicz, Friedland highlights the exceptional incarnation of the *corpus mysticum* (which he dubs "the true object of political re-presentation"[189]) in the convening of the Estates-General. Friedland insists on the actual creation of a national body, both in the procession[190] but also in a national will formed by the drafting of local *cahiers*, which "underwent several rounds of condensation" and were transported by delegates who swore not to alter their contents.[191] Sieyès' expulsion of the nobility from the national body goes along with the move from portrait to tableau. For Friedland, Sieyès' views on proportionate representation signal the death of the mystical

[184] Friedland, 2002, 23.

[185] Friedland, 2002. 23.

[186] Friedland, 2002. 23.

[187] Friedland, 2002. 60, 61.

[188] Friedland, 2002. 61.

[189] Friedland, 2002. 30. Kantorowicz provides examples of the King being kept in check by the idea that his sovereignty came from his second body, that one that was truly *the body politic incarnate*, or to borrow from Elizabethan legal definitions, "consisting of Policy and Government". Kantorowicz, 1957. 7. He highlights a 1489 interaction between the Parlement de Paris and the King's council, during which the Parlement claimed to be itself a mystical body representing the King as "sovereign Justice of the Realm of France" to stop the King's council's interference. Kantorowicz, 1957. 210–11.

[190] Friedland, 2002. 42.

[191] Friedland, 2002. 34.

body and the possibility of its incarnation, its coming into presence, however exceptional.[192] He connects Sieyès to Diderot: "Exactly as on Diderot's theatrical stage, the actors in this pretend Champs-de Mars must pretend that their audience does not exist".[193] The "new political asesthetic" of the revolution signaled that "the people, in whose name representation was predicated, had been cleared from the stage".[194]

The National Assembly would follow the absolutist king and not the older practice of the actual—although exceptional—incarnation of the *corpus mysticum*: "The National Assembly's legitimacy would come not from its cahiers or from its mandates but from the willingness of the people to regard it as legitimate. Exactly as if the deputies had been modern actors on the theatrical stage, it mattered little whether their performance was *real*; but it mattered very much whether the public regarded their performance as vraissemblable".[195] When the National Assembly took the place of king, Friedland says, "…unlike previous political bodies that had claimed to *be* the French nation, the National Assembly merely claimed to speak on the nation's behalf".[196] Buckley remarks that not merely the king but the representative actors themselves lost their credibility following the king's attempt to flee and his being stopped at Varennes. "Not coincidentally," he writes, "it was at this time that David abandoned his painting of the Tennis Court Oath".[197] It is no longer a question here of this or that man being present or absent from the work (as in our reading of the work as Monument above) but of the whole "show" falling apart. For Buckley, the theatrical (or anti-theatrical) aesthetic of the Revolution—in which Diderot's *bourgeois drame* and David's *Oath* were inscribed—was fatally flawed.

2.5 Conclusion: "Actors in Waiting"?

We mentioned above the scholarly debate regarding whether or not Bailly's turning to face the viewer of the painting was the kind of *coup de théatre* Diderot decried that would somehow disqualify David's *Oath* from being a tableau. In her work, Feilla follows Huet in describing Diderot's spectator, the spectator of a tableau,

[192] Friedland, 2002. 123.

[193] Friedland, 2002. 160.

[194] Friedland, 2002. 80.

[195] Friedland, 2002. 141.

[196] Friedland, 2002. 6.

[197] Buckley, 2006. 56. At 49–50, Buckley also points to the October Days of 1789 as signaling an important shift: "With startling rapidity, the Revolution's new leaders found themselves acting not before the limited sphere of informed opinion, an audience apt to sympathize with the Diderotian theater of the Tennis Court, but before a much larger and more diverse audience, and one now informed by a press that was well prepared to critique—and even to try to script—the performance".

as "an actor 'in waiting'".[198] The logic of the tableau is such as to interpellate its spectator as a future actor and to model his future action for him. Following Fried, however, she does not see Bailly's turning as undoing the *Oath* as a tableau, as breaking the spell of absorption. Rather, "in the revolutionary context after 1790 the political mission of David redefined the problem of theatricality".[199] The spectators are to be absorbed not simply through sympathetic identification but, as it were, more directly, more immediately. David's *Oath*, it would seem, accomplishes and politicizes the tableau such that the waiting of the spectator is abolished. In this way, it points forward to attempts to abolish the actor-spectator distinction altogether, for example in the revolutionary festival.[200] In the same way, it points to the electrification or charge-bearing of *all* bodies. For instance, Eric Santner's work turns to David's *Marat* as a pivotal moment in understanding the shift from political theology—in which the king's body is the sole or principal one libidinally charged —to biopolitics. Our chapter suggests that perhaps David's *Oath*, as well as the pre-absolutist *corpus mysticum*, ought to figure in this story too.

If we follow Friedland, however, the "waiting" of the *Oath's* spectator who is an "actor in waiting" is likely to be perpetual, the call to action to be experienced, if immediately, also vicariously. In this way, David's *Oath*, by way of Diderot's *drame*, points also to such things as melodrama in which the intensity of the identification, the immediacy of the experience of the call to action may dis-charge the one being interpellated as much as call him or her to action.[201] In this way too, the *Oath* invites us to consider how successful the pacification of the audience has been, both in Revolutionary times and in our own, in both theatre and in politics. Friedland himself is quite aware of this question.[202] In her reaction to Friedland, Sarah Maslan draws attention to the activity of theatre audiences during the Revolution. In her opinion, "[t]he revolutionary theatre, unlike representative political institutions, was a place in which representation and direct participation were entirely compatible".[203] Bailly himself, she points out, was worried about the mutual electrification that takes place among theatre-goers.[204] Theatrical representation emerges as a potential critique of and alternative to political representation.

[198]Feilla, 2013. 75.

[199]Feilla, 2013. 89.

[200]See Friedland, 2002. 255. See Buckley, 2006. 40.

[201]On the Revolution, melodrama, and the melodramatic body, see Brooks, Peter. 1991. The Revolutionary Body. In *Fictions of the French Revolution*, ed. Bernadette Fort. Evanston, IL: Northwestern University Press. On how melodrama can dis-charge one from action, see chapter 2 of Robert Meister, 2011. *After Evil: A Politics of Human Rights*. New York: Columbia University Press.

[202]See in particular chapter 8 of Friedland, 2002 entitled: "Breaching the Fourth Wall: Spectators Storm the Stage, Actors Invade the Audience".

[203]Maslan, Susan. 2005. *Revolutionary Acts: Theater, Democracy, and the French Revolution*. Baltimore: Johns Hopkins University Press. 17.

[204]Maslan. 2005. 33.

David's *Oath* is both a work that depicts electrification and an electrifying work. As we have seen, its bodies are both eloquent and charged. Bailly's turning to face the spectator raises the questions—directly to each one of us—of the character of the represented electrification and of whether and how, actually or virtually, we participate in it. How are we, and not simply the representatives, "charged" or "discharged," as citizens of republics or democracies? Attending (note the French "attendre") to David's *Oath* may help us experience ourselves as the kind of "actors in waiting" we are.

Acknowledgements We would like to thank Mireille Fournier and Spencer Young for their thoughtful help as well as John-Andrew Petrakis for a few early conversations. We are grateful for the financial support of the Social Sciences and Humanities Research Council of Canada.

References

Agamben, Giorgio. 2010. *The Sacrament of Language: An Archeology of the Oath*. Stanford: Stanford University Press.

Althusser, Louis. 1972. Ideology and Ideological State Apparatuses. In *Lenin and Philosophy and Other Essays*. New York: Monthly Review Press.

Antaki, Mark. 2013. Genre, Critique, and Human Rights. *University of Toronto Quarterly* 82 (4): 974–96.

Apostolidès, Jean-Marie. 1981. *Le Roi-Machine. Spectacle et politique au temps de Louis XIV*. Paris: Editions de Minuit.

Berns, Thomas and Frydman, Benoît. 2005. L'esprit de corps pensé: Généologie de l'esprit de corps. In *L'esprit de corps, démocratie et espace public*, ed. Gilles J. Guglielmi, 159–81. Paris: Presses universitaires de France.

Bordes, Philippe. 1983. *Le Serment du Jeu de Paume de Jacques-Louis David. Le peintre, son milieu et son temps de 1789 à 1792*. Paris: Ministère de la culture. Éditions de la Réunion des musées nationaux.

Brooks, Peter. 1991. The Revolutionary Body. In *Fictions of the French Revolution*, ed. Bernadette Fort. Evanston, IL: Northwestern University Press.

Buckley, Matthew S. 2006. *Tragedy Walks the Streets: The French Revolution in the Making of Modern Drama*. Baltimore: Johns Hopkins University Press.

Caubisen-Lasfargues, Colette. 1961. Le salon de peinture pendant la révolution. In Annales historiques de la révolution française. 164, 193–214.

Chartier, Roger. 1997. *On the Edge of the Cliff: History, Languages, and Practices*. Trans. Lydia G. Cochrane. Baltimore: Johns Hopkins University Press.

Chaudonneret, Marie-Claude. 2010. Les artistes vivant au Louvre (1791-1848): du musée au bazar. In *'Ce salon à quoi tout se ramène': Le Salon de peinture et de sculpture, 1791-1890*, ed. James Kearns and Pierre Vaisse. Bern: Peter Lang. 7–22.

Crow, Thomas. 1985. *Painters and Public Life in Eighteenth-Century Paris*. New Haven: Yale University Press.

De Baecque, Antoine. 1993. *The Body Politic: Corporeal Metaphor in Revolutionary France, 1770-1800*. Stanford: Stanford University Press.

Diderot, Denis. 1966 (1757). *Entretiens sur le fils naturel* in Oeuvres Esthétiques, ed. P. Vernière. Paris: Garnier.

Dowd, David Lloyd. 1948. *Pageant-master of the Republic: Jacques-Louis David and the French Revolution*. Lincoln: University of Nebraska Press.

Dowd, David L. 1960. Art and Theater During the French Revolution: The Role of Louis David. *Art Quarterly* 23 (1): 3–20.
Feillia, Cecilia. 2013. *The Sentimental Theatre of the French Revolution*. Farnham: Ashgate.
Foucault, Michel. 1973. *The Order of Things: An Archeology of the Human Sciences*. New York: Vintage.
Fowler, Alastair. 1982. *Kinds of Literature: An Introduction to the Theory of Genres and Modes*. Cambridge, MA: Harvard University Press.
Fried, Michael. 1988. *Absorption and Theatricality: Painting and Beholder in the Age of Diderot*. Chicago: University of Chicago Press.
Fried, Michel. 1993. David et l'antithéatralité. In *David contre David: Actes du colloque organisé au musée du Louvre par le service culturel du 6 au 10 décembre 1989*, vol. 1, ed. Régis Michel.
Fried, Michael. 2015. *Another Light: Jacques-Louis David to Thomas Demand*. New Haven: Yale University Press.
Friedland, Paul. 2002. *Political Actors: Representative Bodies & Theatricality in the Age of the French Revolution*. Ithaca: Cornell University Press.
Fuhrmeister, Christian. 2009. 'Eripuit caelo fulmen sceptrumque tyrannis': The Political Iconography of Lightning in Europe and North America, 1750-1800. *Transactions of the American Philosophical Society* 99:144–63.
Gauchet, Marcel. 1989. *La Révolution des droits de l'homme*. Paris: Gallimard.
Huet, Marie-Hélène. 1982. *Rehearsing the Revolution: The Staging of Marat's Death 1793-1797*. Berkeley: University of California Press.
Hunt, Lynn. 2008. *Inventing Human Rights: A History*. New York: W.W. Norton & Co.
Johnson, Dorothy. 1993. *Jacques-Louis David: Art in Metamorphosis*. Princeton: Princeton University Press.
Kahn, Victoria. 2004. *Wayward Contracts: The Crisis of Political Obligation in England, 1640–1674*. Princeton: Princeton University Press.
Kantorowicz, Ernst H. 1957. *The King's Two Bodies: A Study in Medieval Political Theology*. Princeton: Princeton University Press.
Kemp, Wolfgang. 1994. The Theatre of Revolution: A New Interpretation of Jacques-Louis David's *Tennis Court Oath*. In *Visual Culture: Images and Interpretations*, ed. Norman Bryson, 202–227. Middletown: Wesleyan University Press.
Landes, Joan B. 2001. *Visualizing the Nation: Gender. Representation, and Revolution in Eighteenth-Century France*. Ithaca: Cornell University Press.
Lefort, Claude. 1988. The Permanence of the Theologico-Political? In *Democracy and Political Theory*. Trans. D. Macey. Minneapolis: University of Minnesota Press.
Loty, Laurent. 2009. L'inachèvement emblématique du serment de jeu de paume. *Dix-huitième siècle* 41 (1): 27–41.
Marin, Louis. 1981. *Le portrait du roi*. Paris: Les éditions de minuit.
Marin, Louis. 1988. *Portrait of the King*. Trans. M. Houle. Minneapolis: University of Minnesota Press.
Marin, Louis. 1997. *Food for Thought*, trans. Mette Hjort. Baltimore: Johns Hopkins University Press.
Maslan, Susan. 2005. *Revolutionary Acts: Theater, Democracy, and the French Revolution*. Baltimore: Johns Hopkins University Press.
Meister, Robert. 2011. *After Evil: A Politics of Human Rights*. New York: Columbia University Press.
Melzer, Sara E., and Kathryn Norberg (eds.). 1988. *From the Royal to the Republican Body: Incorporating the Political in Seventeenth- and Eighteenth-Century France*. Berkeley: University of California Press.
Mondzain, Marie-José. 2005. *Image, Icon, Economy: The Byzantine Origins of the Contemporary Imaginary*. Stanford: Stanford University Press.
Nora, Pierre. 1998. *Realms of Memory: The Construction of the French Past*, vol. 3. New York: Columbia University Press.

Ozouf, Mona. 1998. The Pantheon: The École Normale of the Dead. In *Realms of Memory: The Construction of the French Past*, vol. 3, ed. Pierre Nora, 325–346. Trans. A. Goldhammer. New York: Columbia University Press.

Pommier, Édouard. 1991. *L'art de la liberté: Doctrines et débats de la Révolution française*. Paris: Gallimard.

Propeck, Lina. 1993. David et le portrait du roi. In *David contre David: Actes du colloque organisé au musée du Louvre par le service culturel du 6 au 10 décembre 1989*, vol. 1, ed. Régis Michel, 293–318.

Reichardt, Rolf, and Hubertus Kohle. 2008. *Visualizing the Revolution: Politics and the Pictorial Arts in Late Eighteenth-century France*. London: Reaktion Books.

Roberts, Warren. 2000. *Jacques-Louis David and Jean-Louis Prieur: Revolutionary Artists, The Public, The Populace, and Images of the French Revolution*. Albany: State University of New York Press.

Schmitter, Amy M. 2002. Representation and the Body of Power in French Academic Painting. *Journal of the History of Ideas* 63: 399–424.

Tackett, Timothy. 1996. *Becoming a Revolutionary: The Deputies of the French National Assembly and the Emergence of a Revolutionary Culture (1789-1790)*. Princeton: Princeton University Press.

Thévoz, Michel. 1989. *Le théâtre du crime: essai sur la peinture de David*. Paris: Les éditions de minuit.

Trey, Juliette and de Baecque, Antoine. 2008. *Le Serment du Jeu de paume: quand David réécrit l'histoire*. Versailles: Éditions Artyis.

Undank, Jack. 1986. Diderot and the Phenomenology of the Ordinary. *Diderot Studies* 22: 143–70.

Watelet, *Encyclopédie, Dictionnaire raisonné des sciences, des arts et des métiers, par une Société de Gens de lettres. Tome 7.* [1757] Le Breton 1757.

Williams, Raymond. 1995. *Keywords: A Vocabulary of Culture and Society*. Oxford: Oxford University Press.

Mark Antaki, Ph.D. (University of California, Berkeley 2005), is an Associate Professor in the Faculty of Law at McGill University. His research interests focus on law and the humanities, law and language, as well as the history of ideas. He teaches courses in public and private law as well as legal theory. Some of his publications include: "Declining Accusation" in George Pavlich and Matthew P. Unger, eds., *Accusation: Creating Criminals* (Vancouver, UBC Press, 2016); "Un-stating Law" in Shauna Van Praagh, Lionel Smith and Helge Dedek, eds., *Stateless Law: Evolving Boundaries of a Discipline* (Burlington, VT: Ashgate, 2015); "'No Foundations'? " (2014) 11 No Foundations: Interdisciplinary Journal of Law and Justice 61–77; "Genre, Critique, and Human Rights" (2013) 82 University of Toronto Quarterly 974–996 (special issue on law and literature).

Catherine Le Guerrier is currently pursuing a Master's degree in Philosophy of law at Université de Montréal. She has completed the B.C.L.-LL.B. program of the McGill Faculty of Law where she was awarded the Principal David L. Johnston Medal for Contribution upon her graduation.

Chapter 3
The Quest for the Decisive Constitutional Moment (DCM)

Stefan Huygebaert

Abstract The Constitution, as fundamental, formal law, needs some form of representation in order to gain validity. This chapter demonstrates that, apart from using symbols such as tables of the law, artists alternatively chose for an artistic device, for which the name DCM (Decisive Constitutional Moment) is put forward. This device entails the selection and depiction of a specific, pivotal moment from constitutional history. The definition of this device consists of three parts, drawing on existing theory about the decisive moment by photographer Henri Cartier-Bresson, the constitutional moment of legal scholar Bruce Ackerman, and the depiction and narration of a history and a moment in visual art, with particular attention for the relationship between the depicted moment and the moment of depiction. The chapter's focus is on works of art from the long nineteenth century, the age of revolution, Constitution and a new idiom in art history in which artist took scenes from contemporary life as subject matter, thus combining a journalistic eyewitness account with an academic style. Looking into the main artistic media of this era and their use in DCMs allows for a better understanding of the legitimizing function of the art works under scrutiny. The chapter further develops with an elaborate study of the design entries for the 1849 competition for a constitutional monument in Brussels, Belgium, which demonstrates the variety of possible decisive constitutional moments and the challenges which artists faced when including them in their designs.

3.1 Introduction

Making the Constitution, the fundamental and most elementary of the nation's laws, perceivable to citizens is crucial for it to function. As political theorist Hans Vorländer writes in his 2012 essay *What is Constitutional culture?*, "[c]onstitutions

S. Huygebaert (✉)
Ghent Legal History Institute and Department of Art History, Musicology and Theater Studies, Ghent University and Research Foundation – Flanders (FWO), Ghent, Belgium
e-mail: stefan.huygebaert@ugent.be

S. Huygebaert et al. (eds.), *Sensing the Nation's Law*, Studies in the History of Law and Justice 13, https://doi.org/10.1007/978-3-319-75497-0_3

have to rely on symbolic forms of representation that lend them validity, that is, acceptance and recognition."[1] Therefore, visual artists have been charged with the difficult task of rendering the Constitution visually perceptible in order to communicate it to the population. However, both the abstract nature and the lack of iconographic tradition complicate this depiction of the Constitution.[2] One solution is the use of symbols, as can be seen in the famous painting by Jean-Jacques Francois Le Barbier visualising the *Declaration of the Rights of Man and of the Citizen* (1789, Paris, Carnavalet Museum). Here, amongst many symbols, tables of the law emphasise both the sacral, religious respect for and the everlasting and unchangeable character of the fundamental rights written down in the 1789 *Declaration*.[3]

This chapter deals with another solution for the challenges artists faced when having to depict the Constitution. The object of scrutiny is an artistic device which artists could apply when visualising the Constitution, and which I refer to as the DCM (Decisive Constitutional Moment).[4] I borrow my use of the term "device" from art historian Francis H. Dowley's analysis of the so called significant moment in French eighteenth-century sculpture.[5] Comparable to how the sculptural "significant moment" device (in which a person is depicted during his/her quintessential biographic moment) served to show the essence of a person's contribution to history, the DCM device serves to show the Constitution's essence and its contribution to the nation. "Device" should therefore be understood as a byword for "representational vehicle" or "artistic practice", comparable to a three-quarter view in portraiture or the use of human-like personifications for abstract notions.

Although many examples of DCM use can be found before and after the period, my particular focus lies on works of art from the long nineteenth century, the age of revolution and Constitution, as well as of the start of a new idiom in art history. Following a few isolated uses by late-eighteenth-century painters such as Benjamin West and John Singleton Copley, referred to as the "revolution of history painting"

[1]Vorländer, Hans. 2012. What is "Constitutional Culture"? In *Constitutional Cultures: On the Concept and Representation of Constitutions in the Atlantic World*, eds. Silcke Hensel, Ulrike Bock, Katrin Dircksen, and Hans-Ulrich Thamer, 21–42. Newcastle upon Tyne: Cambridge Scholars Publishing, 28.

[2]Müller, Marion C. 2011. Verfassung. In *Handbuch der politischen Ikonographie*, eds. Uwe Fleckner, Martin Warnke, and Hendrik Ziegler, 514–521. München: C.H. Beck. Green Fryd, Vivien. 2012. Representing the Constitution in the US Capitol Building: Justice, Freedom and Slavery. In *Constitutional Cultures*, 228–229 and 244.

[3]Reichardt, Rolf. 2007. L'imaginaire de la Constitution de 1789 à 1830: symbolique d'union ou de division politique? In *Le combat autour de la Représentation: politique symbolique en France, 1789–1830*, eds. Natalie Scholz, Christina Schröer, and Hans-Ulrich Thamer. Rennes: Presses de l'Université de Bretagne.

[4]For the sake of consistency, in what follows, I use the abbreviation "DCM" when referring to the artistic device, and the written words "decisive constitutional moment" when referring to the actual, historical moment.

[5]Dowley, Francis H. 1957. D'Angiviller's Grands Hommes and the Significant Moment. *The Art Bulletin* 39 (4):259–277.

since art historian Edgar Wind's 1938 article,[6] this idiom really came into vogue during the French Revolution, when artists started to combine journalistic eye-witness accounts with an academic style. The idiom is reflected in painter Jacques-Louis David's words from 1792: "[W]e will (...) no longer have to try to find subjects for our paintings in the history of ancient people".[7] This combination of a sense of historical correctness with high artistic quality was long reserved to battle paintings, and was now being used for contemporary events.[8] For the new idiom, one can think of the many prints showing contemporary, pivotal events such as the attack on the Bastille or Louis XVI's execution.

An image that immediately comes to mind when characterising the long nineteenth century as the age of revolution, Constitution and this new idiom, is David's *The Oath of the Tennis Court* (study persevered in Paris, Louvre Museum), arguably the prototype use of the DCM. A study for this never finished painting, analysed at length by Mark Antaki and Catherine Le Guerrier in this book's second chapter, was presented at the 1791 Parisian salon, the most significant art exhibition at the time. David tried to represent a moment that in historiography came to be seen as crucial for both the French Revolution and its first Constitution (proclaimed on 3 September 1791): the oath pledged by the Third Estate on 20 June 1789 not to leave the assembly before a Constitution would be drafted.[9] David was far from being the single artist in the period between 1789 and 1914 who chose for the DCM. Likewise, he was not the only artists depicting the specific moment. His own student, August Couder, later depicted the same dramatic moment in 1848 (Versailles, Museum of the History of France).

In the first part of this paper, I define this device by focusing on three primary elements—Decisive, Constitutional and Moment—each referring to one of the three words that make up the DCM. This modus operandi is justified because of the fact that both the "decisive moment" and the "constitutional moment" are existing, coined notions, the former by French photographer Henri Cartier-Bresson, the latter by American legal scholar Bruce Ackerman. This paper draws on these two notions and their definitions, as far as possible, although we must remain aware of the limitations in applying them on the device I put forward. Apart from these two, I aim to tackle the issue of depicting a moment in visual art, before finally putting together a definition for the DCM.

---

[6]Wind, Edgar. 1938. The Revolution of History Painting. *Journal of the Warburg Institute* 2 (2):116–127.

[7]Quoted in Johnson, Dorothy. 2006. *Jacques-Louis David. New perspectives*. Newark: University of Deleware Press, 111.

[8]Abrams, Ann Uhry. 1979. Politics, Prints, and John Singleton Copley's Watson and the Shark. *The Art Bulletin* 61 (2):265–276. Reynaerts, Jenny. 2008. Het begin van de vrijheid: "Prise de la Bastille" door Charles Thévenin (1790). *Bulletin van het Rijksmuseum* 56 (1/2): 136–149. Vagts, Alfred. Battle-Scenes and Picture-Politics. 1941. *Military Affairs* 5 (2): 88–90.

[9]Boime, Albert. 1987. *Art in the Age of Revolution 1750–1800*. A social history of modern art. Chicago and London: The University of Chicago Press.

In the second part, I demonstrate how the DCM is used in different media, and how each of these feature their own limitations. The media under scrutiny include painting and its lasting use after the rise of photography, medals with their specific aura of unchangeable sources of the past, and sculpture, more in particular a formula featuring a commemorated, sculpted person and one or more narrative, biographical bas-reliefs in its base.

The third and last part elaborates a case study in which the Belgian government organised a design competition for the Congress Column, a monument dedicated to the 1830–1831 constituent assembly. Analysing the 17 preserved and located designs for this competition helps to gain insight into the variety of possible moments which could serve within a DCM.

For the purpose of this chapter, I apply Hanna Fenichel Pitkin's double definition of what a Constitution is—notably a definition she made at the occasion of the U.S. Constitution's 1987–1988 bicentennial, a moment of commemoration. Pitkin roughly makes the distinction between, on the one hand, a material, Aristotelian *constitutio*, a fundamental make-up of a people; and, on the other, the formal, written Constitution, the result of "something we do", an act of "constituting".[10] These verbs (to do, to constitute) indicate an evolution, a narration, a developing storyline in the creation of the single, written document, known as the formal Constitution. For an artist choosing for a DCM, his or her main concern is: what exact episode or event from this story is crucial, when exactly is a Constitution, or when do or did we constitute?

3.2 Defining a DCM

3.2.1 Decisive: Cartier-Bresson's Decisive Moment

French photographer and co-founder of the Magnum photo agency Henri Cartier-Bresson (1908–2004) had his major photobook *Images à la sauvette*, translated in English as *The Decisive Moment* (both published in 1952). Allegedly, Cartier-Bresson borrowed the term from seventeenth-century French politician Cardinal de Retz' memoires: "There is nothing in this world that has no decisive moment".[11] However, de Retz's decisive moments referred to historical events with a time span varying from several weeks to a single important encounter, whilst Cartier-Bresson had a much more instantaneous interpretation.[12] Cartier-Bresson

[10]Pitkin, Hanna Fenichel 1987. The Idea of a Constitution. *Journal of Legal Education* 37 (2): 167–169.

[11]"Il n'y a rien dans ce monde qui n'ait un moment décisif" Kelsey, Robin. 2009. Of Fish, Birds, Cats, Mice, Spiders, Flies, Pigs, and Chimpanzees: How Chance Casts the Historic Action Photograph into Doubt. *History and Theory* (48): 71. (When the original quote is featured in footnote, the translation is mine)

[12]Kelsey, 2009. 71, note 28.

writes that, for him, "...photography is the simultaneous recognition, in a fraction of a second, of the significance of an event as well as of a precise organization of forms which give that event its proper expression".[13] From Cartier-Bresson, the definition for the DCM can borrow this combination of artist and reporter as well as an event's instantaneousness as crucial elements.

It is necessary to emphasise—and to be fully aware of—the risks of using a twentieth-century term applied in photography, for a nineteenth-century medium and device. Eventually, photography would be able to grasp the split second when a moment or instant unfolds itself, what painting, sculpting and other nineteenth-century media could not. Likewise, the element of truth and eyewitness, so typical for the aura and "indexicality" of photography, is missing in these traditional media. The distinction is adequately formulated by Alan Woods in his essay *Death and the instamatic*: "A painting (if it wishes to) re-states reality, a photograph belongs to the event it describes. (...) The sense is not of time arrested —paintings do not freeze time—but of time denied, transcended (as in an icon or an allegory) or expressed (as in history painting)."[14] This is why art historian Ernst Gombrich distinguishes the photographic instant from the artistic moment, the first (in the case of documentary photography) witnessing an event, the later reconstructing and reinventing it.[15] Both the pregnant and significant moment are more adequate terms for analysing pre-photographic media, as will be made clear below, but by borrowing Cartier-Bresson's adjective, I emphasise the instantaneous and therefore dramatic character of artistically depicted constitutional moments.

3.2.2 Constitutional: Ackerman's Constitutional Moment

American legal scholar Bruce Ackerman (b. 1943) coined the influential notion of a "constitutional moment", an extraordinary moment of popular consensus that leads to constitutional change outside the normal mode of amendment, foreseen in U.S. Constitution's article 5.[16] The dualism in Ackerman's theory refers to the enactment of normal law by the legislature in times of ordinary politics, whereas in times of constitutional politics, constitutional law is enacted by the people, who have turned into mobilised and engaged citizens.[17] In his 1984 Storrs lecture and his book *We the People: Foundations* (1991), Ackerman distinguishes three such "mega-moments" in American history, which he originally referred to as "three

---

[13]Cartier-Bresson, Henri. 1999. *The Mind's Eye: Writings on Photography and Photographers*. New York: Aperture: 42.

[14]Woods, Alan. 1984. Death and the Instamatic. *The Cambridge Quarterly* 13 (2):149, 159.

[15]Gombrich, Ernst Hans. 1982. Moment and movement in art. In *The image and the eye*, ed. Ernst Hans Gombrich, 40–62. Oxford: Phaidon.

[16]Ackerman, Bruce. 1991. *We, the people: Foundations*. Cambridge: Harvard University Press.

[17]Weill, Rivka. 2006. Evolution vs. Revolution: Dueling Models of Dualism. *The American Journal of Comparative Law* 54 (2):429–479.

peaks of high importance that tower over valleys full of more particular meanings".[18] These extraordinary "moments of passionate sacrifice and excited mobilization" culminate in higher law making or a "fundamental reworking of the status quo".[19] Ackerman emphasises the limited window of opportunity of these rare periods of heightened political consciousness during and shortly after a revolution in which a constituent assembly can operate. In other words, the constitutional moment is turned into constitutional momentum, since much depends on the short-lived engagement of the people with public policy, and the legitimation and normative value generated by engagement, mobilisation and popular endorsement.[20] The three moments Ackerman discerns in U.S. history are (1) the Founding and the writing of the Constitution and the Bill of Rights; (2) the Reconstruction era after the Civil War and (3) the New Deal.

Three elements from Ackerman's theory could render it inadequate to the task of this chapter. First, his theory on exceptional moments of higher law making is specifically designed for the American situation. Second, Ackerman himself, in later writings, warned for an overly instantaneous interpretation of constitutional moments as split seconds, comparable to de Retz's reading of decisive moments in history. On the contrary, according to Ackerman, constitutional moments require at least a decade before the popular support is sufficiently demonstrated.[21] Thirdly, Ackerman narrows constitutional moments to cases of constitutional change, a break with the past.[22] An alternative could be Jason Frank's "constituent moments". In his book by that name, Frank argues that "the people" are a vague, almost metaphysical though potent political claim who's power derives from a constitutive surplus from the revolutionary era. Constituent moments differ from Ackerman's constitutional moments because their focus is not on constitutional law and formal political constitutions. Rather, Frank demonstrates how said claim is made time and again during democratic everyday (mirco-)politics, and not just during exceptional historical shifts and radical breaks.[23]

From Ackerman's constitutional moment, I retain the extraordinary character and the popular consensus and endorsement which gives legitimacy to constitutional change.

---

[18]Ackerman, Bruce 1984. Storrs Lectures: Discovering the Constitution. *Faculty Scholarship Series* Paper, 1051.

[19]Ackerman, 1991. 22, 31.

[20]Tushnet, Mark. 2008. Comparative constitutional law. In *The Oxford Handbook of Comparative Law*, eds. Mathias Reimann, and Reinhard Zimmerman, 1226–1257. New York: Oxford University Press, 1235.

[21]Ackerman, Bruce. 2010. *The Decline and Fall of the American Republic*. Cambridge: Harvard University Press, 70–71.

[22]Weill, 2006. 463–464.

[23]Frank, Jason. 2010. *Constituent moments: Enacting the People in Postrevolutionary America*. Durham and London: Duke University Press, 3–4, 31–33, 250–251.

3.2.3 Moment: Visual Narration of a Story and a Moment

It is important to fully realise the difficulties in visual narration of a story or a history as well as the complex relationship between the moment of depiction by an artist, and the historical moment which is depicted. Regarding the first issue, comparing two versions of one and the same story can be revealing. For the sake of this chapter, an example of an exemplum iustitiae will suffice. The story under scrutiny is that of the corrupt judge Sysamnes. As written by Valerius Maximus in his *Factorum et dictorum memorabilium libri IX*, Sysamnes was bribed, arrested, flayed alive and, finally, succeeded by his own son, Otanes, who had to sit on his father's skin when judging. Late-medieval painter Gerard David's rendering of this story in the form of a diptych (Fig. 3.1) shows it in a so called continuous narrative, with a total of four episodes on two panels, repeating certain characters in one and the same panel. From left to right, the corrupt judge is bribed, arrested, punished and succeeded by his son. Pieter Paul Rubens's seventeenth-century version (of which the original is lost, Fig. 3.2) focuses, in a typical baroque mode, on the most dramatic moment that summarises or "essentialises" the entire story. Rubens chose the last of Gerard David's four episodes, where the father's skin draped on Otanes's throne helps to summarise the entire story.[24]

Similarly, telling the story of the Constitution visually can be done by either showing several episodes of the constituent process, or focusing on one dramatic moment. The differences between these two ways of visual story telling were further developed by, amongst others, eighteenth-century writers such as Lord Shaftesburry and Gotthold Ephraim Lessing. In particular, they wrote about the kind of alternative Rubens used. As Lessing put it in his famous treatise on Laocoön: "Painting can (…) only represent a single moment of an action and must therefore select the most pregnant moment which best allows us to infer what has gone before and what follows."[25] Discussions on this "pregnant" moment, this dramatic moment chosen by the painter, are most relevant for the moments that are selected in the device under scrutiny. Shaftesburry and Lessing preferred a moment preceding the drama—indeed: pregnant—whereas baroque and neo-classical or romantic artists such as, respectively, Rubens and Jacques-Louis David chose the climactic, dramatic moment. Still, this will be an "artistic moment" or *punctum temporis*, chosen and constructed by the artist and including inevitable compositional inventions. Art historian Ernst Gombrich emphasised how, ever since photography's exposure time was reduced to a level that allows the creation of the frozen moment so vital to Cartier-Bresson's decisive moment, people tend to forget the often constructed nature of the artistic moment in, for example, painting: "…the instant of which the theoreticians speak, the moment when time stands still, is an

---

[24]Paumen, Vanessa. 2016. The skin of the judge: the judgement of Cambyses. In *The Art of Law: Three Centuries of Justice Depicted*, eds. Stefan Huygebaert, Georges Martyn, Vanessa Paumen, and Tine Van Poucke, 81–90. Tielt: Lannoo.

[25]Quoted in Gombrich, 1982. 42.

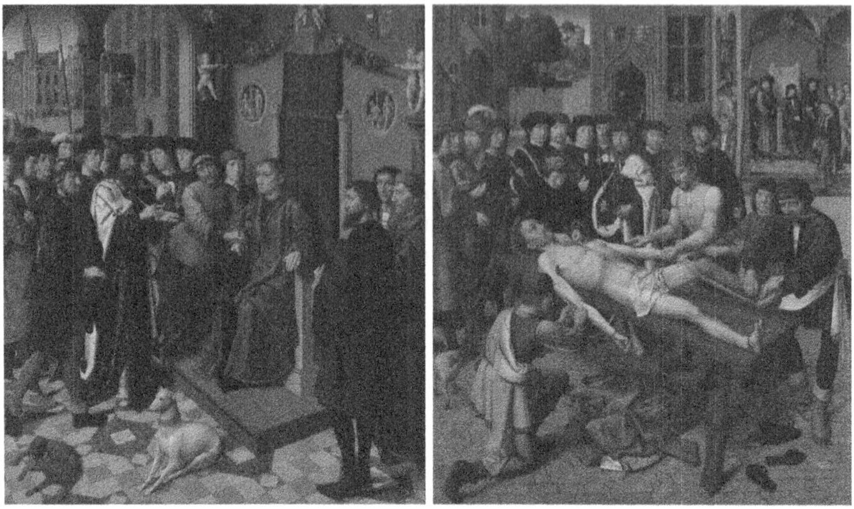

Fig. 3.1 Gerard David, *The judgement of Cambyses*, 1498, oil paint on wood, Groeningemuseum, Brugge © Lukas—Art in Flanders VZW. *Photo* Hugo Maertens

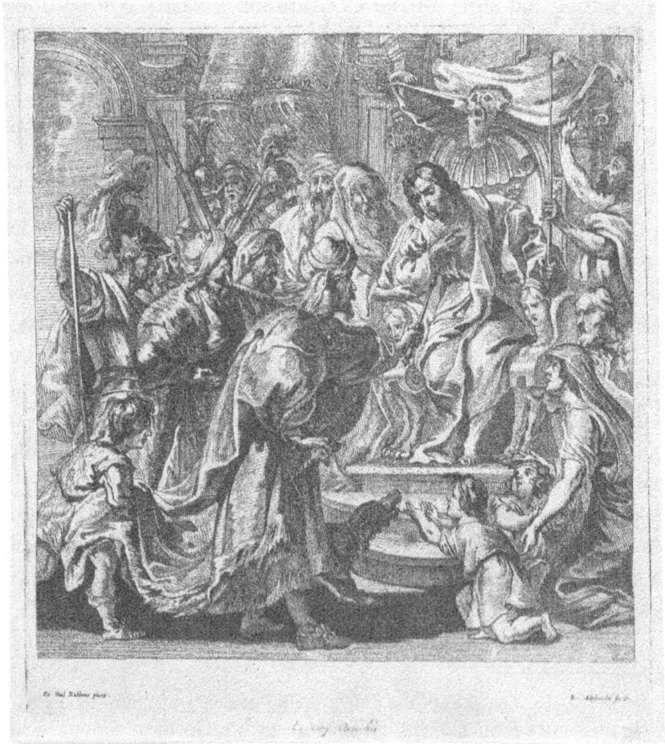

Fig. 3.2 R. Eynhoudts after Pieter-Paul Rubens, *The Judgement of Cambyses*, print, s.d. (seventeenth century). © Rijksmuseum, Amsterdam

illicit extrapolation, despite the specious plausibility which the snapshot has given to this old idea."[26]

Therefore, and for the sake of consistency and analysis, I first distinguish and introduce four chronological relationships between the actual, historical constitutional moment and the moment of its depiction, before finalising the definition of the DCM. These four chronological relationships are reconstruction, recording, staging and inventing. Arguably, each of these four relationships is present, to a certain degree, in any artistic depiction of a historical moment, including one taken from constitutional history, and so the borders between them are not to be understood as strict.

First, the term "reconstruction" reminds us of the fact that nineteenth-century media often depicted constitutional moments days, months or years after their unfolding, often with changed realities, such as the many fractions and hostilities within the group pledging the Tennis Court Oath. For example, Mirabeau is still present in David's picture, although he would later be demonised by Robespierre, making it impossible for David to "keep up (…) with the Revolution", in Antaki and Le Guerrier's words.[27]

As was mentioned earlier, photographic recording or, in Woods's words, "belonging to the event" was impossible for a painter like David. However, many artists who use the DCM try to let their depictions of the moment pass as a neutral recording, for example by including themselves as eyewitness. This sort of "recording" is present in David's other famous masterpiece, *Consecration of the Emperor Napoleon I and Coronation of the Empress Josephine in the Cathedral of Notre-Dame de Paris on 2 December 1804* (1807, Louvre, Paris), where David painted himself in the top left part of the background audience.[28]

Often, events which could pass as decisive constitutional moments are ceremonial in nature, such as singings, oaths or coronations. Their organisers have their future, lasting depictions already in mind. Inviting an artist such as David to be present in the Notre Dame, demonstrates the agenda of these depictions. More generally, one can think of leaders' lingering handshakes and voting gestures at the ballot box, a moment stretched in time in order for photographers to grasp and eternalise it. For these anticipated commemorations I use the word "staging".

Lastly, at the moment of depiction, constitutional moments are (partly) "invented". In some cases they never unfolded. The alleged abdication of Belgian King Leopold I during the revolutionary wave of 1848 certainly never happened in the presence of his family, the military, and the judiciary, which is how a print shows and invented the moment (Brussels, Royal Library, print S.III.100836). In other cases, important elements are changed or added. David, in his *Consecration of the Emperor Napoleon*, added Napoleon's mother and brother, both of whom were

[26]Gombrich, 1982. 53.

[27]See Antaki & Le Guerrier's contribution in this volume.

[28]It should be noted how artists using the DCM or any other device which depicts a specific moment typically need long titles to refer to the actual setting, time and event.

absent from the coronation ceremony. Both family members are included in the painting, to help legitimise Napoleon's imperial ambition. Most of all, however, artistic renderings of contemporary moments and events remain inventions (because of the punctum temporis' constructed nature) and almost always include allegory or intuitive references to famous images, as is the case in Copley's 1778 "prototype" *Watson and the shark* (Washington D.C., National Gallery of Art) and David's use of, for example, the lightning motive in his *Tennis Court Oath*.[29]

The borders between these four categories are fluid, of course. For example, any attempt at recording, due to the limitations of artistic media, will include reconstruction, while any reconstruction necessitates invention, heightened by the essential amount of drama at the climactic turning point which artists aim for when using a DCM. Likewise, staged moments count on recording and reconstruction, and many decisive constitutional moments have a staged, ceremonial nature.

3.2.4 A Definition for the DCM

These theoretical elements and insights are combined in the definition of a DCM which I put forward. The DCM is defined as an artistic device in which a specific, instantaneous and climactic turning point from constitutional history is selected and artistically depicted, recorded, reconstructed, staged and/or invented, as a means to perpetuate, commemorate and ultimately to legitimate the Constitution as fundamental order and law by emphasizing, directly or indirectly, the consensus that lays at the Constitution's origins. The acronym DCM thus does not refer to the specific moment which is depicted (the decisive constitutional moment), but to the act of depicting it. The decisive constitutional moment becomes functional or instrumental by virtue of its depiction in a DCM.

Art works resulting from the use of a DCM can easily be called sites of memory ("lieux de mémoire"), French historian Pierre Nora's influential concept. Nora emphasised how these sites are crystallisations or embodiments of memory. Defining them as "moments of history torn away from the movement of history" Nora also states "Every constitution (…) is a lieu de mémoire".[30] As such, paraphrasing Nora's definition of sites of memory, decisive constitutional moments are moments of constitutional history torn away from the movement of constitutional history. As Cartier-Bresson wrote: "[I]nside movement there is one moment at which the elements in motion are in balance. Photography must seize upon this moment and hold immobile the equilibrium of it."[31] In the evolution of collective memory over time and past generations, only a small set of crucial, important,

[29]Wind 1938. Abrams 1979.

[30]Nora, Pierre. 1989. Between memory and history: les lieux de mémoire. *Representations* (26 special issue: Memory and counter-memory): 7, 21.

[31]Cartier-Bresson, 1999. 33

canonical, say: decisive moments will be withheld from this flux of time. A nineteenth-century artist commissioned to depict constitutional history is faced with the choice of one single moment, often made at a time when this flux was still very recent and featured a much larger quantity of possible decisive moments. This selection process of the ideal moment is an integral part of the device. Therefore, the third main part of this contribution focuses on the variety of possible moments which artists considered. I will do so by scrutinising a case study about a Belgian monument competition in 1849. First, however, it is necessary to analyse the artistic media in which the DCM is used.

3.3 The Medium Constitutes the Message

3.3.1 (Wall-)Painting, Prints and Photography

The best way of demonstrating both the possibilities and aura of painting, is by looking into its use at a time when the photographic alternative existed. Especially in cases of commemorative depictions of official, ceremonial occasions, photography often lost out to painting. The latter was regarded as a higher art form, whereas the former was seen as a mere medium. Such was the case in 1901, at the opening of the first Federal Australian Parliament in the Exhibition Building in Melbourne. Although photographs of the ceremony exist, the Australian Art Association commissioned Tom Roberts to paint an enormous painting, measuring over five by three meters and including more than 260 recognisable portraits (*Opening of the First Parliament of the Commonwealth of Australia by H.R.H. The Duke of Cornwall and York (Later King George V), May 9, 1901*, 1903, Canberra, British Royal Collection—permanent loan to the Parliament of Australia). Roberts was one of the 10.000 people present at the ceremony and afterwards moved his studio into the exhibition building. An important advantage of painting was that the medium allowed Roberts to feature all heads recognisably, which would guarantee sells of prints to the men and women depicted—as was the case with West's *Death of General Wolfe* (1771, Ottawa, National Gallery of Canada) and the intention with David's *Tennis Court Oath*. The medium also allowed for minor inventions, which include turning faces and avoiding overlapping heads. A more elaborate invention, however, can be noted in the upper left section, when comparing the painting with photographs of the actual moment. In reality, the spot on the wall beneath the flags (which, themselves are additions as well) featured a Justitia painting. However, in his painting, Roberts omitted the Justitia, and instead included—that is, invented—a portrait of Henry Parker, often referred to as the "Father of the Federation". Deceased in 1896, the politician was not present at the 1901 opening. Parker's added portrait, therefore, serves as a legitimation for the decisive moment of federation. Robert's anachronistic use of oil paint was "the inherited means of signifying power".[32] Drawing on the aura of the grand genre of history painting, the invention helped seize Australia's decisive constitutional moment in a painting known not as much through its monstrously long title, but by its nickname: *The Big Picture*.

The case of the 1937–1938 sesquicentennial of the adoption and ratification of the U.S. Constitution also demonstrates this combination of aura and possible inventions.[33] For the occasion, American president Franklin Delano Roosevelt personally ordered a change in the composition of the Poughkeepsie Post Office wall painting. The town in New York County housed the New York State ratifying convention back in 1787, where FDR's ancestor, Isaac Roosevelt was part of the Federalist camp. Originally, the 1937 post office mural by Gerald Foster would feature the ratification scene in which the Constitution is signed. FDR had it changed to the moment of compromise between federalists and anti-federalists, a compromise consisting of a promise that a Bill of Rights would be added to the Constitution. This compromise took away anti-federalists' fear of a possibly despotic federal government, and having it depicted in his home state would serve FDR's presidency very well. At the time the painting was made, the democratic president endured severe attacks revolving around the constitutional nature of his New Deal program. Notably, here we see a reconstruction of Ackerman's first constitutional moment (the Founding) during the third (the New Deal) commissioned by a president who wishes to emphasise his own constitutionalism by referring to a story of compromise involving his own bloodline. In a thorough analysis of the Poughkeepsie wall painting, FDR is quoted on the matter: "there 'ain't no such thing' as a masterpiece of permanence in the art of living or the art of government [but] when a great picture has been painted and touched up a little here and there, it becomes at last a permanent contribution to civilization for all time."[34]

These two examples demonstrate how the choice for (wall) painting as a medium indicates the commissioning government's agenda of legitimation and endorsement of the Constitution and their own interpretation and policy, mostly because of the possibilities of invention inherent to painting.

3.3.2 Medals

When it comes to perpetuating historical facts, few media are as renowned as medals, since metal has long been regarded as an incorruptible and unchangeable source of the past, as opposed to modifiable texts. Additionally, medals have the

[32]Spate, Virginia. 1996. Where the Sun never set: Tom Roberts and the British Empire. In *Tom Roberts*, ed. Ron Radford. Adelaide: Art Gallery of South Australia and Art Exhibitions, 86.

[33]Rhoads, William B. 1990. The President and the Sesquicentennial of the Constitution: Franklin Roosevelt's Monument in Poughkeepsie. *New York History* 71 (3):308–321.

[34]Rhoads, 1990. 321.

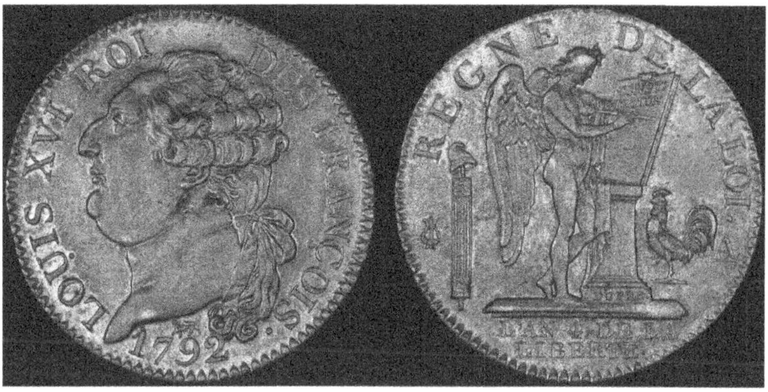

Fig. 3.3 Augustin Dupré, *Louis XVI Roi des François 1792 [obverse] – Règne de la Loi – L'An 4 de la Liberté [reverse]*, coin, 1792. © National Numismatic Collection, National Museum of American History, Smithsonian Institution

advantage of being mobile and reproducible on a large scale. The antique artistic medal genre owed much of its renaissance to the quattrocento artist Pisanello. Like the artworks featuring contemporary events as subject matter, here too, the French Revolution sparked a renewed interest in the medal as medium. First, a competition for the fabrication of new coins was organised in France after the closing of the old monetary administration on 11 January 1791. The instigator of said closing in 1791, Augustin Dupré, won the competition and was elected as Engraver General of the French Mint. Already his first coins as Engraver General commemorated the Constitution, albeit using the French Revolution's allegorical visual language rather than a DCM. Underneath the inscription "Reign of the Law" ("Règne de la Loi"), Dupré's 1792 coin (Fig. 3.3) shows the winged Genius of France[35] writing the word "Constitution" on the table of the law, referring to the short-lived constitutional monarchy of Louis XVI who's head adorns the reverse—at a time when it was still on his shoulders. Louis served as the third element of the new, momentary political trinity featured on the edge lettering: "The Nation, the Law and the King".[36]

On 26 October 1792, David addressed the National Convention and expressed his wish that commemorative medals (lacking nominative value, as opposed to coins) be struck for all glorious events happening in the Republic, imitating, as he saw it, the Greeks and Romans.[37]

Along with a renewed interest in designing and striking medals came a numismatic interest, which interpreted these art works as crucial historical sources.

---

[35]A study for the reverse side of this coin is preserved at Paris, Musée Carnavalet D.3516BIS.

[36]Babelon, Jean. 1927. *La médaille et les médailleurs*. Collection l'Art et le Goût. Paris: Payot. 197–200. *Réimpression de L'ancien moniteur: vol 8: Constituante*. 1861. Paris: Henri Plon. 98.

[37]Babelon, 1927. 199–200.

Given that practically every decisive political, legislative, constitutional, or military moment would end up on the side of a medal, it was possible to write a history of a country by simply listing the medals chronologically, as stepping stones of the past.[38]

An intriguing early example is Antwerp-born numismatist Jacques de Bie's 1636 edition *Metallic France* (*La France métallique*). De Bie had the intention of following the history of France, the new Rome, through its medals all the way back to Charlemagne. The only problem for de Bie was that no such medals existed for much of the historical period. His seventeenth century conception of historical authenticity is far removed from our modern view. De Bie's intention was to simply place the many medals he had "found" in a chronological order, which made his publication a reconstruction even though the medals themselves were presented as recordings of contemporary moments. However, since numerous medals were missing in the chronology, de Bie had to fill gaps with reinvented medals, which made him an inventor. De Bie's *modus operandi* included showing prints after medals that had never materially existed, thus indirectly abusing the tangible medal's aura of authenticity. In other words, he presented reconstructions and inventions as recordings.[39]

Comparable in name, but completely different in conception, was the *Metallic history of Napoleon the Great* (*Histoire métallique de Napoléon le Grand*) which Napoleon issued in 1806, possibly as an answer to David's concern. The intention of Napoleon's *Metallic History* was essentially to record the different—mostly military—moments as they occurred from 1806 onwards by means of medals, and ultimately to legitimise him as emperor.[40] However, due to the speedy succession of events and the slowness of casting medals, the project never progressed past the design stage, with the exception of one medal for the victory of Iena on 14 October 1806. Part of the problem might have been Napoleon's demand to approve every design. Although Napoleon's history was largely a military one (full of decisive battle moments) his many legal efforts were likely to have been part of his *Metallic History*. Thus, during its last session on 18 February 1814, the commission discussed the type and legends for the medal to commemorate the Penal Code. Since this Napoleonic criminal code had been promulgated in 1810, the medal would have been a reconstruction of the legislative moment.[41]

The close link between revolutions and Constitutions, with the first giving popular endorsement to the second, makes a particular, slightly more recent medallic enterprise equally fascinating. Belgian numismatist Louis Guioth

---

[38]Cullen, Lucy, Wendy Fisher, Melissa Hamnett, and Marjorie Trusted. 2007. Medals and plaquettes. In *The making of sculpture: The materials and techniques of European sculpture*, ed. Marjorie Trusted, 86–87. London: Victoria and Albert Museum.

[39]Jones, Mark. 1990. 'Proof stones of history': The status of medals as historical evidence in seventeenth-century France. In *Medals and coins from Budé to Mommsen*, eds. M.H. Crawford, C. R. Ligota, and J.B. Trapp, 53–64. London: The Warburg Institute University of London.

[40]Cullen, Fisher, Hamnett, and Trusted, 2007. 86–87.

[41]Babelon, 1927. 199–201.

published his *Numismatic history of the Belgian Revolution* in 1844, followed by a second volume in 1851.[42] Guioth's objective was to show "the relation between the facts destined to be passed down by means of the burin."[43] With these words, Guioth almost paraphrased his Antwerp predecessor, de Bie, who in his introduction to *Metallic France* in 1636 purported only to have chronologically ordered the many medals he "found" in different cabinets.[44] Guioth was more respectful of historical facts. He based his work entirely on already existing, historical medals, records of past moments. The element of reconstruction was his listing them, and, like any historian, organising the past.

Guioth's case is interesting because it shows two aspects of a DCM when put to use on a medal as a medium. First, the limited amount of space on a medal's surface in fact did not allow for a narrative depiction of a moment or anecdote. Few of the medals Guioth listed had actual scenes on their surfaces. Looking back at Belgium's modern medallic history, Belgian numismatist Babelon wrote in 1927 that medal makers risked falling into boring accuracy when meticulously describing these events, whereas symbols would suggest them far more successfully.[45] Second, when medals were listed chronologically, the question was: where to start? Whatever moment-cast-into-medal would be featured as the first in a history of the revolution, automatically had the connotation of having put the spark to the finder. In his introduction, Guioth wrote that the facts-turned-into-medal were important because they had resulted in Belgium's independence. But what, in other words, had been the decisive revolutionary moment, and how far back did Guioth want to go? *Ab ovo*, "from the egg", the roots of the country, or somewhere *in medias res*, "along the way", when opposition against the regime of King William I was already at hand? A commonly-repeated narrative about the Belgian Revolution situates its origin at a show in the Mint opera house, but Guioth only chose a medal depicting the opera, the *Mute of Portici,* as his ninth. So he situates the decisive moment long before.

As it turned out, for Guioth, the *via media* between *ab ovo* and *in medias res* was… "LEX/REX", Law is King.[46] These Latin words are inscribed in the opening medal (Figs. 3.4 and 3.5) of Guioth's *Numismatic History*, a medal which has the

[42]Guioth, J.L. 1844. *Histoire numismatique de la révolution belge, ou Description raisonnée des médailles, des jetons et des monnaies qui ont été frappés depuis le commencement de cette révolution jusqu'à ce jour.* Hasselt: P.-F. Milis. Guioth, J.L. 1851. *Histoire numismatique de la Belgique, faisant suite à l'histoire numismatique de la Révolution Belge, ou Description raisonnée des médailles, des jetons et des monnaies qui ont été frappés depuis le commencement de cette Révolution jusqu'à ce jour.* Hasselt: Milis.

[43]"la relation des faits destines à être transmis à l'aide du burin" Guioth, 1844. v.

[44]Jones, 1990. 59–61.

[45]Babelon, 1927. 222–223.

[46]Using the words "Lex Rex", the anonymous medal maker probably referred to the 1644 book by the same name written by scottish writer Samuel Rutherford. Rutherford's Presbyterian argument, subsequently secularized by John Locke and used by Thomas Jefferson, was that even the King and government are bound by law. Transferred to the 1829 Belgian case, this means that the King, too, must abide by the Constitution.

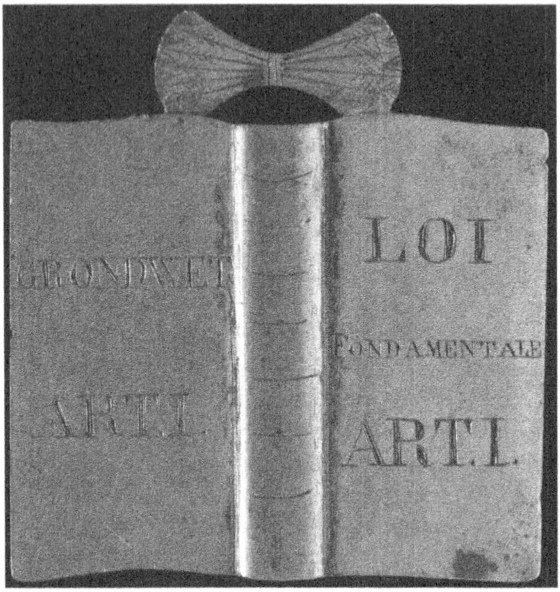

Fig. 3.4 Anonymous, *book-shaped medal from the early days of the Belgian Revolution [obverse]*, 1829. Ghent University Library. Ghent University

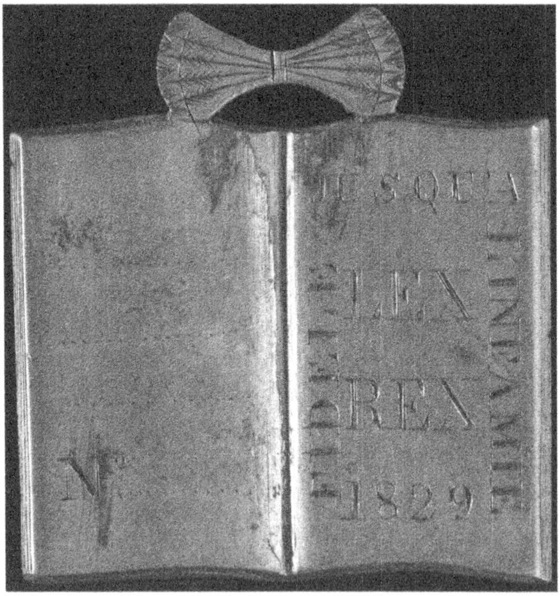

Fig. 3.5 Anonymous, *book-shaped medal from the early days of the Belgian Revolution [reverse]*, 1829. Ghent University Library. Ghent University

shape of an open book with the words "Constitution article 1" in French and Dutch on its front and back cover, respectively. On its reverse, the right hand page of this Constitution features the words "fidelity up to infamy" ("fidèle jusqu'à l'infamie") surrounding the earlier mentioned "LEX/REX/1829". During a speech in Liège on

23 June 1829, William I, King of the United Kingdom of the Netherlands, had referred to the southern—i.e. Belgian—opposition and their petitions and grievances as "infamous" behaviour. As many of the Belgian petitioners noted, this so called infamy was merely a use of their constitutional right to petition, which is declared in article 161 of the 1815 Constitution of the United Kingdom of the Netherlands. The artist behind the medal thus recorded a moment which, by the revolutionaries, was seen as constitutional—or, rather, felt as a violation of their Constitution. Guioth, in his turn, by including the piece as his opening medal, turns the constitutional moment into a decisive constitutional moment. The necessary element of consensus and unity is not so much depicted as it symbolised, by means of a bundle of nine arrows (one arrow is breakable, a bundle is not) which surmounts the open book medal. The number nine refers to the amount of provinces petitioning against King William I.

In short, medals might be the number one medium when using the DCM if it was not for two inherent but paradoxical features: their limited surface space, which does not allow narrative scenes, and their success as recordings of significant moments, which led to accumulations, materially, and collections, on paper (and in cabinets), reducing the extraordinary nature of the many moments they recorded.

3.3.3 *Sculpture*

There are roughly two ways to include specific moments when sculpting a person. The first was used in the eighteenth century and is known as the significant moment. Showing this moment was a device by means of which the portrayed person was sculpted during a biographic moment, a historical turning point in his or her public career. In line with Shaftesbury and Lessing, the sculptors often chose the moment before the action, rather than the climax of the crucial event.[47]

The second way of using narration in monumental sculpture is prevalent within the nineteenth century's so-called *statuomania*, the accumulating erection of public statues. This alternative to significant moments entails the formula in which the statue, equestrian or standing, stands on a plinth adorned with bas-reliefs.[48] These bas-reliefs, then, picture crucial moments from the life of the commemorated person and clarify his or her accomplishments.

An important precedent or prototype for this formula originated in sixteenth-century Florence. Giambologna's equestrian statue of Cosimo I on the Piazza della Signoria has three narrative bas-reliefs, made between 1596 and 1599.

[47]Dowley, 1957.

[48]Nancy Scott, in her study on the Italian sculptor Vincenzo Vela, refers this particular formula, and notes how the narrative or allegorical bas-reliefs had to "suggest the impact of a person's moment in history". Scott, Nancy. 1979. Politics on a Pedestal. *Art Journal* 38 (3): 193. Also see Plotek, Arial. 2008. Allegory in the age of realism. Monumental sculpture in France, 1848–1880: Institute of Fine Arts, New York University.

One of them, at the rear end, features Cosimo's proclamation as Duke in 1537. Young Cosimo's succession of Alessandro de' Medici was precarious. The title of Duke of the Florentine Republic only existed since Alessandro's constitutional reform in 1532. As a solution to this issue, the bas-relief combines two historical events which in reality were separated by several months: Cosimo's proclamation as Duke on 9 January 1537 and the proclamation of the Diploma of Emperor Charles V on 30 September, made public on 16 October 1537, which recognised Cosimo's reign. Giambologna showed Cosimo's proclamation together with Charles V's charter, and the constitutional moment as shown on the relief is invented. Above all, Giambologna's relief shows the succession of Cosimo as based on the broad consensus of the Florentine patriciate, with a Latin inscription referring to a consensus within the Senate's vote.[49] The Duke relief, like the two others, had to help legitimate Cosimo's ascent to power within a recently modified Constitution, and the use of a DCM serves this legitimation fruitfully.

This formula, of narrative bas-reliefs in a statue or monument's plinth, met a renewed interest in the nineteenth century. In 1848, an equestrian statue was erected for Godfrey of Bouillon, the eleventh-century leader of the first crusade, in Brussels's Royal Square. Two of the four sides of the pedestal were destined to feature bas-reliefs showing events from the life of Godfrey, and much like the Giambologna model, the short sides were to receive inscriptions.[50] Godfrey's major accomplishments were military and legislative in nature, and both had their decisive moment. One relief would show Godfrey leading the taking of Jerusalem, the other would focus on his role in the *Assises of Jerusalem* (*Assises de Jérusalem*). An early nineteenth-century narrative interpreted these *Assises* as a code that resulted from Godfrey's order to collect customs and laws for the Kingdom of Jerusalem.[51] Given that "[t]hese laws established the rights of everyone within the feudal system",[52] some simply called the *Assises* a "Code of Constitutional Laws".[53]

Although the consensus about the reliefs' content ("Godfrey warrior—Godfrey legislator"[54]) was reached in 1849, it would take half a century of scientific debates within the Belgian Academy of Sciences to resolve the question how these

[49]Erben, Dietrich. 1996. Die Reiterdenkmäler der Medici in Florenz und ihre politische Bedeutung. *Mitteilungen des Kunsthistorischen Institutes in Florenz* 40 (3), 309.

[50]*Etude épigraphique sur le monument érigé à Bruxelles en 1848 à la mémoire de Godefroid de Bouillon. Extrait de la Revue Générale de Belgique.* 1866. Brussels: Victor Devaux et Cie., 5.

[51]Prawer, Joshua. 1961. Étude sur le droit des Assises de Jérusalem: droit de confiscation et droit d'exhérédation. *Revue historique de droit français et étranger* 39. 520–551 and 40 (1962), 29–42.

[52]"[c]es lois établissaient les droits de tous et de chacun selon le système féodal" Collin de Plancy, J. 1848. *La chronique de Godefroid de Bouillon et du royaume de Jérusalem. Première et Deuxième Croisades (1080–1187) avec l'Histoire de Charles-le-Bon.* Paris: La Librairie des Livres Liturgique Illustrés, 100.

[53]"un code de lois constitutionnelles" *Etude épigraphique,* 1866. 18.

[54]"Godefroi guerrier - Godefrois législateur" De Ram, M. 1849. Rapport sur les questions proposées par M. le Ministre de l'intérieur. *Bulletins de l'Académie royale des Sciences, des Lettres et des Beaux-Arts de Belgique* 16. 203.

moments should be depicted. Allegory and realistic narration constituted the major sides of the arguments. In the end, two narrative bas-reliefs by Guillaume De Groot were added to Godfrey's pedestal as late as 1897.[55] The southern relief shows a chaotic war scene, whilst the northern relief features a scene with an enthroned Godfrey opposite two men with papers. The extraordinary long period of half a century between decision and execution of the bas-reliefs is intriguing, since it bridges the artistic eras of nationalist romanticism and fin-de-siècle symbolism. During this half a century of debates about the reliefs and inscriptions, severe doubts about Godfrey's role in the writing of the code had grown. The liberal newspaper *L'Indépendance Belge* (*Belgian Independence*) wrote in 1895: "In all honesty, today we know that Godfrey (…) did not at all give his subjects a Code (…). But this statue of Godfrey of Bouillon features such archaeological anachronisms, such historical errors, that these subjects will not mar it—quite the contrary!"[56] In this case, the moment which the DCM depicted shifted, thanks to historical research, from reconstruction to invention.

Like a historical person, an entire country or nation has a history. For example, the 1883 Parisian Monument to the Republic (Square of the Republic, Paris) by Léopold Morice, features biographic scenes of the republic in its base. Like Guioth's *Numismatic History*, such narration needs a start. Morice took the *Tennis Court Oath* (20 June 1789) as an outset, in a relief clearly based on David's painting. Other episodes and moments are conspicuously omitted, not the least the 1870–1871 Paris Commune, an unwanted scene for the Third Republic's government.[57]

3.3.4 Moment, Medium and Message

From these examples it is possible to draw three important conclusions. First, it becomes clear how the depiction of a historical moment is limited by material constraints, often urging artists and commissioners to the choice for allegory as opposed to a narrative scene, due to limited space. Second, they demonstrate how the choice of a moment is linked to the moment of choice, such as the new Medici line of Cosimo I and FDR's precarious political situation which spurred them to depict specific historical moments from their constitutional history. Thirdly, they confirm the importance of distinguishing recording, reconstructing, inventing and

[55]Meirsschaut, Pol. 1900. *Sculptures de plein aires à Bruxelles. Guide explicatif.* Brussels: Bruylant, 75.

[56]*L'Indépendance Belge*. 1895. 21 July 1895. "À la vérité, on sait aujourd'hui que Godefroid (…) ne donna point à ses sujets un Code (…). Mais cette statue de Godefroid de Bouillon présente de tels anachronismes archéologiques, consacre de telles erreurs historiques, que ses sujets ne la dépareraient pas – au contraire!"

[57]Best, Janice. 2006. Une Statue monumentale pour la République. *Nineteenth-Century French Studies* 34 (3&4):311–313.

staging as part of the DCM device. Thus, with validation and legitimation as the device's main objective, the (1) mode of depiction, (2) moment of depicting and (3) selection of the historical moment need to be taken into account.

3.4 Moment into Monument: The 1849 Congress Column Competition in Belgium

Godfrey's statue and its bas-reliefs demonstrate that the *Assises* were interpreted as a formal Constitution, understood as a fundamental law, a single written document. Moreover, scholars like Joseph-François Michaud, in his *History of the Crusades*, referred to the *Assises* as a monument of feudal jurisprudence and legislation, like others who called it "a monument of wisdom and humanity".[58] These phrasings make clear how, as Nora stated, every Constitution is indeed a site of memory, a monument to its own importance. Moreover, actual monuments have been raised for Constitutions, and those monuments often feature moments, in the form of dates or narrative bas-reliefs. Because of this, they resemble the Giambologna formula, with the Constitution as the commemorated 'person', and the moments depicted in the bas-reliefs as memorable events in the life of the Constitution, much like how the Paris Monument for the Republic could be interpreted biographically. An in depth study of the Belgian Congress Column case is equally revealing and helps to evaluate the choice (1) for the DCM as a device; (2) for one or more of the many possible moments, and (3) for the specific way of depicting these moments.

3.4.1 The 1849 Competition

The revolutionary wave that struck Europe in 1848 passed remarkably quietly through Belgium.[59] The government, headed by liberal Prime Minister and founding father Charles Rogier, granted a limited number of political concessions to the left-wing agenda, and raised spending on public works in order to lower the amount of potentially risky unemployed labourers. Additionally, there was an electoral reform under which the threshold (tax payment being the primary criterion for suffrage) was lowered to the constitutional minimum, the 40% tax on printed publications was abolished and Parliament was reformed. Most importantly, the freedom fought for in France and other European countries had already been

[58]Michaud, Joseph-François. 1867. *Histoire des croisades*. Paris: Furne, Jouvet et Cie, vol. 1., 466. "un monument de sagesse et d'humanité" *Journal de Bruxelles*, 25 December, 1873, 2 "ce célèbre monument de législation", *Etude épigraphique*, 1866. 18.

[59]For a more elaborate account and references on the post-1848 constitutional cult in Belgium, see Huygebaert, Stefan. 2015. Unshakeable Foundations An Iconological Study of the Belgian Constitutional Cult following the 1848 Revolution. *Journal of Belgian History* 45 (4):10–39.

protected by Belgium's Constitution, written by the country's Constitutional Assembly—called *Congrès National* or National Congress—between 10 November 1830 and 7 February 1831. This assembly was preceded by a provisional government which proclaimed Belgium's independence on 4 October 1830, shortly after a revolution against the regime of William I had split the territory off from the United Kingdom of the Netherlands (1815–1830). Leopold of Saxe-Coburg (1790–1865), who became Louis-Philippe's son-in-law after marrying his daughter Louise of Orléans (1812–1850), was eventually elected the Belgian monarch in a constitutional monarchy.[60]

Despite the relative quietness, Belgium's government seemed very much aware of the possibility of a revolution in 1848, especially from February onwards. The French example of an abdicating King—Leopold's father-in-law—inspired some to produce the earlier mentioned print, featuring the invented moment of Leopold's abdication (Brussels, Royal Library, Print Room, S.II 12680).

The government's awareness of the possibility of political unrest becomes particularly clear through the artistic measures, which were taken in Belgium during and shortly after the 1848 revolutionary wave. In an earlier article, I have analysed the ways in which the Belgian liberal government intensified the celebration and near veneration of the country's Constitution. These artistic measures could be called a constitutional cult, in which the population was reminded of the country's fundamental law and the civic liberties guaranteed therein. The most important and lasting part of this propaganda effort was the monument Rogier erected on a panoramic spot in the Royal Street, in the heart of Brussels. On 13 October 1849 a Ministerial Decree by Rogier announced the organisation of a competition for the design of a column-shaped monument. The Belgian competition in 1849 was presented as democratic, since all citizens could go and look at the different designs. However, it was a carefully selected commission that was tasked with choosing one of the 64 anonymous and numbered designs. Although the specification of the form, namely a column, strongly limited the options for the competitors, their choice of ornaments, symbols, personifications and allegories surrounding and surmounting Brussels's soon-to-be site of memory was almost endless.

3.4.2 A Plenitude of Choices

Equally long was the total list of specific moments from constitutional history, which the competing artists wished to include. Reviewing the entries, the Belgian *Journal de l'Architecture* (*Journal for Architecture*) pitied the competing artists:

> In fact, the work of the Congress that formed Belgium as an independent Kingdom, was not at all characterised by any memorable event, like the ones that often prepare or accompany

[60]Leopold was in fact only the second choice, as the National Congress first elected the Duc de Nemours (1814–1896), son of the French King, who refused this offer.

> the development of a nationality that founds itself, and of a liberty that creates itself. Not a single feat of arms to remember, not a single hero to glorify.[61]

Because of this lack of clearly conventional and dramatic, decisive battle moments, the choice for the artist was ample. The newspaper *L'Indépendance* reminded the competitors of their real task: their design was to feature a summary of the events from the Belgian Revolution (1830) until the signing of the Constitution, as well as the freedoms, powers and provinces. All that, according to *L'Indépendance*, should be made clear by means of allegory, and not—as many competitors had tried—by means of inscriptions, which were deemed easy and hardly ingenious.[62] At the time of the competition, however, the events the artists attempted to bring to mind in their sculptural and architectural sketches had unfolded only two decades earlier. No real canonisation had been established yet, and one generation after the revolution, many of the key actors, such as the revolutionary leaders, many members of the National Congress and the King were still actively involved in politics. The 1849 competition thus served as a filter, a catalyst speeding up a process of selection and elimination of lesser dates, ultimately resulting in a Belgian decisive constitutional moment. 17 designs are preserved, most of which are kept in the Belgian State Archives in Brussels. Of these, 15 are shown in sufficient detail in order to analyse any possibly narrative bas-reliefs. These designs enable me to largely summarise the list of possible moments which could serve in a DCM as follows.

The Revolution (September, 1830)

When writing about revolutionary legitimacy, Ackerman emphasises that in order to gain the authority to speak in the name of the people, the leader(s) of a revolutionary movement must have the support of a significant group of mobilised followers. This constitutional moment is thus a moment of mass mobilisation in its most literal sense, when "We, the People" take up arms against an oppressing force. Moreover, as mentioned above, it was the French Revolution that gave rise to the artistic quest for contemporary decisive moments. Two of the 17 Belgian designs in 1849 included Belgian revolutionaries with canons and bayonets, who fought the oppressing force of the Dutch monarch.[63] Much like design number 39, which features ancient roman weaponry symbolising war and battle in general, these projects recognised the importance of the Belgian Revolution, but their creators refrained from choosing a decisive moment within those revolutionary days.

---

[61]"En effet, l'œuvre du congrès qui constitua la Belgique en royaume indépendant, ne fut point illustrée par les événements mémorables qui souvent préparent ou accompagnent le développement d'une nationalité qui se fonde, d'une liberté qui se crée. Nul fait d'armes à rappeler, nul héros à exalter." La Colonne de la Constitution. 1850. *Journal de l'architecture et des arts relatifs à la construction* 3 (3):34.

[62]*L'Indépendance Belge*. 1850. Monument de la Constitution. 31 January 1850.

[63]La Colonne de la Constitution. 1849. *Journal de l'architecture et des arts relatifs à la construction* 2 (11): 175: "des combattants de septembre semblent danser une ronde".

These moments did exist. Some of them were featured on a monument devoted to the 1830 revolution itself and inaugurated on the Square of the Martyrs in Brussels in 1838, which preceded the Congress Column as the closest to a national monument that Belgium had. A few years after 1838, the Martyrs monument received four bas-reliefs. Of the two added in 1846, the one in front is allegorical and timeless, as it shows liberated Belgium crowning its warriors with laurels. The other one on the back shows a specific moment on 2 October 1830, when the graves of the martyrs on the improvised burial ground of the Square of the Martyrs were consecrated. The reliefs on the sides, added in 1848 and 1849, respectively, feature two more specific moments from the revolution: the attack on the Warande Park led by Juan Van Halen on 25 September 1830, and the oath of the volunteers. In addition to these moments depicted on the bas-reliefs, the surmounting personification of Liberty, a sculpture sometimes interpreted as personifying Belgium, is shown writing down four precise dates (23, 24, 25 and 26 September 1830) in the book of history.[64]

In contrast to the Martyrs Monument, in the Congress Column designs references to the revolution in general are far less ubiquitous, and in some cases completely absent. This corresponds with Jeroen Janssens's observation that, from 1848 onwards, the emphasis of the patriotic rhetoric shifted from revolution to Constitution, with the latter providing the consolidation for the liberal values of the first.[65] Additionally, the Congress Column was to become a monument specifically for the Constitution and the Constituent Assembly, and not so much for the revolution these consolidated. However, those designs that did feature life-size statues of revolutionaries (e.g. numbers 21 and 45), or references to the revolution, such as canons and bayonets (e.g. number 52), showed them at the base of their respective column. These specific column designs feature a vertical chronology—one newspaper discerned a type of "chronological columns" amongst the entries[66]—and thus mark the Belgian Revolution as the foundation and beginning of the process that would eventually lead to the Belgian Constitution and Monarchy, personified on top of the respective columns.

Writing, Voting and Proclaiming: The Constituent Assembly's Plenary Sessions (10 November 1830–7 February 1831)

As they were designing a monument for the Belgian Constituent Assembly, several of the artists, understandably, chose to depict scenes from the assembly, or dates referring to specific votes and decisions in the Constitution's genesis. Théodore Juste, the historian whom Rogier asked to write a *History of the National Congress* in 1849, had already selected (but not illustrated) three main votes from the Congress's history for his 1840 illustrated book *History of Belgium*. These were 18

[64]Goedleven, Edgard. 1996. *Het Martelaarsplein te Brussel: gedenkteken van de Belgische onafhankelijkheid en zetel van de Vlaamse Regering*. Tielt: Lannoo, 123–134.

[65]Janssens, Jeroen. 2001. *De Belgische natie viert: de Belgische nationale feesten 1830–1914*. Leuven: Universitaire pers, 50–52.

[66]*L'Indépendance Belge*. 1850. Monument de la Constitution. 31 January 1850.

November 1830 (the proclamation of Belgium's independence); 22 November 1830 (the vote for a representative monarchy as form of government) and 24 November 1830 (the everlasting exclusion of the house of Orange from the Belgian throne).[67]

Design number 21 (Fig. 3.6) is interesting in this respect, because it features an abundance of royalist iconography. The base of the column shows Belgian revolutionaries honouring—or worshipping—a central personification with a sceptre, globe, cornucopia and scroll. Underneath are the words "Choice of the Belgian people for a Constitutional Monarchy, 22 November 1830".[68] The design thus makes use of an allegory to refer to a specific moment of vote in the constituent process. Moreover, it is interesting to note that the subscript does not have the Congress as its active subject, but the Belgian people. It therefore legitimises the vote by equating the 200 members of the National Congress, elected by a group of 30.000 voters (less than one per cent of the population) with the entire population of Belgium, indeed: "We, the People".

In general, these kind of votes were tedious as subject matter and therefore very much in line with the *Journal de l'Architecture*'s comment. Notably, another voting scene represented on design number 21—in this case one that was actually depicted in a bas relief—was regarded so visually uninteresting that the designer partially hid it behind a statue for the King.

Electing the Monarch: Leopold I (4 June 1831)

The artist behind design number 21 used different words than "the Belgian people" right above the mentioned allegory of the revolution. There, a statue of Leopold I has the words "Leopold I, King of the Belgians, elected by National Congress 4 June 1831" written on its pedestal.[69] This teleological history writing evidently omits to bring up the first vote of the Congress for a Belgian monarch in early February, which chose Louis-Philippe's son, the Duc de Nemours. Behind Leopold's statue a bas-relief shows a voting scene, set in a comfortable, salon-like version of the National Congress. An audience is present in the balcony areas above, and here again, the Belgian people is mentioned, since the entire bas-relief is entitled "The Belgian people at the National Congress".

The entire edifice, according to the artist of this design, was to be crowned literally with a royal crown. This kind of celebration of constitutional monarchy, present in three more designs, would eventually make it to the final monument by Joseph Poelaert, where Leopold's statue replaced an earlier planned personification of the Constitution after a decision by the Chamber of Representatives in 1853.

[67]Juste, Théodore. 1840. *Histoire de Belgique*. Brussels: A. Jamar, 597–598. Belgium's provisional government had already proclaimed the separation from William's United Kingdom of the Netherlands on 4 October 1830.

[68]"Adhésion du people à la monarchie constitutionelle 22 nov. 1830" Design nr. 21, National Archives of Belgium, Brussels, *Kaarten en Plannen*, 762.

[69]"Leopold I Roi des Belges élu par le Congrès National le 4 juin 1831." Author's translation. Design nr. 21, National Archives of Belgium, Brussels, *Kaarten en Plannen*, 762.

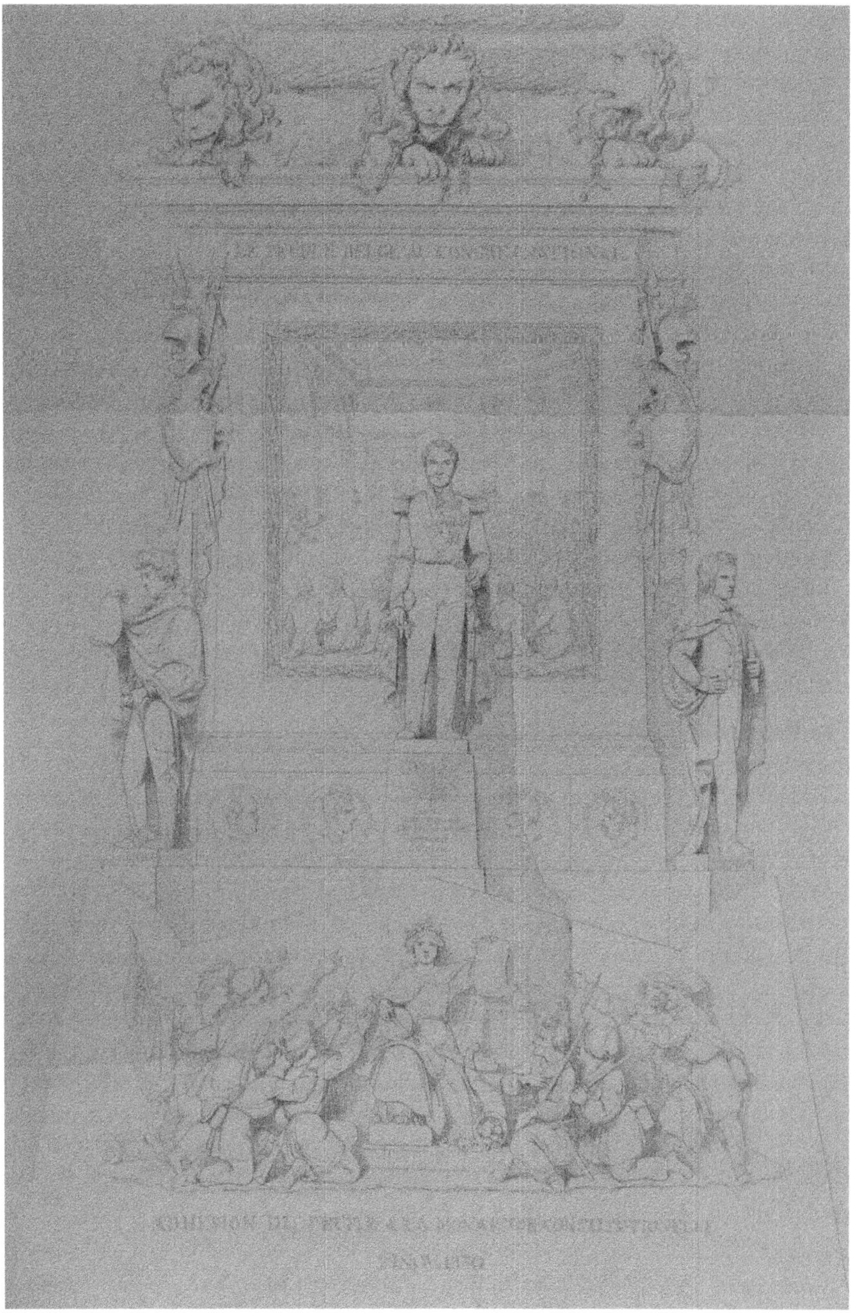

Fig. 3.6 Anonymous Congress Column design nr. 21 (detail: base of the design), National Archives of Belgium, Brussels, *Kaarten en Plannen*, 762. © *photo* Author

This Parliamentary decision demonstrates the weight and importance of the vote for a constitutional monarchy in general and for Leopold's dynasty in particular as Belgian constitutional moments.

In other imagery celebrating the Belgian nation, artists visualised not so much the voting episode of Leopold's election in Congress, as the offering of the Belgian crown in his residence in Marlborough House, London. There is a notable difference between these depictions of the Marlborough House scene and the French imagery that reconstructed the preceding episode, in which the same crown was offered to the Duc de Nemours. Nicolas Gosse's painting (1836, Paris, Castle of Versailles) of Louis-Philippe's grand refusal of the Belgian Crown in February 1831, shows the French perspective with the King and his sons, including the Duc de Nemours, high above Belgium's regent Surlet de Chokier, who respectfully and with a modest bow offers the King a piece of paper. A lithograph by De Doncker shows the scene with Leopold in a much more intimate setting (Brussels, Royal Library—Print Room, S.II 143816). The same can be said about the painting featured on a temporary triumphal arch on the Royal Square at the occasion of Leopold's silver jubilee as Belgian Monarch in 1856. Here, all people involved in the offering of the Belgian crown to Leopold by the deputies of the National Congress were shown in a composition of democratic isocephaly, a stark contrast with Gosse's hierarchic painting. Depicting the offering of the Belgian crown to Leopold clearly had DCM potential, since an inscription below the image on the arch mentioned the exact date of the event: 23 June 1831.

The Royal Entry (21 July 1831)

Royal entries are part of the pomp and circumstance associated with royalty. For example, even as recently as 1999, the Belgian crown prince and his wife Mathilde visited the country's main cities after their royal wedding. Likewise, Leopold I visited Brussels with his second wife, Louise of Orléans, after their wedding on 9 August 1832—a moment commemorated in several medals. Historically, however, an entry of a duke or count in the Low Countries' territories had a strong legal, if not constitutional connotation. During an event known as a joyous entry (Blijde Intrede/Joyeuse Entrée), the citizens and the prince swore to uphold the privileges and duties, which, particularly in Brabant, was accompanied by a written charter.[70] Joyous entries can easily be called pre-modern constitutional moments. This explains the historical weight of the depiction of Leopold's entry into Belgium at the coastal border town of De Panne on 17 July 1831, shortly after his election as King, as well as of his "solemn entry" on horseback into Brussels and in the various cities in between. When, a few days later, the soon-to-be King arrived in Bruges,

[70]Arnade, Peter. 1997. City, State and Public Ritual in the Late-Medieval Burgundian Netherlands. *Comparative Studies in Society and History* 39 (2): 305. Deseure, Brecht. 2015. De lange schaduw van de Blijde Inkomst: Revolutionair discours over de oude grondwetten in België. In *Rechtsgeschiedenis op nieuwe wegen/Legal history, moving in new directions*, ed. Dave De ruysscher, 35–58. Antwerp: Maklu. See also the 1958 special issue on joyous entries of *Standen en Landen* 16.

where medieval joyous entries were part of a celebrated urban history, a priest recalled the medieval Burgundian dukes as friends of the nation. Théodore Juste, in his *History of the Belgian National Congress* written in 1849–1850, recalled the historical reciprocal oaths of the people and sovereigns before describing Leopold's entry into Brussels.[71]

As these facts demonstrate, for a young nation like Belgium, linking contemporary constitutional moments to historical ones was crucial in order to legitimate the new regime. Any depiction of such a moment is, therefore, to some extent an invention. This invention is no different from historians Hobsbawm and Ranger's famous invention of traditions. This is defined as a repeated practice, often of ritual or symbolic nature, which attempts "to establish continuity with a suitable historic past."[72] Royal entries, as well as the imagery depicting them, are specifically analogous to the second type of invented traditions discerned by Hobsbawm and Ranger: the type that legitimises institutions. For DCMs, the repetition of the practices which Hobsbawm and Ranger refer to, is guaranteed by the images depicting the moment over and over again.

Congress Column design number 52 (Fig. 3.7) depicts Leopold's entry centrally on the column's shaft, although it is unclear if the scene is set in De Panne or Brussels. The design is all the more interesting because of its specific narrative device. The entry scene is fit in between two others in a spiral bas-relief or frieze. Above it, an agitated orator speaks to a plenary assembly, whilst underneath a roughly sketched scene possibly shows an oath. The spiral is reminiscent of Trajan's column, a quintessential example of continuous narrative in Roman friezes, since scenes happening in very different settings are shown closely linked.[73] At least one other Congress Column entry (number 44-bis, only known by description) made use of this narrative strategy.[74] Such a spiral creates a teleological effect, with one episode linked to another in a single continuum.

The Constitutional Oath (21 July 1831)

Perhaps the most evident moment from Belgian constitutional history to be commemorated and depicted, is the oath taken by Leopold I on 21 July 1831. Evident, because since 1890 and up until today it is celebrated—although often by Belgians unaware of the exact historical reason—as Belgium's national holiday.[75] Marking the difference with the inauguration ceremony of William I on the same location—the Royal Square in Brussels—in 1815, the absence of a coronation made Leopold's constitutional oath on 21 July 1831 the pivotal moment of his

---

[71]Juste, Théodore. 1850. *Histoire du Congrès national de Belgique, ou de la fondation de la monarchie belge*. Brussels, 352–353.

[72]Hobsbawm, Eric, and Terence O. Ranger. 1983. The Invention of Tradition. Cambridge University Press: Cambridge, 1.

[73]Blanckenhagen, Peter H. von. 1957. Narration in Hellenistic and Roman Art. *American Journal of Archaeology* 61 (1):78–83.

[74]*L'Indépendance Belge*. 1850. Monument de la Constitution. 31 January 1850.

[75]Janssens. 2001, ix.

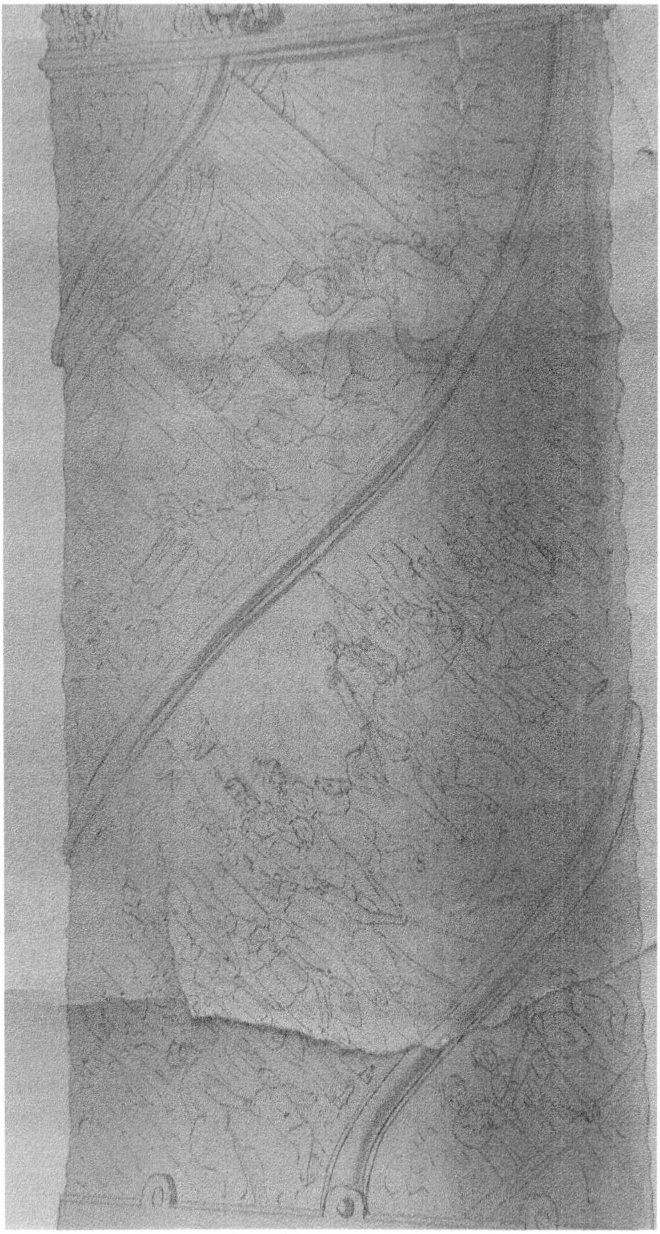

Fig. 3.7 Anonymous Congress Column design nr. 52 (detail: spiral bas-reliefs on the shaft), National Archives of Belgium, Brussels, *Kaarten en Plannen*, 762. © *photo* Author

inauguration. Leopold was King by the grace of the people, as Baron de Gerlache, the president of the National Congress, emphasized at the occasion. Inside the "liturgy of power", the post-revolutionary oath maintained a sacral vigour within a desacralisation of politics, as shown by Paolo Prodi.[76] However, more than religion, history served as a major form of legitimation. Again, as was the case with the royal entries, a historical parallel was made with earlier reciprocal pacts between rulers and the people, such as those of Philip the Good and Charles V.[77]

The King only needed a few seconds to pronounce the words prescribed in article 80 of the 1831 Constitution: "I swear to observe the Constitution and the laws of the Belgian people, to maintain the national independence and the integrity of the territory."[78] Even for an instantaneous moment like the swearing of an oath, the variety of surviving depictions is conspicuous. The oath was featured as a relief on the shaft of an unofficial Congress Column design by architect August Payen and a sculptor named Leclercq, which was picked up in the artistic press in 1849.[79] Their relief on the front shows Leopold, amidst a group of standing people, whilst putting his right hand down and holding his hat with his left. When compared with the many prints and paintings produced shortly after the inauguration in 1831, Payen and Leclercq's choice for the specific moment was less obvious than could be expected. Other depictions feature a surprising variety of poses and compositions, and thereby of actual instants within the moment. Some prints depict Leopold with his hand on the Constitution, other showed him seated on the throne after the regent had granted him to do so. In a history painting from 1831 (Brussels, Royal Museums for Fine Arts of Belgium), Ferdinand de Braekeleer chose the moment of acclamation, when Surlet de Chokier, Belgium's regent, asked the people to welcome their new King with a cheer. In 1856, De Braekeleer reconstructed the moment in a new history painting (Brussels, Royal Museums for Fine Arts of Belgium).[80]

As opposed to painters and printmakers, the Congress Column designers, when showing the oath, were unable to depict the architectural surroundings. Notably, the limited space disabled them to include the main building on the heavily ornamented Royal Square, right behind the ephemeral stage: the church of Saint-James on the

[76]Prodi, Paolo. 1997 (1992). *Das Sakrament der Herrschaft. Der politische Eid in der Verfassungsgeschichte des Okzidents*. Trans. J. Elze. Berlin: Duncker & Humblot, 17, 403.

[77]Deneckere, Gita. 2011. *Leopold I. De eerste koning van Europa*. Antwerpen: De Bezige Bij, 214–215.

[78]"Je jure d'observer la Constitution et les lois du peuple belge, de maintenir l'indépendance nationale et l'intégrité du territoire." In the current version of the Belgian Constitution, this phrase is included in article 91. The official report of the inauguration is included in Huyttens, E. 1844. *Discussions du Congrès national de Belgique*. Brussels: Adolphe Wahlen et Cie, 613–622.

[79]The Payen and Leclercq design was discussed in 'La colonne de la constitution', *Journal d'architecture*, 1850, 34–36. and shown in *La Renaissance*, 1849 (after 140).

[80]Leen, Frederik. 2005. Over revolutie en de stichting van een nieuwe staat. In *De romantiek in België. Tussen werkelijkheid, herinnering en verlangen*, eds. Dominique Marechal, and Gautier Platteau, 72–73. Tielt: Lannoo.

Coudenberg. For printmakers, however, this building allowed to include both time and timelessness in their use of the DCM. In Woods's words: their prints showed time expressed and time transcended. On the one hand, the church's clock made it possible to indicate the exact time (2:15 p.m.) and therefore increased the instantaneity of the depicted instant, as one artist chose to do (Fig. 3.7). Other printmakers framed their print in such ways that the clock was left out, or went so far as to alter the architecture and erase the church tower altogether, thereby erasing time from the image.

On the other hand, the church's pediment offered a means to make the clearly important, if not decisive moment of a constitutional oath last, helping to emphasise its timelessness. Again, and in line with *L'Indépendance*'s earlier mentioned comment, allegory saved the day. Leopold putting his hand on the book, tablet or scroll of the Constitution became the quintessential allegorical image of the day. This representation of Leopold's oath was included in the pediment of the church, as can be seen on a print by Simoneau (Fig. 3.8). The pediment featured Leopold kneeling in front of a personification of Belgium crowning the constitutional tables of the law (upon which was written "Long live the King of the Belgians") with a laurel. In other words: already at the unfolding of the actual historical moment of the constitutional oath, its own timeless image served as its backdrop, making it quintessentially staged. The organizing and commissioning government did not

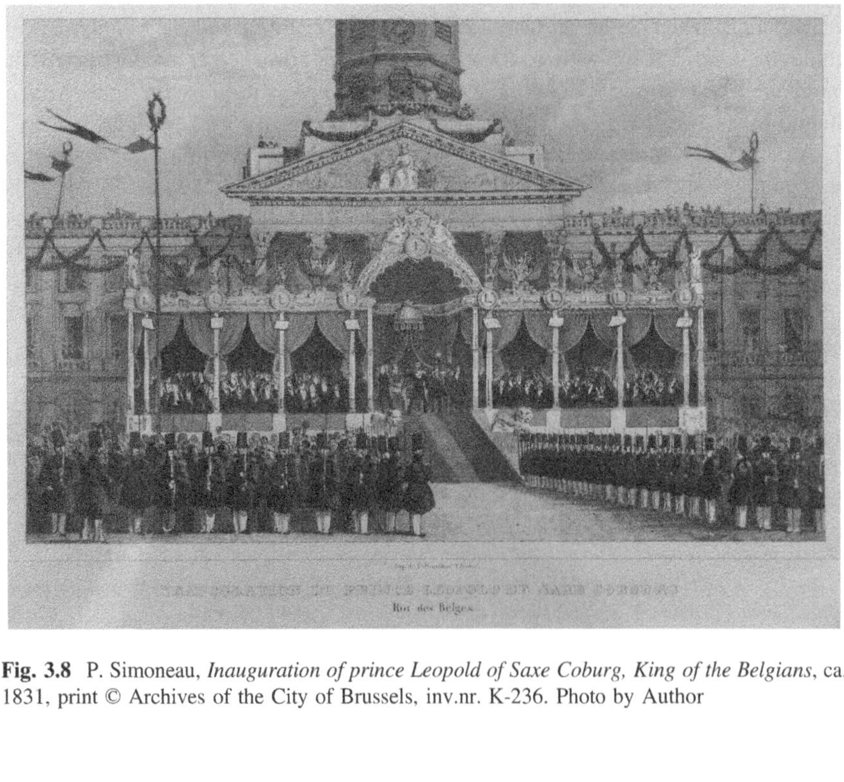

Fig. 3.8 P. Simoneau, *Inauguration of prince Leopold of Saxe Coburg, King of the Belgians*, ca. 1831, print © Archives of the City of Brussels, inv.nr. K-236. Photo by Author

only anticipate the future depiction of the moment, they already had it depicted above Leopold before he had even begun his oath.

This timeless image would indeed survive. For example, one of the Column designs was crowned with a statue of Leopold in an oath taking position (The Hague, Netherlands Institute for Art History, BD/1484). Already before the 1848 Revolution, in 1847, medal artist Laurent Hart designed a medal commemorating Leopold's constitutional oath (Brussels, Royal Library, Print Room, II.4439-4442). The different designs (Fig. 3.9) give an exclusive insight into the genesis of a romantic medal. Balancing between anecdote and allegory, most of Hart's designs lean to the latter, as they include allegorical figures for concepts such as the arts, history, and the Belgian nation. Despite the presence of personifications, the lower right design shows the most realistic scene with the regent holding the Constitution —in its allegorical form of tables of the law—and members of the army standing next to the King. In the background stands a building reminiscent of the church of Saint-James on the Coudenberg, in front of which the actual oath took place.

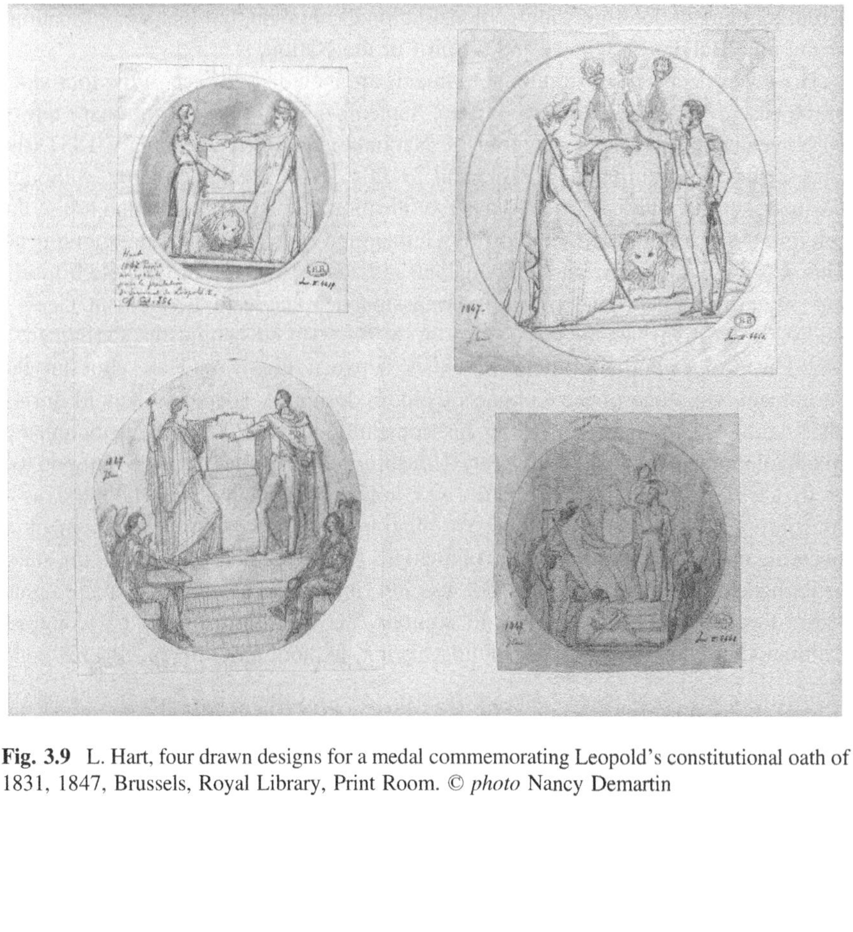

Fig. 3.9 L. Hart, four drawn designs for a medal commemorating Leopold's constitutional oath of 1831, 1847, Brussels, Royal Library, Print Room. © *photo* Nancy Demartin

In the end, Hart chose the most sober design close to the lower left drawing and the 1831 pediment image, with Leopold facing a personification of the Belgian nation: a timeless allegory.

For the depiction of a constitutional oath, artists thus made use of a triple notion of time: the instantaneous, momentary nature of the event, the historical link with the old Constitutions by means of an invented tradition, and the timelessness of an allegory.

3.4.3 The Final Choice: Living in the Moment

After a draw between competing architects Joseph Poelaert (number 46D) and Pierre Dens (number 42) following the competition, it was Poelaert's design that was finally executed and subsequently inaugurated on 26 September 1859 (Fig. 3.10). Naturally, like the date of the first stone, this September day was commemorated by means of medals. More surprisingly, the single frieze on the actual monument does not show a (constitutional) moment, but the personifications of the nine Belgian provinces and a Spirit of the Nation.

However, decisive constitutional moments are included on each of the four sides of the base, by means of inscribed dates: September 1830 (the revolutionary days), 10 November 1830 (the opening of the National Congress), 7 February 1831 (the vote for the Constitution, Fig. 3.11) and 21 July 1831 (Leopold's oath). Although Poelaert's original design featured a personification of the Constitution on top of the column, today a statue of Leopold I by Guillaume Geefs surmounts the monument. This was done after a parliamentary debate and against the will of Leopold himself. The same Parliament had already commissioned a statue of Leopold at Geefs's studio for its own plenary meeting room, to be featured behind the Parliament's president. An important difference exists between the two. The statue in the Parliament—like one of the Congress Column designs[81]—depicts Leopold during his "significant moment" of taking his constitutional oath. Geefs had included a small column and the open book of the Constitution, as well as a crown lying on top of it. Clearly, the Parliament statue was not just Leopold I, but Leopold as a constitutional King, during his decisive biographical and constitutional moment of swearing upon the Constitution that defined his role as the head of the Belgian state. In Parliament, the date 21 July 1831 was inscribed underneath the statue, emphasizing the constitutional moment. In contrast, the statue on top of the Congress Column simply shows Leopold holding his hat, without any reference to his oath.

[81]Anonymous design kept at RKD - Nederlands Instituut voor Kunstgeschiedenis, The Hague, inv./cat.nr. (BD/1484 - NEG/Originelen).

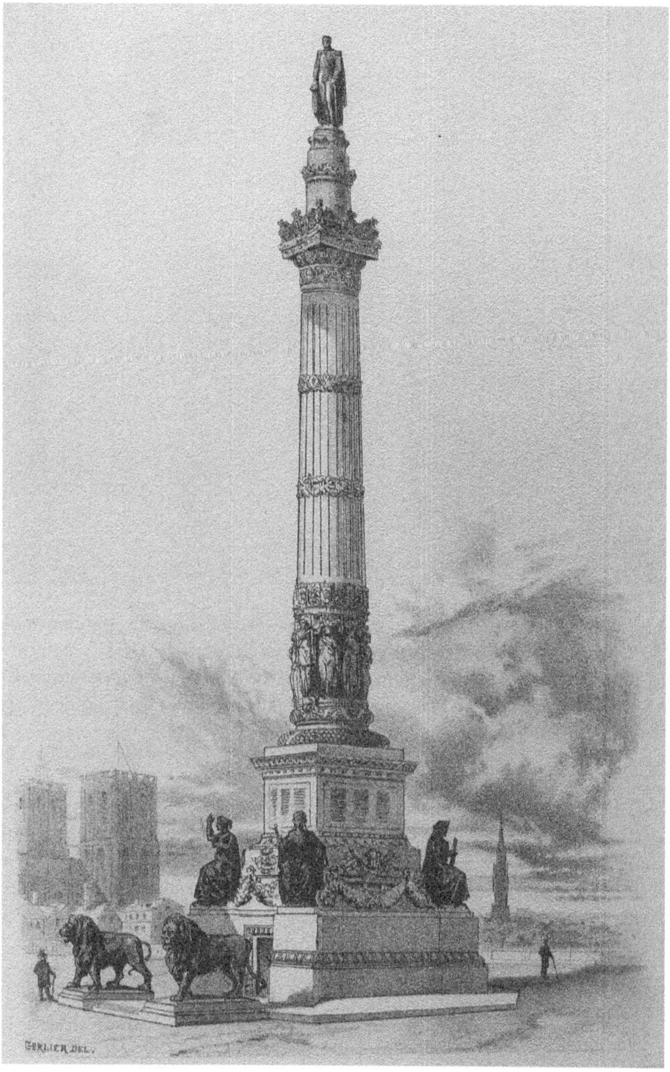

Fig. 3.10 G. Gerlier, *The Congress Column*, illustration for Felix Stappaerts, *La Colonne du Congrès à Bruxelles. Notice historique et descriptive du monument*, Brussels, 1860

In the plenary session on 11 June 1853, during a financial debate concerning the Congress Column and the new church for the Belgian royals (both projects by Joseph Poelaert), Member of Parliament Abbé De Haerne stated:

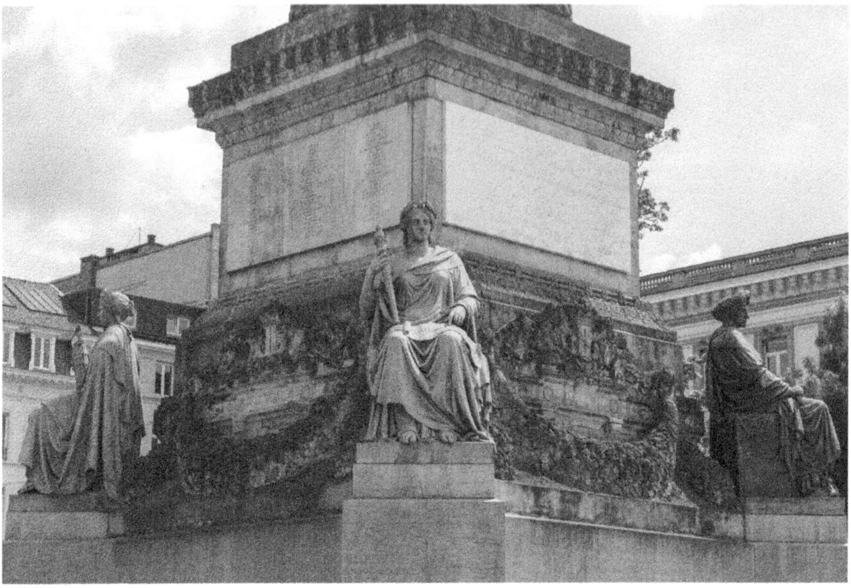

Fig. 3.11 Joseph Poelaert, Congress Column, Brussels, 1859 (detail: inscriptions of the date of 10 November 1830 (opening of the National Congress) and 7 February 1831 (voting of the Belgian Constitution) inscribed in the base, in between personifications of the constitutional freedom of association (l) (by Charles Fraikin); education (m) and press (r) (both by sculptor Joseph Geefs). © Laure Geerts/Collectif Caravane

> Gentlemen, there are in the life of a people, as in the life of individuals, decisive moments, solemn occasions that should be seized to avoid the risk of compromising the future. The constitutional regime is threatened in several countries; for Belgium, this regime is its reason to be, its lifebuoy. Let us show Europe that we hold it more than ever, and that the Constitution, as an immobile column, has unshakeable foundations in the soil of our fatherland.[82]

Apart from the recent death of the Belgian queen and the upcoming wedding of the Belgian crown prince, De Haerne was referring to another decisive moment, unfolding a few years ago and directly linked with the Belgian Constitution.

[82]"*Messieurs, il y a dans la vie des peuples, comme dans la vie des individus, des moments décisifs, des occasions solennelles qu'il faut savoir saisir sous peine de s'exposer à compromettre l'avenir. Le régime constitutionnel est menacé dans plusieurs pays; pour la Belgique, ce régime est sa raison d'être, son ancre de salut. Faisons voir à l'Europe que nous y tenons plus que jamais et que la Constitution, comme une colonne immobile, a des fondements inébranlables dans le sol de la patrie.*"
Annales parlementaires 1852–1853, Chambre des Représentants. 1853. Brussels, 1671 (11 June 1853).

This Constitution had survived the 1848 Revolution that had shook Europe. The wave had not hurt the Belgian Constitution, in neither of Pitkin's meanings, and the stable Congress Column was there to remind everyone of that moment and fact. The Column in Brussels, with its four fundamental freedoms, its crowning hero of the Constitution and a bulk of other iconography, thus grasped more than the four dates inscribed in its base. Above all, it seized and reconstructed (albeit allegorically) the days following the French February Revolution of 1848 as (one of) Belgium's decisive constitutional moment(s). Ackermanian in its non-instantaneousness, this moment was not a constitutional amendment—the electoral threshold was lowered neatly within the constitutional limits set out in then article 47. Instead of one of constitutional change, Belgium's 1848 decisive constitutional moment was a moment of constitutional reaffirmation that was eternalised by means of public art, most notably the Congress Column.

Arguably, this 1848 moment even had its Cartier-Bresson like instant on 1 March 1848 just before 3 pm. In a plenary session—one slightly more agitated than usually—a leftist member, Adelson Castiau, had just warned the Belgian representatives of the fact that the revolutionary ideas from the streets of Paris would make a world tour, and pass through Belgium. In his response, a Catholic Member of Parliament, Auguste Delfosse, stated:

> Liberty, for making its world tour, no longer needs to pass through Belgium. In Belgium, we possess the great principles of liberty and equality; they are inscribed in our Constitution, as they are engraved in our hearts.[83]

Following such a dramatic expression of patriotism, the parliamentary records mention prolonged applause, congratulations and fierce emotion. The quote was picked up by the press, and the instant was soon turned into an allegorical print. The same instant appeared as a quote on a medal commemorating Delfosse and—more importantly—it survived history, at least for a while. In 1880, Frans Vinck turned Delfosse's words into a large history painting (Brussels, Chamber of Representatives, Fig. 3.12). Again, painting allowed for dramatic gestures and recognisable faces of the main participants in that day's debate, and by means of a DCM, the decisive constitutional moment is reconstructed three decades after its dramatic occurrence.[84]

[83]"La liberté pour faire le tour du monde ne doit plus passer par la Belgique. Nous avons en Belgique les grands principes de liberté et d'égalité: ils sont inscrits dans notre Constitution, comme ils sont gravés dans tous nos cœurs". *Annales parlementaires 1847–1848, Chambre des Représentants*, 1848. Brussels, 950 (1 March 1848).

[84]Huygebaert, 2015.

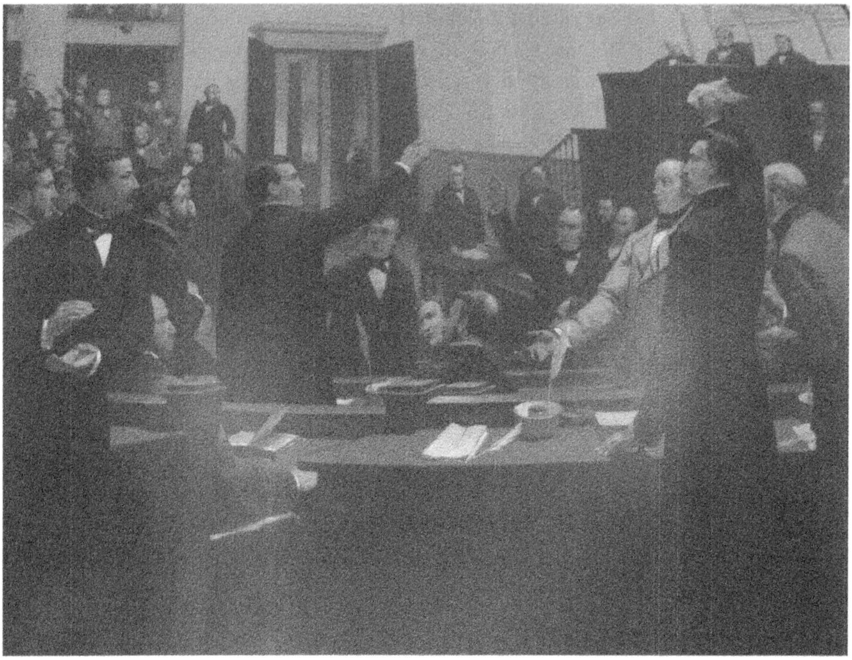

Fig. 3.12 F. Vinck, *The session of 1 March 1848*, 1880 (detail), Chamber of Representatives, Brussels. © photo by Author

3.5 Conclusion

> To constitute, one must not merely become active at some moment but must establish something that lasts, which, in human affairs, inevitably means something that will enlist and be carried forward by others. Unless we succeed in creating – together with others – something lasting, inclusive, principled, and fundamental, we have not succeeded in constituting anything.[85]

Hanna Fenichel Pitkin's interpretation of a Constitution as "something lasting" is no different from what artists have tried to symbolise by means of the stone tables in their artworks representing the Constitution. This chapter demonstrates that, in their search for a symbol for the Constitution, artists saw an alternative potential in what Pitkin first mentions: the moment when one—i.e. the nation—becomes active. Selecting and depicting this moment was an artistic device or practice, in which a focus on the instantaneous allowed artists to create something eternal and lasting: timelessness through a focus on time.

The distinction between the actual, historical moment and its depiction—between the decisive constitutional moment and the DCM—is necessary for the

[85]Pitkin, 1987. 168–169.

analysis of this device and constitutes the essence of how a DCM functions. The artistic media in which the DCM was put to use, allowed artists not only to record, but also to reconstruct and invent parts of the event, and the organising and commissioning government to stage whatever event they interpreted as having potential. The objective and reason for them to use the DCM—or to commission an artist who did so—was the legitimation of the Constitution, or in Vorländer's words: validity, acceptance and recognition.

Moreover, the search for a significant, pregnant or decisive moment from constitutional history, the quest for a constitutional *punctum temporis*, never happens *in tempore non suspecto*, but—quite the contrary—*in tempore opportuno*, at the opportune moment. From Giambologna's relief for Cosimo I's taking of power, over Jacques-Louis David's expression of a Constitutional desire and the monument competition in Belgian following the French February Revolution until FDR's involvement in the sesquicentennial image during his own Ackermanian constitutional moment, time and again it becomes clear that the artistic search for the moment unfolds in moments of constitutional creation, change, threat or crisis. Scrutinising the DCM and its use provides a basis for a deeper understanding of the nation's law and its visual sensation or perception. Therefore, apart from the choice for the moment, we should always look into the moment when that choice is made.

Acknowledgements I warmly thank Judit Beke-Martos, Angela Condello, Bruno Debaenst, Thijs Dekeukeleire, Dirk Heirbaut, Felix Jäger, Georges Martyn, Sarah Marusek, Desmond Manderson, Kenan Van De Mieroop, Toon Moonen, Marjan Sterckx, Yannis Stoyas, Bruno De Wever and Jana Wijnsouw for reading and commenting earlier or oral versions of this text, as well as the anonymous reviewers for their comments. Realised with the support of Research Foundation—Flanders (FWO).

References

Abrams, Ann Uhry. 1979. Politics, prints, and John Singleton Copley's Watson and the Shark. *The Art Bulletin* 61 (2): 265–276.

Ackerman, Bruce. 1984. Storrs lectures: Discovering the constitution. *Faculty Scholarship Series* Paper 149.

Ackerman, Bruce. 1991. *We, the People: Foundations*. Cambridge: Harvard University Press.

Ackerman, Bruce. 2010. *The Decline and Fall of the American Republic*. Cambridge: Harvard University Press.

Annales parlementaires 1847–1848, Chambre des Représentants. 1848. Brussels, 950 (1 March 1848).

Annales parlementaires 1852–1853, Chambre des Représentants. 1853. Brussels, 1671 (11 June 1853).

Anonymous design kept at RKD - Nederlands Instituut voor Kunstgeschiedenis, The Hague, inv./cat.nr. (BD/1484 - NEG/Originelen).

Arnade, Peter. 1997. City, State and Public Ritual in the Late-Medieval Burgundian Netherlands. *Comparative Studies in Society and History* 39 (2): 300–318.

Babelon, Jean. 1927. *La médaille et les médailleurs*. Collection l'Art et le Goût. Paris: Payot.

Best, Janice. 2006. Une Statue monumentale pour la Republique. *Nineteenth-Century French Studies* 34 (3&4): 303–322.

Boime, Albert. 1987. *Art in the age of revolution 1750–1800*. A social history of modern art. Chicago: The University of Chicago Press.

Cartier-Bresson, Henri. 1999. *The mind's eye: writings on photography and photographers*. New York: Aperture.

Collin de Plancy, J. 1848. *La chronique de Godefroid de Bouillon et du royaume de Jérusalem. Première et Deuxième Croisades (1080-1187) avec l'Histoire de Charles-le-Bon*. Paris: La Librairie des Livres Liturgique Illustrés.

Cullen, Lucy, Wendy Fisher, Melissa Hamnett, and Marjorie Trusted. 2007. Medals and plaquettes. In *The making of sculpture: The materials and techniques of European sculpture*, ed. Marjorie Trusted, 75–91. London: Victoria and Albert Museum.

De Ram, M. 1849. Rapport sur les questions proposées par M. le Ministre de l'intérieur. *Bulletins de l'Académie royale des Sciences, des Lettres et des Beaux-Arts de Belgique*.

Deneckere, Gita. 2011. *Leopold I. De eerste koning van Europa*. Antwerpen: De Bezige Bij.

Deseure, Brecht. 2015. De lange schaduw van de Blijde Inkomst: Revolutionair discours over de oude grondwetten in België. In *Rechtsgeschiedenis op nieuwe wegen/Legal history, moving in new directions*, ed. Dave De ruysscher, 35–58. Antwerp: Maklu.

Design nr. 21, National Archives of Belgium, Brussels, *Kaarten en Plannen*, 762.

Dowley, Francis H. 1957. D'Angiviller's Grands Hommes and the significant moment. *The Art Bulletin* 39 (4): 259–277.

Erben, Dietrich. 1996. Die Reiterdenkmäler der Medici in Florenz und ihre politische Bedeutung. *Mitteilungen des Kunsthistorischen Institutes in Florenz* 40 (3): 287–361.

Etude épigraphique sur le monument érigé à Bruxelles en 1848 à la mémoire de Godefroid de Bouillon. Extrait de la Revue Générale de Belgique. 1866. Brussels: Victor Devaux et Cie.

Frank, Jason. 2010. *Constituent Moments: Enacting the people in postrevolutionary America*. Durham: Duke University Press.

Goedleven, Edgard. 1996. *Het Martelaarsplein te Brussel: gedenkteken van de Belgische onafhankelijkheid en zetel van de Vlaamse Regering*. Tielt: Lannoo.

Gombrich, Ernst Hans. 1982. Moment and movement in art. In *The image and the eye*, ed. Ernst Hans Gombrich, 40–62. Oxford: Phaidon.

Green Fryd, Vivien. 2012. Representing the Constitution in the US Capitol Building: Justice, Freedom and Slavery. In *Constitutional cultures: On the concept and representation of constitutions in the Atlantic World*, ed. Silcke Hensel, Ulrike Bock, Katrin Dircksen, and Hans-Ulrich Thamer, 227–249. Newcastle upon Tyne: Camrbidge Scholars Publishing.

Guioth, J.L. 1844. *Histoire numismatique de la révolution belge, ou Description raisonnée des médailles, des jetons et des monnaies qui ont été frappés depuis le commencement de cette révolution jusqu'à ce jour*. Hasselt: P.-F. Milis.

Guioth, J.L. 1851. *Histoire numismatique de la Belgique, faisant suite à l'histoire numismatique de la Révolution Belge, ou Description raisonnée des médailles, des jetons et des monnaies qui ont été frappés depuis le commencement de cette Révolution jusqu'à ce jour*. Hasselt: P.-F. Milis.

Hobsbawm, Eric, and Terence O. Ranger. 1983. *The invention of tradition*. Cambridge: Cambridge University Press.

Huygebaert, Stefan. 2015. Unshakeable foundations an iconological study of the Belgian Constitutional Cult following the 1848 Revolution. *Journal of Belgian History* 45 (4): 10–39.

Huyttens, E. 1844. *Discussions du Congrès national de Belgique*. Brussels: Adolphe Wahlen et Cie.

Janssens, Jeroen. 2001. *De Belgische natie viert: de Belgische nationale feesten 1830-1914*. Leuven: Universitaire pers.

Johnson, Dorothy. 2006. *Jacques-Louis David. New perspectives*. Newark: University of Deleware Press.

Jones, Mark. 1990. 'Proof stones of history': The status of medals as historical evidence in seventeenth-century France. In *Medals and coins from Budé to Mommsen*, ed. M.H. Crawford, C.R. Ligota, and J.B. Trapp, 53–64. London: The Warburg Institute University of London.

Juste, Théodore. 1840. *Histoire de Belgique*. Brussels: A. Jamar.

Juste, Théodore. 1850. *Histoire du Congrès national de Belgique, ou de la fondation de la monarchie belge*. Brussels.

Kelsey, Robin. 2009. Of fish, birds, cats, mice, spiders, flies, pigs, and chimpanzees: How chance casts the historic action photograph into doubt. *History and Theory* 48: 59–76.

La Colonne de la Constitution. 1849. *Journal de l'architecture et des arts relatif à la construction* 2 (11):171–178.

La Colonne de la Constitution. 1850. *Journal de l'architecture et des arts relatif à la construction* 3 (3):33–38.

Leen, Frederik. 2005. Over revolutie en de stichting van een nieuwe staat. In *De romantiek in België. Tussen werkelijkheid, herinnering en verlangen*, eds. Dominique Marechal, and Gautier Platteau, 72–73. Tielt: Lannoo.

L'Indépendance Belge. 1850. Monument de la Constitution. 31 January 1850.

L'Indépendance Belge. 1895. 21 July 1895.

Meirsschaut, Pol. 1900. *Sculptures de plein aires à Bruxelles. Guide explicatif.* Brussels: Bruylant.

Michaud, Joseph-François. 1867. *Histoire des croisades*, vol. 1. Paris: Furne, Jouvet et Cie.

Müller, Marion C. 2011. Verfassung. In *Handbuch der politischen Ikonographie*, ed. Uwe Fleckner, Martin Warnke, and Hendrik Ziegler, 514–521. München: C.H.Beck.

Nora, Pierre. 1989. Between memory and history: les lieux de mémoire. *Representations* (26 special issue: memory and counter-memory): 7–24

Paumen, Vanessa. 2016. The skin of the judge: The judgement of Cambyses. In *The art of law: Three centuries of justice depicted*, ed. Stefan Huygebaert, Georges Martyn, Vanessa Paumen, and Tine Van Poucke, 81–90. Tielt: Lannoo.

Pitkin, Hanna Fenichel. 1987. The idea of a constitution. *Journal of Legal Education* 37 (2): 167–169.

Plotek, Arial. 2008. *Allegory in the age of realism.* Monumental sculpture in France, 1848–1880: Institute of Fine Arts, New York University.

Prawer, Joshua. 1961. Étude sur le droit des Assises de Jérusalem: droit de confiscation et droit d'exhérédation. *Revue historique de droit français et étranger* 39, 520–551 and 40 (1962), 29–42.

Prodi, Paolo. 1997 (1992). *Das Sakrament der Herrschaft. Der politische Eid in der Verfassungsgeschichte des Okzidents*. Trans. J. Elze. Berlin: Duncker & Humblot.

Reichardt, Rolf. 2007. L'imaginaire de la Constitution de 1789 à 1830: symbolique d'union ou de division politique? In *Le combat autour de la Représentation: politique symbolique en France, 1789–1830*, ed. Natalie Scholz, Christina Schröer, and Hans-Ulrich Thamer. Rennes: Presses de l'Université de Bretagne.

Réimpression de L'ancien moniteur: vol 8: Constituante. 1861. Paris: Henri Plon.

Reynaerts, Jenny. 2008. Het begin van de vrijheid: "Prise de la Bastille" door Charles Thévenin (1790). *Bulletin van het Rijksmuseum* 56 (1/2): 136–149.

Rhoads, William B. 1990. The president and the sesquicentennial of the constitution: Franklin Roosevelt's Monument in Poughkeepsie. *New York History* 71 (3): 308–321.

Scott, Nancy. 1979. Politics on a pedestal. *Art Journal* 38 (3): 190–196.

Spate, Virginia. 1996. Where the Sun never set: Tom Roberts and the British Empire. In *Tom Roberts*, ed. Ron Radford, 62–96. Adelaide: Art Gallery of South Australia and Art Exhibitions.

Tushnet, Mark. 2008. Comparative constitutional law. In *The oxford handbook of comparative law*, ed. Mathias Reimann, and Reinhard Zimmerman, 1226–1257. New York: Oxford University Press.

Vagts, Alfred. 1941. Battle-scenes and picture-politics. *Military Affairs* 5 (2): 87–103.

von Blanckenhagen, Peter H. 1957. Narration in hellenistic and Roman art. *American Journal of Archaeology* 61 (1): 78–83.

Vorländer, Hans. 2012. What is "Constitutional Culture"? In *Constitutional cultures: On the concept and representation of constitutions in the Atlantic World*, ed. Silcke Hensel, Ulrike Bock, Katrin Dircksen, and Hans-Ulrich Thamer, 21–42. Newcastle upon Tyne: Camrbidge Scholars Publishing.

Weill, Rivka. 2006. Evolution vs. revolution: Dueling models of dualism. *The American Journal of Comparative Law* 54 (2): 429–479.

Wind, Edgar. 1938. The revolution of history painting. *Journal of the Warburg Institute* 2 (2): 116–127.

Woods, Alan. 1984. Death and the instamatic. *The Cambridge Quarterly* 13 (2): 147–163.

Stefan Huygebaert is a Research Foundation Flanders (FWO) Ph.D. Fellow at the Ghent Legal History Institute and Department of Art History, Musicology and Theatre Studies (Ghent University). His dissertation, entitled *Visual Ideals of Law and Justice* is an iconological study of legal imagery in nineteenth-century Belgium. In 2014–2015, and again in 2016–2017, Stefan was a Ph.D. fellow (Stipendiat) within the Minerva Research Group *The Nomos of Images: Manifestation and Iconology of Law* at the Kunsthistorisches Insitut in Florenz (Max-Planck-Institut). He publishes and teaches on legal iconography and nineteenth-century art, and recently co-edited the catalogue for the exhibition *The Art of Law: Three Centuries of Justice Depicted* (Groeningemuseum, Bruges).

Chapter 4
Courbet and the Nude Republican Master

Oliver Watts

> Carla Bruni: The New Jackie O? How France (and Its President) Fell for Its Enchanting First Lady: Liberté, Égalité, Nudité.
> *Vanity Fair,* September, 2008, (cover page caption).
>
> My love life is terrible. The last time I was inside a woman was when I visited the Statue of Liberty.
> Woody Allen, *Crimes and Misdemeanours,* Metro Goldwyn Meyer, 1989.
>
> It will be a long time before we agree on the true sense of the word "democracy"!
> Gustave Courbet, letter to the Government of National Defence, Paris [5 October 1870] found in ten-Doesschate Chu, Petra. 1992. *Letters of Gustave Courbet.* Chicago: University of Chicago Press, 392.
>
> [They] call me "the socialist painter." I accept that title with pleasure. I am not only a socialist but a democrat and a Republican as well – in a word, a partisan of all the revolution and above all a Realist ... for "Realist" means a sincere lover of the honest truth.
> Quoted in Petra ten-Doesschate Chu, 1992. 97.

Abstract Within the art historical canon, Gustave Courbet is presented as the quintessential autonomous artist. He is seen as part of the seminal modern movement "away" from the courtly in art and towards artistic freedom and critical distance. Reading his work within the discourse of Critical Legal Studies, and in particular psychoanalytical theory, it is clear that an artist is never wholly free of the legal structures that define them. What is the import of that repositioning? In a close reading of Courbet's major work, The Studio, this chapter makes two claims. First that Courbet is actually partisan, imaging very strongly and clearly his Republican values. His work is situated within the language of sovereignty, not outside of it, and represents duelling claims to sovereignty. Second, that in the self portrait, far from positioning the artist at the centre of the world, which is the canonical reading, the work can instead be seen as an attempt to image the position of the legal subject in relation to the law. It is a work that illustrates the process of legal subject formation.

O. Watts (✉)
Sydney College of the Arts, Sydney, NSW, Australia
e-mail: oliwatts@hotmail.com

S. Huygebaert et al. (eds.), *Sensing the Nation's Law*, Studies in the History of Law and Justice 13, https://doi.org/10.1007/978-3-319-75497-0_4

4.1 Introduction

4.1.1 Duelling Masters

In the work of Gustave Courbet, the *genre historique,* the artistic form invented to approximate *juste milieu* values (part bourgeois, part monarchical), of the first half of the nineteenth century found its fullest expression. This tension between the old and the new, between two notions of sovereignty, marks a certain turning point for political history but also for art's role. For many it is art's shift away from courtly patronage to a more freemarket autonomy that delineates the birth of modern art. Courbet has often been seen in the canon of modern art to be one who sums up the moment of this change. This reading, however, makes the case that Courbet is still a court painter but for the other Republican side. Through a Lacanian framework I discover the way ideology and power is signed (and disguised) within one of Courbet's most famous works.

The chapter is a close analysis of one work, *The Artist's Studio: A Real Allegory summing up seven years of my artistic and moral life (The Studio)*, 1855 (Fig. 4.1). A shift occurred during the early years of Louis Napoleon's reign, from the hope of the 1848 revolution to Republican despair over the *coup d'état* of 1851 and the crowning of the President as Emperor Napoleon III. It is no coincidence then that Courbet chose the 1855 Exposition to create his own ideological masterpiece, which this chapter argues should be seen as Republican, seditious and politically emancipatory. Through the lens of art history, coupled with legal theory and legal iconography, a new understanding of the painting becomes available. The more common held view of Realism, Courbet's style, was that it was revolutionary rather than partisan, artistically free rather than at the service of a possible Republican state.

This chapter relies on the definitive reading of the painting by Hélène Toussaint from 1977.[1] Toussaint's reading, which has been largely accepted by art historians, recognised the characters on the left hand side of the painting less as types and more as portraits of actual historical figures. Most importantly, the figure of the "hunter" was seen as the king's effigy, Napoleon III, thinly disguised.

This reading was further theorised by Klaus Herding.[2] The Toussaint/Herding analysis has Courbet as the central fulcrum of the picture, exhorting the ruler to find a peace with other nations of the world during the Exposition of 1855. The painting thus becomes an alternative "king's portrait". *The Studio* is a large, painted caricature and in it the Monarch and the Republic are brought together. In this contribution I suggest an alternative reading, as an extension of the Toussaint/Herding reading, where the connections between law and power are redrawn. I see the nude "model" as a disguised effigy of the Republic or Marianne; this revelation counters

[1]Toussaint, Hélène. 1977. *Gustave Courbet [1819-1877] [exhibition catalogue]*. Paris/London: Grand Palais/Royal Academy of Arts.

[2]Herding, Klaus. 1991. *Courbet: To Venture Independence*. New Haven: Yale: University Press.

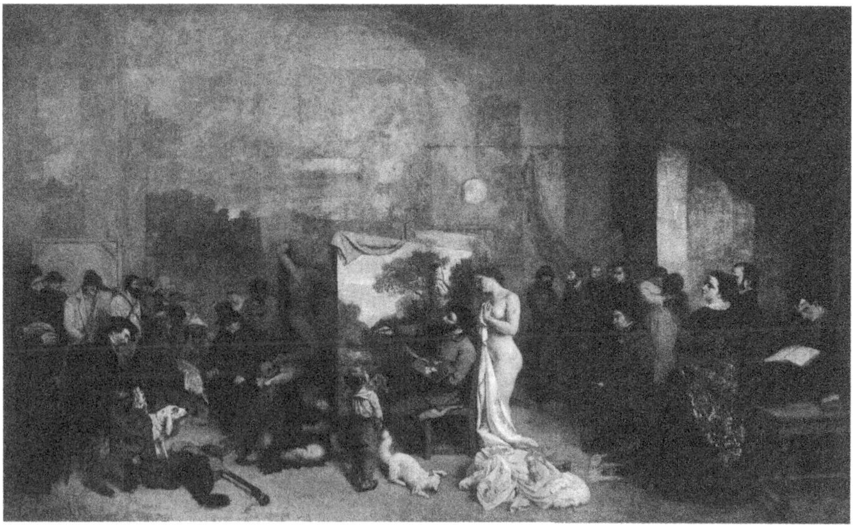

Fig. 4.1 Gustave Courbet, *The artist's studio, a real allegory of a seven year phase in my artistic and moral life*, 1854–1855, 361 cm × 598 cm, oil on canvas. Getty Images

other readings that emphasise the modern genius of Courbet and *The Studio* as a metapicture for the autonomous artist. In Courbet's works we see a duel between the king's monopoly, as sovereign, to give political meaning to the image and another's right, expressed as both the artist's autonomy (artistic sovereignty) and also the Republican alternative to sovereignty. More recent scholarship suggests that perhaps Courbet was not as arrogant and self-centred as he proclaimed—there is evidence that illustrates Courbet was a servant of the Republic and its politics.[3]

Previous readings of the painting are seductive and sound yet are founded on the orthodox modernist belief that the artist is central and autonomous. What if we see Courbet as an early modern author, still within what Jacques Lacan might call the master discourse of the absolute ruler, who is a servant to the political ideology of the day? What if he is merely a painter of effigies, a sovereign portraitist? The reading of the painting as an image of the Republic also suits its framing, in the context of Courbet presenting his Pavilion of Realism at the same time as the great Exposition of 1855. In countering the Exposition, Courbet himself created a theatre, "a comedy", which was not only the clowning reversal of the state-sanctioned paintings of the Exposition but was its Republican other. There is not enough time

[3]Chu, Petra ten-Doesschate. 2008. *The Most Arrogant Man in France: Gustave Courbet and the Nineteenth Century Media Culture*. Princeton & Oxford: Princeton University Press.; his views are consistently political and leftist, the fact that he joined the Commune at such a high administrative level is characteristic of his general political disposition.

to dwell on the ideological underpinning of the Exposition, although a few of the royal portraits will suffice.[4] The effigy maker of the Second Empire was primarily Franz Xaver Winterhalter. Having painted for Louis-Philippe, he was also the favourite of Princess Eugénie of France. The masterpiece painted for the Exposition of 1855 was *The Empress Eugénie Surrounded by her Ladies in Waiting*, 1855. The gleaming dresses represented the wealth of Napoleon III.[5] The image of Napoleon III for the coronation also brought back many monarchical symbols lacking in the royal imagery of Louis-Philippe. I note this to direct the viewer to the reality of the Exposition of 1855 as both the birth of a certain modernity of the Second Empire but also the swansong of a pre-disciplinary society, absolute monarch.

Courbet, however, was presenting a different ideology, the ideology not of a new Napoleon, but of a new gleaming Republic. The monopoly on the state-sanctioned ideology was challenged by Courbet, the self professed "most arrogant man in France" and a "government" in his own right. The whole exercise of the Courbet pavilion was to proclaim independence and autonomy.[6] The revisionist historians, while seeing some social and political content, still worked within a framework that Realism was a modern movement autonomous from the state.[7] Despite its transgressive status, Courbet's work was highly influenced by the state sanctioned reception of art in the Salon. The necessary consequence of reinstating the Republic in an analysis of *The Studio* is that the autonomous artist, the portrait of Courbet, is decentred. Now the central group becomes the landscape, Courbet and Marianne. The painting becomes about the mode in which the subject/artist is the servant of, and subjectivised by the Marianne figure. In this way Courbet is the Republican "Winterhalter" of 1855.

---

[4]See Mainardi, Patricia. 1990. *Art and Politics of the Second Empire: The Universal Expositions of 1855 and 1867*. London and New Haven: Yale University Press.

[5]Boime, Albert. 2008. *Art in an Age of Civil Struggle, 1848-1871*. Chicago: University of Chicago Press, 683–684; Boime even suggests this insinuated to French society that Napoleon III was sleeping with the ladies in waiting.

[6]In a particularly interesting reading Patricia Mainardi sees the commercial autonomy of the "solo exhibition" as another blind spot in traditional art theory. Mainardi, Patricia. 1991 (December). Courbet's Exhibitionism. *Gazette des Beaux-Arts* 118:253–266.

[7]Nochlin, Linda. 1972. *Realism (Style and Civilizations)*. London: Penguin. and Nochlin, Linda. 1966. *Realism and Tradition in Art, 1848-1900*. New Jersey: Prentice Hall College Division.; Reff, Theodore. 1981. Exhibitions of Later Realist Art. New York: Garland.; Rubin, James H. 1981. *Realism and Social Vision in Courbet and Proudhon*. Princeton Essays on the Arts. Princeton: Princeton University Press. Courbet was such a promethean artist that Picasso had a pair of green striped pants made to match those of Courbet's in *The Studio*. Linda Nochlin reports this fact but cannot place where she heard it. Nochlin, Linda. 1988. Courbet's Real Allegory: Reading The Painter's Studio. In *Courbet Reconsidered*, eds. Sarah Faunce, and Linda Nochlin. Yale: Yale University Press. A suggestion may be in Picasso's own poetry where he writes of "Goya" wearing a "pair of striped pants like Courbet and me", in Picasso, Pablo. 2004. *The burial of the Count of Orgaz & Other Poems*. Trans. Jerome Rothenberg, and Pierre Joris. Boston: Exact Change, 292.

4.1.2 Courbet, The Studio and Iconology

Revisionist readings of Courbet re-established Realism as a politically and socially aware art, an art for the people by the people.[8] However, the vestiges of Greenbergian formalism still loomed large, and in all the readings Courbet is the central figure who represents personal and artistic freedom and the political power of art. Linda Nochlin made of the painting a Fourierist allegory based on notions of "work", capital, labour and talent.[9] This reading is heavily reliant on the presence of Proudhon and Francois Sabatier, who were both influenced by Fourier. James Rubin saw *The Studio* as an allegory of Proudhonian notions of work, nature and the artist.[10] Alan Bowness follows this thread that it is about artists' "declaration of independence".[11] A turning point in the analysis of this painting came when the "hunter", the most prominent figure on the left side of the composition was identified as Napoleon III. Hélène Toussaint first suggested this reading for the centenary exhibition catalogue in 1977–8.[12] Contemporary references to the figure used the term "poacher" (*braconnier*), which alluded to Louis-Napoleon's poses as a reformer prior to his election in 1848 and the "stealing" of the government in the coup d'état of 1851.[13]

The scholarship surrounding *The Studio* have all had to come to terms with the readings of the left side figures by Hélène Toussaint. Nochlin and Rubin, most famously, have revisited their initial readings, though they maintain that their prior readings still have import in the area of sociological analysis. Most recently Albert Boime has also disregarded Toussaint's iconological discoveries.[14] Following these readings, Herding produced what has now been received as the definitive iconological analysis of the painting, which relies particularly on a reading of sovereignty and an image that commands.[15] It is this discovery of legal philosophy and exploration of sovereignty within the painting that initially directed my own analysis. Based on the importance of Napoleon III, Herding sees the work as an *adhoratio ad principem,* or an exhortation to the ruler calling for reconciliation and a return to balance. In this the artist is the King's equal, teacher and wise man.

---

[8]Clark, T.J. 1978. *Image of the People: Gustave Courbet and the 1848 Revolution*. Berkeley: University of California Press.; Faunce, Sarah, and Linda Nochlin. 1988. Courbet Reconsidered. Yale: Yale University Press.

[9]Nochlin, Linda 1967. The Invention of the Avant-Garde: France 1830-1880. In *Avant-Garde Art*, eds. Thomas Band Hess, and John Ashbery. New York: Macmillan, 3–24.

[10]Rubin, James. 1981. *Realism and Social Vision in Courbet and Proudhon*. Princeton: Princeton University Press.

[11]Bowness, Alan. 1972. *Courbet's 'Atelier du Peintre', Fiftieth Charlton Lecture on Art* Newcastle upon Tyne: University of Newcastle upon Tyne, 30

[12]Hélène Toussaint, 1977.

[13]Ibid., 145. Worth adding here was Napoleon III's devotion to dogs, which was widely known and often resulted in him being symbolised by the jackboot in cartoons and caricatures.

[14]Albert Boime, 2008. 213.

[15]Klaus Herding, 1991.

Perhaps it is timely to dwell on why there was such a blind spot for art historical analysis in the first place, and why it took until the late seventies to find a definitive reading. The first and perhaps simplest reason was that there was a classic red herring in the form of a letter from Courbet to the novelist and art critic Champfleury, a great supporter of Courbet. In this letter the left hand side was described as the "world of commonplace life".[16] Fried uses this letter to expand on the notion that not all empirical data is useful.[17] The second reason is a reliance on art historical iconography to the expense of the link with more popular culture such as cartoons and caricature. Following Toussaint's analysis Linda Nochlin suggests that the painting can be seen as a "political cartoon writ large".[18] Nochlin, however, dismisses her own intuition and describes the import of Toussaint's analysis:

> Most startling of all, given Courbet's supposed animosity to the Second Empire and all that it stood for, as well as the fact that direct representation of the Imperial person in cartoons and caricatures was forbidden by the regime, was Toussaint's convincing identification of the booted moustachioed figure with the hunting dogs who dominates the left foreground as a covert representation of Emperor Napoleon III himself.[19]

It should not be startling because *The Studio* is in no way a celebration of Napoleon III. Courbet represented the figure of the king disguised because of the strict *lèse majesté* laws and in argument against them. The revolutionary import of the work was dismissed by Nochlin. As I will expand below even the Herding/Toussaint analysis suffers from a heavy traditional iconographic approach. The other major blind spot is centred in the sixties, where Courbet studies were saturated in a Greenbergian-inspired formalism of non-engagement with political matters. Indeed, Michael Fried would have the Napoleonic painting in some way cut from his canonical story of the movement of western art:

> It is as though the rise of Napoleon and the need for propagandist painting not only mobilized a generation of painters (led by the older David, who from the first lent his talents to the Empire) but also placed in abeyance the entire Diderotian project, thereby staving off for more than a decade a representational crisis, the worst of which was yet to come.[20]

For Fried, Courbet becomes the first to join the Diderotian project of absorption (not command); Fried argues through his many books that a battle between theatricality, absorption and anti-theatricality from the eighteenth century onwards is

---

[16]Toussaint suggests that Courbet's letter to Champfleury was purposefully dissembling (274). In another work Toussaint also suggests though that there are clues in the letter for those who have a knowledge of the slang of the period. See Toussaint, Hélène. 1979. 'A propos d'une Critique', Les Amis de Gustave Courbet. *Bulletin de correspondance hellénique* 61:10–13.

[17]Fried, Michael. 1992. *Courbet's Realism*. Chicago: University of Chicago Press. Fried writes, "Courbet's letter to Champfleury thus epitomises the nondecisiveness of exactly the sort of "objective" evidence that positivist art history likes to think would settle all questions of interpretation." 323

[18]Nochlin, 1988. 20.

[19]Ibid. 20

[20]Fried, 1992. 22.

one of the primary concerns of representation and its relationship to the "beholder". Although it is true that full monarchical symbolism never returned after the regicides of 1649 and 1793, many of the rituals of sovereignty were observed, and Courbet's work must also be placed in the complex matrices of patronage and control in the Second Empire.[21] The readings also place too much emphasis on the Romantic notions of Courbet that he was a free and autonomous modern artist. Both Nochlin and Fried seem to dismiss Herding's analysis of the artist as a redemptive force.[22] Fried focuses on the portrait of Courbet and the "representation of the act, the immediate context, and the emerging artefact of representation".[23] For Fried the source of truth and force is the painting itself; Fried sees the work as a self-referential metapicture not directed towards ideology. Nochlin had also argued in an earlier text that:

> It is the artist, Courbet, of course, who plays the central role in the monumental *Painter's Studio,* yet he envisions his role as one both socially more humble and ideologically more grandiose than the usual conception of the term. Courbet sees himself at once as the earthy matter-of-fact painter, a popular craftsman working with tools of brush and canvas and at the same time, in the iconographic context of the *Studio,* as the Harmonian Leader...[24]

In relation to these readings the Toussaint/Herding reading does displace the centrality of the artist but turns the work into a duel between king and artist. This displacement still maintains the fiction of the artist sovereign. The duel is really between the king and the Republic.

4.2 The King and The Artist: A Political Allegory

The main insight of the Toussaint/Herding reading, and underpins my approach, is that the painting is seen as a political statement or cartoon based on national effigies. Furthermore, the artist is seen to be exhorting some values based on natural rights and nature. The 'model' becomes herself a muse or mediator for truth. Toussaint sees the painting as Louis Philippe's *genre historique,* and it was common to paint genre pieces as historical and political points at the scale of history painting; although by any standard *The Studio* was impressive in scale. It is relevant to also connect the painting to an earlier Courbet work, *Firemen Running to a Fire*, 1850–51, which

---

[21]See Crapo, Paul 1995. The Problematics of Artistic Patronage under the Second Empire: Gustave Courbet's Involved Relations with the Regime of Napoleon III. *Zeitschrift für Kunstgeschichte* 58 (2):241–261.

[22]Nochlin, 1988. 20–21. It is Fried who writes "of his own art by virtue of its special relation, emblematised by the easel, to what Herding calls 'primary nature'". Fried, 1992. 158.

[23]Fried, 1992. 158.

[24]Nochlin, Linda. 1971. *Realism*. London: Penguin, 130.

Toussaint reads as a political comment on Napoleon III.[25] Crapo also reads these two paintings together and suggests that whereas the first painting is a propaganda piece for Napoleon III, Courbet's 1855 *The Studio* is highly critical.[26] His major proof is the disguised portraits and national effigies. Herding goes into great detail to describe the commonplace occurrence of such "disguised" meaning. Firstly, in similar vein to those exercised by Honoré Daumier, the political necessity of disguise, especially in regard to the king's effigy, was tantamount. Although a number of new journals started in this period Louis Napoleon, as President, forbade offences against his person in a bill of 17 July 1849 (Article 1). With the Coup d'Etat on 2 December 1851, Emperor Louis Napoleon again took control over the press. Police seized press offices around the country. A Presidential Decree in February 1852 saw a return of similar laws to the July Monarchy's September Laws. Disguise was a common strategy among many cartoonists and artists. Daumier himself invented the Ratapoil character, who was a thug who showed more than a passing resemblance to Napoleon III. Herding also links the genre to *enigmata,* where there is a secondary meaning that must be deciphered as part of spiritual education.[27]

Toussaint saw that Courbet's *The Studio* was populated by recognisable contemporary figures beside Napoleon III. The Jew was the financier Achille Fould who had been the Minister of Finance between 1849 and 1852. The old clothed man was Persigny, a close friend of Louis Napoleon, and the Italian was the military figure Giuseppe Garibaldi. The scythe man was Thaddeus Kosciuszko, a revolutionary figure of the Polish freedom movement,[28] and the labourer was Michael Bakunin, standing for Russian socialism. The Hungarian is Lajos Kossuth. These represent international insurrectionary movements, which formed the revolutionary context for Napoleon III's government. Of the other nations present, the strongman, the nude behind the easel, seems to represent Turkey; the clown refers to Asia; the Irishwoman and her child seem to allude to the British Isles and the conditions brought about through the Industrial Revolution, including the recent Irish potato famine. The "romantic cast-offs" by the Emperor's feet recall Louis Napoleon's membership, as a young man, in the Carbonari, when he fought to liberate Italy from Austria.[29] Fintan Cullen identifies Ireland also as a national figure, if not merely a generalized representation of Britain's poor and

[25]Toussaint, 1977. 110–114. This argument is continued in Toussaint, Hélène. 1981. Le realisme de Courbet au service de la satire politique et de la propagande gouvernementale. *Bulletin de la Société de l'Histoire de l'Art français* Année 1979.

[26]Crapo, 1995. 250. He puts emphasis on this particularly critical approach towards two figures. Two sinister figures, Emile de Girardin (symbolising the pro-Bonaparte press) and the "priest" Louis Veuillot, are represented as the worst of the conservative wing of the Church.

[27]Herding, 1991, 4.

[28]Toussaint mentions that the socialist is Alexander Herzen (256–257), a colleague of Proudhon, but her position was clarified in conversation with Linda Nochlin in *Courbet Reconsidered*, n. 15, 223.

[29]Crapo, 1995. 250.

downtrodden.[30] In relation to my reading of the central nude as an alternative sovereign effigy, there is another figure of the Republic that Toussaint isolates on this left hand side. The presence of the old man, a Republican guard, represents the values of the Republic. Toussaint identifies him as possibly Lazare Carnot, the revolutionary politician and military leader who was one of the original Republicans voting for the execution of Louis XVI. Petra ten-Doesschate Chu sees this figure as Antoine-Claire Thibaudeau, the longest surviving regicide.[31] Exiled until 1830, Napoleon III named Thibaudeau senator and attributed him the *legion d'honneur*. Following this, perhaps Courbet shows that Thibaudeau is one of the Emperor's men. It is notable in this context that Courbet refused his *legion d'honneur* from Napoleon III. The figure of the old Republic is nostalgic and compromised.

The right hand side figures, which Courbet in the Champfleury letter describes as "friends" have been known for some time and are clear portraits. It is a common assumption, and relevant to my reading, that this side does represent "friends" and more broadly the art and politics of the Republican left. There is Champfleury himself, the champion of Realism in prose, Max Buchon the Realist poet and Republican exile,[32] and the revolutionary thinker Pierre Proudhon. Even the representatives of other arts were also politically sympathetic to Courbet. Alphonse Promayet was a musician who set Courbet's ballads to music.[33] Charles Baudelaire and the two "free" lovers seem to represent the values of love, poetry and freedom. The bourgeois couple have been read as patrons of Courbet's art.

Klaus Herding, following Toussaint's empirical and iconographical work sees the painting as an exhortation for the reconciliation between contending nations and parties. Considering that the forum was to be the *Exposition Universelle des Beaux-Arts* to be held in 1855 this seems like a logical conclusion. Rejected from the exhibition, Courbet mounted his own Pavilion of Realism. Herding sees this through the art historical lens of allegory and *adhoratio ad principem*, "an exhortation to the ruler of a kind common in treatises on statecraft down into the nineteenth century".[34] Primarily the painting should be read in relation to other works depicting an artist visited by a king.[35] By reversing the genre Herding sees the artist insisting on his own sovereignty, effectively a modern, autonomous art. I agree with Herding only so far as the painting shows a king visiting the studio of the artist, but it is the Republic that admonishes the king, mediated by the space of the citizen/artist's studio. In an earlier piece of writing, Herding links the nude

---

[30]Cullen, Fintan. 1995. *Visual Politics: Representation of Ireland: 1750–1950*. Cork: Cork University Press, especially Chapter 4.

[31]Chu, 1992 . 134.

[32]Max Buchon was a close friend of Courbet and was exiled to Belgium during the reign of Napoleon III.

[33]Chu, 1992. 55–56.

[34]Herding, 1991. 57.

[35]Herding, 1991. 56. I am thinking of paintings such as François Guillaume Ménageot's *Leonardo Dying in the Arms of Francis I* (c.1781).

figure to the *adhoratio ad principem*. For him it is a muse that connects the figure of the artist and monarch based on the iconography of the triad of Apelles/Campaspe/Alexander.[36] In the story the beautiful Campaspe is Alexander's lover, sacrificed to Apelles who has also fallen for her. So for Herding there is a strong triad created encompassing the artist, "truth"/muse, and the king; the triad is still present in our reading but the artist is the mediator. Finally, Herding fails to come to terms with a question he sets himself: why are the two parts so separated and uncommunicative?[37] Art (artist) and truth (muse) bring everyone together, Herding contends, and the diverse group, from other nations, to Republicans and Bonapartists, speaks of the "peaceful coexistence of diverse opinions and stances".[38] This in the end seems a little forced, given the painting's strict compositional separation. The reading offered below allows us to keep the two halves separate. The right hand side connected to the centre represents the promise of Republican France, while the figures on the other side are in darkness for they are characters that must be enlightened into the "civilising mission" of French liberty.

4.3 Discovering Marianne

4.3.1 The Ideological Context of Art and French Liberty

The shift in my reading is that the nude or "muse" character is Marianne, an alternative sovereign effigy. I see the painting as Courbet's pictorial hope for a future Republican France, and I ground this interpretation on Republican artists' resistance to the hypocrisy of *juste milieu* politics which always tried to "modernise" and "democratise" monarchy enough to make it palatable (as an aside a particularly useful strategy for Britain since Earl Grey's "middle way" of the same period). I will argue that Herding's analysis of an *adhoratio ad principem* is correct, but it is not only to the monarch that this exhortation is directed, but to the Marianne, the body of democratic France. The other art historical blind spot is that to represent France involves a doubling of the sovereign effigy, once the hunter is designated Napoleon III. The latest revisionist history of the salon and other exhibitions is that there were strong ideological differences between the state-sanctioned academicians and the more autonomous, Republican-styled artists. Patricia Mainardi has made a very thorough study of this political manoeuvring

[36]Herding, Klaus. 1978. Das Atelier des Malers - Treffpunkt der Welt und Ort der Versöhnung. In *Realismus al Widerspruch: Die Wirklichkeit in Courbets Malerei*, ed. Klaus Herding. Frankfurt am Main: Suhrkamp, 231, 311 n 45: see also Seibert, Margaret. 1983. Courbet Note. *Art Bulletin*.

[37]Herding, 1991. 46.

[38]Ibid., 57

especially around the Universal Exhibitions.[39] The Fair of 1855 was clearly aimed at re-cementing France as the cultural centre after Britain's success in 1851. Mainardi sees the story of the Salon in the nineteenth century as a fight between the monarchical and legitimist claims and the autonomy of the artist in early capitalism.[40] However, it would be incomplete to see the fight for autonomy merely about artists' rights. Ideologically it was important for the artists to speak for France and as the nineteenth century progressed this "civilising mission" was taken very seriously. By bringing France back to the centre of the work, Courbet showcases "Republican France" in 1855, not the bastardised version of liberty offered by the court of Emperor Napoleon. Between 1855 and 1937 France used the Fairs to position itself as the breadbasket of cultural trends and technologies.[41] For example, the Third Republic (or in this circumstance "the people of France") gifted the *Statue of Liberty* to the United States in 1886, officially titled *Liberty Enlightening the World*. Daumier's famous Marianne, for the revolutionary government of 1848, is suckling the world, which illustrated quite pertinently the image France had of itself within the collection of other nations.[42] I suggest that Courbet can likewise put Republican France at the centre of his work as the superior force over the other nations presented (Hungary, Ireland, Poland etc.) and over the reign of Napoleon III. This reading also makes sense of the artists and patrons on the right hand side of *The Studio*; they are the "facilitators" of French culture. If France is the light of the world then the figures on the right hand side are France's apostles. While Herding sees art as the unifying force, for French politics there has always been a strong notion of the unifying power of democracy.[43] Most recently Pierre Rosanvallon has described this particularly French understanding of democracy as a universalizing force which believes in equality to the point of "univocality"; the point of universal suffrage, enacted in March 1848, was not, Rosanvallon writes, to allow France's diversity of opinions and interests to find political expression. During the Revolution, the goal of universal suffrage was to sublimate that diversity into an undivided popular sovereignty created and expressed by the public ritual of the vote. The embodiment of the mass in a singular body was well within the understanding of Republican sovereignty.

---

[39]Mainardi, 1990.; Herding also reads this battle between the state sanctioned image of the nation and sees it again as the artist's autonomy directly. The mediating master signifier is that Courbet believes he is free based on the values of freedom of speech suggested by the Republic of 1848.

[40]Mainardi, Patricia. 1993. *The End of the Salon: Art and the State in the Early Third Republic*. Cambridge: Cambridge University Press.

[41]Bourdieu, Pierre. 1993. The Field of Cultural Production. In *The Field of Cultural Production*, ed. Randal Johnson, 29–73. New York: Columbia University Press.

[42]Porterfield, Todd. 1998. *The Allure of Empire: Art in the Service of French Imperialism, 1798–1836*. Princeton: Princeton University Press. For the construction of nationalism through culture see Hobsbawm, Eric, and Terence Ranger. 1983. *The Invention of Tradition*. Cambridge UK: Cambridge University Press.

[43]Rosanvallon, Pierre. 2006. Democracy Past and Future, ed. Samuel Moyn. New York: Columbia University Press.

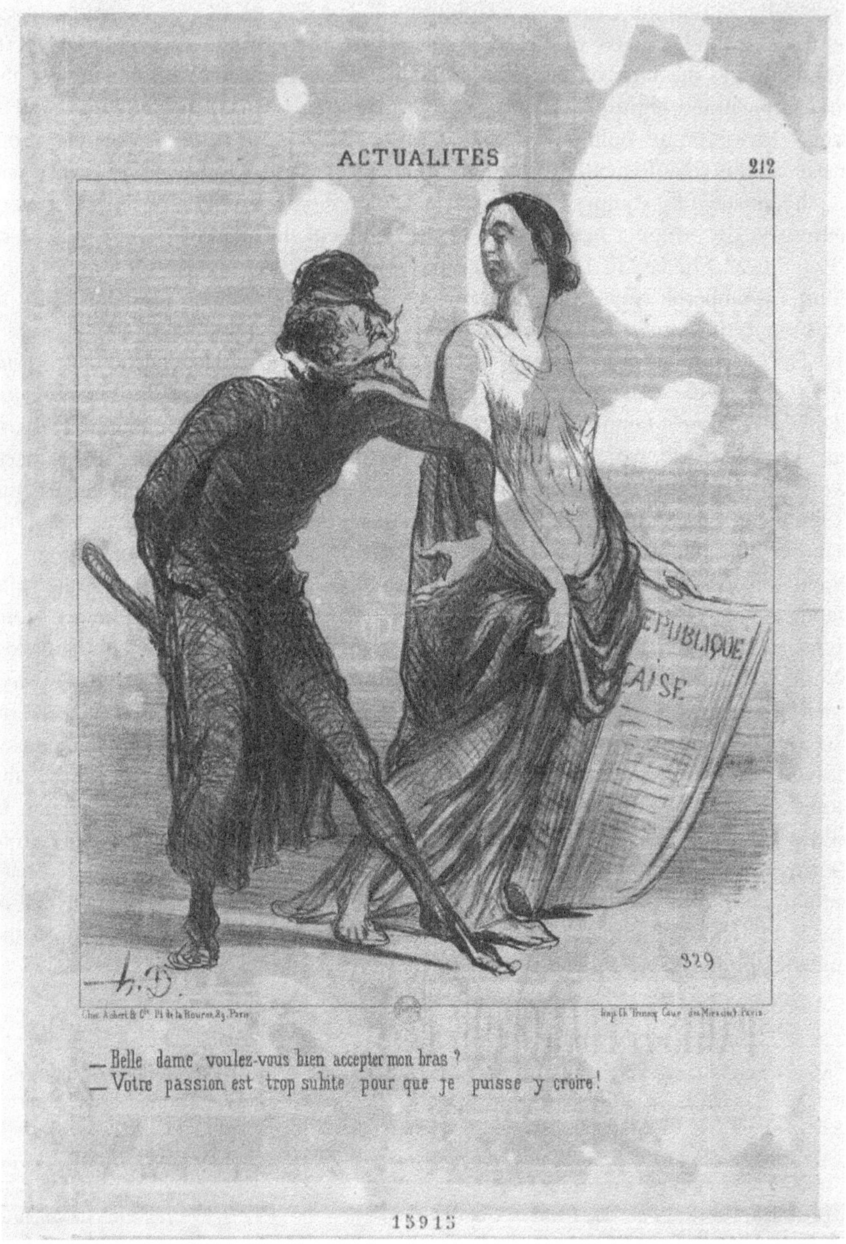

Fig. 4.2 Honoré Daumier, *The Second French Republic is suspicious of the attention of Ratapoil*, 25 September 1851, 25 cm × 20 cm, lithograph. Europeana/Bibiliothèque National de France

Finally the use of cartoons and caricatures show that it is quite possible that *The Studio* has at its centre the effigy of the Republic. A number of cartoons of Daumier for example show Ratapoil (a disguised Napoleon III) at loggerheads with the Republic of France shown as the Marianne. In a classic mirroring of his earlier method Ratapoil asks the Republic whether she wishes to take his arm in *The Second French Republic is suspicious of the attention of Ratapoil*, 1851 (Fig. 4.2); in another, *The vulture-like eagle of Napoleon III eats the liver of France,* 1871 the Republic is represented as Prometheus who has her liver eaten by an Imperial eagle (Fig. 4.3). I would link this to Daumier's strategy of disallowing the approach of *juste milieu* politics, the quilting of Republican virtues to Louis Napoleon.[44] The most recent scholarship suggests that Courbet was more influenced by the popular press than many of his artist contemporaries; we also know that Courbet was friendly with Daumier.[45] Fried and others also suggest that the "issue of sources has been too narrowly conceived".[46]

4.3.2 *Disguising Marianne*

After the Coup d'Etat the *lèse-majesté* rules again forbade direct imaging of the king or the Republic. The use of the Marianne had been intense in the revolutionary period just preceding this between 1848 and 1851; the draped figure could be the Marianne in an extension of this usage. It is not surprising that the nude has been overlooked as an effigy, as the iconology is ambiguous. The timing of the instigation of the Marianne as the Republican symbol in 1848 is alluded to in *The Studio*, which is "seven years" before 1855. In 1848 the Ministry of the Interior launched a sculpture contest to symbolize the Republic. After the fall of the monarchy, the Provisional Government had declared: "The image of liberty should replace everywhere the images of corruption and shame, which have been broken in three days by the magnanimous French people". The replacement occurred directly from one symbol to another. Although the symbol of Marianne is not an official emblem, and only the French Flag is written into Article 2 of the French Constitution, the Marianne has been inscribed into state use. Its first use on a postage stamp was in 1849.[47] The stamp showed the head of Ceres above which is written *République Française*; as an agrarian society the image of Ceres as the

[44]As I discussed in Watts, Oliver. 2014. Daumier and Replacing the King's body. In *Law, Culture and Visual Studies*, eds. Richard K. Sherwin, and Anne Wagner, 421–443. Dordrecht, Heidelberg, New York, London: Springer.

[45]Chu, 2008; Schapiro, Meyer. 1941. Courbet and Popular Imagery: An essay on Realism and Naivete. *Journal of the Warburg and Courtauld Institues* 4:164–191.

[46]Fried, 1992, 128. Another example is how Fried suggests that *After Dinner* (1849) relates to an illustration by Lorentz that appeared in February 1848. See also Schapiro, 1941.

[47]The French National Assembly approved the issue of the first French postage stamp on 24 August 1848. Most recently Marianne was represented in September 1999, used as an official seal

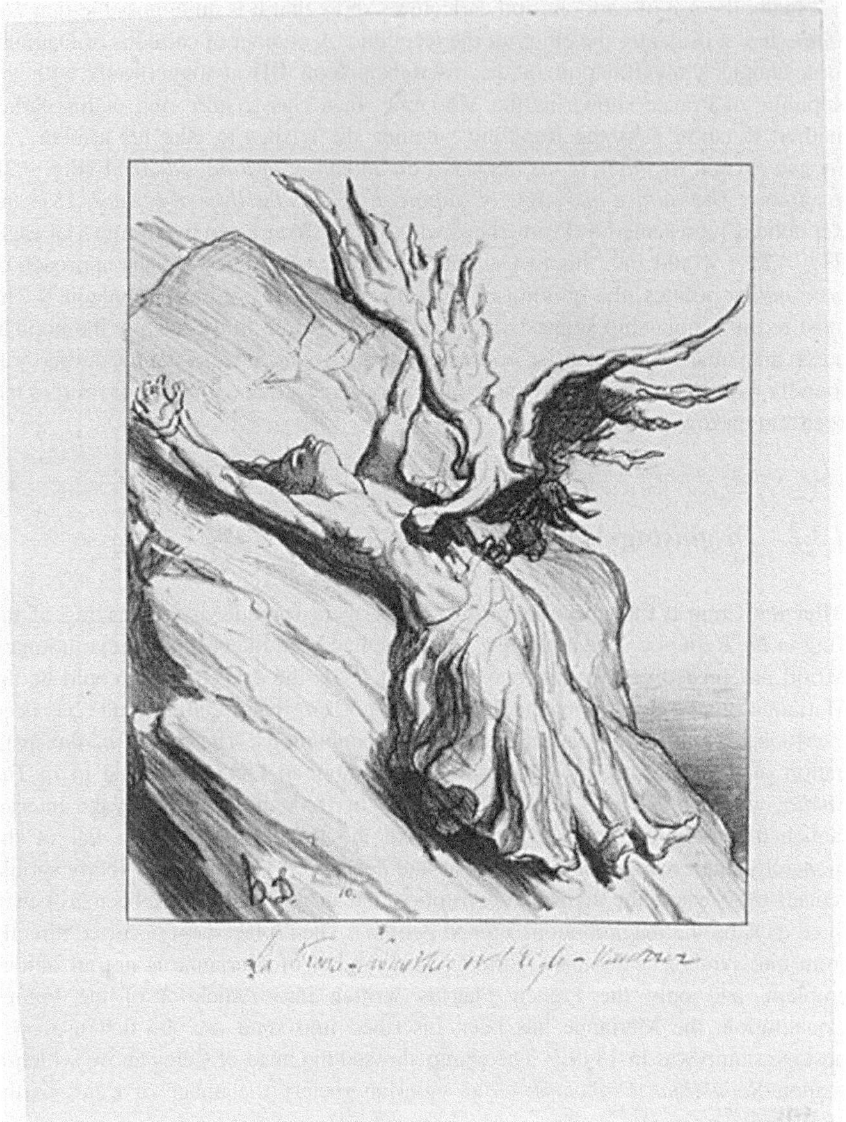

Fig. 4.3 Honoré Daumier, *The vulture-like eagle of Napoleon III eats the liver of France*, 13 February 1871, 25 cm × 21 cm, lithograph. The Metropolitan Museum of Art, The Elisha Whittelsey Collection, The Elisha Whittelsey Fund, 1990

Republic of France was appropriate and a prototype of the Marianne was seen on later stamps. This stamp did not go on sale in French post offices until 1 January 1849. Soon after, it was replaced by the effigy of Napoleon Bonaparte, reflecting the transition of France from Republic to Empire. It is this quick shift from repression in the 1st Empire to the use of the Marianne to her repression again that underpins this work; it is the new threat, from 1852, of *lèse-majesté* charges that animates the political importance of this work and its strategies of disguise.

Returning to the iconological question, the use of the Republic dated back to 1792.[48] The Convention adopted a new seal for the Republic to replace the effigy of the king; although there was a discussion to whether an alternative effigy was needed the convention felt that a replacement was necessary.[49] The axiom, "Archives de la République Française", was framed by a woman dressed in an antique robe, with fasces in her left hand and "holding, in her right hand, a pike topped with a Phrygian cap, the bonnet of liberty".[50] The Roman influence is obvious.[51] Indeed there was another common image of the Republic based more directly on the goddess Helena. This Republic is chastely dressed, stationary and holds no weapon, in contrast to the bare-breasted, combative Republic. The widely reproduced images of Antoin-Jean Gros (*The Republic*, 1794, Versailles, musée national du Château) and Nanine Vallain, show differing ways of representing liberty (*Liberty*, 1793–1794, Vizille, Musée de la Révolution française).

So in this period there had been plenty of models from which to choose. The major reason it has not been seen in Courbet's work is that there were no outward signs of the effigy. Vallain's work for example, include a number of related symbols: a broken crown, money (representing feudal corruption), a Funeral Urn, The Phrygian Cap, a scroll with the *Declaration of the Rights of Man and of the Citizen*, the Laurel Bush and Ivy, Weapons at the ready, fasces, the club of force and defense (sovereignty's monopoly on violence), and a Pyramid. Courbet's contemporary Silvestre suggested that the central nude in *The Studio* was allegorical and a personification of truth, even though there were no symbols of truth such as the mirror or sun.[52] The woman was most probably in reality based on a photo by Julien

---

or logo for the French Government on the European Union stamps. In this way Marianne can be located in relation to other countries use of a sovereign head (i.e. Elizabeth II effigy in the UK).

[48]At the inaugural meeting of the French National Convention there was a discussion concerning the new symbols of the Republic and the destruction of monarchical symbols, 21 September 1792.

[49]In our reading of the effigy the force of the Revolution that founded the Republic needed the same sublimation as monarchy.

[50]Agulhon, Maurice. 1979. *Marianne au combat. L'imagerie et la symbolique républicaines de 1789 à 1880*. Paris: Flammarion, 29.; see also Hunt, Lynn. 1986. *Politics, Culture and Class in the French Revolution*. California: University of California Press, 61.

[51]See for a general discussion of the revolution and its symbols: Gombrich, Ernst Hans. 1979. The Dream of Reason: Symbolism of the French Revolution. *British Journal for Eighteenth-Century Studies* 2 (3):187–205. Ozouf, Mona. 1988. *Festival and the French Revolution*. Trans. Alan Sheridan. Cambridge: Harvard University Press, 240.

[52]Fried, 1992. 158. Silvestre, Theophile. 1948–50. Courbet d'après nature (1865). In *Courbet raconté par lui-même et par ses amis*, ed. Pierre Courthion. Geneva, 47.

Vallou de Villeneuve of a woman called Henriette Bonnion.[53] She is draped with one breast showing which was also quite common for goddesses and other allegorical figures.[54] What is confusing but totally in keeping with the *genre historique*, is that below the classical and traditional drapery, is the fallen dress of the "real" model.

Margaret Seibert and John Moffit place emphasis on the notion of Liberty.[55] Following Silvestre, Seibert sees the nude in Courbet's painting as representing Truth.[56] Seibert also suggests that the central nude can be seen as a personification of Beauty and in this central grouping the cat is the allegory of Liberty.[57] She relies on Theophile Gautier's article on the symbols of the Republic in *L'Artiste*, 1848, which explains that the cat is the symbol of independence and liberty. Seibert writes, "[t]he cat became a part of the Republic's coat-of-arms and appeared at the feet of Liberty in Pierre-Paul Proudhon's *Allegory of the Constitution*... The white cat in Courbet's *Atelier* follows the dictates that Liberty be draped in white, reinforcing the fact that this is her cat, Independence".[58] A logical application of Seibert's own analysis is that the central figure is indeed Liberty and not Truth or Beauty.[59]

Moffit is less circumspect. Crediting and accepting Seibert's analysis that the woman represents "(in part) Truth" Moffit sees the figure also representing Liberty, a composite allegory that he calls "Truth-Liberty". It is Moffit who first takes Seibert's illumination of the symbol of the white cat to its full conclusion.[60] More convincingly, however, Moffit connects the meaning of Courbet's work to the popular print of Claude Niquet, which treats the subject of *La Déclaration des Droits de l'Homme et du Citoyen*. In this print, the element in the centre is not a landscape but a large, tilted sign inscribed with the complete text (17 articles) of the *Declaration*; the similarity of the compositions is uncanny. As in the Courbet

---

[53]Waller, Susan. 2006. *The invention of the model: artists and models in Paris, 1830–1870*. Aldershot: Ashgate Publishing, 73.

[54]Warner, Marina. 1985. *Monuments and Maidens: the allegory of the female form*. London: Weidenfeld and Nicholson, 294–328.; O'Brien, David. 2006. *After the Revolution: Antoine-Jean Gros, painting and propaganda under Napoleon*. Pennsylvania: Penn State Press, 26–28.

[55]Seibert, Margaret. 1983. A Political and a Pictorial Tradition Used in Gustave Courbet's Real Allegory. *The Art Bulletin* 65 (2):311–316.; this was followed by a letter which highlighted the similarity of her approach to Herding which had not been credited (or seen), Seibert, Margaret. 1984. Letter. *The Art Bulletin* 66 (1); Moffit, John. 1987. Art and Politics: An Underlying Pictorial-Political Topos in Courbet's "Real Allegory". *Artibus et Historiae* 8 (15):183–193.

[56]This analysis is supported by a number of writers, see for example Boudaille, Georges. 1969. *Gustave Courbet- Painter in Protest*. Trans. M Bullock. Greenwich, Conn.: New York Graphic Society. 65; Nicholson, Benedict. 1973. *Courbet: The Studio of the Painter*. New York, 31.

[57]Seibert, 1983, 312.

[58]Ibid., 315–316.

[59]Seibert, instead, relying on previous art historical iconography and in particular a close reading of the obscure engraving of Johann Saenredam, *Painter Painting a Young Woman*, the women did represent love but has been 'modernised' and now represents Republican Truth and Beauty.

[60]Moffit, 1987. 184.

painting a woman looks at the *Declaration* as the central nude looks intently at the work on the easel. Moffit suggests, "[i]n effect, instead of functioning as the spokesperson-translator for 'la liberte', as in Niquet's print, in Courbet's *L'Atelier* this woman now *is* Liberty".[61] So Truth-Liberty looks on the artwork, and for Moffit represents the truth of Realist painting and literature. Again, like Herding's definitive iconological reading, Truth and Liberty are connected only to the modernist author and artistic autonomy. Moffit mentions the Toussaint/Herding analysis disparagingly and sees no broader political statement in the work.[62] So for example in the Niquet print there is a side that is unenlightened by the *Declaration*; this corresponds in the composition to the left side of Courbet's painting. Niquet represents the evil of the prior *ancien régime*, by one fallen figure clutching a money bag and lying on top of the crumpled document "droits et privilèges". Moffit reads this unenlightened attitude in relation to the Truth-Liberty expressed by the artists' Realism. Moffit does not feel it necessary to extend his analysis to legal questions. However, Moffit's reading of the work in relation to the *Declaration of the Rights of Man and of the Citizen* is decidedly apt, where the painting *becomes* the symbol of natural rights. Moffit however, focuses on the import of "truth" for Social Realism and is not interested in making any jurisprudential conclusions.

4.4 The Studio Under the Gaze of the Law

4.4.1 Jurisprudence

By a fusion of Herding's muse and *adhoratio ad principem*, Moffit's Truth-Liberty and Toussaint's many national effigies, an aperture is opened to see the central nude as an effigy of the Marianne. In the political context of the time, and the ideological framing of the *Exposition Universelle*, the movement towards a juridical understanding of the piece seems warranted. The final shift that allows for a reevaluation of the sophisticated and knowledgeable iconological readings is the scholarship that has helped us see the birth of Realism in relation to the Salon, cartoons and other contemporary academic and state-sanctioned work. The autonomy of the early moderns was by no means complete and was beholden to many ideological pressures. *The Studio* is not only a metapicture for painting but can be looked at as a metapicture for the ideological power of the sovereign image. Through this reading a number of iconological discoveries become apparent.

[61]Ibid., 188

[62]Ibid., n 24, 193. Moffit finds the reading too 'explicit' and feels that each figure should be seen more as principals of authority. He does not like the Masonic angle of the Toussaint/Herding reading, seeing no internal logic for it.

4.4.2 The Iconology of the Artist as Amanuensis

The iconology supports the reading that the artist is merely the servant of the Republic. Although Picasso was able to see in the green striped pants of Courbet the quintessential garb of a genius, the artist's appearance intimates a working class circumstance.[63] As Nochlin notices, Courbet is the only one "working". This position of art and the artist working and contributing to the public good follows the logic of theorists who see the work illustrating Proudhon's socialist ideas. Rubin for one sees it directly linked to Proudhon's ideology;

> *The Studio* in fact encompassed all aspects of past, present, and the future of their [Courbet and Proudhon's] association: while as we shall see it alluded directly to a history of social development derived form Proudhon's social theory, it showed Courbet as the hero of this development. Thus it represented what for Proudhon would become a problematic interpretation of his own ideas.[64]

In our new analysis Courbet's position squares with Proudhon and Rubin's analysis.[65] The stumbling block for Rubin is that modernist teleology *must* have Courbet as the fulcrum. Even in the letter to Champfleury the work is split into three parts (whether based on the Niquet print or not). My suggestion is that the Republic herself is the centre and the one who is the overall patron/author(ity) of the work. In the letter to Champfleury. Courbet states in regard to the nude:

> ...then comes the canvas on my easel and myself painting, showing the Assyrian profile of my head. Behind my chair is a nude female model. She is leaning on the back of the chair, watching me paint for a while. Her clothes are on the floor in front of the painting. Then there is the white cat close to the chair.[66]

Her expression and gesture is one of deep sympathy with what Courbet is doing; she is almost motherly in her devotion to Courbet's work. This gaze is doubled by the small child also watching. Unlike Seibert, who sees the child as an "innocent eye", it is more likely that he is the hope of a new Republican France. The letter goes on to connect the "nude model" to the "friends" behind them; these are the other artists and allies of the Republic.

The central group therefore concerns the creation of a legal subject through the figure of the Republic and through the image. It is as if the Republic gives meaning to all that is within the frame of the painting and to the others that work in the arts; it is a very Proudhonian thesis. In Freudian terms there even seems to be a simple

---

[63]Picasso apocryphally had a pair of green striped pants made for studio use based on this picture and his adoration of Courbet.

[64]Rubin, James Henry. 1980. Realism and Social Vision in Courbet & Proudhon, 90.

[65]In 1863 the men worked together on what would become *The Principle of Art and Its Social Purpose,* published after Proudhon's death in 1865. Courbet wrote: "It's marvelously funny I am swamped by manuscript; every day I write between five and ten pages of aesthetics. . . . We are at last going to have a real treatise of modern art, and the way, pointed out by me, is to run parallel with the Proudhonian philosophy."

[66]Chu, 1992. 131–133.

triadic group, where the Republic is the superego/sovereign, Courbet is the ego/citizen, and the child is still to be totally symbolically castrated, the Id. The strong and obvious diagonal that links all three faces has hitherto been under theorised, but the effigy of the Republic (not a muse, not truth, or artistic autonomy), political Liberty, is "mother" and "nurturer" to both child and Courbet. The tightness of this group also explains the distance and secondary importance of the Napoleon III character. If the Herding analysis were correct, one would have thought the connection between the artist and the king would have been formally stronger; in this reading the circularity of the central group dismisses the need for any monarchical structures. This is a visual strategy where the Republic is kept separate from the monarch, so that the *juste milieu* is not effective (the *juste milieu* being the middle way meant to contain revolt, fusing republican values subtly with a monarchical reality).[67]

4.4.3 Civilised Landscape and Natural Law

The other element in the central group is the painting itself. The painting is a picture of the Franche-Comté region, where Courbet was born and raised in Ornans. Herding, and many others, see the landscape as a return to this childhood, a primordial nature far from the modernity of the city.[68] Herding locates within his reading of "primary nature", Rousseau's "state of nature". This is linked to his interpretation of Truth and the muse, and elsewhere as a symptom of the anxiety of modernisation.[69] Herding goes on to argue that after 1855—and *The Studio*—Courbet turns more to nature, "in which nature came to stand in for the artist's earlier demands for equality".[70] But a more extended reading would look more seriously at the jurisprudential import of this discovery. The horizontal created by the Republic looking along the brush of Courbet pass his head, threading nature, Courbet and the Republic pictorially together. Beside this obvious compositional link, Fried notes that Courbet almost dissolves *into* the picture plane of the landscape. Conversely the waterfall flows *out* of the painting and seems to continue

[67]See for a further discussion of this in relation to Daumier's work in Watts, 2014.

[68]Herding, 1991, 59. Herding mentions the corroborative sources at n 94; see Schama, Simon. 1995. *Landscape and Memory*. London: Vintage Books for a general discussion of the cultural construction of "nature".

[69]See Herding, 1991, Chapter 4: 'Equality and Authority in Courbet's Landscape Painting'.

[70]Herding, 1991, 64. Fried too noted the turn to landscape after this painting. A reason for this may be the tight censorship of the more political imagery of Courbet's earlier "Realism". Tentatively would also suggest that the *genre historique* became a popular mode of painting *within* the Salon and Expositions. Could the use of a lesser genre, landscape, not continue a trajectory towards disavowing the state sanctioned imagery of industrial capital and modernisation of the city, which it celebrated? That Herding sees the political allusion to Rousseau's "state of nature" confirms this idea.

down the body of the Republic.[71] The painting represents the basis of natural law. In a reanimation of Moffit's analysis (remembering the connections between *The Studio* and the famous Niquet print) not only is the painting compositionally similar but, *contra* Moffit, actually raises the same topic. The landscape is a visual representation, of the *Declaration of the Rights of Man and the Citizen*. The light of Reason emanates from the painting, enlightening the right hand side of the work, as in the Niquet print.

4.5 A Lacanian Artist and Legal Subject Formation

4.5.1 The Studio as an Image of Symbolic Castration

If the painting does represent the idea of natural law *and* the *Declaration* then this helps explain the tightly-connected characters in the centre of the painting. Both the French and American Republics saw natural law underpinning natural *rights*.[72] In other words the social contract is what turns natural *liberty* into a nation-state.[73] For Hobbes it is by foregoing their natural liberty and subjecting themselves to the sovereign that the social contract and nationhood are formed. By extending Herding (who was merely interested in Rousseau's "state of nature") the central group can be explained through Rousseau's *The Social Contract*, the most complex discussion of this process of legal subject-making.[74] The social contract gave over legislative power to the "general will", which subsumed all other individual wills; this would stop corrupted "positive laws" encroaching on natural rights. The triad represents natural law, flowing out into the legal subject and the Nation, who represent this complex social contract; that is, a Nation unified (under the Republic) but nevertheless made up and moving through the legal subject (Courbet). Arguably, this painting becomes a metapicture for the process of symbolic castration. From a primordial state of nature (Courbet's birthplace, the Franche-Comté) the subject is "forced to be free" through the figure of the unified Republic. The Declaration put forward a doctrine of popular sovereignty and the "general will", "The principle of any sovereignty resides essentially in the Nation. No body, no individual can exert authority which does not emanate expressly from it".[75] In a Lacanian sense the

---

[71]Fried, 1992, 160–161.

[72]French Assembly spoke of "simple and indisputable" notions that led to natural rights. See Murphy, Mark C. 2006. *Natural Law in Jurisprudence and Politics*. Cambridge: Cambridge University Press; Finnis, John. 1991. *Natural Law*. New York: New York University Press.

[73]See Hobbes, Thomas. 1998 (1651). *Leviathan or the Matter, Forme and Power of a Common Wealth Ecclesiasticall and Civil* Oxford: Oxford University Press, where the natural liberty, in the state of nature is considered "solitary, poor, nasty, brutish and short".

[74]Rousseau, Jean-Jacques. 1968. *The Social Contract*. Trans. Maurice Cranston. London: Penguin Classics.

[75]Article 3 of the *Declaration*.

subject is castrated and his subjecthood is constructed like language, "negatively". The subject is known only through his relationship with others, and the complex network of "friends" and "enemies", which we see strongly in the setting of the painting. By entering in a relationship with the symbolic order, here Republican France represented by Marianne, the subject must lose something of himself or herself. So far from being the arrogant artist, in this work Courbet not only shows himself as a worker/slave of the Marianne, but in the image loses his leg into the painting (which in this instance represents his primordial childhood which must be left behind as "lack".) By a series of losses shown in this central grouping the subject is born into the French Republic and natural law.

This central grouping shows the circuit between the master signifier and the citizen. Looking at Lacan's master discourse the elements of the central grouping can be teased out. The master signifier, Marianne, (S1) addresses the slave (S2) or Courbet as worker/citizen; this is very simply the idea of Marianne as the patron or commissioner of Courbet's work, the representation of natural law, a projection of Marianne's law. Lacan shows that the slave/Courbet comes to embody knowledge (the knowledge of natural laws/the *Declaration*). But the truth of the master discourse is that the master is also symbolically castrated. The Marianne must also be created in images (and language) and this in the end is what the painting reveals—adding that other ideologies, like that of Napoleon III, must also be painted and shown in their own alternative Expositions. The master will exist if the subject believes, and the Courbet/slave shows his belief through the act of painting, which is an act of faith and submission. In the end the painting shows a doubling of the Marianne (sovereign under natural law) by the landscape (natural law), the process of the painting is the ongoing process of belief and production of the master's power; the master signifier must be obeyed and repeated. Faith in the law is created through images. By corollary the great "I" of modernist art in this reading is established through loss. In *The Studio* the "I" of the Courbet/genius is not complete but only recognized through his devoted position and the way he is "imaged" by the law.

Finally, the side of the image where the "friends" are positioned may be seen as representing the "legislators" or an alternative and incorruptible "national assembly" that actually did represent the general will (as opposed to the corruptible Bonapartist court represented by the figure of Napoleon III, and his assorted cronies). Under the "social contract" the entire body of citizens is responsible for making laws, and are not merely there to *serve* the "general will".[76] Jonathan Ribner has discussed the image of the "legislator" in art at the time and in this reading Courbet is joined by other "poet" legislators. Ribner writes, "[a]s the French Revolution's cult of the law lost steam, the sacred authority of the lawgiver

---

[76]Rousseau, 1968. 146, 151–154.

was transferred to the poet and artist on both sides of the Channel".[77] This work could be linked to Courbet's friend Millet and his self-portrait as Moses in 1841, which Ribner has also discussed at great length.[78] Along these lines Baudelaire's open, empty pages are reminiscent of the "double tablet" motif that commonly linked Moses's commandments to the state's Declaration.[79]

Katherine Taylor puts this appeal to natural law and "good" legislators into context. She suggests there was a consensus that after nineteen failed constitutions (between 1789 and 1848) there was a general distrust of natural law. She proves that more emphasis was being placed on the actual holders of authority, which was exemplified in the *Festival of Justice* that occurred in 1849 in Paris.[80] The judiciary in 1849 was seen as "less an agent of the ruler than as a separate power conferring legitimacy upon the state".[81] Taylor suggests that the Second Republic was a major upheaval, leading to judicial reform, based on "staffing rather than codes" and that an ideal universal text was undermined by 1848 (both through upheaval and philosophical discussion).[82] Taylor makes a close reading of the visual spectacle of President Bonaparte. So perhaps it is in this setting that Courbet would so adamantly proclaim and reassert the possibility of natural justice. The rhetoric of 1848 would of course return in the Third Republic. The import of *The Studio* may have been hard to see since its rediscovery in the 1920s. We link the Master's discourse with total monarchical control (for example the repression of Napoleon III). *The Studio* illustrates the fact that we need the Master (the Marianne) as the founding force, the "patron" of our social worlds.

4.5.2 My Enemy's Enemy

Through the approach of Lacan a few more issues may be teased out. Herding had difficulty understanding the split nature of the work. Courbet wrote "[o]n the right

[77]Ribner, Jonathan C. 1999. Law and Justice in England and France. In *Law and The Image: The Aesthetics of Law and the Authority of Art*, eds. Costas Douzinas, and Lynda Nead. Chicago, London: University of Chicago Press, 192.

[78]Ribner, Jonathan C. 1993. *Broken Tablets. The Cult of the Law in French Art from David To Delacroix*. Berkeley, Los Angeles, Oxford: University of California Press, Chapter 6, 'The Romantic Moses'.

[79]These empty, "to be written on pages" are reminiscent of Peter Goodrich's wonderful analysis of the empty page in Goodrich, Peter. 1999. The Iconography of Nothing: Blank Spaces and the Representation of Law in Edward Vi and the Pope. In *Law and The Image: The Aesthetics of Law and the Authority of Art*, eds. Costas Douzinas, and Lynda Nead, 89–114. Chicago, London: University of Chicago Press.

[80]See Fischer Taylor, Katherine. 1999. The Festival of Justice, Paris, 1849. In *Law and The Image: The Aesthetics of Law and the Authority of Art*, eds. Costas Douzinas, and Lynda Nead, 137–177. Chicago, London: University of Chicago Press.

[81]Taylor, 199, 141; see also Mona Ozouf, 1988.

[82]Ibid., 144.

are the shareholders, that is friends, workers, devotees of the art world. On the left the other side of trivial life, the people, misery, poverty, wealth, the exploited and the exploiters, the people who live off of death".[83] Although these notes may be "disguised" they point to the opposition. Herding had difficulty seeing the logic that bound the two sides together. As we have seen from the cartoons of the day it was not uncommon to have both the Emperor and the Republic within the one frame, united in juxtaposition.[84] *The Studio* has at *least* two effigies. The blind spot may have arisen even in the Herding/Toussaint reading because it was assumed there could be no king's body alongside another sovereign body; in fact the only other "sovereign" body they privileged was that of the autonomous artist. The effigies are master signifiers, but what is this doubling? For Žižek this separation is what helps *form* the meaning of the master signifier. As Žižek suggests, "[t]his tension introduces a kind of reflective distance into the very heart of ideology: ideology is always, by definition, 'ideology of ideology'... There is no ideology that does not assert itself by means of delimiting itself from another mere 'ideology'".[85]

One aspect of the master-signifier is that it must displace others in order to create enemies (and by extension know your friends). That is, there must be space outside the symbolic to inscribe and define the big Other. In this work, like the rhetoric of Universal Exposition, it is France that proclaims herself the leading light that defines democracy and liberty. In Courbet's work France defines herself against the Bonapartists and the other nations and races. He defines the noble culture of France against the industrial capitalism of Napoleon III and the Jewish penny pincher. It is in this violent *exclusion* that France and democracy really shine forth; it is for this reason that Courbet would have seen the Exposition as a perfect place for unveiling this apostolic work.

4.5.3 Nude Law and Jouissance

There are a number of reasons why this reading has not been seen before. From a modernist perspective (the work was only put on public display in the 1920s) the painting shows many formal and "Realist" innovations. By 1920 the interest in the effigy, whether monarchical or republican, had already dissipated. Although the Marianne is still in use and understood in France, without the context of the Herding/Toussaint analysis and appeal to caricature this reading could not have

[83]Courbet letter to Champfleury 1854, published in Courbet, Gustave, and Petra ten Doesschate Chu. 1992. *Letters of Gustave Courbet* Chicago: University of Chicago Press.

[84]Ribner, 1999. Ribner identifies this doubling in many places, for example he discusses a ceiling work of by M-J Blondel titled, *France in the Midst of the Legislator Kings and French Jurisconsults, Receives the Constitutional Charter from Louis XVIII*, (1827). A regal and crowned France humbly receives the Charter, Monetesquieu and *ancien Regime* royals are in attendance. This rather odd piece suggests that both allegories of France and the King are on the same page.

[85]Žižek, Slavoj. 1994. *Mapping Ideology*. London: Verso, 19.

been articulated. The museological approach, for example, is enlightening. The annexed nature of the display of Courbet's work in a "side chapel", apart from other Realists or other displays of contemporary applied arts, suggests that the "genius" Courbet was unaffected by external, political or artistic influences.[86] Or as Mieke Bal has noted, in The Musée d'Orsay since 1995 the *Allegory* has hung next to *The Source*, painted in 1868 and featuring a nude woman seen from behind at a small water fall in the woods. "The nude woman, then is reinstated at the center of the painting by the discursive collocation of these two paintings on the same wall… they make the viewer go from *Allegory's* nude to *The Source*'s in an act of *metonymic* troping".[87] Subsequent readings seem only able to move so far from the traditional art historical iconography and not realize the import of this work as a jurisprudential exploration of the shift from monarchical to democratic power.

It is the nude itself with all its varied connotations that confused the viewer more than anything—that the viewer could engage with a libidinal reaction to power in the age of Foucault's disciplinary power was a considerable problem for its adequate reception. But if we follow Peter Goodrich's assessment of Pierre Legendre the libidinal aspect finds lucidity:

> The image is thus crucial to an understanding of the authority of law, because it is the image, the specularly structure of authority, which generates the subject's submission to law or, to use Legendre's terms, the capture of the subject by the institution. To understand law it is necessary to understand the aesthetics of law, the erotics of attachment to the institution.[88]

On one hand the beauty of the woman alone suggests the sublime nature of the law, and transcendental notions of justice and love. This feeling could be summed up in the Christian coverall of justice: "love thy neighbour".[89] This erotic connection to the law and Nation is secured through a series of "art jokes". Freud links the joke to man's repressed instinctual nature, especially sexual drives, since for Freud the joke is an expression of the repressed in the conscious (symbolic) world via its elliptical thought.[90] Art also mediates, or is able to sublimate the Real or repressed to some extent, and Freud suggests that his work on the joke is closest to an aesthetic theory in his oeuvre. The first joke is that Courbet has made the Republic inordinately sexy.

---

[86]Barker, Emma. 1999. Case Study 2: The Museum in a Postmodern Era: The Musee D'Orsay. In *Contemporary Cultures of Display*, ed. Emma Barker. New York: Yale University Press. Barker writes: "Its overall effect is to reinforce a highly traditional conception of art history made up of individual geniuses whose unique creativity owes nothing to the world in which they lived". 65

[87]Bal, Mieke. 1996. The Discourse of the Museum. In *Thinking about Exhibitions*, eds. Reesa Greenberg, Bruce W. Ferguson, and Sandy Nairne. New York: Routledge, 212.

[88]Legendre, Pierre, and Peter Goodrich. 1997. Glossary: Image. In *Law and the Unconscious; A Legendre Reader*, ed. Peter Goodrich. London: Macmillan, 260.

[89]Michael Detmold in his final lecture series as Emeritus Professor of Law at the University of Adelaide linked natural law, love and the law, Detmold, Michael. 2009. 'Four Lectures on the Law of Love,' March/April 2009: http://www.law.adelaide.edu.au/documents/law_of_love_lectures.pdf.

[90]Freud, Sigmund. 1960 (1905). *Jokes and Their Relation to the Unconscious*. Trans. J. Strachey. New York: W. W. Norton.

As a "real" allegory it is unclear whether the Republic is an effigy or an actual "nude model", as described in the Champfleury letter. The modelling and warmth of the model's skin are particularly noteworthy. Delacroix particularly liked her thighs, "[i] n the later work (*The Studio*) the planes are well understood, there is atmosphere and there are some parts that are important in execution: the haunches, and the thigh of the nude model and her bosom… They have refused one of the most singular works of this period…"[91] There is a supplement to her symbolic drapery which is the pink dress of the real "bohemian" model.[92] But as many have pointed out, the imagery of the Marianne was always libidinal. Joan Landes suggests that in both high and low cultural images the Marianne was drawn in such a way as to seduce.[93] The images allowed men to fall in love with France.[94]

So Courbet's work beautifully shows the workings of the superegoic Marianne. Besides ruling through order and codes (the symbolic order) she asks you to "Enjoy your Nation".[95] It is this "obscene imposition of enjoyment", which can never be fully met, which marks, for Žižek, the "obscene superego supplement".[96] Already we have seen some of this obscenity through the veiled racism in the piece, which was ideologically common at the time. France was seen as hierarchically above other nations and races. These enemies are placed with the skull on the side of death. Similarly the "love" of Nation coincides with Žižek's contention that the carnival and the clamorous sporting event are the true "political" event. In these transgressive acts, against the superego's own rules (against say transgression or propriety), we build a "social contract" on "nightly" laws. Whether unconscious or not, in Courbet's effort to "disguise" Marianne as a "model", the erotic truth of the Nation was disclosed.

Another joke suggests this hidden obscene supplement of the law. If the landscape represents "natural law" then this phrase in the letter to Champfleury is particularly dissembling: "the canvas that I am working on is a painting of an ass driver who is pinching the butt of a girl he meets, and the donkeys loaded with sacks in a landscape with a mill".[97] Is this a joke? Was Courbet's original intention

---

[91]Delacroix, 'Diaries', 3 August 1855 quoted in Harrison, Charles. 1998. Art in Theory, 1815–1900: Wiley-Blackwell, 361.

[92]For these common prejudices at this time see Phillips, Sarah R. 2006. *Modeling life: art models speak about nudity, sexuality, and the creative process*. Washington: SUNY Press.; Waller 2006.

[93]Landes, Joan. 2003. *Visualizing the Nation: Gender, Representation, and Revolution in Eighteenth-Century France*. Cornell: Cornell University Press; Hunt, 1986. 89–95; and Agulhon, 1979.

[94]Hunt, Lynn. 1991. *Eroticism and the Body Politic*. Baltimore: Johns Hopkins University Press.

[95]Here *Enjoy* is connected to the French word *Jouissance*.

[96]Dean, Jodi. 2004. Žižek on Law. *Law and Critique* 15 (1):1–24.; Žižek, Slavoj. 1991. *For They Know Not What They Do: Enjoyment as a Political Factor*. London: Verso.; Žižek, Slavoj. 1989. *The Sublime Object of Ideology*. London: Verso.

[97]Chu, 1992. 132. Chu dryly observes, "Courbet apparently abandoned the idea for the naughty subject of the painting within the painting and decided on a Franche-Comté landscape instead". 133

to have a lewd, puerile scene at the centre of *The Studio*? Obviously this seems to have no connection to reading the landscape as "natural law". As a Freudian slip it points to the "Sadean" side of the "state of nature"; there are links to be made here with Lacan's reading of Kant through Marquis de Sade, to Courbet's Rousseauian vision of nature. Kant and Rousseau's subject in the end participates in an ideal and externalised realm, unattached to teleological, social and practical concerns. Rousseau's notion of the "general will" as a unified and forceful superegoic entity has often been criticised as democratic but wholly totalitarian.[98] The law and our own acts under the law are never a perfect match, and like Kafka's (anti)heroes we are always guilty that we have not met the demand of the Law. Perhaps this is why Courbet (jokingly) suggests that the spectre haunting the landscape is the desire of the ass driver. Similarly the landscape represents the primordial setting of his childhood before submission to the law (and the codes and performances of Paris).

4.6 The Modern Genius Reinstated After All

The central figures create a circuit, however the subjecthood of Courbet is not fully effaced through submission to Marianne. Something of Courbet resists subjection. Natural law speaks through Courbet, where the artist is almost absorbed into the picture plane. On the other side he is bracketed by the "general will" personified by the sovereign figure of the Marianne. Paradoxically, Courbet and his subjecthood is *still* the fulcrum of the painting. He in effect interpellates himself through the image of the law he is painting (and gazing at). The cast of characters around him (both friend and foe) only frame and redouble the processes of interpellation through Nation and the law.

Perhaps this leads to a cynical conclusion for *The Studio*. Courbet was trying to hold on to an illusion of self-identity that had been threatened by Napoleon III's refusal to recognize Courbet's genius. We have to ask: does Courbet produce another Master/Mistress that recognises him in the same way he imagines himself (which is within the definition of the Lacanian master discourse)?[99] There is no hiding: in this work the Republican dream of modernity is universalising. It is a vision of French liberty that is expansionist and culturally imperialistic, which threatens to "teach" and affect *all* nations. Indeed the process illustrated in the

[98]Lacan, Jacques. 1966. Kant avec Sade. In *Écrits*. Paris: Seuil; see Žižek, Slavoj. 1999. Kant with (or against) Sade. In *The Žižek Reader*, eds. Elizabeth Wright, and Edmond Wright. Wiley-Blackwell (Chapter 13), Žižek, Slavoj. 2006. *The Parallax View*. Cambridge/London: The MIT Press, 91–94.; Zupancic, Alenka 2012. *The Ethics of the Real: Kant, Lacan*. London/ New York: Verso, 80–82, Zupancic sees the reading of Sade and Kant together as, "Thus for Kant freedom is susceptible to limitation, either by pleasure (in the form of any pathological motivation) or by death of the subject." 82

[99]By excluding the unconscious the Master discourse represents the other exactly within the S2 (knowledge).

painting belies its hidden "totalitarian" and obscene underbelly. It is a work of a staunch Republican, singing the praises of the hope of 1848 (which was then receding quickly). One year before his overthrow in 1870, in an effort to instigate the *juste milieu,* Napoleon III tried to broaden his base of support by giving amnesty to previous opponents, and he offered both Courbet and Daumier the *légion d'honneur*. Both artists refused.[100] This refusal should not only be perceived as an act against the Master, but also as demonstration that both artists were tied to one another via their aesthetic and political contributions and to the Republic above that.

References

Agulhon, Maurice. 1979. *Marianne au combat. L'imagerie et la symbolique républicaines de 1789 à 1880*. Paris: Flammarion.

Bal, Mieke. 1996. The discourse of the museum. In *Thinking about Exhibitions*, eds. Reesa Greenberg, Bruce W. Ferguson, and Sandy Nairne. New York: Routledge.

Barker, Emma. 1999. Case study 2: The museum in a postmodern era: The Musee D'Orsay. In *Contemporary Cultures of Display*, ed. Emma Barker. New York: Yale University Press.

Boime, Albert. 2008. *Art in an Age of Civil Struggle, 1848-1871*. Chicago: University of Chicago Press.

Boudaille, Georges. 1969. *Gustave Courbet—Painter in Protest*, trans. and ed. M Bullock. Greenwich, Conn.: New York Graphic Society.

Bourdieu, Pierre. 1993. The field of cultural production. In *The Field of Cultural Production*, ed. Randal Johnson, 29–73. New York: Columbia University Press.

Bowness, Alan. 1972. Courbet's 'Atelier du Peintre'. In *Fiftieth Charlton Lecture on Art*. University of Newcastle upon Tyne, Newcastle upon Tyne.

Chu, Petra ten-Doesschate. 1992. *Letters of Gustave Courbet*. Chicago: University of Chicago Press.

Chu, Petra ten-Doesschate. 2008. *The Most Arrogant Man in France: Gustave Courbet and the Nineteenth Century Media Culture*. Princeton & Oxford: Princeton University Press.

Clark, T. J. 1978. *Image of the People: Gustave Courbet and the 1848 Revolution*. Berkeley: University of California Press.

Courbet, Gustave, and Petra ten-Doesschate Chu. 1992. *Letters of Gustave Courbet*. Chicago: University of Chicago Press.

Courbet d'après nature. 1865. In *Courbet raconté par lui-même et par ses amis*, ed. Pierre Courthion, 47. Geneva.

Crapo, Paul. 1995. The problematics of artistic patronage under the second empire: Gustave Courbet's involved relations with the regime of Napoleon III. *Zeitschrift fur Kunstgeschichte* 58 (2): 241–261.

Cullen, Fintan. 1995. *Visual Politics: Representation of Ireland: 1750-1950*. Cork: Cork University Press.

Dean, Jodi. 2004. Žižek on law. *Law and Critique* 15 (1): 1–24.

Detmold, Michael. 2009. *Four Lectures on the Law of Love*. March/April 2009: http://www.law.adelaide.edu.au/documents/law_of_love_lectures.pdf.

---

[100]Milner, John. 2000. *Art, War and Revolution in France, 1870–1871: Myth, Reportage and Reality* Yale: Yale University Press, 26; Milner suggests Courbet's friends and supporters were very appreciative of this snub to the Emperor and held a dinner in his honour at 10 francs a head, in 1870.

Faunce, Sarah, and Linda Nochlin. 1988. *Courbet Reconsidered*. Yale: Yale University Press.
Finnis, John. 1991. *Natural Law*. New York: New York University Press.
Freud, Sigmund. 1960 (1905). *Jokes and Their Relation to the Unconscious*, trans. and ed. J. Strachey. New York: W. W. Norton.
Fried, Michael. 1992. *Courbet's Realism*. Chicago: University of Chicago Press.
Gombrich, Ernst Hans. 1979. The dream of reason: Symbolism of the French revolution. *British Journal for Eighteenth-Century Studies* 2 (3): 187–205.
Goodrich, Peter. 1999. The iconography of nothing: Blank spaces and the representation of law in Edward Vi and the Pope. In *Law and The Image: The Aesthetics of Law and the Authority of Art*, eds. Costas Douzinas, and Lynda Nead, 89–114. Chicago, London: University of Chicago Press.
Gustave Courbet, letter to the Government of National Defence, Paris [5 October 1870] found in Chu, Petra ten-Doesschate. 1992. *Letters of Gustave Courbet*, 392. Chicago: University of Chicago Press.
Harrison, Charles. 1998. *Art in Theory, 1815-1900*. Wiley-Blackwell.
Herding, Klaus. 1978. Das Atelier des Malers - Treffpunkt der Welt und Ort der Versöhnung. In *Realismus als Widerspruch: Die Wirklichkeit in Courbets Malerei*, ed. Klaus Herding, 223–247. Frankfurt am Main: Suhrkamp.
Herding, Klaus. 1991. *Courbet: To Venture Independence*. New Haven: Yale: University Press.
Hobbes, Thomas. 1998 (1651). *Leviathan or the Matter, Forme and Power of a Common Wealth Ecclesiasticall and Civil*. Oxford: Oxford University Press.
Hobsbawm, Eric, and Terence Ranger. 1983. *The Invention of Tradition*. Cambridge UK: Cambridge University Press.
Hunt, Lynn. 1986. *Politics, Culture and Class in the French Revolution*. California: University of California Press.
Hunt, Lynn. 1991. *Eroticism and the Body Politic*. Baltimore: Johns Hopkins University Press.
Lacan, Jacques. 1966. Kant avec Sade. In *Écrits*. Paris: Seuil.
Landes, Joan. 2003. *Visualizing the Nation: Gender, Representation, and Revolution in Eighteenth-Century France*. Cornell: Cornell University Press, Hunt, 1986.
Legendre, Pierre, and Peter Goodrich. 1997. Glossary: Image. In *Law and the Unconscious; A Legendre Reader*, ed. Peter Goodrich. London: Macmillan.
Mainardi, Patricia. 1990. *Art and Politics of the Second Empire: The Universal Expositions of 1855 and 1867*. London and New Haven: Yale University Press.
Mainardi, Patricia. 1991 (December). Courbet's Exhibitionism. *Gazette des Beaux-Arts* 118: 253–266.
Mainardi, Patricia. 1993. *The End of the Salon: Art and the State in the Early Third Republic*. Cambridge: Cambridge University Press.
Milner, John. 2000. *Art, War and Revolution in France, 1870-1871: Myth, Reportage and Reality* Yale: Yale University Press.
Moffit, John. 1987. Art and politics: An underlying pictorial-political topos in Courbet's "Real allegory". *Artibus et Historiae* 8 (15): 183–193.
Murphy, Mark C. 2006. *Natural Law in Jurisprudence and Politics*. Cambridge: Cambridge University Press.
Nicholson, Benedict. 1973. *Courbet: The Studio of the Painter*. New York.
Nochlin, Linda. 1966. *Realism and Tradition in Art, 1848-1900*. New Jersey: Prentice Hall College Division.
Nochlin, Linda. 1972. *Realism (Style and Civilizations)*. London: Penguin.
Nochlin, Linda. 1988. Courbet's real allegory: Reading the painter's studio. In *Courbet Reconsidered*, eds. Sarah Faunce, and Linda Nochlin. Yale: Yale University Press.
Nochlin, Linda. 1967. The invention of the Avant-Garde: France 1830-1880. In *Avant-Garde Art*, eds. Thomas Band Hess, and John Ashbery, 3–24. New York: Macmillan.
O'Brien, David. 2006. *After the Revolution: Antoine-Jean Gros, painting and propaganda under Napoleon*. Pennsylvania: Penn State Press.

Ozouf, Mona. 1988. *Festival and the French Revolution*, trans. and ed. Alan Sheridan. Cambridge: Harvard University Press.

Phillips, Sarah R. 2006. *Modeling life: Art Models Speak About Nudity, Sexuality, and the Creative Process*. Washington: SUNY Press.; Waller 2006.

Picasso, Pablo. 2004. *The Burial of the Count of Orgaz & Other Poems*, trans. and eds. Jerome Rothenberg, and Pierre Joris. Boston: Exact Change.

Porterfield, Todd. 1998. *The Allure of Empire: Art in the Service of French Imperialism, 1798–1836*. Princeton: Princeton University Press.

Reff, Theodore. 1981. *Exhibitions of Later Realist Art*. New York: Garland.

Ribner, Jonathan C. 1993. *Broken Tablets. The Cult of the Law in French Art from David To Delacroix*. Berkeley, Los Angeles, Oxford: University of California Press.

Ribner, Jonathan C. 1999. Law and justice in England and France. In *Law and The Image: The Aesthetics of Law and the Authority of Art*, eds. Costas Douzinas, and Lynda Nead, 178–199. Chicago, London: University of Chicago Press.

Rosanvallon, Pierre. 2006. *Democracy Past and Future*, ed. Samuel Moyn. New York: Columbia University Press.

Rousseau, Jean-Jacques. 1968. *The Social Contract*, trans. and ed. Maurice Cranston. London: Penguin Classics.

Rubin, James H. 1981. Realism and social vision in Courbet and Proudhon. In *Princeton Essays on the Arts*. Princeton: Princeton University Press.

Schama, Simon. 1995. *Landscape and Memory*. London: Vintage Books.

Seibert, Margaret. 1983. A political and a pictorial tradition used in Gustave Courbet's Real allegory. *The Art Bulletin* 65 (2): 311–316.

Seibert, Margaret. 1984. Letter. *The Art Bulletin* 66 (1).

Taylor, Katherine. 1999. The festival of justice, Paris, 1849. In *Law and The Image: The Aesthetics of Law and the Authority of Art*, eds. Costas Douzinas, and Lynda Nead, 137–177. Chicago, London: University of Chicago Press.

Toussaint, Hélène. 1977. *Gustave Courbet [1819-1877] [exhibition catalogue]*. Paris/London: Grand Palais/Royal Academy of Arts.

Toussaint, Hélène. 1981. Le réalisme de Courbet au service de la satire politique et de la propagande gouvernementale. *Bulletin de la Société de l'Histoire de l'Art français* Année 1979.

Vanity Fair, September 2008, (cover page caption).

Waller, Susan. 2006. *The Invention of the Model: Artists and Models in Paris, 1830-1870*. Aldershot: Ashgate Publishing.

Warner, Marina. 1985. *Monuments and Maidens: The Allegory of the Female Form*. London: Weidenfeld and Nicholson.

Watts, Oliver. 2014. Daumier and replacing the King's body. In *Law, Culture and Visual Studies*, eds. Richard K. Sherwin, and Anne Wagner, 421–443. Dordrecht, Heidelberg, New York, London: Springer.

Woody Allen. 1989. *Crimes and Misdemeanours*. Metro Goldwyn Meyer.

Žižek, Slavoj. 1989. *The Sublime Object of Ideology*. London: Verso.

Žižek, Slavoj. 1991. *For They Know Not What They Do: Enjoyment as a Political Factor*. London: Verso.

Žižek, Slavoj. 1994. *Mapping Ideology*. London: Verso.

Žižek, Slavoj. 1999. Kant with (or against) sade. In *The Žižek Reader*, eds. Elizabeth Wright, and Edmond Wright. Wiley-Blackwell.

Žižek, Slavoj. 2006. *The Parallax View*. Cambridge/London: The MIT Press.

Zupancic, Alenka. 2012. *The Ethics of the Real: Kant, Lacan*. London/New York: Verso.

Oliver Watts is Senior Lecturer and Head of Performance Practices at the National Institute of Dramatic Arts, Sydney Australia. He is an Honorary Associate at Sydney College of Arts, University of Sydney, Sydney Australia. Watts is an academic and artist who works on the nexus of art and law. His current research interest is modes of resistance in Contemporary Indigenous Australian art and performance.

Part II
The Aesthetic Constitution of Office

Chapter 5
Justice Petrified: The Seat of the Italian Supreme Court between Law, Architecture and Iconography

Stefania Gialdroni

And they hoped for a resurgence in Italy of the former power of Rome. This was a rhetorical illusion springing from self-deception and [...] from a desire to mitigate the defeats and the civil strife of their country.

Giuseppe Prezzolini[1].

Abstract "Rome was not the world of religion, of abstract sciences, of literature, of fine arts, because in all those fields other people could defeat it; Rome was the world of law. For law, Romans had a historical vocation, deriving from their intellectual genius, from their moral virtue, from their character, from the force and the persistency of will". These words, pronounced by the Italian Minister of Justice Giuseppe Zanardelli during the foundation stone-laying ceremony of the Palace of Justice (now seat of the Supreme Court of Cassation) in 1889, summarize his ideological program: to make the law one of the cornerstones of unified Italy (1861) with Rome, and especially its glorious and lay legal tradition, as its geographical as well as ideological center. During his long service as Minister of Justice, Zanardelli demonstrated his faith in law as a tool for unifying territories and people, realizing two great works: the first Italian Criminal Code and the Palace of Justice. This chapter aims to describe the events that led to the definition of the very peculiar

[1]Prezzolini, Giuseppe. 1948. The Origins: Why Italians are not Romans. In *The Legacy of Italy*. 7–16. New York: S.F. Vanni. 7. All translations are by the author of this article. Citation in the abstract: "Roma non fu il mondo della religione, delle scienze astratte, delle lettere, delle arti belle, poiché in ciascuno di que' campi altre genti la vincono; Roma fu il mondo del diritto. Pel diritto i romani ebbero una vocazione storica, derivante dal loro genio intellettuale, dalla loro virtù morale, dal loro carattere, dalla forza e costanza della volontà": Zanardelli, Giuseppe. 1889. *Pel collocamento della prima pietra del Palazzo di Giustizia in Roma: discorso pronunziato dal Ministro guardasigilli G. Zanardelli il 14. marzo 1889*. Roma: Forzani e C. x.

S. Gialdroni (✉)
Department of Law, Roma Tre University, Rome, Italy
e-mail: stefania.gialdroni@uniroma3.it

S. Huygebaert et al. (eds.), *Sensing the Nation's Law*, Studies in the History of Law and Justice 13, https://doi.org/10.1007/978-3-319-75497-0_5

iconographical plan of the Italian Supreme Court building, meaningfully known to the people of Rome as *er Palazzaccio*: "the bad palace".

5.1 Law and the City in Context: From the "Sanctuary of Justice" to *er Palazzaccio*

To the people of Rome, the gigantic, probably excessive, white travertine building dominating the right bank of the Tiber, just one kilometre from Saint Peter's Dome and from Castel Sant'Angelo (the ancient prison of the Papal State), is commonly known as *er Palazzaccio*. To translate into English the nickname of the Italian Supreme Court of Cassation (*Corte Suprema di Cassazione*) is no easy task. What is certain is that the suffix—*accio*, in Italian, has a pejorative meaning.[1] It can refer to the building itself—which is a very convincing hypothesis as its architecture has been unanimously criticized both by art historians and by the population of Rome for decades[2]—or to the very concept of justice, which it is meant to represent.

In the first case, we could translate "Palazzaccio" as "the ugly building". After the enthusiasm that surrounded the work of architect Guglielmo Calderini (Perugia, 1837-Rome, 1916) at the time of its inauguration (1911), the building has been commonly despised for being too heavy, confusing, imposing. The same fate occurred to another monument built in exactly the same period, within the very same project of making Rome the capital of a secular Kingdom of Italy, young, modern but at the same time heir of a great past[3]: the *Vittoriano*.[4] On the occasion

---

[1]Quite isolated is the interpretation of the former Secretary General of the Court, Giovanni Longo, according to whom the nickname reveals rather a sort of affection of the Roman people for the palace. Longo, Giovanni E. 1997. Prefazione. In *Il Palazzo di giustizia di Roma*, ed. Marcello Fabbri, Roma: Gangemi 6.

[2]When it comes to the denigration of the monument, the letter sent by Bruno Zevi to Terry Rossi Kirk in 1992, in which the former accused the latter of being attracted by something "horrible and monstrous" (i.e. the Supreme Court building) is quintessential: Rossi Kirk, Terry. 1996. Roman Architecture before the Lateran Pact: Architectural Symbols of Reconciliation in the Competitions for the Palazzo di Giustizia, 1883–87. In *Guglielmo Calderini. La costruzione di un'architettura nel progetto di una Capitale*. Atti del Convegno, Roma, Palazzo delle Esposizioni, 23 settembre 1995. 83–125. Roma: Gangemi. 83. See also, for example, the lines devoted by Pigafetta to the nineteenth-century Roman government buildings: Pigafetta, Giorgio. 2007. *Storia dell'architettura moderna. Imitazione e invenzione fra xv e xx secolo*. Vol. 2. Torino: Bollati Boringhieri. 749.

[3]See also: Berggren, Lars and Sjöstedt, Lennart. 1996. *L'ombra dei grandi: monumenti e politica monumentale a Roma (1870–1895)*. Roma: Artemide; Rossi Kirk, Terry. 1997. The Politicization of the Landscape of Roma Capitale and the Symbolic Role of the Palazzo di Giustizia. In *Mélanges de l'École française de Rome. Italie et Méditerranée*. 109 (1): 89–114. http://www.persee.fr/web/revues/home/prescript/article/mefr_1123-9891_1997_num_109_1_4480?_Prescripts_Search_tabs1=standard&. Accessed 30 June 2015.

[4]The second competition (1884) was won by the project submitted by architect Giuseppe Sacconi, inspired by the Pergamon Altar. When Sacconi died, in 1905, the works were finished by Gaetano

of the fiftieth anniversary of the unification of Italy, in fact, the monument dedicated to Victor Emmanuel II, the first King of Italy, built in Piazza Venezia, near the Capitoline Hill, was also inaugurated. It is commonly known as *Altare della patria* (Altar of the Fatherland) but also as "the typewriter" or "the wedding cake".[5]

If, alternatively, the criticism refers to the function of the palace, i.e. to be the seat of the Italian Supreme Court, a possible translation could be "the bad palace". Today the building houses the Supreme Court of Cassation, the *Tribunale Superiore delle Acque Pubbliche* (i.e. the "Superior Tribunal of Public Waters"), the Council of the Bar Association of Rome (*Consiglio dell'Ordine degli Avvocati*), and the Central Law Library. Inside, there are also a bank, a post office, an office of the National Health Service (ASL), a restaurant/bar, a tobacconist and a kind of stationary store where lawyers can hire a robe for a few euros. When it was planned, though, the building was supposed to house not only the Court of Cassation, but to reunite all the Roman district courts: the civil, criminal and commercial tribunals and courts of appeal.[6] Briefly, it was a kind of concentration of everything that was secular justice in the perception of the Roman population.

But when and how did this almost sacred building, welcomed by the jury that approved the project as having "such merits that it" had to be "placed among the

---

Koch, Pio Piacentini and Manfredo Manfredi. See for example: Acciaresi, Primo. 1911. *Giuseppe Sacconi e l'opera sua massima. Cronaca dei lavori del Monumento nazionale a Vittorio Emanuele II.* Roma: Tipografia dell'Unione editrice; Sapori, Francesco. 1946. *Il Vittoriano.* Roma: Libreria dello Stato; Venturoli, Marcello. 1957. *La patria di marmo (1870–1911).* Pisa: Nistri-Lischi; Rodiek, Thorsten. 1983. *Das Monumento Nazionale Vittorio Emanuele II. in Rom.* Frankfurt a.M. - Bern - Berlin: Peter Lang; Tobia, Bruno. 2013 (2011). *L'altare della patria.* Bologna: Il Mulino; Ugolini, Romano (ed.). 2012. *Cento anni del Vittoriano 1911–2011.* Atti della giornata di studio tenutasi il 4 giugno 2011 al Vittoriano in occasione del Centenario dell'inaugurazione del Monumento. Roma: Gangemi. Particularly complete: Porzio, Pier Luigi (ed.). 1986-88. *Il Vittoriano. Materiali per una storia.* Voll. 1–2. Roma: Fratelli Palombi.

[5]The altar is only part of the monumental complex but, by metonymy, the entire *Vittoriano* has come to be known as *Altare della Patria*, especially after 1921, when the body of the Unknown Soldier was buried here. The two monuments differ in one crucial aspect: Sacconi, architect of the *Vittoriano*, embraced the neo-Hellenistic style at that time fashionable in Berlin, Munich and Vienna while Calderini chose a very "Italian" neo-Cinquecento style: Marconi, Paolo. 2006. L'ispirazione stilistica del "Palazzaccio" e il suo cantiere: un progetto e un simbolo. In *I tesori nascosti della Corte di Cassazione. Fotografie e disegni del Palazzo di Giustizia di Roma*, ed. Carolina Marconi, 11–18. Roma: Gangemi; Pizzo, Marco. 2006. Il Palazzo di Giustizia: un percorso iconografico. In ibid. 51–58. Catherine Brice defines it "cold and rhetorical": Brice, Catherine. 1996. De l'usage politique de l'architecture: le projet de Guglielmo Calderini au premier concours pour le monument à Victor-Emmanuel II, à Rome. In *Guglielmo Calderini. La costruzione di un'architettura.* Cit. 1–4. 2.

[6]"Art. 2. Nel Palazzo di Giustizia avranno sede: la Corte e la Procura generale di cassazione, la Corte e la Procura generale d'appello, le Corti d'assise, il Tribunale civile e correzionale e la Procura del Re, il Tribunale di commercio, la Pretura Urbana, il Consiglio dell'Ordine degli avvocati, il Consiglio di disciplina dei procuratori e l'ufficio di registro per gli atti giudiziari": Regio decreto (Royal decree) n. 1309, "Gazzetta ufficiale del Regno d'Italia" n. 120 (23 May 1883), 2235–2237. 2235. file:///C:/Users/Utente/Downloads/RG1883_05_23_120_PM.pdf. Accessed 14 August 2015.

most important and artistic works of modern art" become the "bad palace"?[7] Very soon probably, thanks maybe also to the uncontrolled increase of the costs (from 16 to 40 millions) of this gigantic work. For this scandal, Calderini was removed from the artistic direction and was also put under investigation, even though he was finally found not guilty.[8] But the criticism goes obviously to the judiciary system as a whole, to its mistakes and slowness. According to the statistics of the European Court of Human Rights, covering the period 1959–2014, Italy violated the right to fair trial due to the length of proceedings in 1.462 out of 2.312 decided cases.[9] Even considering only this fact, it has been a short step for the *Palazzo di Giustizia* to become, in the eyes of the Roman and of the Italian people as a whole, *er Palazzaccio*, the Kafkaesque place of all possible in-justices, of which the length of proceedings is only one of the most ill-famed.[10] This is something really different from the "sanctuary of justice"[11] that Giuseppe Zanardelli (Brescia, 1826—Maderno, 1903), one of the political leaders of the Liberal or Historical Left (*Sinistra storica*) and the real mind behind the project[12], wanted to realize.

This monument provides a privileged and original perspective to amplify our understanding of the search for a national identity typical of the cultural, political and social "Resurgence" (*Risorgimento*) that led to the unification of Italy (1861), in which law and lawyers played a crucial role. This movement cannot be fully understood without considering the role played by the Italian Freemasonry, of which many political leaders and artists were members, including Zanardelli and Calderini.

However, the masonic lodges that developed after the unification of Italy had different characters as compared to those of the previous century. The leading principles were the same (universal brotherhood, cosmopolitan humanitarianism, progress, secularization, anticlericalism) but the social background of their members was changing. They no longer attracted only aristocrats and intellectuals but

---

[7]"il progetto definitivo (...) ha pregi tali da collocarlo tra le opere più importanti ed artistiche dell'arte moderna". These words were pronounced by the Jury on 5 October 1888: Calderini, Guglielmo. 1908. *La improvvisa soppressione della direzione artistica dei lavori del palazzo di giustizia presentata al giudizio della Camera e del Senato.* Roma: Casa editrice italiana. 4.

[8]Ibid.

[9]Human Rights Center of the University of Padua: http://unipd-centrodirittiumani.it/en/news/European-Court-of-Human-Rights-Italy-condemned-for-the-violation-of-the-right-to-respect-for-family-and-private-life/3610. Accessed 30 June 2015.

[10]The interiors of the building, which someone has compared to the "Carceri d'invenzione" by the eighteenth-century artist Giovanni Battista Piranesi, have been used by Orson Welles as a set design for his adaptation of "The Trial" by Franz Kafka (1962).

[11]"Sire, È degno, è lieto, è fausto l'avvenimento, per quale oggi in Roma nel natalizio Vostro, festeggiato dalla Nazione, ottiene fortunatamente i proprii natali il *santuario della giustizia*. (...)." Zanardelli, 1889. v.

[12]Not surprisingly, a recently edited volume on the Supreme Court refers to the "masterpiece *of* Giuseppe Zanardelli *and* Guglielmo Calderini": Pisani, Mario (ed.). 2009. *La corte di cassazione. I progetti e l'architettura del capolavoro di Giuseppe Zanardelli e Guglielmo Calderini.* Roma: Gangemi.

rather members of the middle and lower bourgeoisie, often committed in politics, who helped and protected each other. Over the course of time this "nepotistic" trend led the public opinion to look at Freemasonry with suspicion. This attitude, supported by the "traditional" hostility of the Catholic Church, also retrospectively influenced the historiography on Italian Liberalism, which has often described the Freemasonry of the period as mysterious and shady, lacking in a clear political project except for an exasperated anticlericalism.[13] In fact, many of the political and legal battles of the second half of the nineteenth century cannot be understood if not in the context of the various lay associations created to pursue many social aims and born within the framework of the masonic lodges, including those supporting the abolition of death penalty, the introduction of universal suffrage and divorce, the abolition of prostitution[14]. Many important politicians of the *Sinistra storica*, the party that led the Italian Government from 1876 to 1896, were members of the "Grande Oriente"[15], as were Prime Ministers Agostino Depretis, Francesco Crispi and Giuseppe Zanardelli. If it cannot be sustained that all their behaviours and decisions were influenced by this affiliation, when analysing some features of Zanardelli's undertakings, one can certainly recognize some topics that Freemasons felt strongly about, as the abolition of the temporal power of the Church and the abolition of death penalty. However, his first and main aim was to make the Kingdom of Italy a united and proud country, worthy of its glorious past. The famous maxim "We have made Italy. Now we must make Italians", which is commonly (and erroneously) attributed to the politician, novelist and painter Massimo D'Azeglio (Turin, 1798—Turin, 1866)[16], very effectively summarizes the main problem of the founding fathers of the new-born Kingdom: to unify a very fragmented population, i.e. to create a national identity. We will demonstrate that Zanardelli tried to solve this problem using tools able to reach all levels of the population: law and, especially, architecture and iconography.

5.2 Giuseppe Zanardelli and the Pivotal Year 1889

Both from the point of view of legal history and in terms of the "politicization" of the landscape of Rome after the unification of Italy, 1889 can be considered a pivotal year, one of those crucial moments that can influence all the following

[13]Conti, Fulvio. 2003. *Storia della massoneria italiana. Dal Risorgimento al fascismo*. Bologna: Il Mulino. 8.

[14]Ibid. 10.

[15]The "Grande Oriente d'Italia" had between 4.000 and 5.000 members in the period 1860–1900, distributed in 100–150 lodges. Ibid.

[16]This is a translation of the sentence "Fatta l'Italia, bisogna fare gli Italiani" which, in reality, cannot be found "word for word" in D'Azeglio's memoirs (*I miei ricordi*, 1867). For an in-depth analysis of this oft-cited maxim see: Hom, Stephanie Malia. 2013. On the origins of making Italy: Massimo D'Azeglio and "Fatta l'Italia, bisogna fare gli Italiani". In *Italian Culture*. 31(1):1–16.

developments of a certain phenomenon and that, quite often, galvanize historians. The inauguration of the monument to Giordano Bruno in Campo de' Fiori, the promulgation of the new criminal code and the foundation stone-laying ceremony of the Supreme Court building are all complex phenomena but they are certainly connected and have something in common: an active, if not leading, role played by Giuseppe Zanardelli. His personality, both as a man and as a politician, can be described as turning around two principles: liberty and fatherland. They represent his two souls: the enlightened one and the romantic one. As a son of the Enlightenment, he had a profound faith in individual liberties as well as in the necessity of the state to be secular or even anticlerical in order to see those liberties respected. On the other hand, his aspiration for independence and his love for Italy, demonstrated both in his writings and by means of his actions, constitute the romantic side of his personality.[17]

5.2.1 Giordano Bruno in Campo de' Fiori

The monument devoted to the monk Giordano Bruno, condemned for heresy and sent to the stake in 1600, in the very same square where now its bronze double stands severe and thoughtful amid the yells of the market and the glances of tourists and tipsy night owls, has a quite complicated and certainly fascinating story. The initiative to erect a monument was taken by a group of bold students of the University "La Sapienza" who fought for years to provide the city with this strong symbol of liberty, maybe the only statue of this period which has maintained unaltered its powerful message. But they would not have reached their goal without the support of favorable circumstances: the falling authority of the upper echelons of ecclesiastical power, the support of the more progressive politicians (including Zanardelli) and of Freemasonry as well as the talent of Ettore Ferrari, its sculptor.[18]

Scholars disagree on who first thought to dedicate a monument to Giordano Bruno in Rome: someone says that the idea came from Turin, thanks to the fact that after centuries of oblivion new researches on the philosopher were undertaken by scholars such as Domenico Berti.[19] Very recently Massimo Bucciantini—who has put into perspective the role played by Freemasonry—has very convincingly demonstrated that the mind behind the project was the French Jewish refugee from the Paris Commune, philosopher, patriot and philanthropist Armand Lévy. His idea

[17] Sanesi, Elena. 1967. *Giuseppe Zanardelli dalla giovinezza alla maturità (con documenti inediti)*. Brescia: Ateneo di Brescia. 182–183.

[18] Passalalpi Ferrari, Ettore. 2009. *Il monumento a Giordano Bruno in Campo de' Fiori di Ettore Ferrari*. Roma: Associazione culturale Ettore Ferrari. Very recently the story of the monument has been described almost in the form of an adventure novel: Bucciantini, Massimo. 2015. *Campo dei fiori: storia di un monumento maledetto*. Torino: Einaudi.

[19] Passalalpi Ferrari, 2009. 13.

was then pursued by the University committee led by the law students Adriano Colucci and Alfredo Comandini.

What is certain is that the manifesto written by the organizing committee and subscribed by twenty-five students from the faculties of Law, Liberal Arts, Mathematics, Medicine, Natural Sciences and Engineering is dated 1876. In the manifesto, they asked for subscriptions (i.e. funding) from all over the world but they initially obtained only small amounts of money from the Ministry of Justice, of Education, of Public Works and the Home Office, as well as from masonic lodges and some foreign benefactors (especially English liberals). Furthermore, the municipality of Rome only very reluctantly supported the project. Two years later, many of the members of the committee had finished their studies and proposals to erect the statue in places other than Campo de' Fiori (like the courtyard of the university) scandalized the 1876 promoters. The location, as it was the case of all other monuments of the period, was crucial and in this very case essential. In 1884 a new, much larger university committee, led by Giuseppe Vernazzi, was founded. It included subscribers from France, England, Germany and Spain as well as university professors and members of Parliament. However, of most important significance is that the International Committee of Honor was made of leading intellectuals such as Victor Hugo, Rudolf von Jhering and Ferdinand Gregorovius. Among those stars, the name of Giuseppe Zanardelli appears for the first time. Ten years after the first manifesto, in June 1886, the committee, having collected enough money, formally asked the municipality for the piece of land on which the monument was to be erected. Even though the request was subscribed to by many important political leaders, including Zanardelli[20], the municipality resisted again: the proposed statue, representing Bruno while exposing his thought to the people, was still considered too provocative. Many compromises later, and in spite of Pope Leo XIII threatening to leave Rome for Austria if the monument were unveiled[21], the appointment of the anticlerical freemason Francesco Crispi as Prime Minister got things moving again and the monument was finally inaugurated on 9 June 1889. For this occasion, Mameli's Hymn, Italy's national anthem, of which the music was almost unknown until that moment, was "resurrected". [22]

In spite of all the difficulties, the promoters had convinced a very powerful "sponsor" already in 1876. The telegram sent by Giuseppe Garibaldi, Italy's national hero[23], was revealed only on the day of the inauguration:

---

[20]Passalalpi Ferrari, 2009. 40.

[21]Ponziani, Daniel. 2003. Il monumento a Giordano Bruno. In *Giuseppe Zanardelli, 1826–1903. Il coraggio della coerenza*. 114–116. Milano: Skira. 116.

[22]Porena, Manfredi. 1957. *Roma capitale nel decennio della sua adolescenza (1880–1890)*. Roma: Edizioni di storia e letteratura. 116.

[23]Giuseppe Garibaldi (Nice, 1807—Caprera, 1882) was a general, patriot and politician. It is commonly said that the Italian "Risorgimento" was "made" by four persons: Victor Emmanuel II (the king), Camillo Cavour (the politician and diplomat), Giuseppe Mazzini (the thinker) and Giuseppe Garibaldi (the soldier). This last one is certainly the most famous and beloved one. He was called the "Hero of Two Worlds" as he fought for the liberty and self-determination of the

> My dear friends, You have undertaken a holy action; a monument to Giordano Bruno, burned alive having the only fault of being a just man, a lover of Italy and of humankind. May the monument that you will erect for the great thinker and martyr deliver the final blow to the circus of these clowns who holiday on the right bank of the Tiber. I send you five liras for the monument, and I am, for the rest of my life, yours G. Garibaldi.[24]

5.2.2 The New Criminal Code

1889 was not only the year in which the personification of "pro-freedom of thought" and "anti-death penalty" ideals stood out in the heart of Rome. It was also the year of the promulgation of the so-called "Code Zanardelli", the first criminal code of unified Italy.

As a code is not only a body of laws elaborated by professional jurists but also a historical and cultural process which reflects political reasons and ideological concepts[25], this event has to be considered fundamental to fully understand the genesis of the Italian Supreme Court building. It bears the name of the Minister of Justice, who studied law at the University of Pavia (*Collegio Ghislieri*) for four years, until the university was closed because of the anti-Austrian rallies of 1848. He later obtained his degree from the University of Pisa.[26]

After the political unification, the main issue was to determine the legal system of the new kingdom. There were several possibilities: to extend Piedmont's legal system to the other regions, to preserve, as much as possible, the pre-unification structures or to create brand new laws.[27] The last alternative prevailed and in only four years Italy had its first four codes: the civil code, the commercial code, the code of civil procedure and the code of criminal procedure. Despite this very quick

---

people both in Europe and South America. His almost mythical figure is usually associated with the military enterprises that he undertook with his 1000 volunteers, known as "camicie rosse" because of the red shirts they used to wear instead of uniforms. Monsagrati, Giuseppe. 1999. Garibaldi, Giuseppe. In: *Dizionario Biografico degli Italiani* 52. Roma: Istituto dell'Enciclopedia Italiana. http://www.treccani.it/enciclopedia/giuseppe-garibaldi_%28Dizionario-Biografico%29/. Accessed 10 July 2016.

[24] "*Miei cari amici, Voi avete iniziato un'opera santa; un monumento a Giordano Bruno, bruciato vivo colla sola colpa di essere stato un uomo onesto ed amante dell'Italia e della umanità. Possa il monumento da voi eretto al gran pensatore e martire essere il colpo di grazia alla baracca di cotesti pagliacci che villeggiano sulla sponda destra del Tevere. Vi mando lire cinque pel monumento, e sono per la vita, vostro G. Garibaldi*": Bucciantini, 2015. 249.

[25] Lacché, Luigi. 1997. Un code pénal pour l'unité italienne: le Code Zanardelli (1889). La genèse, le débat, le projet juridique. In *Le pénal dans tous ses États. Justice, États et Sociétés en Europe (XIIe-XXe siècles)*, eds. Xavier Rousseaux, and René Levy, 303–319. Bruxelles: Facultés universitaires Saint-Louis. 303.

[26] Chiarini, Roberto. 2003. Biografia di Giuseppe Zanardelli. In *Giuseppe Zanardelli, 1826–1903. Il coraggio della coerenza*. Cit. 43–80.

[27] Padoa Schioppa, Antonio. 2007. *Storia del diritto in Europa. Dal medioevo all'età contemporanea*. Bologna: Il Mulino. 522–523.

legal unification, which nevertheless excluded criminal law for many years, obtaining a united judicial system was no easy task and Italy maintained five Courts of Cassation for criminal jurisdiction until 1888 (Turin, Florence, Naples, Palermo and Rome) and for civil jurisdiction until 1923. Rome was of course added only after 1870, when the territory of the future capital city was also conquered. In 1871 the relationships between the Kingdom of Italy and the Holy See were established by the so-called *Legge delle Guarentigie* ("Law of the Papal Guarantees"), according to which the Pope maintained complete freedom as a spiritual leader and the legal condition of a head of state. However, Pope Pius IX did not recognize this law and prevented Catholics from political activities for a long period of time (*bulla Non expedit*). The tension ended only in 1929, with the Lateran Pacts signed by Mussolini and Pope Pius XI.

Nevertheless, Italy had to wait almost thirty years for a new criminal code. What has been called "Beccaria's effect", i.e. the very early abolition of the death penalty in Tuscany thanks to the criminal code known as "Leopoldina" (1786), produced a disproportion between the various pre-unification Italian states and led to a debate that was destined to last for one century. After 1861, three criminal codes were in force in the Kingdom of Italy. The criminal code of the former Kingdom of Sardinia (1859) was extended to the Reign of Italy, except for the territory of the ex-Grand duchy of Tuscany, which maintained its 1853 code. The same code of the Kingdom of Sardinia was then modified to be applied in the Naples provinces and in Sicily.[28] The two main reasons for this lack of uniformity—not too unexpected for a nation that had still to be "invented" despite a common cultural background—, were the peculiarities of the Tuscan code (which did not foresee the death penalty) and the need to maintain public order in southern Italy, where the problem of brigandage was destined to trouble the minds of Italy's rulers for many decades. The debate regarding the death penalty in those years has been defined as the most topical among all debates that involved jurists (e.g. Pietro Ellero and Francesco Carrara) and public opinion.[29] In 1877, when the Chamber of Deputies approved the first book of the Criminal Code (only the last of many projects) as amended by the Minister of Justice Pasquale Stanislao Mancini, the jurist who "wrote little but did a lot against capital punishment"[30], the death penalty had already been de facto abolished in Italy thanks to the general pardon granted by King Umberto I. In 1883 Zanardelli had submitted a project very much inspired by the work of Luigi Lucchini, founder of the *Rivista penale*, member of Parliament, professor of criminal law, one of the leading figures of criminal law doctrine in nineteenth-century Italy. But it was only in 1887, when he was re-appointed Minister of Justice after four years that the project, conveniently modified, was ready to be approved. Also in this case Lucchini played

[28]Lacché, 1997. 305.

[29]Lacché, 1997. 307.

[30]See Mancini's speech: "Discorso al Parlamento sulla pena di morte" (Turin, 1865): Sbriccoli, Mario. 1990. La penalistica civile. Teorie e ideologie del diritto penale nell'Italia unita. In *Stato e cultura giuridica in Italia dalla Unità alla Repubblica*, ed. Aldo Schiavone, 147–232. Bari: Laterza. Footnote 31.

a leading role. On 30 June 1889, after the approval of the Chamber of Deputies and of the Senate, Zanardelli presented the code to the king, and it entered into force on 1 January 1890.

After thirty years of debates, this liberal-moderate code, an expression of the so called "Classic School" of criminal law, introduced many novelties (e.g. the distinction between crime and offence, a mitigation of the—typically French—severity towards crimes against property, an increase of the punishments for habitual criminals, the grant of a limited right to strike, etc.) but its most famous and symbolic feature is certainly the abolition of the death penalty. In the same year in which the construction of Zanardelli's "temple of justice" began, Italy had achieved complete legislative unification.

5.2.3 *Justice in Piazza Cavour*

Finally, 1889 was also the year in which the construction of the new Palace of Justice began. The day was 14 March, the birthday of King Umberto I. Twenty-two years later, on 11 January 1911, in time for the celebrations for the fifty years of the Reign of Italy, the building was inaugurated. Just a few months before the presentation of the new criminal code to the king, Zanardelli reached another goal: to build the temple of "his" liberal, secular and modern justice just next to the Vatican.

The competition for the Palace of Justice was won by Guglielmo Calderini, a fifty-year-old architect (and engineer) from Perugia, professor in several Italian universities, later author of the new *quadriportico* of the Basilica of Saint Paul outside the Walls (1890s). He conquered Zanardelli, who wanted, directed and controlled the competition in order to realize a monument that matched his idea of a "magnificent and severe" palace.[31]

The choice of the winning project had been difficult as several different juries discussed, argued and questioned the proposals over a period of five years. Some members of the commissions died in the meanwhile (Andrea Busiri-Vici replaced Giovanni Montiroli, president of the first artistic jury), some others renounced the task (Francesco Vespignani and Giuseppe Sacconi were respectively replaced by Enrico Gui and Gateano Koch). Those projects remained a dream in the head of their creators but nevertheless each of them shows a precise idea of justice. Furthermore, many other cities in Europe renovated or built their palaces of justice in the very same period, revealing different ways to glorify and legitimize the judiciary in the century of the struggles for national identities.

[31]Zanardelli, Giuseppe. *Relazione sull'approvazione del decreto*, (n.d. [30 June 1882]), p. 12, ms., in "Carte Zanardelli", b. 851, AS, Brescia. Quoted in: Rossi Kirk, 1996. 84. Footnote 5.

5.2.4 A Wind of Change? New Palaces of Justice in Nineteenth-Century Europe

In the century of romantic nationalisms, a wind of architectural renovation and construction involving the palaces of justice of many states blew over Europe. Zanardelli himself, on the occasion of the foundation stone-laying ceremony, compared Rome, the city which gave legal knowledge to "all nations", with Vienna, Brussels, London, Paris and Leipzig, all cities which, in those very years, built or renovated their "admired and superb" palaces of justice.[32] And he underlined how, in Vienna and Brussels, they used the effigies of "*our* jurists and orators" in order to symbolize the glory of legal disciplines.[33]

In the introduction of the important work "La justice en ses temples", Alain Girardet, in 1992 Secretary general of the French Association for the History of Justice, complained about the absence of comprehensive and interdisciplinary studies on the architecture of the "cathedrals of justice" in France.[34] Apparently, the same fate occurred to all palaces of justice that will be briefly described here, a fate that is probably to be ascribed to the severe judgment that very rapidly followed the triumph of eclecticism. This was not an exclusively European feature. For instance, in the United States, the courthouses "were wildly eclectic—multi-storied, turreted, towered, gabled—as various architects embellished styles known as Greek Revival, French Second Empire, Italianate, Gothic, Neoclassical, Victorian, and Beaux-Arts".[35] In 1953 Marcello Piacentini, one of the leading architects of Italian rationalism, despite his admiration for the *Palais the Justice* in Brussels, described the period between 1860 and 1880 as "narrow" and "desperate", a kind of Greco-Roman catastrophe necessary to finally "liberate" architecture in order to let it fly towards the clear skies of modernity.[36]

---

[32]For a brief overview see: Pevsner, Nikolaus. 1976. *A History of Building Types*. Princeton University Press. Italian edition: Pevsner. Nikolaus. 1986. *Storia e caratteri degli edifici*. Trans. G. Bestelli. Roma: Fratelli Palombi. 71–82.

[33]Zanardelli, 1889. ix.

[34]"Or, ces bâtiments imposants, situés au cœur de la cité et qui semblent s'adosser à une légitimité éternelle, tels des cathédrales du droit, n'ont paradoxalement pas trouvé la place qui leur revient dans l'ensemble des études architecturales portant sur le XIXe siècle": Girardet, Alain. 1992. *La justice en ses temples. Regards sur l'architecture judiciaire en France*, 15–19. Poitiers: Brissaud. 15.

[35]Resnik, Judith and Curtis, Dennis. 2011. *Representing Justice. Invention, Controversy, and Rights in City-States and Democratic Courtrooms*. New Haven - London: Yale University Press. 137.

[36]"Nella seconda metà del secolo XIX, dunque, prima ancora della sazietà del classicismo, dal 1860 al 1880, si videro gli ultimi sprazzi della tradizione, le ultime scintille greco-romane, una esplosione definitiva, quasi a fissare la fine di un periodo, di un'epoca. E appunto per questo, un'èra non serena, non pronta ad una lunga e lenta maturazione, sana e consapevole; ma un periodo stretto, disperato, che si avvicinava allo sfacelo e preparava, con la catastrofe, l'avvento della liberazione, verso cieli limpidi e chiarissimi, additati poco dopo dal Ruskin, dall'Olbrich,

5.2.5 Outside Italy

London chose the Victorian gothic style for its Royal Courts of Justice, which house the High Court and Court of Appeal of England and Wales. George Edmund Street prevailed among the group of eleven architects competing for the contract and in less than ten years (1874–1882), Queen Victoria could inaugurate the Law Courts located on the Strand, near the border with the City of London but still within the City of Westminster, and surrounded by the four Inns of Court.[37] The iconographical project, even though it included the heads of important judges and lawyers carved over the outer porch, was more related to divine justice, embracing a tradition well established in northern Europe[38], with Jesus (the Supreme Judge of the Last Judgement) represented at the top of the upper arch while Solomon (the wise judge) and Alfred the Great (the learned and merciful king) were positioned at a lower level.

Paris opted for a fusion of late Renaissance architecture and neo-classicism cleverly reinvented.[39] The Parisian Palace of Justice, located in the very center of the city, on the *Île de la Cité*, has a very long history, dating back to the Gallo-Roman period. The Merovingian dynasty rebuilt the Roman palace, which became the first building permanently occupied by the Frankish Realm ready to conquer and unify France. The last important transformation took place between 1835 and 1914, involving four generations of architects who interpreted, according to the changing political and cultural environment, the project laid down by Jean-Nicolas Huyot between 1835 and 1840. The names of Joseph-Louis Duc, Honoré Daumet and Albert Tournaire emerge among the others. Thirty years after the re-organization of the French legal system under Napoleon, the government finally decided to renovate the *Palais*, which had to host the *Prefecture de police* of Paris, the courts and tribunals of the city, of the department and of the region and finally the Court of Cassation. This renovation of a preexisting complex of buildings has been interpreted both as a point of departure for a post-revolutionary institutional architecture and, in particular in the western façade designed by Duc (in front of *Rue de Harlay*), as a creative fusion of classical order and more "romantic" elements, such as arcades divided into segments and vaults representing, respectively, the Code Napoleon (and indirectly the Justinian Code) and its strict interpretation (exacerbated by the *École de l'exégèse*), and the need for equity in its widest sense. Also the Court of Cassation was "re-invented", in the very same

dall'Hoffman". Piacentini, Marcello. 1953. *Considerazioni sull'Urbanistica e l'Architettura di Roma e altrove*. Roma: Ars Nova. 124.

[37]1883 (repr. 1977). *The Royal Courts of Justice. Illustrated Handbook*. London: Wildy & Sons Ltd.

[38]See for example: Martyn, Georges. 2006. Painted *Exempla Iustitiae* in the Southern Netherlands. In *Symbolische Kommunikation vor Gericht in der frühen Neuzeit*, ed. Reiner Schulze, 335–356. Berlin: Duncker & Humblot.

[39]Taylor, Katherine Fisher. 1992. Le code et l'équité. La transformation du Palais de Justice de Paris au XIXe siècle. In *La justice en ses temples*. Cit. 83–127.

period, by Joseph-Louis Duc. Located on the *Quai de l'Horloge*, it reminds one much more of the late French Renaissance.

The Palace of Justice (*Oberster Gerichtshof*) of the Austro-Hungarian Empire was inaugurated on 22 May 1881 by Emperor Franz Josef I, seven years after the Imperial Ruling which decreed that it had to be constructed in Vienna "in permanent solicitude for the needs of the administration of justice and the population in its quest for justice".[40] The architect was the Viennese Alexander Wielemans, Edler von Monteforte, who realized what is considered (again) a major example of historicism, i.e., eclecticism.

In Leipzig, the new seat of the *Reichsgerichtshof* (Imperial Court of Justice) of the German Reich (established in 1879, the same year in which the Imperial Justice Laws came into effect) was designed by two architects: Ludwig Hoffmann and Peter Dybwad. It was built between 1888 and 1895 and housed the supreme criminal and civil courts until 1945. The design was, once more, the result of a mixture of architectural models: the Italian Renaissance style on one hand—but in this case enriched by a central dome and a large portico on the main façade—, and the French Baroque on the other. It is now the seat of the Federal Administrative Court.

Among the palaces of justice mentioned by Zanardelli, Brussels' *Palais de Justice* (Fig. 5.2) is certainly the one that really influenced Calderini. Also known as "the Mammoth", the masterpiece of architect Joseph Poelaert (supported by the technical skills of engineer François Wellens) is a triumph of eclecticism, which combines classical elements with a taste for Mesopotamic and Hellenistic orientalism[41]. The program was established by a committee of magistrates and was approved by the government. It had to host all the civil and military jurisdictions covering an area of 26.000 m^2 on the *Galgenberg* hill (the "Mount of gallows", where once criminals were hanged), thus dominating, until today, the entire city. Two elements particularly characterize the building: the imposing dome (realized after Poelaert's death and surrounded by four bronze statues representing Strength, Justice, Royal Mercy and Law), and the central portico, pediment and attic, balcony and balustrade, with the bust of the goddess Athena on top. According to the Minister of Justice Jules Bara it was destined to become "the most beautiful, not to say the *only* monument of the nineteenth century"[42] and seventy years after the inauguration (15 October 1883) Marcello Piacentini still considered it the "most significant and representative" architectural achievement of the nineteenth century.[43] Nevertheless, it was harshly criticized for having costed 50 million Belgian francs, for having no concept and no soul, for not containing any clear symbol

[40]http://ogh.gv.at/en/palace-of-justice/construction. Accessed 24 August 2015.

[41]Marconi, 2006. 14.

[42]*Le Palais de Justice*. 2012 (2001). Bruxelles ville d'art et d'histoire 31. Bruxelles: Ministère de la Région Bruxelles-Capitale et al. 23.

[43]"una delle opere architettoniche più importanti del mondo, certamente la più significativa e rappresentativa del secolo scorso". Piacentini, 1953. 126.

explaining its function. In a word, for being "monstrously babelish".[44] Almost thirty years later, Calderini had to face most of these critiques too.

5.2.6 *The Failing Projects for the Italian Palace of Justice: Looking for a "National Style"*

As mentioned above, many western countries that built new courthouses during the second half of the nineteenth century identified their "national style" with eclecticism, often referring to ancient Rome. Paradoxically, eclecticism seems therefore to have been the "national style" of many different nations. Italy's real peculiarity was to emphasize reference to historical figures rather than focus only on abstract concepts such as law and justice.

In May 1881, when a specific *Concorso dello Stato* foreseeing the construction of a new courthouse was approved[45] with the idea of rejecting "well-connected persons" and opening the doors to architects and artists chosen through public competitions (foreigners excluded), Zanardelli was about to be appointed Minister of Justice for the first time (29 May 1881–25 May 1883). The building had to be "grand and severe".[46] In 1882, in accordance with the Mayor of Rome Luigi Pianciani and with the "activist in Roman art and reconciliatory politics" Prince Baldassarre Odescalchi[47], he decided that the location of the new building should be in the area of *Prati di Castello*, on the other side of the river Tiber with respect to the city centre: a place of fields and vineyards very near to St. Peter's Basilica. He resigned before the end of the first, inconclusive, competition, but regained his role in time for the second one, and was reappointed Minister of Justice from April 1887 until February 1891.

After the location was soon decided, the real problem was to define a "national style", not only for the "temple of justice" but for the whole new kingdom.

The *Sinistra storica* has been described as having a real obsession for flamboyant buildings and imposing monuments, especially if compared to the lack of interest of the *Destra storica* (Liberal or Historical Right) for this rhetorical architectural language, perhaps partly motivated by the will to limit conflicts with

---

[44]*Le Palais de Justice*, 42. See also: Piacentini, 1953. 126–127. According to Verlaine: "C'est babélique, et Michel-Angesque, avec du Piranesi, et un peu, peut-on dire, de folie... Extérieurement c'est un colosse, intérieurement c'est un monstre; se veut être immense, et ce l'est", quoted in: Pevsner, 1986. 77.

[45]Legge 14 maggio (Law 14 May) 1881 n. 209: Regio decreto (Royal decree) n. 1309, "Gazzetta ufficiale del Regno d'Italia" n. 120 (23 May 1883), 2235–2237.

[46]"dovrà presentare un aspetto grandioso e severo". Ibid.

[47]Rossi Kirk, 1996. 84.

the Pope. The decision to adopt a kind of imperial style for the new kingdom was not necessary nor unavoidable, considering the very strong municipal and regional Italian roots.[48]

The political leaders of the *Sinistra* and their architects decided to refer to ancient Rome or to the Renaissance period but the dilemma was how to do so in an innovative way. This choice determined the failure of all projects that evoked a different idea of "national style" and in particular those referring to local peculiarities. For reasons related to the secularization of the new kingdom, all projects reminiscent of elements typical of the Catholic architecture were refused: domes and bell towers above all. The Roman landscape had been dominated by "papal monuments" for centuries and this image had to be changed.[49]

The first architectural competition (1883–84) did not result in any winner. As in the very same months other architectural competitions were underway (Monument to Victor Emanuel II and renovation of Palazzo Montecitorio), many of the most prominent architects of the period did not participate and only twenty-six projects were submitted to a jury of twenty-four members (one-third architects, two-thirds bureaucratic officials) and chaired by the Minister of Justice.[50] Architects of the *Accademia di San Luca* constituted the artistic subcommittee. Each project had a title and in theory its architects were anonymous. In practice, it was usually known who were the architects behind the designs, as Ernesto Basile ironically pointed out, entitling his project "Basile". Just to give a few examples of the entries: entry n. 21 "SPQR" was considered too late-baroque to give severity to a grand building; entry n. 14 "Elsa" was dominated by an iron and glass dome, reminding of Antonelli's synagogue in Turin (1863) and Wallot's *Reichstag* in Berlin (competition of 1882); entry n. 16 "Iustitia" opted for a Doric temple portico and a tall clock tower; entry n. 4 "Giustizia", with its Corinthian temple main entrance and its eclectic references to Byzantine churches and Piranesian fascinations was described by some critics as resulting in the "mausoleum of justice" rather than in its temple[51]; entry 15 "Basile" opted for a Florentine Quattrocento style. Being characterized by elements referable to the Catholic Church's architecture (domes) or to "not-enough-national" styles (Greek/Roman temples) or to regional traditions (the *Palazzo della Signoria* in Florence), all the projects of the first competition failed.

[48]According to Robin Williams, before 1876, government buildings and palaces in Rome as well as in Italy were designed according to the neo-Cinquecento style. In practice, they were not distinguishable from the *real* Cinquecento buildings. Williams, Robin. 1996. The image of secular power: The *Romanità* of Italian state architecture under the Sinistra, 1876–90. In *Guglielmo Calderini. La costruzione di un'architettura*. Cit. 9–23. 9.

[49]On 4 April 1861 Ferdinand Gregorovius still noted (a few lines after having criticized the decision to make "the moral center of the world" the capital city of a *too young* Reign of Italy: "… auf jedem Schritt nur Erinnerungen und Monumente der Päpste (…), Kirchen, Klöster, Museen, Fontänen, Paläste, Obelisken mit dem Kreuz..": Kruft, Hanno-Walter and Völkel, Markus (eds.). 1991. *Gregorovius, Ferdinand. Römische Tagebücher (1852–1889)*. München: Beck. 129.

[50]According to art. 10 of the Law 14 May 1881 n. 209. Cit.

[51]Rossi Kirk, 1996. 88.

The jury members "insisted upon three, continuous floor levels, rejected towers and cupolas and were generally negative on all elements that broke the horizontal line of the cornice and challenged the traditional architectural image of churches".[52]

The forty-four participants of the second competition (1885–87)[53] took advantage, as it was often the case at that time, of the publicly exhibited projects of their predecessors: some ideas were copied, and the evaluation criteria were now clearer. The artistic subcommittee, when the jury was reconvened on 30 May 1886, was almost entirely changed. The president, architect Andrea Busiri-Vici, was elected during the first meeting. The jury explicitly stated its criteria: the building had to be stable and apt to assure a peaceful and comfortable use as well as appropriate to its function without resembling a prison or a fortress.[54] But these were still very vague criteria and they certainly evolved during the process of examination. Apparently domes and bell towers were not sanctioned because they were non-appropriate but simply for aesthetic reasons: because they were considered ugly or not sufficiently "grand and severe". What was mainly sanctioned, however, was the wrong distribution of spaces and the lack of light. Entry n. 6 "Qui adspicis benevolus esto" was considered incomplete and defective in the distribution of space; entry n. 7 "Currite sedit" lacked of some of the locations required and was insufficiently illuminated; entry n. 8 "Amore all'arte" did not have the necessary magnificence and entry n. 12 "Arme nuove" no artistic value at all; entry n. 14 "Aria e luce" did not provide comfortable communications between the parts open to the public; entry n. 35 "Irnerio" presented many locations that were considered too small (e.g. corridors or the records office) or not conveniently located (e.g. the public toilets) and so on. First seven projects were selected and finally only four remained: n. 15 "Areopago" (A. Guerra); n. 18 "Imponente" (G. Calderini); n. 19 "Ernesto Basile" and n. 41 "Ape" (A. Marchesi).[55]

Even though they differed in many aspects, they all had in common to be horizontal, without domes or towers and with large courtyards: "all the architects chosen as finalists proposed images that gave to the secular institution an identity in contrast to Saint Peter's [Basilica]".[56]

The full commission had waited seven months for the artistic deliberations but, apparently, the bureaucrats suspected that no project was really worth developing as four finalists were too many. Once again, the competition did not lead to any

[52]Ibid. 92.

[53]All the details of the competition were described on the "Gazzetta ufficiale": *Commissione ministeriale per il secondo concorso del Palazzo di Giustizia da erigersi in Roma*, in "Gazzetta ufficiale", n. 70 (25 March 1887), Date 5 February 1887. 1652–59. file:///C:/Users/Utente/Downloads/RG1887_03_25_070_PM.pdf. Accessed 14 August 2015.

[54]"(…) l'edificio dovrà offrire, e nell'insieme, e nei particolari, dimensioni e forme tali che, mentre ne assicurino la stabilità permanente ed il tranquillo e comodo uso, contribuiscano nel tempo stesso a dargli il carattere richiesto dall'alta sua destinazione; senza che perciò abbia l'aspetto di un carcere o di un fortilizio": *Commissione ministeriale per il secondo concorso*. Cit. 1652.

[55]Ibid.

[56]Rossi Kirk, 1996. 109.

decision. As a consequence, the members of the *Accademia di San Luca* who were also members of the artistic jury not only resigned from any further involvement in the competition but also asked Prime Minister Agostino Depretis to choose the definitive project using his executive powers. On 4 April 1887, only a few days after Busiri's letter to Depretis, Diego Tajani was ousted and Zanardelli reinstalled as Minister of Justice.[57] He took things in hand.

Zanardelli, in fact, opened a third competition on 25 May 1887, this time limited to (probably) seven finalists who were invited (by means of a letter of the Minister of Justice and not through a ministerial or royal decree) to rework their designs by the end of September[58]. He took the entire responsibility and completely renewed the artistic jury, excluding the academicians who had resigned. Andrea Scala, a prominent architect of theatres, became the president, Giuseppe Sacconi replaced Gaetano Koch and Antonio Tagliaferri, the most important architect in late-nineteenth-century Brescia, designer of Zanardelli's country villa in Maderno, was invited to join the jury. It was completed by two engineers and by two members of the mayor's office. Some of the candidates did not participate and the competition was narrowed to Calderini, Basile and Manfredo Manfredi (entry n. 37: "ΔIKH"). The artistic jury rejected the temple-style façade with external stairs and the central transverse hall proposed by Manfredi and on 19 October 1887 the full commission engaged Calderini and Basile in a "head-to-head final run-off competition"[59]: they had forty days to rework their designs again. Zanardelli took care of this "final rush" at the point that he met both architects in order to explain how, according to his opinion, their projects should be improved. *He* imposed the open central courtyard instead of the central covered space and *he* decreed that the top-most floor did not need to extend the entire width of the building. The result was communicated on 4 November 1887: Calderini won six votes to two. The jury unanimously approved the executive project on 5 October 1888 only after some modifications proposed by a specially appointed commission (and, as usual, by Zanardelli himself) were introduced.

---

[57]Busiri-Vici, Andrea. Letter to A. Depretis. Rome, 26 March 1887. In PMC, 1889, b. 100, f. 4, d. 15, ACS Roma. Quoted in Rossi Kirk, 1996. Footnote 168.

[58]According to Terry Rossi Kirk the commission admitted seven finalists even though the former artistic commission had already excluded n. 37 ΔIKH, n. 38 "Giustiniano" and n. 40 "Comodità, salubrità e decoro". Rossi Kirk, 1996. 110–111. The various competitions are cleverly summarized by Calderini himself: "Il programma del concorso nazionale per ottenere il progetto del Palazzo di Giustizia fu inizialmente preparato da S.E. *Zanardelli*; e durante i Ministri *Pessina* e *Tajani* si mandarono ad effetto due concorsi architettonici senza alcun frutto. Tornato Zanardelli al potere, emanò un invito, in data 25 maggio 1887, agli architetti italiani, onde prendessero parte alla gara (…). Tre gare ebbero luogo, dove i concorrenti migliori furono ridotti prima a *sette*, poi a *quattro* ed infine a *due* (…).": Calderini, 1908. 3–4.

[59]Rossi Kirk, 1996. 115.

5.2.7 Zanardelli's Concept and Calderini's Vision

It has been observed that "architecture is the vehicle of the myth", that the very building housing a court creates a boundary in which "legal ritual is circumscribed in initiatory and institutional terms" and that it is thanks to architecture that the "invisible reality of Law is anchored to the immediacy of the physical and social order"[60]. In the case of the Italian Supreme Court the myths were two: Italy and Rome, its geographical as well as ideological centre.

When the Supreme Court was finally inaugurated in 1911, Senator Oronzo Quarta, General Prosecutor of the Court of Cassation, made a speech during which he reminded his audience that "if we look back at our history we will clearly see how times of light and darkness, of rebirth and decay, of glory and obscurantism, followed the fact that we referred to or we departed from Romanism"[61]. Furthermore, in exalting the majesty and perfection of the new building, he could not avoid making reference to the man that "made" the Court as it was and died before seeing it completed, the "great Lombard soul" who took care of the building with love and waited for its completion with feverish anxiety[62]. The "great Lombard soul" was of course Giuseppe Zanardelli who, twenty-three years before, in a speech made before the Italian Senate about the necessity of a *unique* criminal Supreme Court, clearly stated that it had to have its seat in Rome, the new capital, the origin of legal learning:

> ...if the Italian cities can recognize a supremacy to Rome, this supremacy belongs to jurisprudence; if there is a field in which Rome has to represent Italy, this is precisely the field of law[63].

One year later, when the first stone of the new palace was laid down, he was asked to make a speech before the king. He could finally express all his ideas on what he defined the "sanctuary of justice"[64]:

---

[60]Evans, David. 1999. Theatre of deferral: The image of the law and the architecture of the Inns of Court. In *Law and Critique* 10: 1–25. 8.

[61]Quarta, Oronzo. 1911. *Discorso pronunciato dal Senatore Oronzo Quarta, Procuratore generale presso la Corte di Cassazione di Roma, per la inaugurazione del Palazzo di Giustizia di Roma il giorno XI gennaio MDCCCCXI.* Roma: Tipografia dell'Unione Editrice. 6–7. "Se volgiamo lo sguardo alla nostra istoria ci apparirà chiaro, come i tempi di luce e di tenebre, di rinascimento e di decadenza, di gloria e di oscurantismo, seguirono sempre secondo che ci volgemmo al Romanesimo, o dal Romanesimo di dipartimmo".

[62]"antesignano la grande anima lombarda di Giuseppe Zanardelli, che ne promosse e sospinse sempre con sentimento di forte, profonda italianità, e, sino agli estremi momenti della sua vita curò con amore, ed attese con ansia febbrile la desiata attuazione". Ibid. 4.

[63]"...se le città italiane possono consentire a Roma un primato è appunto questo della giurisprudenza; se havvi campo in cui a Roma s'addice di rappresentare l'Italia, è precisamente il campo del diritto": 13 March 1888, Discourse at the Italian Senate, in Zanardelli, Giuseppe. 1905. *Discorsi parlamentari di Giuseppe Zanardelli pubblicati per deliberazione della Camera dei Deputati.* Roma: Tipografia della Camera dei Deputati. Vol. 2. 373–389. 388.

[64]Zanardelli, 1889. v.

> [...] here where law had its cradle and its glory, the Palace of justice has to rise up not unequal to those built in the other metropolises of the civilized world. By now, in this Capital of the Kingdom, Tribunals and Courts have such disproportioned and indecorous seats that all the dignity of the place appears to be lost. Therefore, one could almost say that it would be preferable to administer justice in the open air, as Saint Louis King of France did under the historical oak of Vincennes.[65]

Finally, as we have seen, Claderini's project "Imponente" (Imposing) was chosen to represent justice in the city where "law had its cradle and its glory", successfully combining, as Zanardelli wanted, art and utility, hygiene and comfort.[66]

Calderini was one of the oldest participants and, thanks to his experience, he probably had a leg up on most of the other architects. He proposed—only in the second competition—a heavily rusticated neo-Cinquecento style building, exposed by means of twenty-one very much appreciated presentation drawings realized with the help of a talented student assistant, Ulpiano Bucci. The plan presented four courtyards distributed around a central cross, containing the areas open to public circulation with a covered *salle des pas perdus* at the centre. He explicitly referred to other European courts (Paris, Brussels, Vienna, Berlin, London and Leipzig) in supporting the utility of this space but he renamed it with the Italian words *ambulatorio centrale* and added some Doric rusticated details that gave the space a less "foreign" touch. In the major open space (*cortile d'onore*) he added a *scalone d'onore* (main staircase) that was destined to remain one of the most original and appreciated features of the building. In order to match the required severity and secularity, he studied selected architectural models such as those of Palladio and Vignola, the sixteenth-century masters whose architectural treatises were part of Italian academic education. Their works, certainly together with the works that Galeazzo Alessi realized in Perugia, forged Calderini's imaginary. As those artists came from northern Italy, Calderini tried to make his project more "Roman" by underlining the connection to Palazzo Farnese and Palazzo della Cancelleria[67], especially with reference to the proportions of the building and the *cortile d'onore*.

---

[65](...) qui dove il diritto ebbe la sua culla e la sua gloria, il Palazzo di giustizia sorga non impari a quelli edificati nelle altre metropoli del mondo civile. Al presente, in questa Capitale del Regno i Tribunali e le Corti hanno sedi così sproporzionate ed indecorose che ogni dignità del luogo appare perduta, sicché quasi potrebbe dirsi preferibile che la giustizia venisse resa all'aperto, come da San Luigi re di Francia sotto la storica quercia di Vincennes". Ibid. vii.

[66]"Arduo era il problema a sciogliere, poiché colle ragioni dell'arte, meno che mai trascurabili in un monumento che deve sorgere presso alla mole Adriana, non lungi dalla sublime cupola di Michelangelo, dovevansi conciliare le ragioni eminentissime dell'utilità pratica, dell'igiene, della comodità, della sicurezza indispensabili in un palazzo di giustizia, e i quali, per i limiti e le condizioni che impongono nella costruzione e distribuzione delle parti, frenano e mortificano la fantasia dell'artista". Ibid. vi.

[67]Rossi Kirk, 1997. 107.

The rusticated style inspired to sixteenth-century secular architecture particularly convinced the jury of the second competition: Gaetano Koch defined it magnificent, noble and severe[68].

However, because of the third competition and of the final head-to-head match with Ernesto Basile, the project had to be reworked twice before being approved. For the third competition, Calderini seriously took into account the critiques he received from the jury. One crucial point was that the building risked being too dark and he therefore aimed to create a plan that allowed the building to be clear, spontaneous, airy and easily accessible from all sides, avoiding mazy paths. "Light and air everywhere"! he wrote.[69] In particular, he designed eight big courtyards instead of four, maintaining the same dimensions of the four original by removing some porticos.[70] To connect the different parts of the building, he preferred wide galleries with windows: our ancestors, he wrote, used and even abused porticos, but they had a much stronger constitution. The open air was not convenient for magistrates and clerks used to sitting in well-heated rooms.[71] He then substituted the tall covered hall (the *salle des pas perdus*), with three one-story "ambulatories" in order to separate very clearly the *collegi giudiziari*, this way obtaining wide spaces before all courtrooms. From a stylistic point of view, he even emphasized the use of rustication, trying to imitate the grandiosity and severity of famous non-religious constructions and creating at the same time a contrast with the smooth surfaces of Saint Peter's Basilica. Finally, he very much focused on the importance of the

[68]"Grandioso è lo stile, carattere nobile e severo". Ibid. 103.

[69]"Siano dunque rispettati tutti i dogmi del buon organismo onde la pianta riesca semplice, chiara, spontanea, ariosa, e di facile accesso a tutte le parti (…). Luce ed aria dappertutto, perché questa è condizione precipua degli edifici da edificarsi in qualsiasi città del regno, ma è indispensabile in Roma e, ciò che più conta, in un edificio che, in questa città, è destinato a raccogliere a massa la gente. Questi furono i criteri che mi servirono di base per incarnare il secondo progetto che oggi presento". Calderini, Guglielmo. 1887. *Relazione esplicativa del progetto per il palazzo di giustizia in Roma, modificato e ripresentato per invito di s. E. Il Ministro di Grazia e giustizia*, Perugia: Tilli. 4.

[70]Ibid. 5.

[71]"I nostri antichi fecero, più che un uso, un abuso de porticati da tener luogo interamente di corridoi di comunicazione, ed io stesso, nel primo progetto, introdussi i portici per le comunicazioni tra i diversi offici interni: facendo però così, io feci omaggio all'arte, ma tradii il comodo. I nostri maggiori erano di fibra più forte di noi; i tempi in cui vissero non faceano sentire il bisogno dei mille comodi e dei tanti riguardi che noi oggi esigiamo; l'aria era il miglior ospite degli appartamenti; ma noi, delicati bocchini e stomacuzzi di molli cenci e di non nata carta (come ci chiama il Gozzi) non possiamo seguire lo stesso concetto architettonico, e l'arte della sesta, che è lo specchio ed il teatro della società, bisogna che appunto in questo proposito cambi la massima. Perché sia salva l'igiene, ai porticati aperti devono sostituirsi gallerie chiuse da finestre, non essendo certo salutare che i Magistrati ed impiegati, chiusi tutto il giorno entro offici corredati di caminetti e stufe, abbiano poi da trovarsi improvvisamente esposti alle forti correnti aree di un porticato aperto per recarsi da un officio all'altro come sempre loro ne accada il bisogno". Ibid. 23.

scalone d'onore and on its symbolic value as it had to lead the visitor to the *piano nobile* and then to the *Aula Massima* (later frescoed by Cesare Maccari and Paride Pascucci) which constitutes the very heart of the whole building.[72]

In October 1887, when the jury selected Calderini's and Basile's projects for the head-to-head final match, Calderini took advantage of Zanardelli's "suggestion" not to extend the top-most floor to the entire building. This way, the monumentality augmented but the façade remained essentially horizontal, as requested. He reintroduced, for the main entrance, the wide arch (*grande arcone centrale*) of his very first project and maintained the rusticated surfaces for the lower portion of the building while for the upper floors he opted for "ashlar masonry walls on the piano nobile and an Ionic columnar order".[73] In this case too, the idea to "soften" the building came from the Minister of Justice.

The final result was a kind of "baroque classicism", contaminated by Piranesi's drawings (see for example his "Carceri") and by Mesopotamic fascinations, which were fashionable in the French area.[74] The drawings still preserved in the archives of the Supreme Court testify that Calderini wanted to create a complete artwork, which included sculptures, decorations and furniture, all designed by the architect himself or under his control.[75] Calderini certainly could not imagine that nowadays the main entrance is located in Piazza Cavour. As a result, his beloved open courtyard remains oddly relegated to a kind of backyard.

5.3 Talking Statues: The Legal-Historical Iconography of the Supreme Court[76]

The architecture of the palaces of justice is certainly to be considered a "talking" architecture, destined to give a message concerning a certain idea or ideal of justice. In the Italian Supreme Court this effect is multiplied by the presence of its peculiar

[72]"E' questa la sede della suprema autorità giudiziaria, e quivi l'architetto è d'uopo s'inchini, offrendo a questa parte più eletta del tempio di Temi la grazia migliori dell'arte della sesta. Grandiosità, severità e decoro devono accumunarsi insieme per rendere i primi onori a questa benemerita istituzione della civiltà, che sopra ogni altra com'aquila vola". Ibid. 18–19.

[73]Rossi Kirk, 1996. 118.

[74]Marconi, 2006. 14.

[75]Neri, Maria Luisa. 2006. Forma esistenziale e forma effettuale: dal disegno alla realtà. I dettagli decorativi del Palazzo di Giustizia. In *I tesori nascosti della Corte di Cassazione*. Cit. 43–50.

[76]For a unique collection of beautiful pictures of the statues of the Supreme Court see those by Mauro Margutti in: Manodori Sagredo, Alberto (ed.). 2007. *La Corte di Cassazione. Le opera d'arte del Palazzo di Giustizia di Roma*. Roma: Gangemi. See also the website of the Supreme Court: http://www.cortedicassazione.it/corte-di-cassazione/it/statue.page. Accessed 24 August 2015.

decoration, made of a kind of procession of jurists.[77] Some of them are placed directly on the street, strangely reminiscent of a very rooted feature of the eternal city: its talking statues.

5.3.1 From Pasquino to Ulpian

The famous Pasquino but also "il Babuino", "Madama Lucrezia", "Marforio", "il Facchino" and "l'Abate Luigi" are statues that have embodied for centuries the ironic, critical, even vulgar spirit of the Roman people.[78] The city cannot be fully understood without considering the role they played since the sixteenth century, when anonymous authors started to attach to the statues satiric messages (often verses), in Italian or Latin, to criticize the authorities. The best-known one is located near Piazza Navona and is called "Pasquino". For this reason, all the jokes, opinions and proposals that suddenly appear on the statues even today are called "pasquinate".[79]

The numerous statues that decorate the Supreme Court (Figs. 5.1, 5.3, 5.4 and 5.5) were certainly thought to give a different message: they are not there to criticize the institutions but rather to support and legitimize them. Nevertheless, they are talking statues too and some similarities with their less dignified "relatives" can be drawn. The attitude of the Roman jurists, portrayed both on the side of the court which was originally designed as the main entrance and in the open courtyard, is indeed very peculiar. They seem to talk to the man of the street, to ask him if he needs their advice, to suggest a winning defense strategy. While the statues attached to the wall of the building are standing in more imposing positions, the statues at the feet of the steps are sitting, as if lawyers waiting for their clients to be received. Licinius Crassus (Fig. 5.4) turns his head as someone who has just been called or wants to hear or look at someone in a relaxed and serious attitude; Salvius Iulianus (Fig. 5.1) is deeply immersed in his thoughts; Modestinus is an old man concentrated in reading and Gaius (Fig. 5.5) a very young lawyer looking towards the future with a papyrus scroll in his right hand.

In a certain sense, they are not talking *for* the people (like Pasquino) but *to* the people.

In telling the adventurous story that led to the erection of the statue of Giordano Bruno in Campo de' Fiori, we did not refer to the statue dedicated to the rebel monk by Pietro Masulli and positioned in 1865 in the *Cortile del Salvatore* of the University of Naples. That monument has been described by Massimo Bucciantini

[77]According to Catherine Brice, the Italian *statuomanie* of the end of the nineteenth century is the result of two heritages: the one of the French Revolution and the one of the Catholic Church, in particular of its baroque dimension. Brice, 1996. 1.

[78]For an overview of the talking statues see the website created by a group of residents of Rome's historical center: http://www.statueparlantiroma.it/index.htm. Accessed 17 July 2016.

[79]Giannottu, Caterina. 2011. Un narratore arguto e antichissimo. Pasquino in Parione e la satira in Roma fra tradizione e modernità. In *Clio. Rivista trimestrale di Studi Storici*. 47 (1): 123–145.

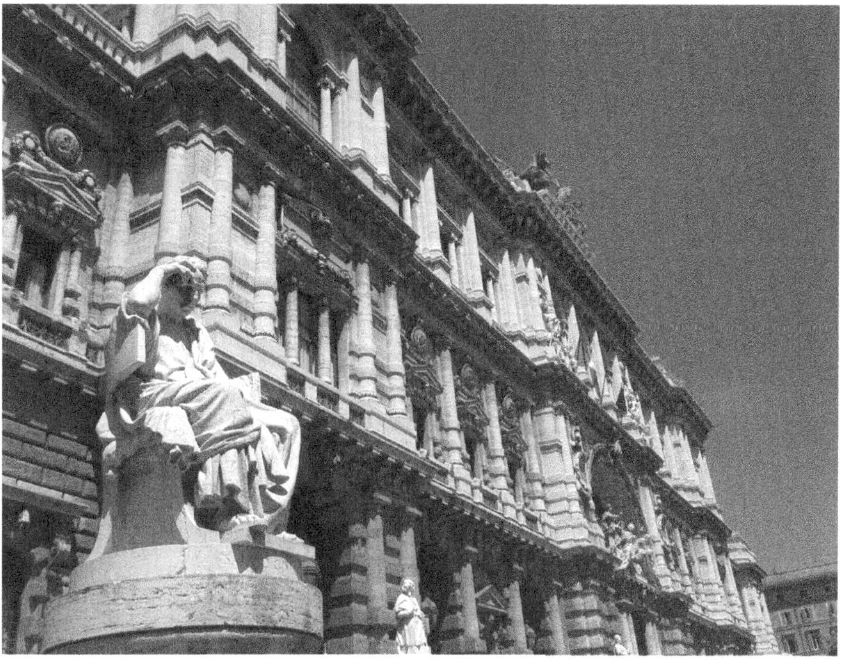

Fig. 5.1 Former main entrance of the Italian Supreme Court of Cassation on the Tiber bank (Piazza dei Tribunali). Emilio P. Gallori: Statue of Salvius Iulianus. All pictures by Stefania Gialdroni

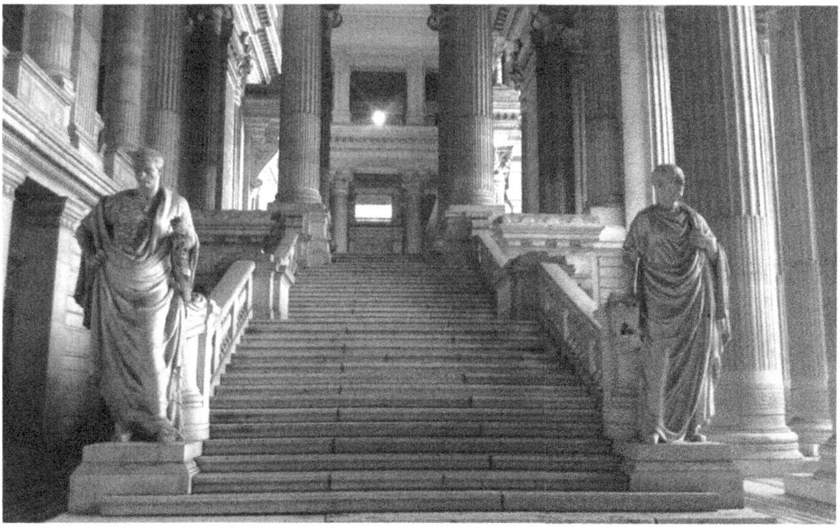

Fig. 5.2 *Palais de Justice*, Brussels. Peristyle. One of the two monumental stairs leading to the first floor. Antoine-Félix Bouré (1883), statues of Ulpian (left) and Cicero (right)

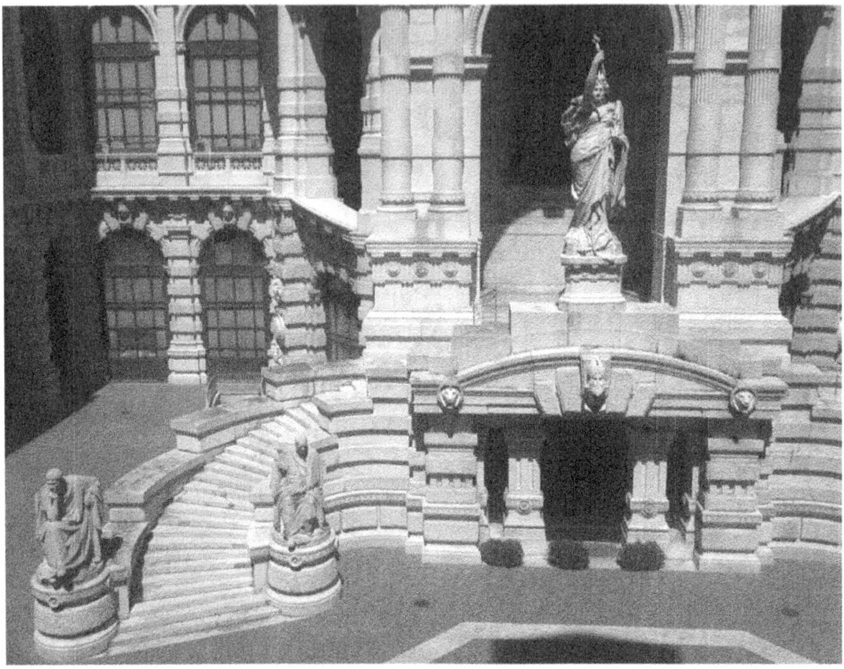

Fig. 5.3 Guglielmo Calderini, open courtyard with the main staircase. In the center: Enrico Quattrini, statue of the Law (or the Triumph of Justice). On the left: Michele Tripisciano, statues of Quintus Hortensius and Paulus

as a "talking statue" that seems to portray the philosopher in the very moment in which he pronounced the famous reply to the cardinals of the Sant'Uffizio who were condemning him: "Maiori forsan cum timore sententiam in me fertis quam ego accipiam" ("Perhaps you pronounce this sentence against me with greater fear than I receive it").[80] A few days after the inauguration, the Naples students burned the new encyclical *Quanta cura* by pope Pius IX and the "Syllabus of Errors" in front of the statue: it was a very powerful and almost peaceful attack on the temporal power of the Catholic Church and a celebration of freedom of thought. These are the same ideas that the statue positioned in Campo de' Fiori had to transmit and the statues of the Supreme Court could suggest. Because the Court was built attached to the Vatican but in a way that does not create any visual connection between Saint Peter's Dome and the Palace of Justice. Because the most important statues represent all secular jurists, leaving the portraits of those linked to the Church to an absolutely marginal role (the only ecclesiastical figure that can be found among the statues is Cardinal Giovanni Battista De Luca while a low-relief on the top of the building features, in a row of famous jurists, the author of the

[80]See: Bucciantini, 2015. 9.

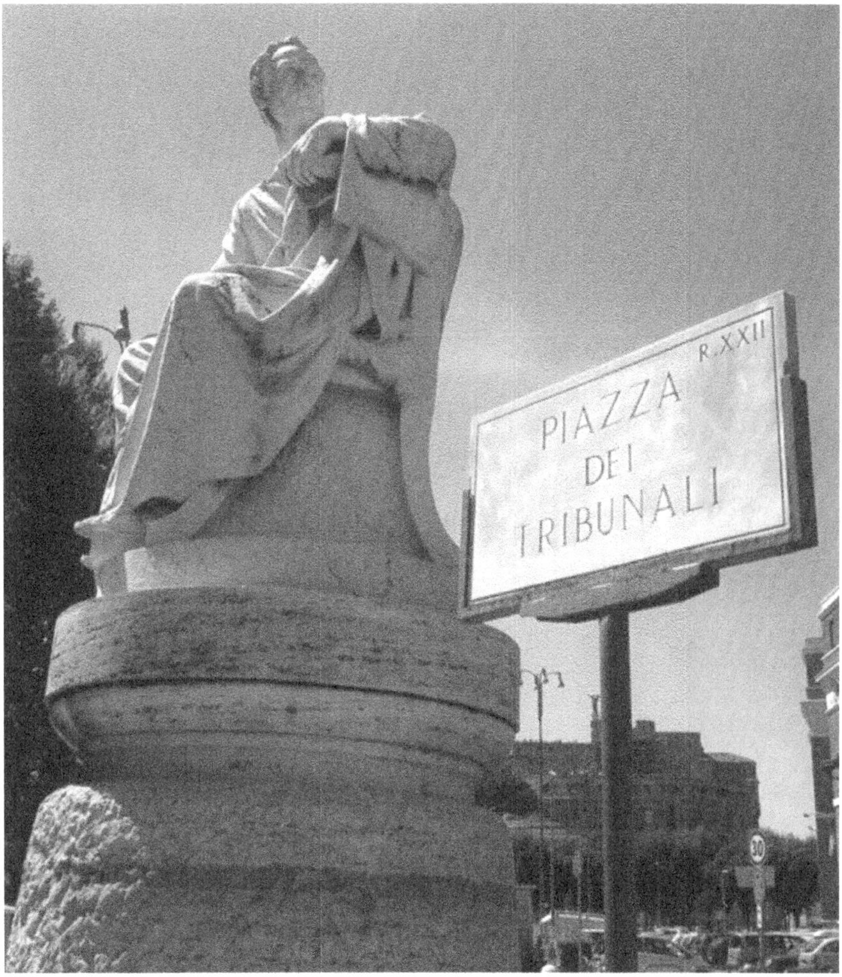

Fig. 5.4 Emilio P. Gallori: Statue of Licinius Crassus. In the background: Castel Sant'Angelo

foundation stone of the *Corpus Iuris Canonici*, the Camaldolese monk Gratian). Because justice is not to be found in heaven but here and now.

5.4 A Procession of Orators and Jurists

The competition for the realization of the sculptures which had to decorate the façade of the Supreme Court building was announced in 1898, ten years after the beginning of the construction. They had to express the historical continuity between Roman law and contemporary legislation. Enrico Quattrini, fellow countryman and

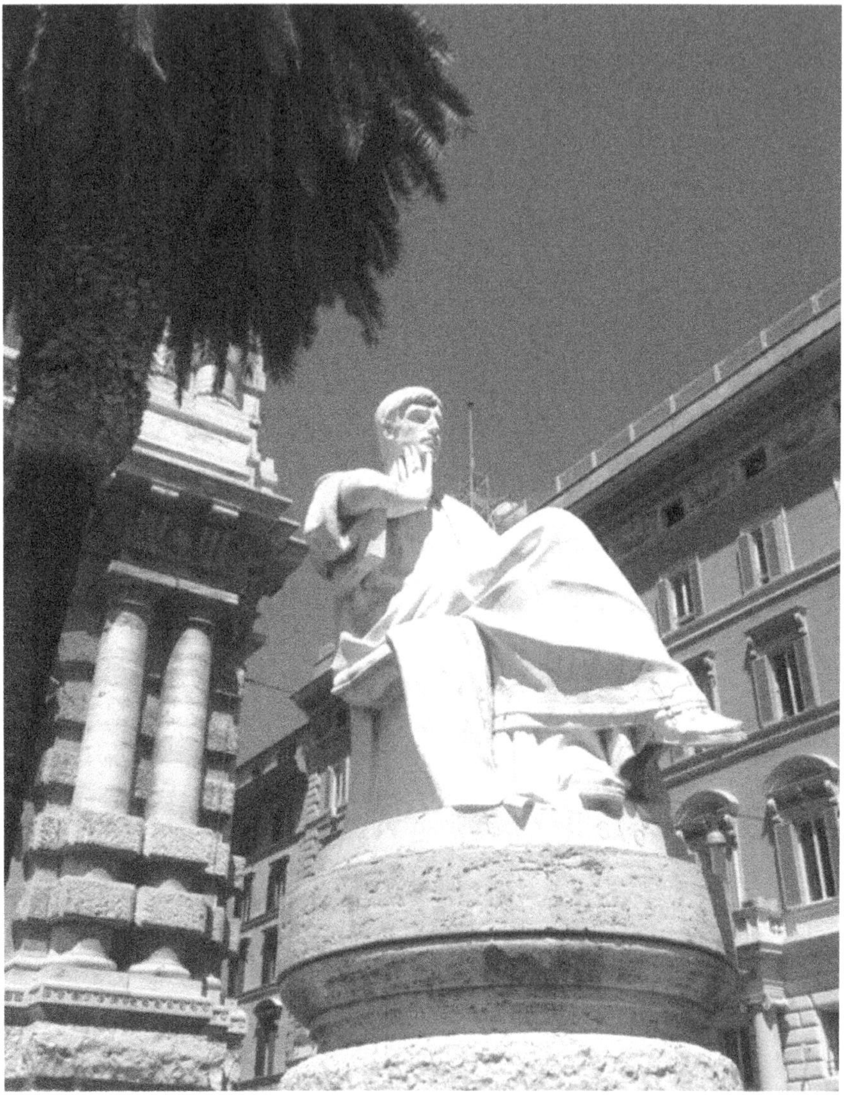

Fig. 5.5 Ernesto Biondi: Statue of Gaius

friend—even though a clericalist—of Calderini, is the eclectic artist behind two of these artworks: the group at the top of the arch which frames the main entrance representing Lady Justice between Law and Strength (Fig. 5.6) [81] and the statue of

[81]A special competition was quickly organized for this sculptural group (29 November–27 June 1900).

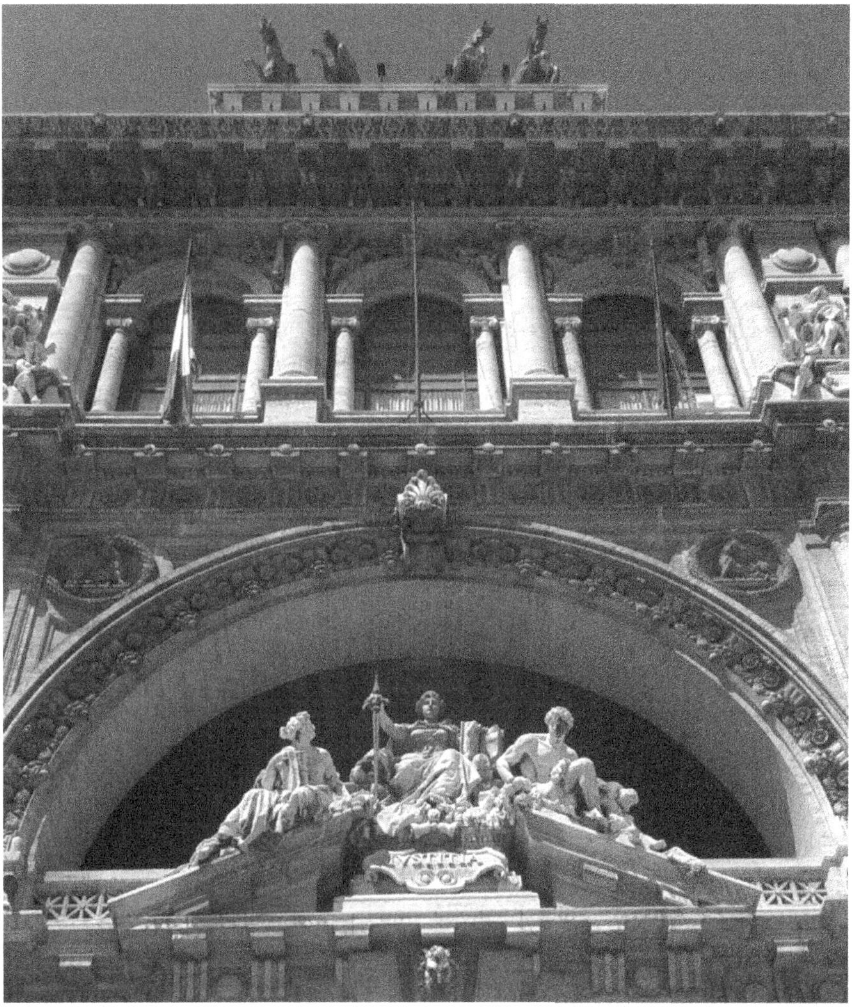

Fig. 5.6 Enrico Quattrini, Lady Justice between Law (left) and Strength (right) on the top of the wide arch dominating the former main entrance. On the top of the building: Ettore Ximenes, bronze quadriga

the Law at the center of the *cortile d'onore*, like a contemporary goddess in this *sancta sanctorum* of the temple of justice (Fig. 5.3).[82]

As the other sculptors chosen by the Jury (composed by G. Monteverde, A. Balzico, C. Boito, G. Sacconi, O. Tabacchi and Calderini, who was a member of the Advisory Commission and was always present in an informal way), he was not

[82]It is interesting to notice that the room under the statue of the Law has been "converted" into the chapel of the Supreme Court. It is a very small space with a cross, an altar and a few chairs.

Roman. In general, minor artists, coming from the provinces, gave their contributions, rather than the "big stars" chosen instead for the contemporary *Palazzo delle Belle Arti*.[83] Zanardelli influenced, as usual, all choices: from the iconographical project to the selection of the artists.

The opinion of art historians was in general severe as the statues were not considered at all. In his famous "Scultura italiana moderna" Francesco Sapori quotes only five out of the (at least) thirteen sculptors involved and only two of them, Ximenes and Biondi, with a quick reference to the Supreme Court. The only positive comment is referred to Biondi and his statue of Gaius "full of thoughtfulness".[84]

The four Roman jurists of the courtyard were thus carved by the Sicilian Michele Tripisciano and by the Tuscan Mauro Benini. Paulus (the most quoted jurist in Justinian's *Corpus Iuris Civilis*) and Quintus Hortensius (great orator and jurist of the late Republic) by the first one and Ulpian (the prevailing jurist among Papinianus, Paulus, Gaius and Modestinus, according to Valentinian III's famous "Law of quotations") and Labeo (probably the most productive jurist of the first imperial period) by the second one. A new competition was quickly published (10 June–23 November 1899) to select the artists in charge of the standing statues of the façade. The winners were Ubaldo Pizzichelli for Cicero and Silvio Sbricoli for Papinianus, famous for his moral qualities as well as for being a great lawyer. The idea of putting these very two effigies at the entrance of the court had been in the mind of Zanardelli for many years. Already in 1889, in fact, during the discourse for the foundation stone-laying ceremony he stated:

> When in the vast propylaeum of this Palace two great statues will rise, the one of Papinianus and the one of Cicero, we will be able to tell ourselves that all the nations of the world united could not offer anything capable of representing, in such a complete and august manner, jurisprudence and eloquence, deepness of thought and excellence of speech.[85]

The bronze quadriga at the top of the building is instead the artwork of a very famous artist of the period, Ettore Ximenes. If all authors agree that it clearly was intended to remind one of or to communicate with the quadrigas on the top of the *Vittoriano*, scholars disagree on who leads the quadriga: Law[86] or a Winged Victory. The mystery can be solved only by taking a close look at the monument, which seems to represent a Winged Victory holding in her right hand the emblem of Roman law (*ius*) and in her left hand a globe. On the globe stands a figure that can

---

[83]Zappia, Caterina. 1996. Gli artisti di Calderini: arte e architettura in età umbertina. In *Guglielmo Calderini. La costruzione di un'architettura*. Cit. 75–82. 79.

[84]"piena di raccoglimento": Sapori, Francesco. 1949. *Scultura italiana moderna*. Roma: Libreria dello Stato. 30.

[85]"Quando nel vasto propilèo di questo Palazzo sorgano due grandi statue, quelle di Papiniano e di Cicerone, noi potrem dire a noi stessi che tutte le nazioni del mondo unite insieme nulla potrebbero offrire che rappresenti, in modo altrettanto completo ed augusto, giurisprudenza ed eloquenza, profondità di pensiero ed altezza della parola": Zanardelli, 1889. ix.

[86]Pizzo, 2006. 55.

be interpreted as Law, who seems to have the very same features as Victory, but without wings.[87]

For the remaining statues Zanardelli decided to avoid the slowness of public competitions and opted for direct assignments: Augusto Rivalta for Modestinus, Ernesto Biondi for Gaius, Emilio P. Gallori for Licinius Crassus and Salvius Iulianus. But the age of Zanardelli was fading. His last direct assignment (two lions by Achille D'Orsi) was blocked by the Ministry of Public Works as a consequence of the protests that Zanarelli's "relaxed management" had raised. When Zanardelli died in 1903 his successor, Scipione Ronchetti, announced a new competition. The new Jury, made of Calderini, Ximenes and Pietro Canonica, chose the artists for the remaining standing statues, representing medieval and modern lawyers: Bartolus (Mauro Benini), Giovanni Battista De Luca (Arturo Dazzi), Giambattista Vico (Luigi De Luca) and Gian Domenico Romagnosi (Augusto Rivalta).

The iconographical project, even considering only the outside of the building, was completed by an overwhelming variety of full, low and high relief sculptures: dozens of jurists right under the upper-most cornice, the she-wolf feeding Romulus and Remus, and then dozens of Savoy crests, Athena/Minerva's heads, scales, lions, eagles and garlands all over the building. The only religious references seem to be the low-reliefs of the ten commandments tablets: a powerful representation of written law. The upper-most cornice, not even visible from the street, is made up of an uninterrupted line of kneeling bulls, yoked with laden garlands, representing the motto *sub jugo legis* ("under the yoke of the law").[88] This repeated reference to the necessity of a complete "submission" to the law appears as an ideal framework at the top of Zanardelli's palace.

5.5 Conclusion: From Hyper-symbolism to Hypo-symbolism

Italy is both an old nation and a young state. The common linguistic, religious, legal and artistic background shared by the Italian population can be certainly questioned, thanks to the peculiar and very fragmentary history of the Italian peninsula, but a certain cultural unity cannot be denied. The founding fathers of the Reign of Italy needed to express the unity of the new reign by means of an aesthetic procedure, the only mean to reach all levels of the population.

[87]See pictures and descriptions in: Manodori. 2007. 29–37.

[88]Marconi, Paolo. 2002 (1997). Il "Palazzaccio": storia e architettura. In *Il Palazzo di Giustizia di Roma*. Cit. 25–40. 39.

It was particularly important that this be done in Rome, designated as the new capital city according to Cavour's[89] project, a city that was at the same time the cradle of the Roman legal-political culture and the seat of the head of the Catholic Church. In order to state the unity of the new kingdom as well as its lay nature, a precise iconographical project was implemented, consisting of a series of buildings and statues, which together referred to the famous motto *Libera Chiesa in libero Stato* ("A free Church in a free State").[90]

On the basis of public competitions, the most important Italian architects and artists of the period worked hard in order to make abstract concepts tangible: *unity* and *liberty* (*Vittoriano* by Giuseppe Sacconi, 1885–1911), *economy* (*Banca d'Italia*[91] by Gaetano Koch, 1886–92), *art* (*Palazzo delle Esposizioni*[92] by Pio Piacentini, 1877–83) and *justice* had suddenly all their "temples", like new deities of a brand new world. Or, using Pierre Legendre's words, the above-mentioned palaces became "the living Emblems of these names".[93] In all those cases the abstract concept was portrayed through a reference to history. As the nineteenth century used history as the principal means to understand humankind and interpret reality, art-works became signs of a process of (supposed) continuous cultural progress.[94]

In accordance with this tendency, the city was studded with statues of the heroes of the *Risorgimento* and in some cases with symbols of the oppression and obscurantism of the Papal State. The statues of Giuseppe Garibaldi on the

[89]Camillo Benso Count of Cavour, one of the founding fathers of the Reign of Italy and first Prime Minister until his death in 1861. Passerin d'Entrèves, Ettore. Cavour, Camillo Benso Conte di. 1979. In: *Dizionario Biografico degli Italiani* 23. Roma: Istituto dell'Enciclopedia Italiana. http://www.treccani.it/enciclopedia/camillo-benso-conte-di-cavour/. Accessed 28 June 2015.

[90]This formula is usually attributed to the French politician and journalist Charles Forbes de Montalembert but it is undeniable that Cavour (at that time not only Prime Minister but also Minister of Foreign Affairs and of the Navy) used it several times, meaning the necessity of a complete separation between secular and spiritual power and not the subjection of the state to the Church. Cavour also pronounced this formula during the speech he gave at the Chamber of Deputies to sustain the decision to make Rome the Capital of unified Italy (27 March 1861). He sustained (25 March 1861), in fact, that "in Roma concorrono tutte le circostanze storiche, intellettuali, morali che devono determinare le condizioni della capitale di un grande Stato" ("all the historical, intellectual and moral circumstances which have to determine the conditions of the capital city of a great State converge in Rome"). See: 1872. *Discorsi parlamentari del Conte Camillo di Cavour raccolti e pubblicati per ordine della Camera dei Deputati*. Roma: Botta, Tipografi della Camera dei Deputati. Now available at: http://www.cavour150.it/scritti2.html. Accessed 3 November 2015.

http://www.sba.unifi.it/upload/scienzesociali/mostre/costruire_italia/discorso_cavour.pdf. Accessed 26 June 2015.

[91]Bank of Italy.

[92]Palace of Exhibitions.

[93]Legendre, Pierre. 2004. *Ce que l'Occident ne voit pas de l'Occident. Conférences au Japon*. Paris: Fayard. Quoted in: Heritier, Paolo. 2014. Law and image: Towards a theory of nomograms. In *Law, Culture and Visual Studies*, eds. A. Wagner, and R.K. Sherwin, 25–48. Heidelberg - New York - London: Springer. 27. Heritier convincingly states the necessity that legal theory not refer solely to the concepts of text and norm but also to the connection between image and law.

[94]Pigafetta, 2007. Vol. 2. Cit. 655.

Gianicolo[95], of Cavour in the new neighborhood of Prati[96], of Marco Minghetti in Corso Vittorio Emanuele II[97], of King Victor Emmanuel II at the center of the *Vittoriano*[98], are examples of the first group. On the other hand, the statues representing Giordano Bruno in Campo de' Fiori and Cola di Rienzo near the *Campidoglio*[99] gave a message of liberty and anti-clericalism. All these statues were connected to each other, in a kind of mute dialogue in which their orientation was crucial. This kind of urbanistic language can likewise be observed in the very structure of the neighborhood of Prati[100], from which it is not possible to see Saint Peter's Dome, even though the area is attached to the Vatican.

After the period of the so called "monumentomania" Rome did not experience any remarkable intervention from the point of view of the relationship between *law and architecture*. Not even Mussolini's megalomania left its traces in Rome, if we exclude the building of the law faculty in the new university campus (*città universitaria*) not far away from Termini Station[101]. After the end of WWII nothing

[95]By Emilio P. Gallori (1895).

[96]By Stefano Galletti (1895).

[97]By Lio Gangeri (1895).

[98]By Enrico Chiaradia (1888–1901, finished by Emilio P. Gallori).

[99]By Girolamo Masini (1871).

[100]See for example the structure of Piazza Cavour, a square dominated by the statue of the famous political leader, where both the current main entrance of the Court of Cassation and the Valdese Church (1911–14) are located. In particular, the fact that a huge non-Catholic church was built in an important square is emblematic. The piece of land chosen, acquired thanks to the generosity of Mrs. Stewart Kennedy, was located near to the Vatican and therefore to Castel Sant'Angelo, where, in 1560, the Valdese pastor Gian Luigi Pascale was burned as a heretic. Architect Paolo Bonci and engineer Emanuele Rutelli were the authors of the project while the internal decoration was entrusted to Paolo Paschetto. Many years later, in 1947, Paschetto won the public competition for the "Emblem of the Italian Republic", approved by the Constituent Assembly. His drawing, even though modified, is still displayed in all Italian public buildings (Silvestri, Silvia. 2014. Paschetto, Paolo Antonio. In: *Dizionario Biografico degli Italiani* 81. Roma: Istituto dell'Enciclopedia Italiana. http://www.treccani.it/enciclopedia/paolo-antonio-paschetto_(Dizionario-Biografico/). Accessed 26 June 2015. See also the emblem's description on the internet website of the "Quirinale", the seat of the Italian President of the Republic: http://www.quirinale.it/qrnw/statico/simboli/emblema/emblema.htm. Accessed 3 November 2015). The emblem is made of four elements: a star (associated to the personification of Italy), a gear wheel (labor), an olive branch (peace) and an oak branch (strength and dignity).

[101]Rationalist architecture and its relationship with the fascist regime are of course a huge topic that cannot be treated here. It is sufficient to underline that several palaces of justice were built in that period in different cities but not in Rome. The most famous one is the Palace of Justice in Milan by Marcello Piacentini and Ernesto Rapisardi (1929–47). Linked to the legal world is nevertheless the construction of the new seat of the University "La Sapienza" in Rome, including the Law Faculty. It was built during the years 1932–35, once more under the direction of Marcello Piacentini, who gave to Gaetano Rapisardi (Ernesto's brother) the task of designing, among others, the Law Faculty building (*Giurisprudenza*). However, projects had been proposed since 1888 (e.g. the proposal by Valentino Cerruti in the area of Castro Pretorio, where the campus will be then realized in the 1930s). Also Calderini had submitted a proposal in 1906. He wrote to Giovanni Giolitti, the Prime Minister, supporting the idea of a university campus according to the "American style", with gyms, laboratories, homes for the faculty and dormitories. Surprisingly, he thought it

even comparable was undertaken and, even though a new court was built in the 1960s (the Criminal Court in Piazzale Clodio, 1963–66[102]), no Cicero, Baldus or Gentili, no personification of Justice, Law or Strength was intended to "keep an eye" on the behaviors of men, to warn them or to assist them.

Symbols are hermeneutic devices that lead from physical experiences and rational activities to a metaphysical reality.[103] Human beings, united in a society, create their "social objects" by means of symbols and, in turn, the objects symbolized shape human beings as part of a community.[104] The Supreme Court building, overloaded with symbols, is a symbol itself: it does not express truths but collective beliefs. It alludes (as symbols affect our intuition rather than our rationality) to the glorious past of a nation finally freed from foreign oppressors and unified, as well as to a new, lay and enlightened justice. However, symbols rise and fall and sometimes evolve, as in the very case of the Italian Supreme Court. They act on the mind of the collectivity, which is influenced by all possible spiritual and material factors. Therefore the meaning of a symbol can change.[105] As aforesaid, the nickname of the building, *Palazzaccio*, has a double meaning: "the ugly building" but also "the bad building", an evident allusion to the injustice and slowness of the Italian judicial system as commonly perceived by the community: Zanardelli's dream has crashed under the weight of Calderini's project.

Nowadays, symbols of what one could or should consider the founding values of the state have disappeared from Rome's landscape and the debate about the reasons for this absence is open.

It has been argued, for example, that the absence of symbols denotes a political vacuum, which can be replaced either by sheer administration or by brute power. In brief, there is no more political (and juridical) meaning to be communicated as we live in a world dominated by financial capitalism, in which politics and law are relegated to a mere executive role[106].

On the contrary, as John Quincy Adams suggested already in 1831, the absence of symbols can be interpreted as the very essence of democracy:

> Democracy has no monuments; it strikes no medals; it bears the head of no man on a coin; its very essence is iconoclastic.[107]

---

could be done in the seventeenth-century Palazzo Altieri. See: Di Marco, Fabrizio. 2012. La città universitaria di Roma. Dal progetto Botto-Giovannoni alle ultime proposte prima di Piacentini. In *L'altra modernità nella cultura architettonica del XX secolo*, ed. Laura Marcucci, 79–100. Roma: Gangemi, 82.

[102]Nicoletti, Manfredi. 1978. *Continuità, evoluzione, architettura*. Bari: Dedalo Libri, 70.

[103]Zagrebelsky, Gustavo. 2012. *Simboli al potere. Politica, fiducia, speranza*. Torino: Einaudi, 7.

[104]Zagrebelsky, 2012. 15.

[105]Zagrebelsky, 2012. 25 ff.

[106]Zagrebelsky, 2012. 17 and 81 ff.

[107]This very famous phrase of the sixth President of the United States is usually quoted without any reference to its origin. It can be found in Adam's diaries, within an entry dated 11 December 1831: Adams, Charles Francis (ed.). 1876. *Memoirs of John Quincy Adams. Comprising Portions of his Diary from 1795 to 1848*. Vol. 8. Philadelphia: J.B. Lippincott. 433. https://archive.org/stream/memoirsofjohnqui08adamuoft#page/432/mode/2up. Accessed 29 June 2015.

According to this interpretation, in a true democracy all ideas and ideologies have the same dignity, as far as they respect the fundamental values of a nation or, more concretely, the constitution (written or unwritten) of the state that embodies the nation. After WWII the dark shadow of the strong symbols of the totalitarianisms of the first half of the twentieth century seems to have cancelled from Europe most symbols related to politics and justice. The only value that the new building hosting judicial courts still embody seems to be "transparency". Glass walls, mirrors and water characterize for example the Seat of the European Court of Human Rights in Strasbourg, designed by the British architect Lord Richard Rogers (1994).[108] Here and there, a Lady Justice survives, sometimes beautifully reinterpreted.[109]

But if we focus on symbols related to history, another explanation is possible.

Zanardelli was a lawyer educated in the shadow of Friedrich Carl von Savigny's idea that *"die ganze Rechtswissenschaft selbst nichts Anderes ist, als Rechtsgeschichte"* ("The whole of jurisprudence itself is just legal history").[110] The universities of the Lombardo-Venetian Kingdom (Padua and Pavia, where Zanardelli studied) were the only ones which Savigny did not criticize in his famous 1828 essay on the state of education in Italy[111], as they provided the students with a solid Roman law background, on the basis of the assumption that Roman law was the foundation of any code.[112]

Starting from this assumption, the Liberal Left "petrified" history in order to justify new political and legal institutions, this way trying to "make Italians" after having "made Italy", or simply trying to make Italians accept the new legal framework *they* had created.

---

[108]For an interesting comparative overview of National Courts in the twentieth century and the efforts made to reinvent courthouse architecture see: Resnik, Judith and Curtis, Dennis. 2011. *Representing Justice*. Cit. Chap. 10 and also: Resnik, Judith; Dennis, Curtis and Tait, Allison. 2014. Constructing courts: Architecture, the Ideology of Judging, and the Public Sphere. In *Law, Culture and Visual Studies*. Cit. 515–545. The authors hold that on one hand glass facades should represent the accessibility and transparency of modern democracies even though, on the other hand, courthouse interiors appear more and more characterized by segregated passageways.

[109]On the iconography of Justice see: Resnik and Curtis, 2011. For an alternative interpretation of the blindfold see: Prosperi, Adriano. 2008. *Giustizia bendata. Percorsi storici di un'immagine*. Torino: Einaudi.

[110]Savigny, Friedrich Carl von. 1806. *Recension des Lehrbuchs der Geschichte des römischen Rechts von Gustav Hugo*. 2te Ausg. Berlin 1799, 3te Ausg. Berlin 1806. In *Allgemeine Literatur Zeitung* 20. 21. Oct. 1806, Num. 251–252, S. 129–144. Now in: *Vermischte Schriften*. 1950. Vol. 5, 1–36. Berlin: Deit und Comp. 2.

[111]Savigny, Friedrich Carl von. 1828. Über den juristischen Unterricht in Italien. In *Zeitschrift für geschichtliche Rechtswissenschaft*. 6: 201–228.

[112]Di Renzo Villata, Gigliola. 2004. La formazione del giurista in Italia e l'influenza culturale europea tra Sette e Ottocento. Introduction to: *Formare il giurista. Esperienze nell'area lombarda tra Sette e Ottocento*, ed. G. Di Renzo Villata, 1–105. Milano: Giuffrè, 85.

References

Acciaresi, Primo. 1911. *Giuseppe Sacconi e l'opera sua massima. Cronaca dei lavori del Monumento nazionale a Vittorio Emanuele II.* Roma: Tipografia dell'Unione editrice.

Adams, Charles Francis (ed.). 1876. *Memoirs of John Quincy Adams. Comprising portions of his Diary from 1795 to 1848.*, vol. 8. Philadelphia: J.B. Lippincott.

Berggren, Lars, and Lennart Sjöstedt. 1996. *L'ombra dei grandi: monumenti e politica monumentale a Roma (1870–1895).* Roma: Artemide.

Brice, Catherine. 1996. De l'usage politique de l'architecture: le projet de Guglielmo Calderini au premier concours pour le monument à Victor-Emmanuel II, à Rome. In *Guglielmo Calderini. La costruzione di un'architettura nel progetto di una Capitale.* Atti del Convegno, Roma, Palazzo delle Esposizioni, 23 settembre 1995, 1–4. Roma: Gangemi.

Bucciantini, Massimo. 2015. *Campo dei fiori: storia di un monumento maledetto.* Torino: Einaudi.

Calderini, Guglielmo. 1887. *Relazione esplicativa del progetto per il palazzo di giustizia in Roma, modificato e ripresentato per invito di s. E. Il Ministro di Grazia e giustizia.* Perugia: Tilli.

Calderini, Guglielmo. 1908. *La improvvisa soppressione della direzione artistica dei lavori del palazzo di giustizia presentata al giudizio della Camera e del Senato.* Roma: Casa editrice italiana.

Chiarini, Roberto. 2003. Biografia di Giuseppe Zanardelli. In *Giuseppe Zanardelli, 1826–1903. Il coraggio della coerenza*, 43–80. Milano: Skira.

Conti, Fulvio. 2003. *Storia della massoneria italiana. Dal Risorgimento al fascismo.* Bologna: Il Mulino.

Passerin d'Entrèves, Ettore. 1979. Cavour, Camillo Benso Conte di. In *Dizionario Biografico degli Italiani* 23. Roma: Istituto dell'Enciclopedia Italiana.

Di Marco, Fabrizio. 2012. La città universitaria di Roma. Dal progetto Botto-Giovannoni alle ultime proposte prima di Piacentini. In *L'altra modernità nella cultura architettonica del XX secolo*, ed. Laura Marcucci, 79–100. Roma: Gangemi.

Di Renzo Villata, Gigliola. 2004. La formazione del giurista in Italia e l'influenza culturale europea tra Sette e Ottocento. Introduction to: *Formare il giurista. Esperienze nell'area lombarda tra Sette e Ottocento*, ed. G. Di Renzo Villata, 1–105. Milano: Giuffré.

Discorsi parlamentari del Conte Camillo di Cavour raccolti e pubblicati per ordine della Camera dei Deputati. 1872. Roma: Botta, Tipografi della Camera dei Deputati.

Evans, David. 1999. Theatre of deferral: the image of the law and the architecture of the Inns of Court. *Law and Critique* 10: 1–25.

Passalalpi Ferrari, Ettore. 2009. *Il monumento a Giordano Bruno in Campo de' Fiori di Ettore Ferrari.* Roma: Associazione culturale Ettore Ferrari.

Giannottu, Caterina. 2011. Un narratore arguto e antichissimo. Pasquino in Parione e la satira in Roma fra tradizione e modernità. *In Clio. Rivista trimestrale di Studi Storici.* 47 (1): 123–145.

Girardet, Alain. 1992. Introduction. In *La justice en ses temples. Regards sur l'architecture judiciaire en France*, 15–19. Poitiers: Brissaud.

Heritier, Paolo. 2014. Law and image: towards a theory of nomograms. In *Law, Culture and Visual Studies*, ed. A. Wagner, and R.K. Sherwin, 25–48. Heidelberg: Springer.

Hom, Stephanie Malia. 2013. On the origins of making Italy: Massimo D'Azeglio and "Fatta l'Italia, bisogna fare gli Italiani". *Italian Culture* 31 (1): 1–16.

Kruft, Hanno-Walter, and Markus Völkel (eds.). 1991. *Gregorovius, Ferdinand. Römische Tagebücher (1852–1889).* München: Beck.

Lacché, Luigi. 1997. Un code pénal pour l'unité italienne: le Code Zanardelli (1889). La genèse, le débat, le projet juridique. In *Le pénal dans tous ses États. Justice, États et Sociétés en Europe (XIIe-XXe siècles),* eds. Xavier Rousseaux, and René Levy, 303–319. Bruxelles: Facultés universitaires Saint-Louis.

Le Palais de Justice. 2012 (2001). Bruxelles ville d'art et d'histoire 31. Bruxelles: Ministère de la Région Bruxelles-Capitale et al.

Longo, Giovanni E. 2002 (1997). Prefazione. In *Il Palazzo di giustizia di Roma*, ed. Marcello Fabbri. Roma: Gangemi.

Manodori Sagredo, Alberto (ed.). 2007. *La Corte di Cassazione. Le opera d'arte del Palazzo di Giustizia di Roma*. Roma: Gangemi.
Marconi, Paolo. 2002 (1997). Il "Palazzaccio": storia e architettura. In *Il Palazzo di Giustizia di Roma*, ed. Marcello Fabbri, 25–40. Roma: Gangemi.
Marconi, Paolo. 2006. L'ispirazione stilistica del "Palazzaccio" e il suo cantiere: un progetto e un simbolo. In *I tesori nascosti della Corte di Cassazione. Fotografie e disegni del Palazzo di Giustizia di Roma*, ed. Carolina Marconi, 11–18. Roma: Gangemi.
Martyn, Georges. 2006. Painted *Exempla Iustitiae* in the Southern Netherlands. In *Symbolische Kimmunikation vor Gericht in der frühen Neuzeit*, ed. Reiner Schulze, 335–356. Berlin: Duncker & Humblot.
Monsagrati, Giuseppe. 1999. Garibaldi, Giuseppe. In *Dizionario Biografico degli Italiani* 52. Roma: Istituto dell'Enciclopedia Italiana.
Neri, Maria Luisa. 2006. Forma esistenziale e forma effettuale: dal disegno alla realtà. I dettagli decorativi del Palazzo di Giustizia. In *I tesori nascosti della Corte di Cassazione. Fotografie e disegni del Palazzo di Giustizia di Roma*, ed. Carolina Marconi, 43–50. Roma: Gangemi.
Nicoletti, Manfredi. 1978. *Continuità, evoluzione, architettura*. Bari: Dedalo Libri.
Padoa Schioppa, Antonio. 2007. *Storia del diritto in Europa. Dal medioevo all'età contemporanea*. Bologna: Il Mulino.
Pevsner, Nikolaus. 1976. *A History of Building Types*. Princeton University Press. Italian edition: Pevsner. Nikolaus. 1986. *Storia e caratteri degli edifici*. Trans. G. Bestelli. Roma: Fratelli Palombi.
Piacentini, Marcello. 1953. *Considerazioni sull'Urbanistica e l'Architettura di Roma e altrove*. Roma: Ars Nova.
Pigafetta, Giorgio. 2007. *Storia dell'architettura moderna. Imitazione e invenzione fra xv e xx secolo*, vol. 2. Torino: Bollati Boringhieri.
Pisani, Mario (ed.). 2009. *La corte di cassazione. I progetti e l'architettura del capolavoro di Giuseppe Zanardelli e Guglielmo Calderini*. Roma: Gangemi.
Pizzo, Marco. 2006. Il Palazzo di Giustizia: un percorso iconografico. In *I tesori nascosti della Corte di Cassazione. Fotografie e disegni del Palazzo di Giustizia di Roma*, ed. Carolina Marconi, 51–58. Roma: Gangemi.
Ponziani, Daniel. 2003. Il monumento a Giordano Bruno. In *Giuseppe Zanardelli, 1826–1903. Il coraggio della coerenza*, 114–116. Milano: Skira.
Porena, Manfredi. 1957. *Roma capitale nel decennio della sua adolescenza (1880–1890)*. Roma: Edizioni di storia e letteratura.
Porzio, Pier Luigi (ed.). 1986-88. *Il Vittoriano. Materiali per una storia*, vols. 1–2. Roma: Fratelli Palombi.
Prezzolini, Giuseppe. 1948. The origins: Why Italians are not Romans. In *The Legacy of Italy*, 7–16. New York: S.F. Vanni.
Prosperi, Adriano. 2008. *Giustizia bendata. Percorsi storici di un'immagine*. Torino: Einaudi.
Quarta, Oronzo. 1911. *Discorso pronunciato dal Senatore Oronzo Quarta, Procuratore generale presso la Corte di Cassazione di Roma, per la inaugurazione del Palazzo di Giustizia di Roma il giorno XI gennaio MDCCCCXI*. Roma: Tipografia dell'Unione Editrice.
Resnik, Judith, and Curtis, Dennis. 2011. *Representing Justice. Invention, Controversy, and Rights in City-States and Democratic Courtrooms*. New Haven: Yale University Press.
Resnik, Judith; Dennis, Curtis and Tait, Allison. 2014. Constructing courts: Architecture, the ideology of judging, and the public sphere. In *Law, Culture and Visual Studies*, eds. A. Wagner, and R.K. Sherwin, 515–545. Heidelberg: Springer.
Rodiek, Thorsten. 1983. *Das Monumento Nazionale Vittorio Emanuele II: in Rom*. Berlin: Peter Lang.
Rossi Kirk, Terry. 1996. Roman Architecture before the Lateran Pact: Architectural Symbols of Reconciliation in the Competitions for the Palazzo di Giustizia, 1883–87. In *Guglielmo Calderini. La costruzione di un'architettura nel progetto di una Capitale*. Atti del Convegno, Roma, Palazzo delle Esposizioni, 23 settembre 1995, 83–125. Roma: Gangemi.

Rossi Kirk, Terry. 1997. The Politicization of the Landscape of Roma Capitale and the Symbolic Role of the Palazzo di Giustizia. *Mélanges de l'École française de Rome. Italie et Méditerranée*. 109 (1): 89–114.
Sanesi, Elena. 1967. *Giuseppe Zanardelli dalla giovinezza alla maturità (con documenti inediti)*. Brescia: Ateneo di Brescia.
Sapori, Francesco. 1946. *Il Vittoriano*. Roma: Libreria dello Stato.
Sapori, Francesco. 1949. *Scultura italiana moderna*. Roma: Libreria dello Stato.
Sbriccoli, Mario. 1990. La penalistica civile. Teorie e ideologie del diritto penale nell'Italia unita. In *Stato e cultura giuridica in Italia dalla Unità alla Repubblica*, ed. Aldo Schiavone, 147–232. Bari: Laterza.
Silvestri, Silvia. 2014. Paschetto, Paolo Antonio. In *Dizionario Biografico degli Italiani* 81. Roma: Istituto dell'Enciclopedia Italiana.
Taylor, Katherine Fisher. 1992. Le code et l'équité. La transformation du Palais de Justice de Paris au XIXe siècle. In *La justice en ses temples. Regards sur l'architecture judiciaire en France*, 83–127. Poitiers: Brissaud
The Royal Courts of Justice. Illustrated Handbook. 1883 (repr. 1977). London: Wildy & Sons Ltd.
Tobia, Bruno. 2013 (2011). *L'altare della patria*. Bologna: Il Mulino.
Ugolini, Romano (ed.). 2012. *Cento anni del Vittoriano 1911–2011*. Atti della giornata di studio tenutasi il 4 giugno 2011 al Vittoriano in occasione del Centenario dell'inaugurazione del Monumento. Roma: Gangemi.
Venturoli, Marcello. 1957. *La patria di marmo (1870–1911)*. Pisa: Nistri-Lischi.
Savigny, Friedrich Carl von. 1806. *Recension des Lehrbuchs der Geschichte des römischen Rechts von Gustav Hugo*. 2te Ausg. Berlin 1799, 3te Ausg. Berlin 1806. In *Allgemeine Literatur Zeitung* 20. 21. Oct. 1806, Num. 251–252, S. 129–144. Now in: *Vermischte Schriften*. 1950. vol. 5, 1–36. Berlin: Deit und Comp.
Savigny, Friedrich Carl von. 1828. Über den juristischen Unterricht in Italien. *Zeitschrift für geschichtliche Rechtswissenschaft*. 6: 201–228.
Williams, Robin. 1996. The image of secular power: The *Romanità* of Italian state architecture under the Sinistra, 1876–90. In *Guglielmo Calderini. La costruzione di un'architettura nel progetto di una Capitale*. Atti del Convegno, Roma, Palazzo delle Esposizioni, 23 settembre 1995, 9–23. Roma: Gangemi.
Zagrebelsky, Gustavo. 2012. *Simboli al potere. Politica, fiducia, speranza*. Torino: Einaudi.
Zanardelli, Giuseppe. 1889. *Pel collocamento della prima pietra del Palazzo di Giustizia in Roma: discorso pronunziato dal Ministro guardasigilli G. Zanardelli il 14. marzo 1889*. Roma: Forzani e C.
Zanardelli, Giuseppe. 1905. *Discorsi parlamentari di Giuseppe Zanardelli pubblicati per deliberazione della Camera dei Deputati*. Voll. 1-3. Roma: Tipografia della Camera dei Deputati.
Zappia, Caterina. 1996. Gli artisti di Calderini: arte e architettura in età umbertina. In *Guglielmo Calderini. La costruzione di un'architettura nel progetto di una Capitale*. Atti del Convegno, Roma, Palazzo delle Esposizioni, 23 settembre 1995, 75–82. Roma: Gangemi.

Stefania Gialdroni is currently instructor of "The Legal Protection of Cultural Heritage" at the RomaTre University. She graduated cum laude in 2003 (RomaTre University, Law Department) and in 2009 she received her Ph.D. in legal history "en cotutelle" between the Universities of Milano-Bicocca and the EHESS in Paris. Since 2008 she has been coordinator and instructor of the "Law and the Humanities" course at the RomaTre University. She has published articles on legal history and on law and the humanities and has presented papers in several countries in Europe (including France, Germany, Belgium, the Netherlands, Finland) and South America (Argentina).

Chapter 6
Visual Rhetoric as "A Space-in-Between": Semiotic Account of French Official Presidential Photographs

Anne Wagner

"The soul never thinks without a picture" (Aristotle).

Abstract This chapter deals with the concept of the French national spirit for the construction of the national identity of France. Some of the most typical French official presidential photographs reveal a hidden discourse, a '*Space-in-between*'. These official photographs are part of French history and are also displayed in town halls even though there is no compulsory obligation to do so. However, some legal regulations have to be respected when shooting their portraits, but artists are also free to adapt their styles owing to each President's will. Studying the visual and hidden discursive implications sheds light on semiotic, philosophical, and legal issues, as well as impacts on our legal culture, tradition and system. Taking into account space and time, the chapter proposes a reflection on the function, role, and limits of these visual and discursive representations, as well as impacts, recognitions and obligations deriving from them.

6.1 Third Space as A Space-in-Between in Visual Rhetoric

The analysis of visual rhetoric as a transfer of cultural values can be observed at different points in time and can lead to the theory of "Third Space"[1] where there exists an obvious correlation between the binary code, which comprises here visual arguments and rational claims, and the 'third space'—a space-in-between[2]—where viewers can assume identical or even opposite cohesion in order to determine what they should believe in. The impact of these analyses over the 'space-in-between'

[1] Wagner, Anne. 2016. A Space in-Between: Legal Translation as a 'Third Space'. Journal of Civil Law Studies 29(1):167–190.
[2] Wagner, 2016.

A. Wagner (✉)
Centre Droits et Perspectives du Droit, équipe René Demogue, Université Lille—Nord de France, Lille, France
e-mail: valwagnerfr@yahoo.com

S. Huygebaert et al. (eds.), *Sensing the Nation's Law*, Studies in the History of Law and Justice 13, https://doi.org/10.1007/978-3-319-75497-0_6

can be documented by producing diverse visual sets of elements having emotional, cultural and identity impacts on people (i.e. the viewers).

These analyses can be used to illustrate the process by which visual rhetoric can be applied in the correlated time and space framework. This step in our investigation always involves careful scrutiny of visual data over a specific period. Accordingly, the time and space approach is generally motivated by the presumption of viewers' cohesions between adjacent points in terms of cultural, national and historical values. Besides, this approach assumes the primary characteristics of interest in our analyses. These periodic variations are often caused by a shift in these values.

State portraits of the Presidents of the V Republic convey the meaning of their political lives and representations in France and far beyond. Visual arguments demonstrate how French Presidential photographs are socially coded to represent their positions in society. Rather than depict reality, the photographer assembles and arranges or rearranges several codes of meaning so that the portrait becomes yet another means of communicating power. These visual "blocks of meaning" are rhetorical acts, but viewers should avoid seeking the transparent and fluid relationship between image and referent.[3] They encourage visual persuasion. A state portrait "*points* but does not tell".[4] Indeed the power of persuasion is promoted by visual rhetoric with state portraits, and could lead to an explanation of how persuasive images are being perceived by citizens.

A series of visual data may influence certain areas of the brain and may affect this "third space".[5] The main goal is to activate the visual memory system in responding with the generation of a mental image for the French collective memory. As Soja mentioned, "each standing [is] clear, but also [has] a secret and conjectured object, filled with allusions and illusions".[6] These fears of miscomprehension, misinterpretation relate to insecurity in visual rhetoric. Memory will therefore operate on a cultural level. Indeed,

> Collective memories allow the fabrication, rearrangement, elaboration, and omission of details about the past, often pushing aside accuracy and authenticity so as to accommodate broader issues of identity formation, power and authority, and political affiliation.[7]

This space-in-between is under constant mutation and flux, and has no rigid borders. Reality is always framed by codes of what viewers believe is worthy of vision, feeling, sensation, and representation. Mitchell talks therefore about

---

[3]Barthes, Roland. 1974. *S/Z: An Essay*. New York: Farrar, Straus and Giroux.

[4]Barthes, 1974. 62.

[5]Wagner, Anne. 2014. Game of Power within the French Urban Landscape: A Socio-Legal Semiotic Analysis of Communication, Vision and Space. *International Journal for the Semiotics of Law* 27(1): 167.

[6]Soja, E.W. 1996. *Third Space - Journeys to Los Angeles and Other Real-and-Imagined Places*. Cambridge: Blackwell Publishers, 56.

[7]Zelizer, Barbie. 1992. *Covering the Body: The Kennedy Assassination, the Media, and the Shaping of Collective Memory*. Chicago: Chicago University Press, 3.

indiscipline, "a moment of breakage or rupture, when the continuity is broken and the practice comes into question".[8] He therefore insists on the "pictorial turn"[9] and the plurality in meaning of images and the importance of disseminating information, ideas, cultures, and opinions with images only, like state or royal portraits.

The mode of visual communication is obviously complex. Representational images tend to prompt emotional reactions, *vividness*.[10] This chapter will not consider psychological research and data analysis, but will focus on analyzing visual data and their variations in time and space so as to envisage (1) discrete visual elements and (2) fundamental visual characteristics still pervading over time and space.

6.1.1 Visualizing Effectively Presidential Photographs

Photographers are faced with the problem of how to efficiently show a wide spectrum of data on a limited display area.[11] Within this framework where viewers are not in the capacity of zooming in for real, they are provided with effective access to visual information in different layers of representation. These layers consist in organizing the photograph itself with a specific background inserting discrete visual elements and with a foreground displaying fundamental visual characteristics. This organization leads to the nonverbal triadic structure[12] where are visible

- *Ideology* relating to the sense of national identity,
- *Aesthetics* referring to the setting of visual elements within the photograph, and
- *Shape* as a visual persuasive tool.

Barthes rightly points out a new mode of observation of images with two concepts: the *studium* and the *punctum*. *Studium* refers to a straightforward common understanding of elements within an image whereas *Punctum* refers to a "partial element" in the picture that "pricks, wounds or stings".[13] *Punctum* simply emphasizes on the viewers' capacity of zooming in, of paying more attention to

---

[8]Mitchell, W.J.T. 1995. Interdisciplinarity and Visual Culture. *Art Bulletin* 70(4): 541.

[9]Mitchell, W.J.T. 1994. *Picture Theory: Essays on Verbal and Visual Representation*. Chicago: University of Chicago Press.

[10]Nissbett, Richard E. and Lee Ross. 1980. *Human Inference: Strategies and Shortcomings of Social Judgment*. Chapel Hill: University of North Carolina Press.

[11]Wagner, Anne and Bozzo-Rey Malik. 2013. French commemorative postage stamps: A means of legal culture and memory. In *Law, culture and visual studies*, eds. Anne Wagner and Richard K. Sherwin, 313. The Netherlands: Springer.

[12]Wagner, Anne. 2011. French Urban Space Management: A Visual Semiotic Approach behind Power and Control. *International Journal for the Semiotics of Law* 24(2):229–230.

[13]Barthes, Roland. 2000. *Camera Lucida*. London: Vintage Books. 28.

some elements than others, and "these elements, which rises from the scene, shoots out of it like an arrow, and pierces [...]" the viewers.[14]

6.1.2 Visual Elements as Consensual Symbolism

Similarly to the translatability process,[15] visual messages need to be 'transplanted', translated and naturalized by being associated with one or several given perceptual elements within the photographs. Images have thus a rhetorical power with "a set of socially constructed meanings or norms [...] to the extent that they become invisible or common sense",[16] "a set of conceptual lenses through which visual images become knowable as communicative or rhetorical phenomena".[17] They become rhetorical images being altogether ubiquitous, influential and important.

"Such a choice endows these elements with a presence",[18] consisting in the photographer's projection to organize the setting of the official presidential photograph. What is essential indeed is the ease with which viewers can connect visual elements—be their presence discrete or fundamental—to national identity almost effortlessly on a general scale, even though some discrete elements may not be well understood, perceived and interpreted. "The notion of resource accounts for change and power imbalance in the visual signification process, as defined by its two ends: representation (or, encoding) and interpretation (decoding)"[19].

This consensual symbolism[20] is a key concept as it leads to the formation of a rational consensus, a set of reasons in the multiplicity of displayed visual elements owing to the viewership's experience, expertise and knowledge (see Fig. 6.1). Consensual symbolism is thus pliable, porous, adaptable to people's perception, and usable over time and space. It thus becomes obvious that the whole set of visual claims in official presidential photographs should be discerned with care. Visual data provided in them are not chosen at random and play important ideological roles in French viewers' memory. The idea of deciphering images is not to influence

---

[14]Barthes, Roland, 2000. 26.

[15]Wagner, Anne and Gémar Jean-Claude. 2014. Decision-Making in Legal Translation, Interpretation and Speech Act: Legal Semiotic Culture-Mediation Techniques. *Semiotica* 201(1/4).

[16]Aiello, Georgia. 2006. Theoretical Advances in Critical Visual Analysis: Perception, Ideology, Mythologies, and Social Semiotics. *Journal of Visual Literacy* 26(2): 92.

[17]Foss, Sonja K. 2005. Theory of visual rhetoric. In *Handbook of visual communication: Theory, methods, and media*, eds. Ken Smith, Sandra Moriarty, Gretchen Barbatsis, and Keith Kenney, 145. Mahwah: Lawrence Erlbaum.

[18]Perelman, Chaim, and Lucie Olbrechts-Tyteca. 1971. *The New Rhetoric: A Treatise on Argumentation*. Trans. John Wilkinson and Purcell Weaver. Notre Dame: University of Notre Dame Press. 116.

[19]Aiello, 2006. 90.

[20]Pearce, Lynne. 1991. *Woman, Image, Text: Readings in Pre-Raphaelite Art and Literature*. Buffalo: University of Toronto Press. 34.

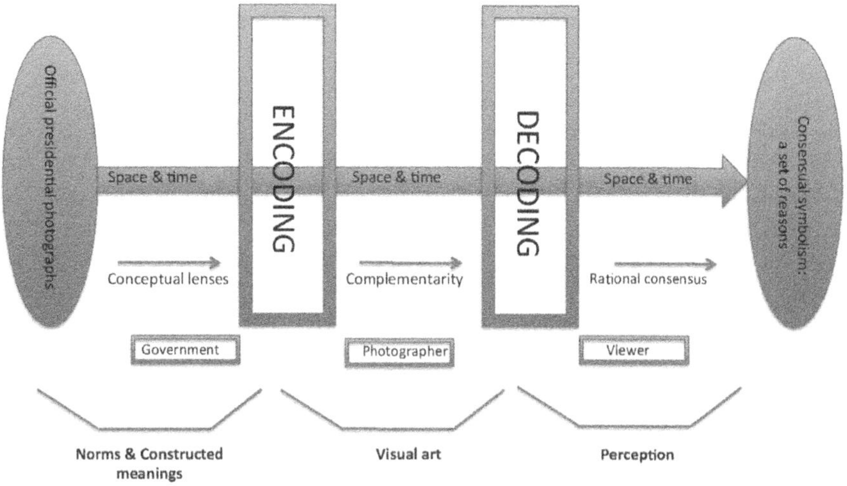

Fig. 6.1 Consensual symbolism in presidential photographs. Figure by the author

citizens but to create a cultural transfer of values. These persuasive elements immediately lead to strong feelings of national identity. So, there is a complex set of relationships between images and their viewers.

Indeed, official presidential photographs transcend the boundary of a particular audience to provide a universal message to the viewers. However this visual-cultural equation is difficult to assess, as there are no verbal elements in these photographs. Accordingly, the viewer "becomes complicit with the [photographer] in telling the story, creating a discourse, and [...] defining a cause that generates the narratives that will unfold".[21]

Barthes complexifies the analysis of photographs when he states "the viewer of the image receives at one and the same time the perceptual message and the cultural message".[22] For this reason, visual elements argue and communicate cultural codes with cultural specific meanings,[23] similarly to jurilinguistics.[24] Accordingly official presidential photographs are treated as language-like symbols in which "visual elements overlie, accentuate, render vivid and immediate, and otherwise elevate in forcefulness [...]"[25] national French ideals.

[21]Lewis, Suzanne. 1999. *The Rhetoric of Power in the Bayeux Tapestry*. Cambridge: Cambridge University Press. 33.

[22]Barthes, Roland. 1967. The rhetoric of the image. In *Elements of semiology*, trans. J. Cape, 9–34. New York: Hill and Wang. (Orig. 1964). 36.

[23]Aiello, 2006. 90.

[24]Gémar and Wagner, 2015.

[25]Blair, J. Anthony. 2004. The rhetoric of visual arguments. In *Defining visual rhetorics*, ed. Charles A. Hill and Marguerite Helmers, 50. Mahwah: Lawrence Erlbaum Associates.

6.2 French Presidential Photographs as Elements of Visual Persuasion

Shooting presidential photographs dates back to Adolphe Thiers (1871–1873) who was the first President of the III Republic. He established this tradition of a full state portrait using photography, a modern and fast means of communication, to expose the grandeur and authority of the French Republic, though no specific rules, at that time, for shooting were established. He even copied the posture of painted portraits. Hence state portraits derive from the official painted Royal portraits being exposed in the Kingdom and even beyond French borders; especially the one from the famous French painter—Hyacinthe Rigaud (1659–1743)—who painted the full-length portrait of King Louis XIV having similar resemblances as the style being used in state portraits.

Obviously Presidential photographs perform several important public functions. They reflect social knowledge and are potent symbols conveying the authority of the French institution. It is a specific genre photograph. Therefore, this genre operationalizes particular ideas in viewers' consciousness; i.e. the way visual elements are coded, and the social conventions linking signs with meaning. Meaning is thus intrinsic to the displayed elements and alludes to the "space-in-between", a porous and pliable interpretation and/or comprehension from viewers of visual items displayed in state portraits.

Descriptions of this specific genre involve attention to the identification and decoding of (1) fundamental visual characteristics forming the major physical fabric of these photographs, and of (2) discrete visual elements, which allude to cultural knowledge (Fig. 6.2).

The approaches chosen in this chapter present both elements being displayed in harmony, balance and integration in a specific space and time framework, with specific regulations. Mitchell explains the reason why "visual culture [...] is a site of convergence and conversation across disciplinary lines".[26] Indeed, within this space and time approach, objectivity is being completed with subjectivity where photographers organize, reorganize or even erase some elements to create new ways of looking, to challenge a rigid visual French ideal, and to reveal that citizens are socially conditioned:

> Whatever the pictorial turn is, then, it should be clear that it is not a return to naïve mimesis, copy or correspondence theories of representation, or a renewed metaphysics of pictorial "presence": it is rather a postlinguistic, postsemiotic rediscovery of the picture as a complex interplay between visuality, apparatus, institutions, discourse, bodies, and figurality.[27]

As already said, official French photographs are important visual sets of elements contributing to the presidential function. These photographs are displayed in all public administrations and town halls. They convey altogether an honorific

[26]Mitchell, 1995. 540.

[27]Mitchell, 1994. 16.

Period	(1) Fundamental visual characteristics	(2) Discrete visual elements
1958–1969 **Charles de Gaulle**	Formal attire Library of the Elysée Order of Liberation Red cord with the medal of the Legion of Honor	Book on the "Constitution of the V Republic" Book on the "History of the French Army"
1969–1974 **Georges Pompidou**	Black suit Library of the Elysée Red Cord with the medal of the Legion of Honor	
1974–1981 **Valéry Giscard d'Estaing**	French flag Black suit and tie	Rosette of the Legion of Honor
1981–1995 **François Mitterrand**	Black suit and tie Book of Montaigne "Essays"	Library of the Elysée Rosette of the Legion of Honor
1995–2007 **Jacques Chirac**	Garden of the Elysée Dark red suit and tie	Rosette of the Legion of Honor Colors: Blue, Red and White French flag
2007–2012 **Nicolas Sarkozy**	Black suit and tie European and French flags	Rosette of the Legion of Honor Library of the Elysée Symbol of France – 1912
2012– **François Hollande**	Garden of the Elysée Black suit and tie	Rosette of the Legion of Honor French and European flags

Fig. 6.2 Fundamental visual characteristics versus discrete elements. Figure by author

function with symbolic powers "that aims at imposing the vision of legitimate division".[28] Therefore, the symbols being displayed in these photographs consist in uniting the French people and in leading to a greater visual intensity over national identity. This identity is the embodiment of national spirit "to make the relevant object, concept of value fill the audience's entire 'field of consciousness'".[29] In other words, it is a portrait both in conformity with the norms and with the ideal of the state function, the garment 'summarizing' both these requirements.

State portraits mark a special selection of a French reality within a specific space and time framework that intensifies the function of the President of the French Republic. This genre is not about facial expressions like in family photographs but about the powerful visual representations of the French national identity and body expression, shaping an influential communicative role. These expressions may differ from one presidential period to another.

6.2.1 Charles de Gaulle (1958–1969) and Georges Pompidou (1969–1974)

If we consider the photographs of Charles de Gaulle and Georges Pompidou (Figs. 6.6 and 6.7), their posture is equivalent to Bourgeois photographs. Charles de Gaulle and Georges Pompidou stand in upright position in the Elysée library, and

[28]Bourdieu, Pierre. 1989. Social Space and Symbolic Power. *Sociological Theory* 7(1): 22.

[29]Perelman and Olbrechts-Tyceta, 1971. 118.

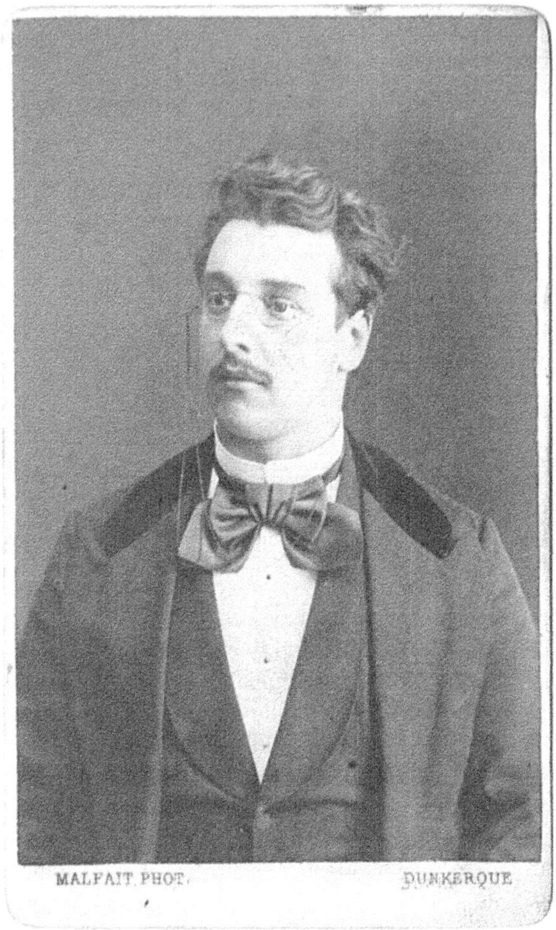

Fig. 6.3 Gentlemen (1874) © Wagner Family Collection/ Boulogne/Mer

they are not facing the camera. They do not smile on this solemn moment like the Bourgeois in 1874 (Fig. 6.3) or the soldier of World War I (Figs. 6.4 and 6.5).

Besides, Charles de Gaulle is dressed in formal attire with discrete military visual elements (epaulettes and metal buttons on his jacket) recalling his high-ranked military status (General). We consider that other photographs of soldiers, the display and their formal attires are always there to show the prominence of their ranks and this unique moment in their lives and/or careers (Figs. 6.4 and 6.5).

Under Charles de Gaulle's right hand, two leather-bound books are shown. Both of them are important in terms of the historical period in which the photograph was taken. The *Constitution of the V Republic* (1958) shows that he is the bearer and founding father of this Constitution. The second book entitled *History of the French Army* is a reminder of his military past as the General who actively participated to

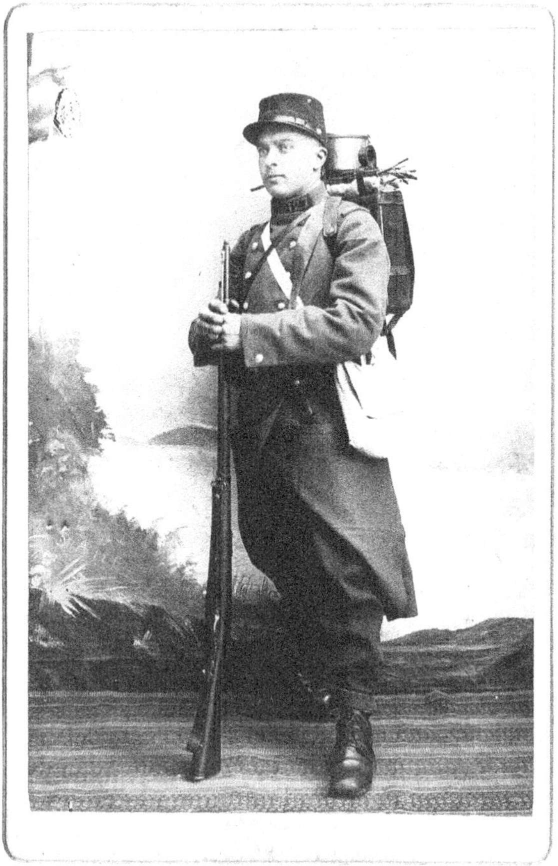

Fig. 6.4 Soldier, World War 1 © Wagner Family Collection/Boulogne/Mer

the Liberation of France during World War II. These two books, even though they are not in the foreground, not only secure the French citizens' rights but also constitute two elements that show Charles de Gaulle's sole authority to govern. Charles de Gaulle also wears the highest honors of the French Republic; i.e. the "Order of Liberation" and the "Red cord with the medal of the Legion of Honor". Contrary to Charles de Gaulle, Georges Pompidou has no military career. Therefore he wears only civil decorations on his black suit. He does not have under his right hand the book of the V Constitution, as it is now a standard practice.

The library where both Presidents stand is a place of power, dating back from Napoleon III who initiated its construction. Though it is rather small in shape with a precious material—mahogany—, the photographer focuses on this stylish element with the President in front creating an illusion of magnificence with plentiful red leather-bound books.

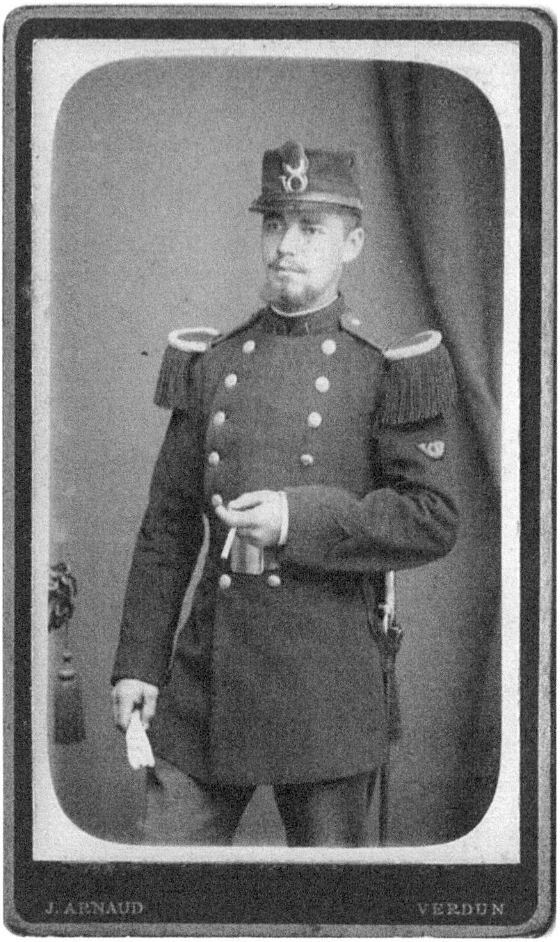

Fig. 6.5 Military officer (nineteenth century) © Wagner Family Collection/ Boulogne/Mer

6.2.2 Valéry Giscard d'Estaing (1974–1981)

This is a period of modernism, which radically differs from former state portraits. Undeniably time has changed and they are no longer referring to the Bourgeois pause of the early nineteenth century (see Figs. 6.3, 6.4 and 6.5). It is a head-and-shoulder portrait with only one discrete visual element—the Rosette of the Legion of Honor on his black suit. Indeed, under Giscard d'Estaing's presidency, abortion was legalized and the age of majority was set at 18 years. This portrait radically differs from the two former ones. Zooming in is horizontal and the photographer only focuses on his shoulders and tanned face. The President looks at the camera.

This photographic image (Fig. 6.8) desacralizes the presidential function and shows a young and smiling man of the present. President Valéry Giscard d'Estaing

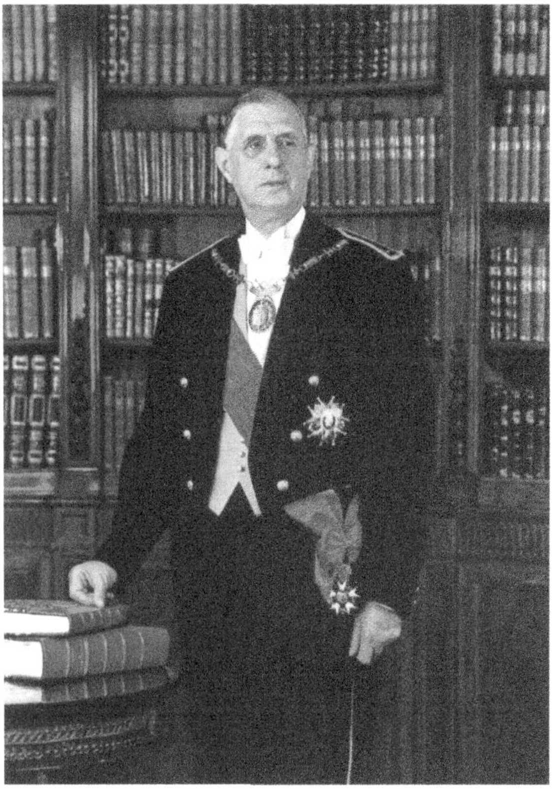

Fig. 6.6 Portrait officiel de Charles de Gaulle, Président de la République française (1958–1969), © La Documentation française. *Photo* Jean-Marie Marcel

is smiling, giving the idea to viewers that he may be more accessible, which is in continuity with his presidential campaign title: "*France dans les yeux*". In order to set aside rank, privilege and other advantages as shown with the two first Presidents of the V Republic, and to try to find an egalitarian appeal with citizens, it resembles more a family photograph.

The French tricolor flag is displayed behind him as an evocation of his highest duty for France. This flag is a fundamental visual characteristic as it is the ambassador, and so it activates a mighty mode of interpellation of citizenship, pride and identification. Indeed as it is the only visual element, the flag does not stand only for the French Republic, but also for all the values and conventions of civil society. It gives a particular inflection to this official presidential photograph.

6.2.3 François Mitterrand (1981–1995)

This portrait (Fig. 6.9) is an articulation, a synthesis between the three former ones (Charles de Gaulle, Georges Pompidou and Valéry Giscard d'Estaing). It fills the

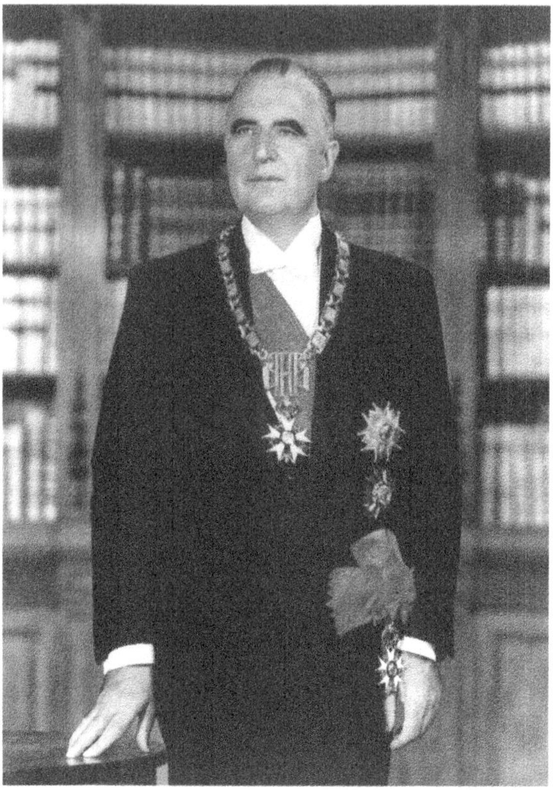

Fig. 6.7 Portrait officiel de Georges Pompidou, Président de la République française (1969–1974), © La Documentation française. *Photo* François Pagès/Paris-Match

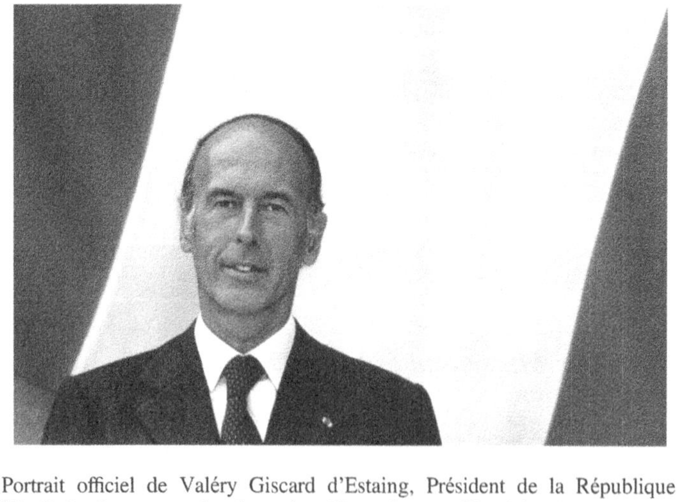

Fig. 6.8 Portrait officiel de Valéry Giscard d'Estaing, Président de la République française (1974–1981), © *La Documentation française. Photo Jacques-Henri Lartigue*

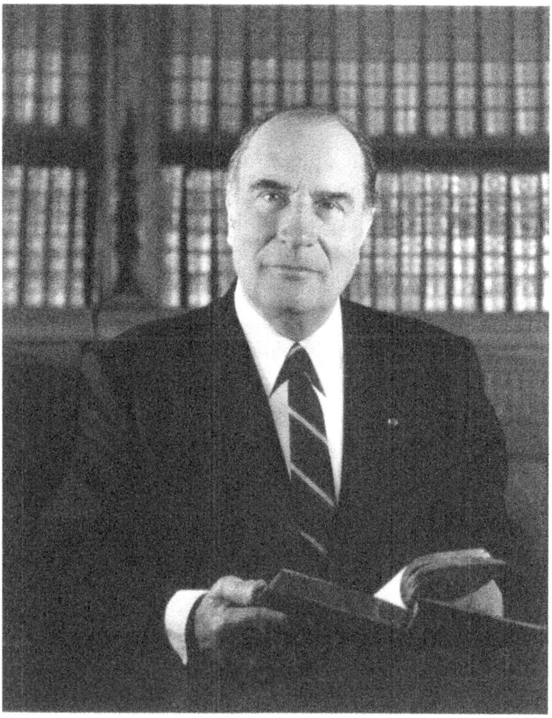

Fig. 6.9 Portrait officiel de François Mitterrand, Président de la République française (1981–1995), © *La Documentation française. Photo Gisèle Freund*

gap between tradition expressed in the official photographs of Charles de Gaulle and Georges Pompidou, and modernism shown in the official portrait of Valéry Giscard d'Estaing. The French flag has disappeared, but François Mitterrand still wears the Rosette of the Legion of Honor on his black suit.

Only the Elysée Library slightly appears in the background, the foreground being the President himself. François Mitterrand is in a sitting position surrounded by famous French history and literature books. He is smiling at viewers, giving a sense of intimacy as if people were invited to listen to a public reading. Indeed, he is shown as a knowledgeable man with one famous piece of literature opened in his hands—"The Essays" of Montaigne. This book was not chosen at random; Stefan Zweig's review argued that its reading permits "the individual, who freely thinks, [to honor] all freedom on earth".[30]

[30]Zweig, Stefan. 1935. *Montaigne*. Paris: PUF.

6.2.4 *Jacques Chirac (1995–2007)*

For the first time under the V Republic, the French President is portrayed in the garden of the Elysée with his hands behind his back (Fig. 6.10). He wears a dark red suit and tie with a blue shirt and the Rosette of the Legion of Honor, having then a similar resemblance to the French flag. Zooming differs from others. On the foreground, the most important visual element is the President in the garden of the Elysée—also known as the People's House—where all Presidents usually exercise political power and take important decisions.

This state portrait also integrates other discrete visual elements, which constitute motifs of political representation including nationalism and civic republicanism. Though they are secondary icons, they still constitute necessary principles of design and appeal. The flag rising behind him and high above the Elysée federates all the French historical values and conventions of civil society. Besides, the wind is flowing in the right direction giving the flag a particular inflection with a sense of destiny to the official photograph.

The blue shirt is a reminder of a Paris blue sky with Jacques Chirac standing in a freshly-mowed green lawn with shadows of age-old trees in the summer season. Furthermore, all the colors representing the history of France are visible in the background with blue on the roof, white on some windows and red on the façade of

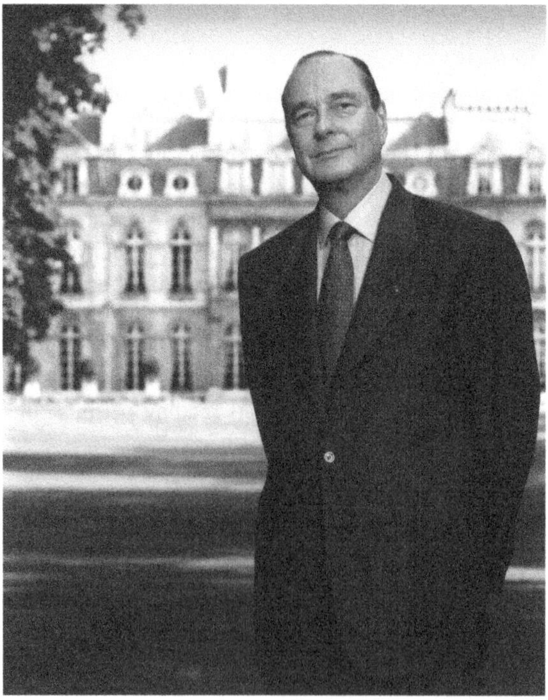

Fig. 6.10 Portrait officiel de Jacques Chirac, Président de la République française (1995–2007), © *La Documentation française. Photo Bettina Rheims*

the Elysée. All these colors were not displayed at random and were shown in a specific order as a reminder of the French flag (blue first, white second and red third).

The way perspectives are widened in the official state portrait permits the photographer to encompass a broader French national vision, to brush with touches of natural elements (colors, shadows of trees and lawn) rendering the moment alive and more prestigious. To put the final touch, President Jacques Chirac is smiling on the sunny solemn moment.

6.2.5 Nicolas Sarkozy (2007–2012)

With the election of Nicolas Sarkozy as the French President in 2007, the official state portrait changes style again. Nicolas Sarkozy is back in the Elysée library (Fig. 6.11)—a magnificent place of knowledge and know-how. Contrary to official portraits of the first two Presidents of the V Republic, the zooming has a wider focus on part of the Napoleonic library. The French President is facing the camera, smiling, with the bourgeois pause of the early nineteenth century. On his right,

Fig. 6.11 Portrait officiel de Nicolas Sarkozy, Président de la République française (2007), © *La Documentation française. Photo Philippe Warrin*

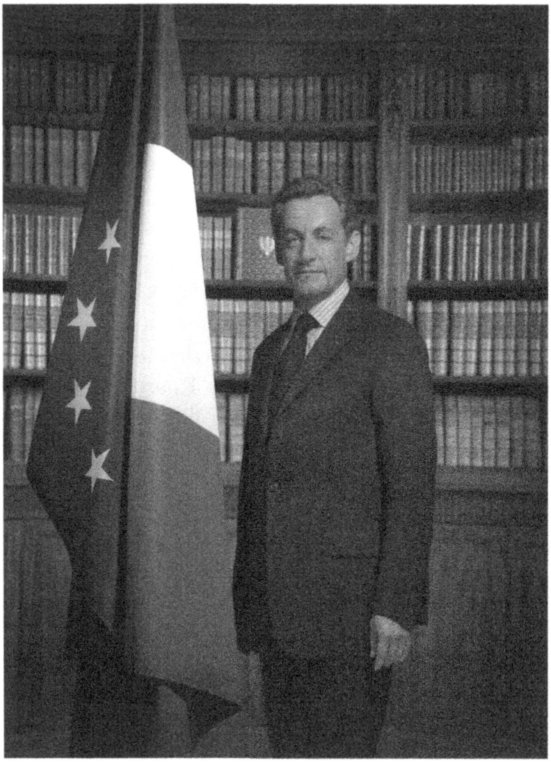

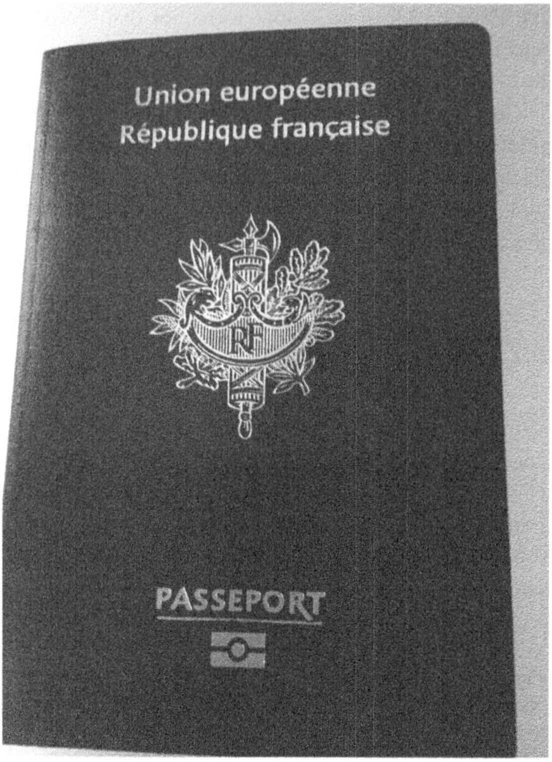

Fig. 6.12 French passport. Photograph by author

two flags appear. They are fundamental visual characteristics showing the importance of both France and Europe for the new resident of the Elysée in terms of national and European political powers. Contrary to the Presidential photograph of Jacques Chirac, the flag is not waving in the wind. And if we consider the photograph of Valéry Giscard d'Estaing, it is not shown in the same way. Furthermore, if we turn to the European flag the photographer has not shown it in full, as only four stars are visible. Like his predecessor, he is wearing a suit and tie with a blue and white striped shirt, with the Rosette of the Legion of Honor—in red—completing the coding of the French flag.

This portrait operates two important functions. The first one is to allow Sarkozy to root himself in the most solid historical tradition of France with the Elysée library—as a place of power and knowledge—and with one very discrete element at the same level as his eyes. This visual sign is not displayed accidentally indeed and appears on the cover of a book, the only one to be shown in this position. It represents the symbol of France, dating back from 1912 and still visible on all French passports, seen in Fig. 6.12.

6.2.6 François Hollande (2012–2017)

When François Hollande is elected in 2012, the state portrait is radically modified with fewer visual elements. The garden of the Elysée constitutes a scenic space outside of all political conventions, knowledge and power. President François Hollande stands in the sunny garden of the Elysée wearing a black suit and tie with the Rosette of the Legion of Honor (Fig. 6.13)—nearly invisible to the eyes. The portrait conveys an impression of movement as if he were walking towards us with his arms hanging down in a sense of simplicity and easy access to people. Indeed when campaigning, François Hollande presented himself as a "normal man", close to people. Therefore, Raymond Depardon's main goal is to faithfully transpose this notion of the political game strategy within the official state portrait. Besides, this sense of movement towards people has a high communicative effect. As all official photographs are displayed in French official buildings and town halls, it gives an impression of a normal man coming towards people to talk and discuss.

On the right-hand side of the photograph, the French and European flags decorate the Banquet Hall of the Elysée. However, their presentation is particular. The French National Convention adopted the modern blue-white-red flag as the national French flag on 15 February 1794 (27 pluviôse an II) stipulating that "The national flag shall be formed of the three national colors, set in three equal bands, *vertically*[31] arranged so that the blue is nearest to the staff, the white in the middle, and the red flying". Today the French flag enshrined in the French Constitution 1958

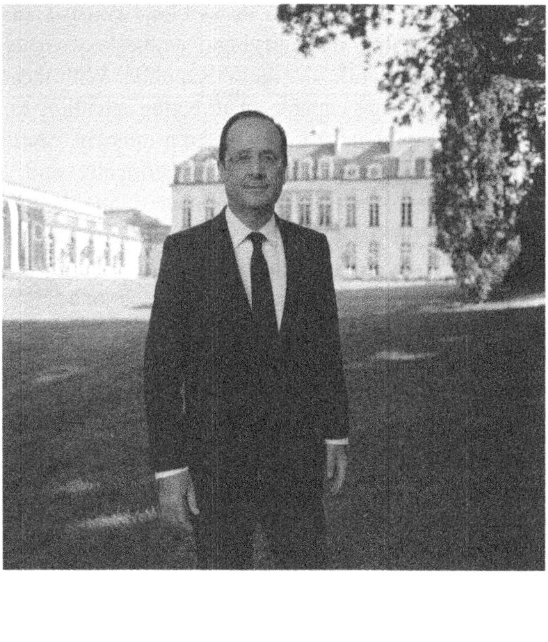

Fig. 6.13 Portrait officiel de François Hollande, Président de la République française (2012), © *DILA-La Documentation française. Photo Raymond Depardon*

[31]my emphasis.

(art. 2) is flown on all public buildings for special events and/or ceremonies as an ambassador of the French identity. When looking at the Presidential photograph of François Hollande, it is displayed horizontally with blue (first), white (second) and red (third). But if the flag is set in the vertical plane, the colors are then shown as red first, white second and blue third. Accordingly, it creates confusion with the Dutch flag as rightly expressed by Kauffer, an expert who recently published the history of the French flag.[32] Besides, the European flag appears first on the photograph, which is contrary to Decree 4 May 1963[33] stipulating that the European flag should be situated on the right of the French flag. So if we look at a public building, it means on our left.

6.3 Official Photographs as Symbols of the French Heritage

With these analyses over time and space, the idea is to explore how focus, context visualization and signs are displayed to enhance a significant communicative power. These state portraits show a particular selection of reality in order to acquire greater intensity and prominence for the viewers, and provide a special opportunity to explore visual imagery and ideological articulation in French culture. They are monumental photographs extending across the entire public space and through historical time, as they will remain important political and cultural French heritage over the long term.

Visualizing France and its symbols consists in separating, reuniting, decomposing, re-creating and carrying a synthesis of visual symbols over a specific space and time framework, i.e. the V Republic. With these analyses, it is noticeable that photographers are capable of directing attention to fundamental visual characteristics as they intersect in this solemn moment. *Studium*[34] is the only valid concept here as everything is socially, historically and legally grounded and coded. Photographers' main goal is to render visible the most relevant and identifying sets of elements in the foreground so that the main cultural and political articulations and transfers of knowledge are not lost in the mix. Therefore, photographers operate a cultural transfer of visual information among this 'space-in-between', and ground national symbols in the social experience of everyday life.

Hence, state portraits like Royal portraits build historical momentum. Such portraits are regarded as encapsulating a specific moment in time and history. The political and social imagery of a President, a King or a Queen shows the prestige of their roles vesting them with visual images expressing particulars to evoke the

---

[32]Kauffer, Rémi. 2012. *La Fabuleuse Histoire du Drapeau Français*. Quai de Scène: Paris.

[33]http://www.defense.gouv.fr/site-memoire-et-patrimoine/memoire/ceremonies/pavoisement-des-edifices-publics.

[34]Barthes, 2000. 28.

universal. Further citizens witness history and may engage their own feelings through the stimulation of official portraits and the displayed visual elements therein.

Accordingly, portraits offer a visual rhetorical complexity, a figurative speech, which deeply entangles codes of visual presentations. Osborn emphasizes "depictive rhetoric" which is a strategic mode of visual communication that "lingers in the collective memory of audiences as representative of their subjects".[35] Visual rhetoric is therefore a mode of inquiry to explore our understandings of this "space-in-between" within visual culture.

References

Aiello Georgia. Spring 2006. Theoretical advances in critical visual analysis: Perception, ideology, mythologies, and social semiotics. *Journal of Visual Literacy* 26(2): 82–102.

Barthes Roland. 1967. "The rhetoric of the image". In *Elements of Semiology*. Translated by J. Cape, New York: Hill and Wang. (Orig. 1964).

Barthes, Roland. 1974. *S/Z: an essay*. New York: Farrar, Straus and Giroux.

Barthes, Roland. 2000. *Camera Lucida*. London: Vintage Books.

Blair, J.Anthony. 2004. "The rhetoric of visual arguments" in defining visual rhetorics. In *Hill and Marguerite Helmers*, ed. A. Charles. Mahwah NJ: Lawrence Erlbaum Associates.

Bourdieu, Pierre. 1989. Social space and symbolic power. *Sociological Theory* 7 (1): 14–25.

Foss, Sonja K. 2005. Theory of visual rhetoric. In *Handbook of Visual Communication: Theory, Methods, and Media*. ed. Ken Smith, Sandra Moriarty, Gretchen Barbatsis, and Keith Kenney, 141–152. Mahwah, New Jersey: Lawrence Erlbaum.

Gémar Jean-Claude, Wagner Anne (eds). 2015. Special Issue. Traduction juridique et jurilinguistique: discipline en voie de mondialisation. États et perspectives / Legal Translation and Jurilinguistics: Globalizing Disciplines. Retrospects and Prospects. *International Journal for the Semiotics of Law* 28(1).

http://www.defense.gouv.fr/site-memoire-et-patrimoine/memoire/ceremonies/pavoisement-des-edifices-publics

Kauffer, Rémi. 2012. *La fabuleuse histoire du drapeau français*. Paris: Quai de Scène.

Lewis, Suzanne. 1999. *The Rhetoric of Power in the Bayeux Tapestry*. Cambridge: Cambridge University Press.

Mitchell, W.J.T. 1994. *Picture Theory: Essays on Verbal and Visual Representation*. Chicago: University of Chicago Press.

Mitchell, W.J.T. 1995. Interdisciplinarity and visual culture. *Art Bulletin* 70 (4): 540–544.

Nissbett, Richard E., and Lee Ross. 1980. *Human Inference: Strategies and Shortcomings of Social Judgment*. Chapell Hill: University of North Carolina Press.

Osborn Michael M. 1986. Rhetorical depiction. In *Form, Genre, and the Study of Political Discourse*. ed. Herbert, Simons, and Aram Aghazarian. Columbia: University of South Carolina Press.

Pearce, Lynne. 1991. *Woman, Image, Text: Readings in Pre-Raphaelite Art and Literature*. Buffalo: University of Toronto Press.

[35]Osborn, Michael M. 1986. Rhetorical depiction. In *Form, genre, and the study of political discourse*, eds. Herbert Simons and Aram Aghazarian, 79. Columbia: University of South Carolina Press.

Perelman, Chaim, and Lucie Olbrechts-Tyteca. 1971. *The New Rhetoric: A Treatise on Argumentation*. Translated by John Wilkinson and Purcell Weaver. Notre Dame: University of Notre Dame Press.
Soja, E.W. 1996. *Third Space—Journeys to Los Angeles and other real—and Imagined Places*. Cambridge: Blackwell Publishers.
Wagner Anne and Bozzo-Rey Malik. 2013. French commemorative postage stamps— Means of legal culture and memory. In *Law, Culture and Visual Studies* ed.Wagner Anne, and Sherwin Richard K. The Netherlands: Springer.
Wagner, Anne. 2011. French urban space management—A visual semiotic approach behind power and control. *International Journal for the Semiotics of Law* 24 (2): 227–242.
Wagner, Anne. 2014. Game of power within the French urban landscape: a socio-legal semiotic analysis of communication, vision and space. *International Journal for the Semiotics of Law* 27 (1): 161–182.
Wagner, Anne. 2016. A space in-between: legal translation as a 'third space'. *Journal of Civil Law Studies* 29 (1): 167–190.
Wagner, Anne, and Gémar Jean-Claude (eds). 2014. Decision-making in legal translation, interpretation and Speech Act—legal semiotic culture-mediation techniques. *Semiotica* 201(1/4)
Zelizer, Barbie. 1992. *Covering the Body: The Kennedy Assassination, the Media, and the Shaping of Collective Memory*. Chicago: Chicago University Press.
Zweig. Stefan. 1935. *Montaigne*. Paris: PUF.

Anne Wagner is an associate professor at the Université Lille—Nord de France (Centre de Recherche Droits et Perspectives du Droit, équipe René Demogue). She is the Editor-in-Chief of the *International Journal for the Semiotics of Law and Series Editor of Law, Language and Communication*. She is President of the *International Roundtables for the Semiotics of Law*, Vice-President of the *Multicultural Association of Law and Language* (Hong Kong). She has lectured in Asia, Australia, Europe, and North America. She has extensively published research papers in legal cultural and visual studies, law and semiotics, legal discourse analyses, and legal translation.

Part III
Untimely Reflections on the Nation's Law

Chapter 7
Here and Now: From "Aestheticizing Politics" to "Politicizing Art"

Desmond Manderson

Abstract The relationship between art, law, and politics reached its zenith in the 1930s. This essay takes as its point of departure Walter Benjamin's celebrated essay on the subject, and draws it into a dialogue with two key events that occurred at the same time and that shed new light on Benjamin's work. This intersection has not previously been explored. A year before Benjamin's essay was published, the Mexican mural movement was already wracked by a debate that prefigures his central themes and concerns. A year after Benjamin's essay, the Paris World's Fair perfectly exemplifies his thesis and his prognosis. Yet both these episodes invite us to reconsider Benjamin's too-reductive contrast between 'fascism' and 'communism.' Instead, the interplay between 1935, 1936, and 1937 reflects a much more universal shift in the dynamic between aesthetics, nation, politics and law. In particular, the real distinction lies in how the work of art relates to the 'here and now', to time and place. Reading these three events together illuminates the importance of different modes of temporal and spatial instantiation if we are to resist an 'aestheticizing politics,' by 'politicizing art'.

7.1 The Work of Art

The nation is not a natural construction. It is, as this volume has insisted, mediated through representations and particularly through representations with a sensory component. Images therefore are primary means through which a collective identity is established. They serve to constitute myths of belonging; to distinguish friend from enemy, as Schmitt put it.[1] They tell stories; they create models and examples that frame our social existence. But they also generate the icons and symbols whose

[1]Schmitt, Carl. 2008. *Concept of the Political*. Trans. George Schwab. Chicago: University of Chicago Press.

D. Manderson (✉)
ANU College of Law, Australian National University, Canberra, Australia
e-mail: desmond.manderson@anu.edu.au

S. Huygebaert et al. (eds.), *Sensing the Nation's Law*, Studies in the History of Law and Justice 13, https://doi.org/10.1007/978-3-319-75497-0_7

repetition and familiarity—flags, monuments, even colour combinations[2]—etch habits of feeling and mental associations deep into our psyche. While this has long been and remains true, one moment of our recent history stands out in its commitment to the constitution of national identity through the fusion of art, law, and politics. I mean, of course, the period between the wars. Carl Schmitt was not an outlier in his conceptualization of "political theology".[3] On the contrary, evidence of the link he traced there was everywhere around him. Not just in the calculated exploitation of aesthetic forms of authority in Fascist Italy after 1922 or Nazi Germany after 1933; but no less in Socialist Realism, or in Mexico where the work of the Mexican mural movement was self-consciously advanced as a key agent in the constitution of post-revolutionary nationalism.

It comes as no surprise then that Walter Benjamin, whose ability to detect the faintest breeze of the *Zeitgeist* was so keen, should choose to write on the subject. In *The Work of Art in the Age of its Mechanical Reproducibility*, first published in 1936, Walter Benjamin pens the obituary of the artwork: the death of its presence and the implications of its absence.[4]

> That which withers in the age of mechanical reproduction is the aura of the work of art. This is a symptomatic process whose significance points beyond the realm of art [...]. Both processes are intimately connected with the contemporary mass movements. Their most powerful agent is the film.[5]

This does not amount to a species of technological determinism.[6] On the contrary, the reproducibility of photography and, even more importantly, of film, is "*symptomatic*" of a broader process "whose significance points *beyond* the realm of art". Indeed, elsewhere he describes the notion of "art for art's sake" as a doomed response to a much earlier crisis in the relationship of aesthetics and politics,

---

[2]For discussions of the political power of colours, see the use of gold and red in Aeschylus' *Oresteia*; Desmond Manderson on the use of imperial gold, red and black in Gustav Klimt's *Jurisprudence*; or Morgan Thomas on David's use of red, white and blue colour fields for the French flag: see Lebeck, Anne. 1971. *The Oresteia: A Study in language and structure*. Cambridge: Harvard University Press.; Manderson, Desmond. 2015. Klimt's Jurisprudence: Sovereign Violence and the Rule of Law. *Oxford Journal of Legal Studies* 35 1–28.; Thomas, Morgan. 2017. Law and the Revolutionary Motif after Jacques Louis David. In *Law and the Visual: Transition, Transmission, Transformation*, ed. Desmond Manderson. Toronto: University of Toronto Press [forthcoming].

[3]Schmitt, Carl. 1985. *Political Theology*. Trans. George Schwab. Chicago: University of Chicago Press.

[4]Benjamin, Walter. 2006a. 'The Work of Art in the Age of Its Mechanical Reproducibility' Zeitschfirt fur Sozialfoschung (May 1936). In *Walter Benjamin, Selected Writings Volume 3, 1935-38*, eds. Howard Eiland, and Michael Jennings, 101–133. Cambridge, Mass.: Belknap Press. As is conventional, quotations are, unless otherwise indicated, taken from the slightly modified Third Version, in 2006, *Walter Benjamin, Selected Writings Volume 4, 1938-40*, eds. Howard Eiland, and Michael Jennings, 251–283. Cambridge, Mass.: Belknap Press.

[5]Ibid. 254.

[6]Eagleton, Terry. 1981. *Walter Benjamin: Towards a Revolutionary Criticism*. London: Verso, 176.

"a crisis which was by no means occasioned exclusively by photography but rather *in a relatively independent manner* by the appeal of art works to the masses".[7] Mass media, mass production, and "mass movements" are both fruits and seeds, not just of a technological but a social and just as importantly an aesthetic revolution.

In the inter-war period, art's new relationship to masses, to mass production, and to mass circulation, was a critical component of the ritual constitution of social and political identities. The emotive paraphernalia of fascism—propaganda films, marching troops, flags, insignia, and the rest—clearly unleashed the potential of aesthetics to harness collective experience as a powerful social force.[8] But fascism, as Benjamin makes clear, was merely exploiting wider aesthetic trends. Marinetti's futurist manifestoes embraced the world war as a "cleansing purge", "the most beautiful Futurist poem to date". "Take out your pick-axes, your axes and hammers and wreck, wreck the venerable cities, pitilessly".[9] George Sorel's *Reflections on Violence* (1908) offered a more intellectual account of the same visceral desire, blaming the atomized individual and materialist culture for a widespread social malaise, and advocating instead an intuitive, collective, psychological—in other words mass and aesthetic—consciousness.[10] The World War only intensified these links between violence, suffering, and redemption. Sorel's contribution was to shift the discourse from class conflict to "national regeneration" and from reason and history to psychology and myth. His definition of myth as "a system of images" gave art a central role in the revolution to come.[11] We may even say that the aesthetic mediation of the representation of power and law, organized specifically around mass identities in the form of the nation-state, and exploited through the new technologies of mass media, became central features of modern sovereignty.

Benjamin observes that, by using aesthetics to repress, sublimate, or indeed to exacerbate the underlying social tensions in society, the inevitable outcome—nay, the necessary *purpose*—of fascism was war. He concludes with a clarion call: "Such is the aestheticizing of politics as practiced by Fascism. Communism replies by politicizing art".[12] Benjamin implies two different approaches to the relationship between art, politics, and the nation. But given how widespread the aesthetic

---

[7]Ibid. 264.

[8]Mosse, George. 1996. Fascist aesthetics and society: some considerations. *Journal of contemporary history*: 245–252.; Strathausen, Carsten. 1999. Nazi aesthetics. *Culture, Theory and Critique* 42 (1):5–19.

[9]Eagleton, 1981. 269–270; Braun, Emily. 2000. *Mario Sironi and Italian Modernism: Art and Politics under Fascism*. Cambridge: Cambridge University Press, 31–32. See also Affron, Matthew, and Mark Antliff. 1997. *Fascist Visions: Art and Ideology in France and Italy*. Princeton: Princeton University Press.

[10]Sorel, George. 2004 [1908]. *Reflections on Violence*. Trans. T. E. Hulme, and J. Roth. Mineola, NY: Dover. Antliff, Mark. La Cité française. In Affron and Antliff, 1997, 134–170, at 140.

[11]Sorel, 2004. quoted in Braun, Emily. Mario Sironi's Urban Landscapes. In Affron and Antliff, 1997, 101–133 at 101. See Emilio Gentile, The Myth of National Regeneration in Italy. In Affron and Antliff, 1997, 25–45, at 36–38.

[12]Benjamin, 2006a (The Work of Art…). 270.

constitution of the nation had become, it would be a mistake to take the contrast between fascism and communism at face value. A clue to the true distinction can be found in Benjamin's references, in *The Work of Art* and then again in *On the Concept of History*, to *Jetztzeit*, "here and now", time and place.[13] The "political theology" of art situates representations in a mythological framework, outside of place or time. This rhetoric of eternity attempts to shield political claims from scrutiny or context. Art that resists this ideological appropriation, functions in the *opposite* way, testing political mythology against its precise contexts, times, and consequences. To return to Benjamin's terms, "aestheticizing politics" turns visual representation into something a-temporal and u-topian—literally, timeless and placeless. "Politicizing art" on the contrary, involves returning the image to the temporal and spatial specificities of its origin, with a vengeance. Thus is made possible an art that can hold politics to account rather than simply exult in it.

7.2 Myth, Legend and Utopia

Benjamin was not the first person to note and critique this problematic relationship. The question had already been raised—not in Berlin or Paris or Moscow but in "faraway Mexico", as Leon Trotsky put it.

> The official art of the Soviet Union – and there is no other over there - resembles totalitarian justice; that is to say, it is based on lies and deceit [...]. Do you wish to see with your own eyes the hidden springs of the social revolution? Look at the frescoes of Rivera. Do you wish to know what revolutionary art is like? Look at the frescoes of Rivera."[14]

Aesthetically sophisticated and emotionally powerful as they undoubtedly were, Rivera's murals have left an ambivalent legacy.[15] In the aftermath of the fratricidal

---

[13]Benjamin, 2006a.; Benjamin, Walter. 2006b. On the Concept of History (May 1940). In *Walter Benjamin, Selected Writings Volume 4, 1938-40*, eds. Howard Eiland, and Michael Jennings, 389–400. Cambridge, Mass.: Belknap Press. at XIV, 395.

[14]Trotsky, Leon. 1938 Art and Politics in our Epoch (letter). *Partisan Review*, June 18. Reprinted in 1950. *Fourth International* 11 (2): 61–64.

[15]See Craven, David. 1997. *Diego Rivera as Epic Modernist*. New York: GL Hall.; Rochfort, Desmond. 1987. *The Murals of Diego Rivera*. London: Journeyman.; Craven, David. 2001. Recent literature on Diego Rivera and Mexican muralism. *Latin American Research Review* 36 (3):221–237.; Coffey, Mary Katherine. 2002. Muralism and the people: Culture, popular citizenship, and government in post-revolutionary Mexico. *The Communication Review* 5 (1):7–38.; Lopez, Rick, Desmond Rochfort, Mary Vaughan, and Stephen Lewis. 2006. The Eagle and the Virgin: Nation and Cultural Revolution in Mexico, 1920-1940. Durham: Duke University Press.; Paz, Octavio. 1967. Re/Visions. In *Labyrinth of Solitude*. London: Allen Lane.; Folgarait, Leonard. 1998. *Mural Painting and Social Revolution in Mexico, 1920-1940*. Cambridge: Cambridge University Press.; Anreus, Alejandro, Leonard Folgarait, and Robin Adeleeds Greeley. 2012. Mexican Muralism—A Critical History. Berkeley: University of California Press.; Coffey, Mary Katherine. 2012. *How a Revolutionary Art became Official Culture: Murals, Museums, and the Mexican State*. Durham & London: Duke University Press.

revolutionary war that shook Mexico from 1910 to 1920, the post-revolutionary government of Alvaro Obregón and his successors sought to bind together the state, the nation, and the party into a unified body politic. A highly ambitious program of publicly funded art was central to this goal. It conceived of the promotion and dissemination of a distinctively Mexican art movement as essential to forging a national ideology, and to legitimating the Mexican State.[16] Muralists, notably Rivera, José Orozco, and David Siqueiros, received enormous commissions to realize their work on the walls of government complexes and in public spaces, such as the Palacio de Bellas Artes, the Ministry of Public Education,[17] and the National Palace.[18] As Octavio Paz put it, "that was the way in which a mistake began which ended with the perversion of Mexican mural painting: on the one hand, it was a revolutionary art, or one that called itself revolutionary; on the other, it was an official art".[19] In terms of this chapter and this volume, in Mexico even more than in Germany or Italy or the Soviet Union, the representation of a body of images from the nation's past created a set of founding myths and linked them to rituals, to collective identity, to political legitimacy and to sensory experience.

In an essay entitled *Rivera's Counter-Revolutionary Road*[20] Siqueiros demurred from Trotsky's rapturous enthusiasm. In 1935, the conflict between the two artists boiled over at the Palacio de Bellas Artes. Rivera was coerced or persuaded to sign an artistic *mea culpa*, conceding that his "art has served the demagogic interests of the government", and that it was "an error to realize murals almost exclusively in the interiors of grand buildings".[21] Notwithstanding its edge of Stalinist menace, Siqueiros' critique was astute. In treating Rivera's work as essentially ideologically reactionary, his critique draws attention to the very problem that Benjamin was to address a year later.

In particular, what makes Rivera's work troubling from Benjamin's and Siqueiros' point of view is its lack of a coherent position in time. Elsewhere in this volume, Angela Condello insists that a distinct feature of the function of the work of art in the field of political identity lies in its ability to operate as a "paradigm", meaningfully linking "the concreteness of the specific instance and the universality

[16]See for example discussions in Folgarait, 1998.; Coffey, 2002.

[17]Diego Rivera, murals (Mexico City: Secretariat of Public Education (SEP) Main Headquarters, 1923-28).

[18]Diego Rivera, *The History of Mexico from the Conquest to the Future,* staircase triptych, (Mexico City: Palacio Nacional, 1929-35); *From Pre-Hispanic Civilization to the Conquest,* eleven patio corridor murals (Mexico City: Palacio Nacional, 1942-51).

[19]Quoted in Mary Coffey, 2002. 1.

[20]Siqueiros, David. 1934. Rivera's Counter-Revolutionary Road. *New Masses,* May 29. See also Siqueiros, David. 1975. *Art and Revolution.* New York: Lawrence and Wishart, 332–334.

[21]See Jolly, Jennifer. 2012. Siqueiros' Communist proposition for Mexican Muralism. In *Mexican Muralism—A Critical History*, eds. Alejandro Anreus, Leonard Folgarait, and Robin Adele Greeley, 75–92. Berkeley: University of California Press.; Coffey, 2012.; González Cruz Manjarrez, Maricela. 1996. *La polémica Siqueiros-Rivera: planteamientos estético-políticos 1934-1935.* Mexico D.F.: Museo Dolores Olmedo Patiño.

of the value that is transmitted". The work of art brings together the abstract *through* the concrete, and the universal *through* the particular. One can hear in this echoes of Derrida's reflections on the relationship between law and literature, in Kafka's *Before the Law*.[22]

> There is no literature without a work, without an absolutely singular performance, and this necessary irreplaceability again recalls with the man from the country asks when the singular crosses the universal, when the categorical engages the idiomatic, as a literature always must. The man from the country had difficulty in grasping that an entrance was singular or unique when it should have been universal as in truth it was. He had difficulty with literature.

Literature, like legal aesthetics, is a process which both realizes the contingent historical moment—the "here and now" of an historical crossroads—and at the same time transcends it.

Yet there is another side to this story that bears our sustained attention in this volume. What distinguishes the aesthetic nationalism that succumbs to ideology is its effort to short-circuit this process. In the 1930s, art regularly refused to engage with the contingency of time and place, moving directly to abstract or universal claims of nationhood, identity, and belonging. That is what Benjamin attacks by "aestheticizing the political", and what Siqueiros condemns as "counter-revolutionary".

In all the great artists of Mexican mural renaissance—Rivera, Siqueiros, Orozco—mythology substitutes for critique. The mythic register of the Mexican muralists postulates a rhythm that swells up from out of the deep past, and that still endures.[23] Myth knots together the past and the present into an eternal truth, treating history and politics as epiphenomenal. It is a question of the disavowal of time.[24]

In José Orozco in particular, political action is depicted as a kind of futile striving that is incapable of modifying the mythic structures of the land or the people.[25] The dark stains of violence, death, and corruption are never far from the surface in his work, and no amount of scrubbing will remove them. Many of his works lift their subjects out of a particular historical moment and use them as the medium to deliver a timeless message. What makes *The Trench* (Fig. 7.1) so moving, for example, is the way it abstracts from a specific soldier or war to make a statement that transcends the particulars of a battle.[26] Some have read the three

---

[22]Derrida, Jacques. 1992. Before the Law. In *Acts of Literature*, ed. Derek Attridge, 181–220. London: Routledge. at 213.

[23]Coffey, 2012. 33, 64.

[24]This argument is developed at greater length in the chapter on Mexican muralism in Manderson, Desmond. 2017. *Concepts of Law and Time in the Visual Arts*. Cambridge: Cambridge University Press.

[25]Rochfort, Desmond. 1998. *Mexican Muralists: Orozco, Rivera, Siqueiros*. San Francisco: Chronicle Books., e.g. 99, 118, 140. See Greeley, Robin. 2012. Nietzsche contra Marx in Mexico. In *Mexican Muralism—A Critical History*, eds. Alejandro Anreus, Leonard Folgarait, and Robin Adele Greeley, 148–173. Berkeley: University of California Press. at 158.

[26]José Orozco, *The Trench*, mural (Mexico City: Colegio San Ildefenso, 1922-24).

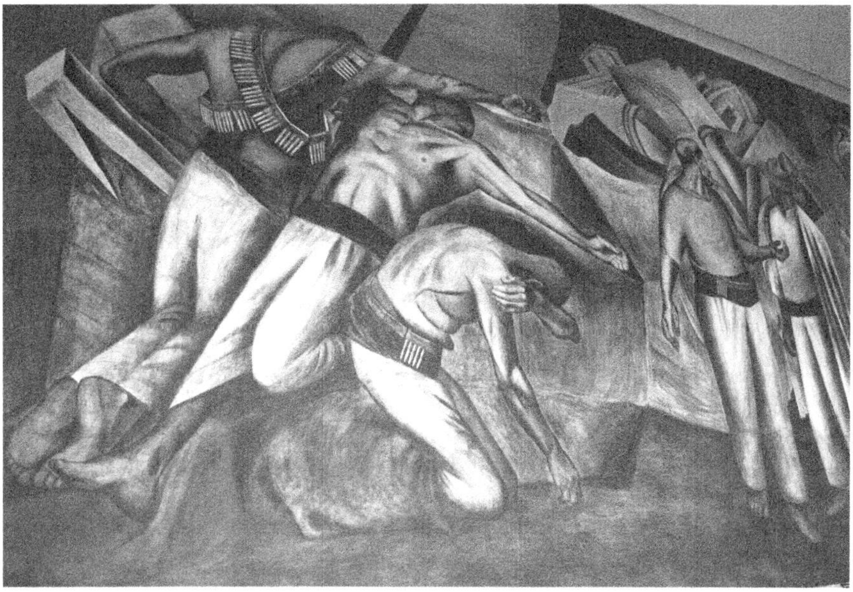

Fig. 7.1 José Clemente Orozco, *The Trench*. Mural, Colegio San Ildefenso, Mexico City. (1922–24) Wikimedia Commons

overlapping figures as a freeze-frame that traces the fall of a body in time and space. But it seems to me that Orozco's point of reference here is not so much slo-mo, but montage.

The three men represent not a single human being falling, but three positions of abjection, all devoid of face or identity, all lost, three snapshots from the eternal tragedy of war. The murals in the Palacio de Gobierno in Guadalajara likewise treat ideology, whether Christian, communist, or fascist, as equally destructive and eternally at war.[27] Even when he portrays specifically historical figures, such as *Hidalgo*,[28] he tends to surround them with the trappings of myth and work them loose from their social and political context. The juxtaposition of Father Hidalgo, brandishing a burning torch (a reference to a famous act that touched off the war of independence in 1811) alongside communist and fascist warmongers from a century later, implies that the apocalyptic fire he lit still burns.

The timelessness of myth is not a distance but a presence; not a lesson of change but of the illusory nature of change. As Roland Barthes puts it, myth transforms historical intention into a natural justification, "making contingency appear eternal" and reducing human decisions to "the simplicity of essences". "For the very end of myths is to immobilize the world: they must suggest and mimic a universal

[27]See in particular Rochfort, 1998. 83–120, 161–84.

[28]Orozco, *Hidalgo*, mural (Guadalajara, Mexico: Government Palace, 1949).

order".[29] This universal order is of course the very opposite of politics which treats the established order as contingent and seeks to intervene in it. A *political* reading of Hidalgo would think about what he did that changed history; Orozco thinks about what he did that didn't.

In Diego Rivera, above all, time is made up of a series of unbridgeable abysses. Take the *History of Mexico* series, comprising the large triptych on the ground floor of the Palacio Nacional and eleven vignettes on the patio balcony above.[30] Here we have three different temporal frameworks, each of which disavow the concrete and particular realities of history. On the right-hand wing of the triptych, and in the scenes above depicting pre-Columbian life, the Aztecs are associated with femininity, craft, and harmony with nature.[31] The violence associated with the Aztecs, their imperial ambitions, ritual sacrifices and authoritarian social structure, are completely ignored.[32] This is not so much myth as legend. A legend does not transcend time, like a myth; on the contrary, it is *trapped* in it. A legend belongs to a specific time and place; it may well be based on real historical figures or events. As opposed to a myth then, the legend does not continue to exist; it is expressed as loss or displacement. Myth is epic; legend is elegaic. Here too then, all temporal links between past and present are severed.

On the other hand—the "left wing" of the triptych, to be precise—Rivera presents the 1911 Revolution as an incomplete event, whose promises of development, prosperity, and equality have yet to be fulfilled.[33] But the Utopia of a unified national community in which the capitalists have been overthrown and a peaceful Mexico prevails, lacks any sense of specificity, any precise political program, or any sense of the conflicts and differences that might need to be addressed along the way. Rivera's Utopia is no less fanciful than his Paradise. If legend severs the past from the present, utopia severs the present from the future. Both myth and utopia, as Barthes wrote, "immobilize the world" and "mimic a universal order".[34]

Between Paradise and Utopia lies *History*, which commands the vast central stage of Rivera's triptych.[35] But here too the static poses, the flat surface and the two-dimensionality of the representations together produce a sense of a "chronological itinerary", as Siqueiros put it[36]—an inexorable movement towards ever

[29]Barthes, Roland. 1972. Myth today. In *Mythologies*. London: Paladin, 142, 155.

[30]Rivera, *History of Mexico*.

[31]See for example, *The Aztec World,* right hand stairwell of *History of Mexico; The Great City of Tenochtitlan; Totanc Civilization; Huastec Civilization; The Papermakers*, and others, all in patio corridor, (Mexico City: Palacio Nacional, 1942-50).

[32]See Rochfort, 1998, 81. See also discussion in Folgarait, Vaughan, and Coffey, 2012.

[33]Rivera, *Mexico Today and Tomorrow*, in *History of Mexico*. For utopia in the work of Rivera, see Rochfort, 1998, 81–160.

[34]Barthes, 1972. 142, 155.

[35]Rivera, *History of Mexico*.

[36]Quoted in Coffey, 2012. 42.

greater unity, progress, and modernity, culminating in the national triumph of the Revolution.[37] In the highly critical words of Leonard Folgarait,

> The figure now functions as a juridical emblem and itself becomes flat, disembodied, and glyph-like. Writing has labelled and supervised the behaviour of its subordinate. Its ownership of the image is both juridical and economic.[38]

In short, Rivera’s work and the history of the Mexican mural movement demonstrates that the problem with the relationship between aesthetics and politics lies in its refusal to engage with particular, concrete, time. Whether as legend, myth, apocalypse, or utopia, an art that ignores the contingencies of history and politics “aestheticizes the political”, functioning in an impoverished ideological register.

7.3 Eternity and Contingency

One year after the publication of Benjamin’s essay, the *Exposition Internationale des Arts et Techniques dans la Vie Moderne,* opened in Paris.[39] Benjamin now lived there, working on the Arcades Project[40] he would never finish. Although he was in San Remo that summer, and in July 1937 confessed that he was “yet to set foot on the grounds of the world’s fair”, he returned to the city in September, worrying about its effects on his accommodation costs.[41] No doubt at some time over the next few months, however, he joined the hundreds of thousands of *flâneurs* who wandered the site from the Trocadero to the Eiffel Tower. As he did so, what must have struck him was how closely the displays confirmed his predictions of the menacing entwinement of art and politics. Art served as the sensory vanguard for ideological representations of the nation. And here too, it is striking how the predominant register is not that of the paradigm but of myth, utopia, and timelessness.

On either side of the *Champs-de-Mars*—a battlefield by any other name—loomed the rival monoliths of Nazi Germany and Soviet Russia. As seen in Fig. 7.2, on one side, Albert Speer’s outsized neo-classical monument to Nazi power was crowned by the eagle and the swastika. On the other side, the Soviet edifice, equally imposing, was topped by the dynamic image of a male worker and a female peasant, hands clasped together, thrusting forward into the future clutching a hammer and a sickle. The Italian pavilion featured *Fascist Work,* a vast mural by

---

[37]See in particular Folgarait, 1998. 110–5.

[38]Ibid. 115.

[39]25 May–25 November, 1937; see Herbert, James. 1997. *Paris 1937: Worlds on Exhibition.* Ithaca: Cornell University Press.

[40]Benjamin, Walter. 2002. *The Arcades Project.* Trans. Howard Eiland, and Kevin McLaughlin. Cambridge, Mass: Belknap Press.

[41]Benjamin, Walter. 1994. Letter 287 to Gershom Scholem, 2 July 1937. In *The Correspondence of Walter Benjamin.* Trans. Manfred and Evelyn Jacobson. eds. Gershom Sholem, and Theodore Adorno, 540. Chicago: University of Chicago Press.

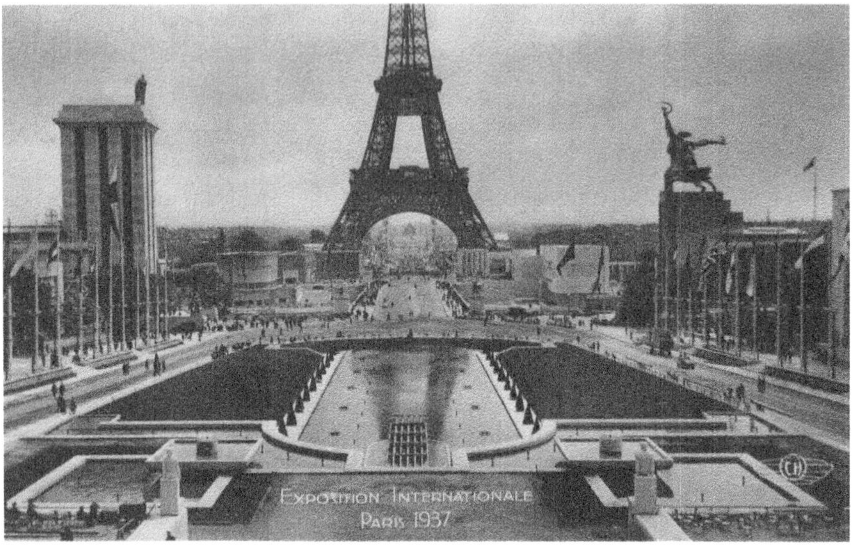

Fig. 7.2 *Exposition Internationale, Paris.* Postcard. (1937) Collection S.H

Mario Sironi, again expressing the kind of archaic never-land beloved of fascist fantasy, its oversized figures apparently stamped out of the primordial clay.[42] The Paris Exhibition presents us with an aesthetic rivalry that surely portends the military one soon to come; or to put it another way, it dramatized how central were the aesthetics of the nation to the furtherance of ideological disputes. These regimes all shared a belief in the key role of the artist in mobilizing mass social change: perhaps ironically, and despite their ideological differences, all sought both to engage the artist politically and to reconstitute him as a humble worker for the betterment of the masses, rather than as an individual aesthete. And in each case, the artistic rhetoric of the nation was seen to demand a move straight to the realm of universality and eternity, circumventing the mediation of a particular story or event. Political theology is achieved by a short cut which is explicitly opposed to singularity, rather than traversing it.

Benjamin's concerns for the implications for art of its reproducibility, its generic repetitiveness, are exactly on point. It marks for Benjamin less a technological than an ontological crisis. As James Herbert explains, something essential was *lost* at the World's Fair which endeavoured to recreate "replica states" in miniaturized form, and thereby shrink them to size capable of apprehension, consumption and purchase.[43] "In a few hours we have just completed a genuine world tour!" gushed one critic.[44] The whole principle of the Pavilions followed the logic of reproducibility—

[42]See Braun, 2000. 198–200.

[43]Herbert, 1997. 50.

[44]Quoted in Ibid. 4.

the annihilation of singularities of time and space, compression into the genre of montage, and the amusement of a mass public. What was lost was the specific experience of those nation-states, both universalized and shrunk beyond recognition.

Two exhibitions outside the grounds of the World's Fair suffered from the same problem. *Musée des monuments francais* did not offer up original architectural features, but merely reproductions, mini-me's that reduced even the cathedral at Rouen to yet another spectacle for mass consumption.[45] At the *Musée de l'homme*, "primitive" cultures from around the world were distilled into specimens and artefacts contained in long lines of identical vitrines.[46] These objects existed not as unique individual artworks but as samples or types, for which many others could easily have been substituted. One mask signifying "Africa" is much like another. Their function may have been ritual, cultic, or aesthetic in their own cultures. But in the museum environment, as Benjamin put it—a year previously—"the whole social function of art is revolutionized. Instead of being founded on ritual, it is based on a different practice: politics".[47] What is on offer is the objectification of archaic others in the interests of the modern subject. Like the *Exposition Internationale,* the *Musée des monuments français* and the *Musée de l'homme* attempt to do away with the constraints of time in the first case, and space in the second.

> As soon as you pass through its gates [...] you are [...] in a land that is located nowhere and everywhere at the same time. A land where all notions of distance and time are confounded.[48]

Benjamin writes: "In even the most perfect reproduction *one* thing is lacking—the here and now of the work of art—its unique existence in a particular place".[49] Benjamin uses the same temporal phrase—*Jetztzeit*—in the essay *On the Concept of History*, written in the year of his death, after the outbreak of the Second World War. In this late work, his references to the "here and now" express an understanding of history as urgent and as particular—the very contingency which the aesthetic commodification of the World's Fair sought to trump. "Here and now" positions history as a crisis which demands our response and implicates our responsibility. It is not "homogeneous, empty time", like myth or legend or utopia – inexorable and unalterable, always already settled. "For every second", he concluded, "was the small gateway in time through which the Messiah might enter".[50]

The abolition of art's singular aura, as we have seen, imports a compensatory power of dissipation, dissemination, and distraction. Art's form and function are

---

[45]Ibid. 41–70.

[46]Ibid.

[47]Benjamin, 2006a. 257.

[48]Quoted in *Ibid*. 6, 14.

[49]Ibid. 253.

[50]Benjamin, 2006b (On the Concept of History). 397. The phrase "homogeneous, empty time" is repeated several times in the course of the essay, e.g. 395, 396, 397.

reframed by and for the mass politics of the nation, and constructed by machines—by films and displays if possible, and with bombs where necessary. With uncanny foresight, Benjamin had predicted in 1936: "instead of promoting power stations across the land, society deploys manpower in the form of armies. Instead of promoting air traffic, it promotes traffic in shells",[51] before concluding that, against the fascist strategy of rendering politics aesthetic, "communism responds by politicizing art".

This clash of positions was nowhere better evidenced than on the *Champs-de-Mars.* In the very shadow of this aesthetico-political clash of the titans, Picasso inserts the "here and now" of a specific historical contingency: Guernica, 1 May 1937. The Pavilion of the doomed Spanish Republic housed *Guernica,* a vast mural created in barely four weeks in response to the carpet-bombing of the Basque town by German and Italian airplanes.[52] Indeed, when he came to revise *The Work of Art* in 1938, Benjamin inserted a specific reference, with Franco's Guernica and Picasso's surely in mind: "Instead of dropping seeds from airplanes, it drops incendiary bombs over cities". [53]

Only Picasso succeeded in returning our senses to the immediacy of an experience from which the mythic tropes of modernist national representations purported to float free. He does so in three ways. First, his cubist forms dismember the body in a manner that exactly complements the effects of the incendiary bombs dropped over the city. As Berger says,—"what has happened to them in being painted is the imaginative equivalent of what happened to them in sensation in the flesh".[54] Second, *Guernica* references the black and white photo-journalism of the newsreels, with its appeal to an immediate, objective and disseminated reality. Third, the violent cuts and rapid compression of montage are a necessary point of reference if we are to understand the painting's poly-perspectival composition. They also provide a further layer that chillingly parallels political and aesthetic violence. The shrapnel's cut, the cubist cut—and now the director's cut.

If Picasso exemplifies Benjamin's demand that the aestheticization of politics must be countered by "politicizing art", this is not a matter of political labels. Certainly the various monuments to ideology on show in Paris reveal the irrelevance of such distinctions. Rather, an "aestheticizing politics" is purposely unanchored in time and place. A "politicizing art" *uses* the specifics of time and place in order to expose the concrete implications swept under the carpet by mythological

[51]Benjamin, 2006a (Second Version). 122.

[52]Pablo Picasso, *Guernica*, 349.3 × 776.6 cm (Madrid: Museo Reina Sofia, 1937). See Opler, Ellen C. 1988. *Picasso's Guernica*. New York: WW Norton.; Clark, Vernon. 1941. The Guernica Mural-Picasso and Social Protest. *Science and Society* 5 (1):72–78.; Berger, John. 1965. *The Success and Failure of Picasso*. New York: Pantheon Books., Arnheim, Rudolf. 1980. *The genesis of a painting: Picasso's Guernica*. Berkeley: University of California Press.; Chipp, Herschel, and Javier Tusell. 1988. *Picasso's Guernica: History, Transformations, Meanings*. Berkeley: University of California Press.

[53]Benjamin, 2006a. 270.

[54]John Berger, 1965, 169; see Opler, 1988. 271.

thinking. Picasso interpellates our political commitments via a single, particular, contemporary event. He returns to art the *Jetztzeit* and fills it with a moral and historical urgency.

Yet he remained acutely aware of the limits of the project. By combining traditional artistic tropes, such as the *Pietà* and the *Madonna*—some might say, parodying them—with a personal psycho-symbolism he had recently explored in *Minotauromachy*,[55] *Guernica* confronts the limit of art's capacity to represent suffering.[56] Recycling of familiar gestures universalizes language to the point of banality, while the artist's mythopoesis personalizes language to the point of impenetrability. The mural leaves us wondering how close art can ever truly get to real life. Although trying to bring so close an event—the title itself points to it, identifying a particular place and a particular date—Picasso's *Guernica* can do no more than recall it from faraway.[57] The more that Picasso tries to make pain present by citing the long tradition of the representation of pain in Western art, the more reality slips through his fingers.[58] Picasso's black and white painting is an image comprised of copies of other images; a picture, of a newsreel, of a memory, of an event. Four degrees of separation.[59]

Art's power to connect the universal and the particular is perhaps less constructive than deconstructive. As the story goes, a visiting German officer asks Picasso, "did you do this?" "No, *you* did", replies Picasso. The joke hinges on whether what is "done" in the artwork is done by the artist or only represented by him, and done by others, politicians and soldiers. By drawing attention to the historical and political context that the works around him steadfastly withheld, Picasso stimulates a critique of the mutual complicity of aesthetics and politics, and reminds viewers of the physical brutality hidden beneath the skirts of fascism's transcendental aesthetics. Picasso's *Guernica* is essentially "queer"; it works not by how you look at the wall on which it is placed, but how you look at all the other

[55]Pablo Picasso, *La Minotauromachie*, etching, 57.4 × 74.2 cm (Paris: Musée Picasso, 1935); see Opler, 1988. 100. See also Emma Crichton-Miller, 2013. 'La Minotauromachie'. 74–75; Damian, Rodica Ioana, and Dean Keith Simonton. 2011. From past to future art: The creative impact of Picasso's 1935 Minotauromachy on his 1937 Guernica. *Psychology of Aesthetics, Creativity, and the Arts* 5 (4):360–369 at 360.; Weisberg, Robert. 2004. On structure in the creative process: A quantitative case-study of the creation of Picasso's Guernica. *Empirical Studies of the Arts* 22 (1):23–54.

[56]Opler, 1988. 207. See Zervos, Christian. 1986. *The Story of a Painting: Picasso's Guernica*. New York: Norton & Company, 206–209; and for a comprehensive discussion of other sources, see Opler, 1988. 253–302.

[57]The reference here and in the title of this essay is to Wim Wenders, dir., *Faraway, So Close!* (Road Movies, 1993).

[58]But see Scarry, Elaine. 1985. *The Body in Pain*. Oxford: Oxford University Press.

[59]Belting, Hans. 1996. *Likeness and Presence*. Trans. Edmund Jephcott. Chicago: University of Chicago Press.

walls on which it is *not* placed.[60] It queered the Paris World's Fair, savagely dismembering its aesthetic ideology of national unity.

The fusion of national identity, law, and art that was so prevalent in the early twentieth century—and which is around us still—did not by any means tend to fulfil the aspiration which elsewhere in this volume is associated with the power of the paradigm or the example to bridge the universal and the particular, the abstract and the concrete. On the contrary, the alliance between art and politics has often functioned ideologically, that is, by a calculated preference for myth and the repression of history. It was Picasso who attempted to say something universal by showing something particular; to say something eternal by showing something *Jetztzeitlichen*. Picasso therefore makes visible the link between Benjamin's understanding of time and the possibilities for an aesthetic-political relation, a middle term in his argument to which Benjamin alluded in his essays on the *Work of Art* and on the *Concept of History*[61], without ever quite spelling out. In stark contrast to the timeless mythologizing—the temporizing move—of fascist art and politics alike, the temporal pressure exerted by the 'here and now,' allows the work of art's aesthetic and political dimensions not to undermine but rather to intensify each other. In the process, he allows us to see that art's relevance lies not just in its capacity to embody and unify the nation, but to disturb and critique it, perhaps even to prise open, just a fraction, that "gateway in time through which the Messiah might enter".[62]

References

Affron M, Antliff M (1997) Fascist visions: art and ideology in France and Italy. Princeton University Press, Princeton

Anreus A, Folgarait L, Greeley RA (2012) Mexican Muralism—a critical history. University of California Press, Berkeley

Antliff M (1997) La Cité française. In: Affron M, Antliff M (eds) Fascist visions: art and ideology in France and Italy. Princeton University Press, Princeton, pp 134–170

Arnheim R (1980) The genesis of a painting: Picasso's Guernica. University of California Press, Berkeley

Barthes R (1972) Myth today. In: Mythologies. Paladin, London

Belting H (1996) Likeness and presence (trans: Jephcott E). University of Chicago Press, Chicago

Benjamin W (1994) Letter 287 to Gershom Scholem, 2 July 1937. In: Sholem G, Adorno T (eds) The correspondence of Walter Benjamin (trans: Manfred and Evelyn Jacobson). University of Chicago Press, Chicago, p 540

Benjamin W (2002) The arcades project (trans: Eiland H, Kevin ML). Belknap Press, Cambridge, Mass

[60]See for example, Sullivan, Nikki. 2003. *A Critical Introduction to Queer Theory*. New York: NYU Press.; Butler, Judith. 1993. Critically queer. *GLQ-NEW YORK* 1:17–32. Butler, Judith. 1990. *Feminism and the Subversion of Identity*. New York: Routledge.

[61]Benjamin, 2006a.; Benjamin, Walter. 2006b.

[62]Benjamin, 2006b. 397.

Benjamin W (2006a) 'The work of art in the age of its mechanical reproducibility' Zeitschfirt fur Sozialfoschung (May 1936). In: Eiland H, Jennings H (eds), Selected writings vol 3, 1935–38. Belknap Press, Cambridge, Mass, pp 101–133
Benjamin W (2006b) On the concept of history (May 1940). In: Eiland H, Jennings H (eds) Selected writings, vol 4, 1938–40. Belknap Press, Cambridge, Mass, pp 389–400
Berger J (1965) The success and failure of Picasso. Pantheon Books, New York
Braun E (1997) Mario Sironi's urban landscapes. In: Affron M, Antliff M (eds) Fascist visions: art and ideology in France and Italy. Princeton University Press, Princeton, pp 101–133
Braun E (2000) Mario Sironi and Italian modernism: art and politics under fascism. Cambridge University Press, Cambridge
Butler Judith (1990) Feminism and the subversion of identity. Routledge, New York
Butler J (1993) Critically queer. GLQ-New York 1:17–32
Chipp H, Tusell J (1988) Picasso's Guernica: history, transformations, meanings. University of California Press, Berkeley
Clark V (1941) The Guernica Mural-Picasso and social protest. Science and Society 5(1):72–78
Coffey MK (2002) Muralism and the people: culture, popular citizenship, and government in post-revolutionary Mexico. Commun Rev 5(1):7–38
Coffey MK (2012) How a revolutionary art became official culture: Murals, Museums, and the Mexican State. Duke University Press, Durham & London
Craven D (1997) Diego Rivera as epic modernist. GL Hall, New York
Craven D (2001) Recent literature on Diego Rivera and Mexican muralism. Lat Am Res Rev 36(3):221–237
Crichton-Miller E (2013) La Minotauromachie
Damian RI, Simonton DK (2011) From past to future art: the creative impact of Picasso's 1935 Minotauromachy on his 1937 Guernica. Psychol Aesthetics Creativity Arts 5(4):360–369
Derrida J (1992) Before the law. In: Attridge D (ed) Acts of literature. Routledge, London, pp 181–220
Eagleton T (1981) Walter Benjamin: towards a revolutionary criticism. Verso, London
Folgarait L (1998) Mural painting and social revolution in Mexico, 1920-1940. Cambridge University Press, Cambridge
Gentile E (1997) The myth of national regeneration in Italy. In: Affron M, Antliff M (eds) Fascist visions: art and ideology in France and Italy. Princeton University Press, Princeton, pp 25–45
Greeley R (2012) Nietzsche contra Marx in Mexico. In: Anreus A, Folgarait L, Greeley RA (eds) Mexican Muralism—a critical history. University of California Press, Berkeley, pp 148–173
Herbert J (1997) Paris 1937: worlds on exhibition. Cornell University Press, Ithaca
Jolly J (2012) Siqueiros' communist proposition for Mexican Muralism. In: Anreus A, Folgarait L, Greeley RA (eds) Mexican Muralism—a critical history. University of California Press, Berkeley, pp 75–92
Lebeck A (1971) The Oresteia: a study in language and structure. Harvard University Press, Cambridge
Lopez R, Rochfort D, Vaughan M, Lewis S (2006) The eagle and the virgin: nation and cultural revolution in Mexico, 1920-1940. Duke University Press, Durham
Manderson D (2015) Klimt's jurisprudence: sovereign violence and the rule of law. Oxf J Leg Stud 35:1–28
Manjarrez MGC (1996) La polémica Siqueiros-Rivera: planteamientos estético-políticos 1934-1935. Museo Dolores Olmedo Patiño, Mexico D.F
Mosse G (1996) Fascist aesthetics and society: some considerations. J Contemp Hist: 245–252
Opler EC (1988) Picasso's Guernica. WW Norton, New York
Paz O (1967) Re/Visions. In: Labyrinth of solitude. Allen Lane, London
Rochfort D (1987) The Murals of Diego Rivera. Journeyman, London
Rochfort D (1998) Mexican Muralists: Orozco, Rivera, Siqueiros. Chronicle Books, San Francisco
Scarry E (1985) The body in pain. Oxford University Press, Oxford
Schmitt C (1985) Political theology (trans: Schwab G). University of Chicago Press, Chicago

Siqueiros D (1934) Rivera's counter-revolutionary road. New masses, May 29
Siqueiros D (1975) Art and revolution. Lawrence and Wishart, New York
Sorel G (2004) [1908] Reflections on violence (trans: Hulme TE, Roth J). Dover, Mineola, NY
Strathausen C (1999) Nazi aesthetics. Cult Theor Critique 42(1):5–19
Sullivan N (2003) A critical introduction to Queer theory. NYU Press, New York
Thomas M (2017) Law and the revolutionary Motif after Jacques Louis David. In: Manderson D (ed) Law and the visual: transition, transmission, transformation. University of Toronto Press, Toronto
Trotsky L (1938) Art and politics in our Epoch (letter). Partisan Rev, June 18. Reprinted in 1950. Fourth Int 11(2):61–64
Weisberg R (2004) On structure in the creative process: a quantitative case-study of the creation of Picasso's Guernica. Empirical Stud Arts 22(1):23–54
Wenders W (1993) Faraway, so close! Road Movies
Zervos C (1986) The story of a painting: Picasso's Guernica. Norton & Company, New York

Professor Desmond Manderson is jointly appointed in the ANU Colleges of Law and of Arts & Social Sciences at the Australian National University, where he directs the Centre for Law, Arts and the Humanities. His books include *From Mr. Sin to Mr. Big (1993); Songs Without Music: Aesthetic dimensions of law and justice* (2000); *Proximity, Levinas, and the Soul of Law (2006); and Kangaroo Courts and the Rule of Law* (2012). His recent work examines the intersection of law and the visual arts, notably *Law and the Visual: Representations, Technologies and Critique* (Toronto 2017); and *Temporalities of Law in the Visual Arts* (Cambridge, early 2018).

Chapter 8
A Hypothesis on the Genealogy of the Motto "In God We Trust" and the Emergence of the Identity of the Church

Paolo Napoli

Abstract The aim of this chapter is to reconstruct a hypothetical genealogy of the U.S. national motto "in God we Trust" by comparing the juridical and theological concept of "depositum". According to Philo of Alexandria, the deposit was the most sacred institutional act of ancient social life, because it had both a religious and a sociological function. According to the *Epistulae* to Timothy (1 Tm 6,20) the term 'deposit' defined the legacy of the Christian faith of which the disciple of St. Paul was entrusted. His task was to manage this legacy and to spread it among the others. Hence the deposit defined at the same time a contract based upon good faith and a symbolic space of "security", namely a container that protected an unchangeable content: the oral knowledge transmitted by Christ to the Apostoles and, indirectly, to St. Paul. The *depositum* was also the procedure through which the word of Christ would acquire all its potential. On the other hand, the contract defined as "*depositum*" by Roman law was characterized by a centrality of the so-called *bona fides* ("good faith") and by the distinction between regular and irregular deposit. This means that the principle of good faith should lead the conducts of the manager whose task is exactly to look after an object called Christian faith. How can we interpret the word '*trust*' according to the juridico-political remarks? The purpose of this chapter is to explain all these related issues.

Section 8.1 has been discussed and co-authored with Angela Condello to whom I express my deep gratitude.

P. Napoli (✉)
EHESS, CENJ, Paris, France
e-mail: napoli@ehess.fr

S. Huygebaert et al. (eds.), *Sensing the Nation's Law*, Studies in the History of Law and Justice 13, https://doi.org/10.1007/978-3-319-75497-0_8

8.1 Introduction—In God We Trust

In this Chapter, I reconstruct the genealogy of the juridical and theological institution called 'deposit' by connecting it to the genealogy of the U.S. national motto "in God we Trust".

Before the well-known motto "In God We Trust" first appeared on American coinage, a very close version of this phrase appeared in a poem (afterwards: a song) that acquired in time an equally iconic status: "The Star-Spangled Banner." As a matter of fact, the words in the American national anthem served as a model for the motto that ended up on U.S. coins and, eventually, U.S. paper money. This thesis is suggested by the words of a document written in 1863 by James Pollock, Director of the United States Mint at the time who had previously served as both Governor of Pennsylvania and a Congressman from that state. Pollock was a close friend of Abraham Lincoln and had been active in the anti-slavery movement in the years leading up to the Civil War. He had strong religious beliefs and this might explain his role in selecting the phrase that expressed Americans' faith in God to characterize and identify money. His idea was that the trust of Americans in God (and, at a more metaphorical level, in a common political-institutional project) should have been declared on the new national coins. At that time, Secretary of the Treasury Salmon P. Chase received many appeals from devout persons throughout the country, urging that the United States recognize the Deity on United States coins.[1] Chase thus instructed Pollock to prepare a motto in a letter dated November 20, 1861:

"Dear Sir: No nation can be strong except in the strength of God, or safe except in His defense. The trust of our people in God should be declared on our national coins.

You will cause a device to be prepared without unnecessary delay with a motto expressing in the fewest and tersest words possible this national recognition."

---

[1]The first such appeal came in a letter dated November 13, 1861. It was written to Secretary Chase by Rev. M. R. Watkinson, Minister of the Gospel from Ridleyville, Pennsylvania, and read:

Dear Sir: You are about to submit your annual report to the Congress respecting the affairs of the national finances.

One fact touching our currency has hitherto been seriously overlooked. I mean the recognition of the Almighty God in some form on our coins.

You are probably a Christian. What if our Republic were not shattered beyond reconstruction? Would not the antiquaries of succeeding centuries rightly reason from our past that we were a heathen nation? What I propose is that instead of the goddess of liberty we shall have next inside the 13 stars a ring inscribed with the words PERPETUAL UNION; within the ring the allseeing eye, crowned with a halo; beneath this eye the American flag, bearing in its field stars equal to the number of the States united; in the folds of the bars the words GOD, LIBERTY, LAW.

This would make a beautiful coin, to which no possible citizen could object. This would relieve us from the ignominy of heathenism. This would place us openly under the Divine protection we have personally claimed. From my hearth I have felt our national shame in disowning God as not the least of our present national disasters.

To you first I address a subject that must be agitated.

Source: https://www.treasury.gov/about/education/Pages/in-god-we-trust.aspx.

In 1863, the Director of the Mint submitted designs for new one-cent coin, two-cent coin, and three-cent coin to Secretary Chase for approval. He proposed that upon the designs either "OUR COUNTRY"; "OUR GOD" or "GOD, OUR TRUST" should appear as a motto on the coins.

In the penultimate sentence of "The Star-Spangled Banner" we still find the set of lyrics that inspired Pollock's choice for a short but powerful reference to the Almighty: "then conquer we must, when our cause is just, and this be our motto: 'In God is our trust".

The search for an appropriate coinage motto began in 1861, after the Civil War had started. Many different mottoes were considered for use on U.S. coinage before officials and responsibles settled upon "In God We Trust" for placement on the new bronze two-cent piece in 1864. The lyrics of "The Star-Spangled Banner" were written in 1814, shortly before the end of the War of 1812 between the fledgling United States and the former mother country, Great Britain. The author (Key) and other American negotiators were on a truce ship when British warships in the bay launched the famous bombardment of Fort McHenry (in front of Baltimore Harbor) and they were forced to witness the fearsome onslaught from a powerless position on the British side of the fray. However, their frustration turned to nationalistic enthusiasm when the dawn's early light on the following day revealed that the large, newly sewn U.S. flag atop Fort McHenry had emerged intact from the fight and the British were forced to withdraw. In the following years and during the whole century after it was written, "The Star-Spangled Banner" was considered the American national anthem: however, it did not attain that status officially until the beginning of the twentieth century. In 1931 the Congress *performatively* approved a legislation that formally declared it to be the national anthem.

In 1956, President Dwight D. Eisenhower established that "In God We Trust" should also become the nation's official motto. A year earlier, in 1955, Congress had mandated use of "In God We Trust" on all U.S. paper money.

We can thus conclude that the motto "in God we Trust" was placed on U.S. coinage essentially because of the increased religious sentiment existing during the Civil War.

8.2 Common Identity Through Common Trust

Since antiquity, when we pronounce the expression "in God *we* Trust", we are always in front of a reciprocal experience. Inasmuch as God has entrusted us with faith, a faith spread and contained in the written and spoken word, we are also the depositary of a *common* trust. It is this *common* trust that constitutes a *common* identity, which has both a juridical and a theologico-political nature. The concept of trust has historically proved that often individual and collective belonging to an institution are contemporaneous. Only after having recognized the belonging to an institution in which many people can recognize themselves can the word of God (*didaskalia*) be spread.

In the construction of a common trust, the process of the deposit has acquired a central relevance. Deposit has a performative force since it constitutes, modifies and enforces the community to which we consign our belonging and trust. Trust is not infinite nor can it change: it preserves the message that has been transmitted, and every shade of meaning in the message cannot betray the message (*didaskalia*) that has originally been given by Christ. The performativity of the message remains constant: the meaning of the religious concept (deposit of faith, trust) informed the juridical evolution of deposit as a social object: through the deposit, through this passage, a new object is constituted. I claim that a similar process occurs in the construction of a common political identity (like in the birth of the American nation), and it is interesting that it was the motto recalling religious trust that was chosen to represent a political identity under construction.

I focus in particular on the deposit of faith (or other value or goods) in its interconnection with the creation of a common and shared identity inside a community. In the specific genealogy of the deposit of faith, it is the Church that is instituted. The *exemplum* of the institution of the Church can symbolically represent the institution of the nation-state. I offer a historico-conceptual analysis based on primary sources in order to describe the emergence of the Church as an institution. The documents analyzed offer a picture of a social phenomenon that started spreading around the first century AD and that allows for a reflection on how material and intellectual constructions converge towards the achievement of a defined goal: the social institution of a legally grounded religion.

Three books, which were to be rechristened the *Pastoral Epistles* during the eighteenth century, were presumably written at the turn of the period generically referred to as Early Christianity (between the first and second centuries AD). The writings in question are three pseudo-epigraphic epistles addressed to St. Paul's most loyal disciples, Timothy (two) and Titus, written by an unknown author, concealing himself behind a famous name such as the apostle's.[2] The false attribution of paternity to leading figures who were able to make the content of writings more prestigious was often employed to communicate important principles involving all Christians. The fundamental idea set forth in the two letters to Timothy most definitely stands out among those expressed in the numerous working recommendations Paul offers to his disciples. In the first letter (I *Tm* 6,20), Paul delivers the following order when taking leave from his emissary in Ephesus: "Timothy, guard what has been entrusted to your care" (*tên parathêkên phýlaxon*). In the second letter, the deposit is mentioned in two occasions, one after another: in 2 *Tm* I,12, Paul has complete trust in Christ's work which is able to "guard what has been entrusted me until that day" (*tên parathêkên mou phyláxai eisekéinên*

[2]As regards pseudo-epigraphy widely used in the Christian cultural environment from 60 to 100 AD, cf. Penna, R. 2011. *Le prime comunità cristiane. Persone, tempi, luoghi, forme, credenze.* Rome: Carocci: 171–180. As regards the question of Pauline authorship of the Pastoral Epistles, called into question at the start of the 1800s by Schleiermacher among others, cf. the detailed critical review by Marcheselli-Casale, C. 2008 (1995). *Le lettere pastorali.* Bologna: Edizioni Dehoniane: 21–44.

hêméran). A little further on, in 2 *Tm* I,14, he once again urges Timothy to take care of the same object whose value is also qualified by an adjective: "Guard the good deposit that was entrusted to you (*tên kalên parathêkên phýlaxon*) with the help of the Holy Spirit who lives in us".[3]

Some key characteristics of sub-apostolic Christianity need to be explained in order to understand the theoretical and practical importance of this metaphor, which appears for the first time in these writings, within a Christian literature where it was to become a constant point of reference. The *Pastoral Epistles* are an important expression of sub-apostolic Christianity. It goes without saying that historians, theologians and commentators have produced an immense bibliography in this regard and that, given the different educational background, I cannot help but benefit from said valuable resources. Nevertheless, acknowledgement of some historical and conceptual features of Early Christianity is useful in order to clarify the atypical use we would like to put forward of sources traditionally employed to develop theological and historical studies. Therefore the use of these materials in a history of administrative normativity cannot exclude suitable contextualisation without which said atypical use may prove to be completely arbitrary. So, firstly the deposit must be placed within its historical scriptural location and hence considered a significant problem for the history of administrative rationality and normativity. Because Paul's disciple and any modern-day financial advisor share an ethical constant: receiving a deposit means managing said deposit.

8.3 The Context of the Pastoral Epistles

It is no coincidence that, within the Pauline corpus, the concept of "deposit" features in the two epistles to Timothy. Just as is not surprising that, within the perspective of a history of normativity, the *Pastoral Epistles* instinctively capture the legal scholar's interest. The exhaustive array of encouragements offered to the two individuals responsible for the correct functioning of the young communities founded by the apostle, prevail over the doctrinal strength and spiritual afflatus which reign in the authentic context of the Pauline epistles. It is as if, alongside the immense theological structure outlined in the letters to the Romans and the Galatians, the person going by the name of Paul felt the need to reflect on the operating means needed to truly achieve the principles of faith. It is no coincidence that the abundance of organisational and technocratic observations seemed a suspicious incongruence and together with other references that are incompatible with the period Paul lived in, encouraged the majority of commentators to date the writing of the *Pastoral Epistles* to the turn of the first century. For us, the problem of authenticity has a relative value, while it is important to examine the genesis of

[3]For the english version cf. Towner, Ph. H. 2006. The Letters to Timothy and Titus. Grand Rapids: Eerdmans: 429 and 456.

the ecclesiastical institution that features widely in the pastoral epistles. The setting-up of the life of a community, equipping it with an operating structure and planning its functions in order to meet the goals it sets itself: all these phases mark out the framework within which the concept of deposit exhibits its irreplaceable role in defining the theological and juridical economy of the growing *ekklesia* (Church).

The letters to Timothy and Titus belong to the "epistolary directive" literary genre, a form of communication used by Hellenistic bureaucracies of the time to give orders to their officials and urge application and zeal. As noted by Cesles Spicq, one of the most respected Catholic commentators of these documents, the style of the *Pastoral Epistles* is not prescriptive, but paraenetic. The precept is addressed in the indirect form of the sentence, of the advice, rather than in the direct form of the command.[4] The three letters are motivated by the prevailing concern of protecting the Christian communities founded by Paul in Ephesus and Crete from the threat of false scholars that corrupted the authenticity of Christ's message. This type of anxiety is typical of Paul, and the apostle had already demonstrated this between 54 and 55 AD after his time spent in Galatia where the evangelised population was exposed to the influence of Judaizer preachers who urged Christians to continue to observe the Law of Moses (*Gal* I,7; 2,4; 3,I).[5] This was the same concern that he expressed with regard to the Christians of Corinth, threatened by the danger of internal factions and hence of divisions (I *Cor* I,10–13). After all, the fear that communities could be easy prey for malicious teachers, apostles and prophets was a common motif in Early Christianity, including outside Pauline environments. One need only recall the number of references contained in a key work such as *Didache or Teaching Twelve Apostles*, posterior to Pauline epistles but most likely contemporary to or slightly earlier than the *Pastoral Epistles* and synoptic gospels.[6]

The birth of a movement of thought or faith is accompanied, out of physiological need, by the imposition of a borderline that clearly distinguishes sound doctrine from mystification. The *Pastoral Epistles* denounced the misleading Gnostic and Judaizer tendencies that generated division, and the term *aíresis* already used in I *Cor* II,19 and *Gal* 5,20 took on the adjectival form of *airetikòn anthropon* (*Tt* 3,10). This figure had already been used in a pejorative sense, but not yet to technically define those who err in their faith. Here, the term heretic refers to the person who feels free to choose the way in which to interpret the evangelical message to the point of being separated from others.

In the *Pastoral Epistles*, this focus on safeguarding the authenticity of the Christian revelation resurfaced around an inflexible methodical aim. In order to consolidate the fragile foundations of the new religious creed, clear directives and suitable leaders were needed for the important task which the letters constantly recall to Paul's two young disciples, wandering emissaries in the local

---

[4]Spicq, C. 1969. *Les Épîtres pastorales* (2 vol.). Paris: Gabalda. I, 34 et seq.

[5]Penna, 2011. 127 et seq.

[6]Rordorf, W., and A. Tuilier. 1998 (second edition) *La Doctrine des Douze Apôtres (Didaché)*. Paris: Éditions du Cerf.

communities.[7] Timothy's task seemed to be especially onerous. Sent to Ephesus, a cosmopolitan city and worthy rival of Rome, he had to tackle a variety of schools of thought, often tending towards syncretism, that took root in the cultural crossroads of Asia Minor. Titus' mission on the island of Crete was of a similar nature, where he stayed to "put in order" (*Tt* I,5) what had been started by Paul himself, in other words to teach the new converts and entrust them to capable ministers.

The concept of "deposit" takes on its weightiest technical and historical meaning against the background of the first "hierarchy" of the church set forth in the *Pastoral Epistles*, organised around the three figures of bishop, presbyters and deacons. A key issue for the form of Early Christianity came to light in this situation: the "ministry" or "office",[8] and theological and exegetical studies have continued to examine this from the second half of the nineteenth century on. This concept in turn may not be understood in full unless placed in comparison with "*charisma*", usually looked on as the fluid and anarchic alternative to the juridical and hierarchical vision innate in "ministry-office". Genuine communicating vessels for which an increase in one corresponds to a decrease in the other, *charisma* and ministry-office lend the history of Christianity its more dialectic rhythm and likewise reveal its varied normative potential. The organisation of the Church was fuelled by the concurrence of these specular forms of governance, in accordance with what Carl Schmitt considered the most surprising *complexio oppositorum* of Catholic rationalism.[9]

This is not the occasion for retracing the debate that developed above all within the Protestantism of *Kulturkampf*. The latter, adopting an anti-Catholic stance, questioned the nature of Early Christianity and, consequently, its real value, destined as such to characterise the phenomenon's deep and indelible truth. Putting to one side the political and ideological reasons that drove Wilhelmine theology to provide legitimisation to the Reich, also with regard to religious specificity, the specific intellectual position that identifies the truest core of a historical experience with its origin comes to light. Once identified—given that this is possible—the latter serves as a litmus test for adopting a critical stance with regard to the real events the Christian religion has experienced throughout the centuries. So, every event can be assessed in relation to its level of correspondence with the primordial appearance of Christianity: not an autonomous historical enhancement but a variation of an essence called the start. Tracing back to origins and historical observation are the two sides of the same intellectual operation aimed at distinguishing the real truth from its deviations. The debate on Early Christianity through to the early decades of the twentieth century can also be interpreted in light of the desire to

[7]Timothy is considered an "evangelist", in other words a second-level apostle (I *Tm* I,18) and, as such, invested with a charismatic office (I *Tm* 4,14). Cf. von Harnack, A. 1902. *Die Mission und Ausbreitung des Christentums in den ersten drei Jahrhunderten*. Leipzig.

[8]For a general overview on Catholic, Protestant and Anglican commentators, cf. Burtchaell, J.T. 1992. *From Synagogue to Church. Public Services and Offices in the Earliest Christian Communities*. Cambridge: Cambridge University Press.

[9]Schmitt, C. 1996 (1923). *Roman Catholicism and political form*. Westport: Greenwood Press.

moralise its origin, as if the "goodness" of its history were stored in a dawning nature, transformed once and for all into a quality, but heavily imbued with nostalgic longing.[10]

From this viewpoint, the position of a legal expert such as Rudolph Sohm is especially emblematic since the origin of Christianity is identified with a level of pre-institutional purity, of non-involvement with any mediation not based on *charis*, in other words on the grace dispensed by the Holy Spirit. However, according to Sohm, the lack of a juridical dimension and lasting institutions was not the straightforward consequence of a society waiting for *parousia* and the end of time. In other words, the charismatic form was not a conjunctural necessity, but the fundamental essence of *Ekklèsia* and therefore it benefitted from a permanent theological superiority,[11] regardless of a history that saw the new religion establishing bodies, hierarchies and governance duties as from the second century on. All of this led Sohm to proclaim Christianity's structural incompatibility with juridical structures (*ist der rechtlichen Organisation unfähig*), given that its only law is the law of love.[12] This is the meaning of the charismatic moment which Weber was to model his well-known type of domination on, nevertheless turning a concept that was basically of anti-normative and anti-hierarchical importance for the Protestant jurist into a figure of power. Hence the oxymoron, "charismatic power", that was to become a constant of political lexis, based however on the nonchalant removal of the conflict present in the parts of the syntagm.

Prior to Weber's intentionally misleading gesture, charisma had been interpreted by Protestant theological and juridical commentators as the countermodel of a ministerial church, the first traces of which can be seen in the *Pastoral Epistles*. It is not a matter of debating herein the historical validity of the charisma-office binary opposition. We will only take into account the fact that the three epistles examine some devices that launched the process of ministerialisation of the *Ekklèsia* in the juridical sense described by Sohm. In this context, the deposit played an all-important role in conceiving the birth of an *institution*. Schematically, we can find some turning points in the three letters that reflect the way in which *Ekklèsia* took shape conceptually and developed the administrative position that was to remain one of its dominant features.

Alongside the deposit, which stands for the original accumulation of an ideal capital entrusted to individuals appointed to manage it, at least two other passages of the *Pastoral Epistles* play a key role in defining the new organisational structure: a reward-retribution system for the services rendered by these individuals, and more generally, by all the members of the Christian society. A kind of specific

---

[10]With regard to this cult of origin as purity of experience and as such qualitatively superior, cf. the criticism by Adorno, T.W. 1973. *The Jargon of Autenticity*. Chicago: Northwestern University Press.

[11]Sohm, R. 1892 (1923). *Kirchenrecht. Band. 1: Die geschichtlichen Grundlagen*. München & Leipzig: Duncker & Humblot: § 2: Der Begriff der Ekklésia.

[12]*Ibidem*, 22.

relationship established between individuals and assets, not only in economic terms, but also in more generally existential terms.

As regards the first aspect, the rendering of service by deacons offered the author of the first letter to Timothy the opportunity to clarify a key principle of New Testament morals. In any case, the performance of a service, even for an edifying cause such as that building God's house on the earth ("I am writing you these instructions so that, if I am delayed, you will know how people ought to conduct themselves in God's household, which is the church of the living God, the pillar and foundation of the truth.", I *Tm* 3,15), requires a motivation which Paul's pastoral wisdom clearly highlights. For example, the deacon does not obey supinely for the purpose written in the service, but is also drawn into a possible exchange. According to I *Tm* 3,13, those who perform their ministry well (οἱ καλῶς διακονήσαντες), gain an excellent standing (βαθμὸν ἑαυτοῖς καλὸν περιποιοῦνται), as well as great assurance (πολλὴν παρρησίαν) in their faith in Christ Jesus. The term βαθμός, which the Vulgate translates as *gradum bonum*, is the reward obtained by the deacon for having performed his service well. It is a metaphor borrowed from architectural language where it defines an elevation, a step, in other words a raised threshold which gives access to a door, a temple, a staircase, a building. In a figurative sense, said step corresponds to an honorary rank and hence to a leading position within the community.[13]

The third element which completes the institutional structure of the *Pastoral Epistles* is the type of relationship which Christians establish with assets. This is what the *Vulgate* sums up in the verse: "*Nemo militans implicat se negotiis secularibus*" (2 *Tm* 2,4), translating the greek text: Οὐδείς στρατευόμενος ἐμπλέκεται ταιίς τοῦ βτοῦ πραγματείαις: no-one serving as a soldier gets entangled with civilian affairs. This is a genuine programme of existence, an essential life conduct and not just a way to organise the division of work within a society. The key words are πραγματείαις and ἐμπλέκεται. The πραγματείαι, as recalls Spicq, with reference to Philo of Alexandria (*Life of Moses*) and studies by L. Robert, are the affairs which allow us to live and not those resulting from an activity such as commerce, in other words they are limited to subsistence.[14] As regards the verb ἐμπλέκεται, which Spicq does not stop to examine, ἐμπλέκω means to imply, but also to "confuse, embroil" in the active form, while the Latin passive *implicari*, in other words "to be involved in such a way as not be able to disentangle oneself" corresponds to the middle form ἐμπλέκεσθαι.[15] The exegesis of the verse has lessened the total sense of vocation described therein, also because the *Vulgate*'s choice to render ἐμπλέκεται with the reflexive form "implicat se" and not with the passive "implicatur" ended up generating ambiguity that did not elude the cunning genius of Thomas Aquinas. The latter drew consequences from the *Vulgate*'s rendering in a highly skilful manner, maintaining that the ban on negotiating deals

[13]Spicq, 1969., I, 462.

[14]*Ibidem*, II, 741.

[15]Stephanus, *Thesaurus graecae linguae*, III/I, 887.

only concerns actions performed deliberately by Christians since the reflexive form "implicat se" calls to mind a voluntary decision.[16] Therefore, all deals which Christians find themselves involved in without wanting to be—out of pity or as a result of their office—would be excluded from the ban. It goes without saying that this paved the way for an array of exceptions with not-so-easily predictable boundaries.

A fund as a starting capital to be drawn upon to help stabilise the enterprise known as the Church; an acknowledgement of the work performed by each of its members thus motivated to obey; an attitude towards civilian affairs that implies a relative refusal by the Christian militant and, indirectly, the obligation within the community to support him, to keep him on the payroll, as occurs with all soldiers involved in wartime campaigns. We can understand that the starting capital, in other words the deposit, represents the engine of this enterprise which consists in institutionalizing a faith into a church. All that remains is to examine more closely the characteristics of this fund which the Christian religion draws its lifeblood from.

8.4 Genealogy of the Deposit

If παραθήκε, with its specific technical and metaphorical nature, emerged in the Biblical lexicon with the two epistles to Timothy, the ideal and same term were, nevertheless, already widely shaped in the Old Testament. In the Old Testament we can find an outline of the legal physiognomy of the social practice, even if the figurative value it will later be given by Christian acceptance is absent. On several occasions we can find the juridical situation which consists in the consignment of an object to someone in order for the latter to conserve it intact and return it at the right moment. For example, in *Ex*, XXII, 10–12, there is a perfect overview of the dialectic between the owner's rights and the obligations of the guardian the asset has been entrusted to in accordance with the law of the deposit:

"If anyone gives a donkey, an ox, a sheep or any other animal to their neighbour for safekeeping (the *Vulgate* translates as *commendaverit ad custodiam* while the *Septaguint* uses the compound *παρακαταθήκης*) and it dies or is injured or is taken away while no one is looking, the issue between them will be settled by the taking of an oath before the Lord that the neighbour did not lay hands on the other person's property. The owner is to accept this, and no restitution is required. But if the animal was stolen from the neighbour, restitution must be made to the owner."

In *Lv*, V, 21–24 it is recalled that "if anyone sins and is unfaithful to the Lord by deceiving a neighbour about something entrusted to them—(*depositum quod fidei ejus creditum fuerat*, according to the *Vulgate*, while the *Septaguint*, VI, 2,7, uses the expression *εν παραθήκε*) they must make restitution in full, add a fifth of the

---

[16]Super 2 *Tm* I, l. 4. Aquinas, Thomas. 1902. *In omnes S. Pauli apostoli epistolas commentaria*. Turin: Marietti, II: 237.

value to it." The "deposit" referred to in this verse of *Leviticus*, as has been noted, translates the Hebrew term *piqqadôn* which in *Gn* XLI, 36 indicates the food held in reserve during periods of plenty in order to deal with famines.[17] The passage in question is a genuine handbook of economic politics because when explaining to the Pharaoh his dream about the seven fat cows eaten by the seven thin cows, Joseph was telling him the preventive measures to be taken to mitigate the devastating effects of the famine that would have lasted for seven years following on from seven years of plenty. The creation of a reserve of food to be used in times of famine is exactly the reason that justifies the setting-up of a "deposit". The latter's prudent nature explains the strategic role it plays in the fight against the adversities of fate, but it also shows its all-important bond with the existence of the political community. The deposit feeds a starving population just as, in the Deuter-Pauline metaphor, it will nourish Christians' faith.

In *2 Mac 3*,10, faced with Heliodorus' desire to seize the money stored in the temple, the high priest of the temple of Jerusalem recalls how the sums «deposited» therein (*deposita* in the *Vulgate*, *παραθήκας* in the *Septaguint*) are needed to maintain widows and orphans. In the face of Heliodorus' forceful demands (2 *Mac 3*,15), the priests *invocabant de coelo eum, qui de depositis legem posuit, ut his qui deposuerant ea salva custodiret.* The *Septaguint* uses the unequivocal wording τὸν περὶ παραθήκης νομοθετήσαντα τοῖς παρακαταθεμένοις ταῦτα σῶα διαφυλάξαι, "prostrated themselves before the altar and called toward heaven for the one who had given the law about deposits to keep the deposits safe for those who had made them". Thus another semantic value is specified for the concept of deposit. Not only is it the act by which the custody of an item is transferred to a trustworthy person, but it is also the physical and symbolic condition that guarantees the safety and unavailability of the item itself. In fact, the money could not be touched because it was stored in a holy place.[18]

In light of the similar characteristics, it is clear that in his comment on the Decalogue, Philo of Alexandria (start of first century AD ca.) was able to confirm that "the deposit is the most sacred institutional act of the life of a society (Ιερώτατον παρακαταθῆκε τῶν ἐν κοινωνία πραγμάτων) because it rests on the good faith of the depositary (ἐπι τῇ τοῦ λαβόντος κειμένη πίστει)". The observation is both sociological and religious. Not betraying the trust of others is clearly a fundamental requisite for good social order. However, this is not sufficient to justify Philo's emphasis which, instead, focuses on another aspect. Unlike other contractual forms of credit, for example loans, which are documented or confirmed by witnesses, the deposit is something confidential between the parties involved, with God being the only witness that approves the agreement between the depositor and the depositary. So, not only does the dishonest depositary fail to meet the

[17]Médebielle, P. 1930–1934. Dépôt de la foi. In *Dictionnaire de la Bible, suppl. vol. II*, 374–375. Paris Letouzey et Ané.

[18]As regards Jewish-Greek history of the ethical and juridical notion of παραθήκη cf. Ehrhardt, A. 1958. Parakatathke. *Zeitschrift der Savigny Stiftung für Rechtsgeschichte (Rom. Abt.)* 75:32–90.

expectations of the depositor who expects the item in question to be returned, but he also violates the divine law because he fails to respect the higher witness who is the only, inevitable guarantor of the agreement.[19] During the second half of the first century, Titus Flavius Jospehus was to confirm the sacred nature of the deposit involving privates (παρακαταθήκην δὲ ὥσπερ ιερόν τι καὶ θεῖον χρῆμα) and the offence caused to God by the fraudulent depositary.[20]

When the individual called Paul orders Timothy to take care of the παραθήκε, he placed himself within a semantic field, already tilled in part by the scriptural precedents mentioned above, upon using a word, the choice of which was not casual. The biographical aspects of the real Paul are also linked to said precedents. Paul, as Spicq recalls, came from a well-off family and had received an education which also included law. Another factor to be taken into account was the influence of Jewish theology which, during the first century, was increasingly focused on case law and jurisprudence, thus affecting the mindset and language of who had become familiar with Roman laws thanks to frequent appearances in courts. While as far as his Greek background is concerned, it must be recalled that according to first-century Attic law, the refusal to return an item received as a deposit meant committing a crime punishable by religious law, civil law and public opinion.[21] Therefore, all of these factors together make the use of specific legal terminology in the Pastoral Epistles highly plausible.

Obviously it is Roman law which paid witness to the most interesting developments of this institution: the *depositor* (creditor) hands over a moveable item to the *depositary* (debtor) who undertakes to keep it safe and return it at the former's request. According to reconstruction by Roman law historians,[22] legal protection of the deposit was not originally granted under civil law (*formula in ius concepta*), but it was thanks to action by the praetor adopting *formula in factum concepta* that the unlawful depositary was obliged to return the item held, as if it were a formal obligation approved under civil law. Later, during the early decades of the Roman Empire, with increased legal knowledge of the importance of providing judicial protection for these types of situations, the deposit became a real, genuine contract of good faith: the agreement was completed with straightforward handing over of the item, without any specific formalities and expression of consent. And the diffusion of Roman law throughout the Roman Empire's provinces also dates from this period, so it is fairly probable that this fairly recent type of contract had also been adopted in the region where Paul was educated and worked.[23]

The relationship's main characteristics lies in the unalterable conservation of the deposited item and in the consequent ban on use by the depositary. If the latter made use of the item, he was asked to respond to the action of theft, as can also be

[19]Philo of Alexandria, *De specialibus legibus*, IV, 30–32.

[20]T. Flavius Josephus, *Antiquities of the Jews*, IV, 8. 38, 285.

[21]Spicq, C. 1931. Saint Paul et la loi des dépôts. *Revue biblique* 40, 482 et seq.

[22]See Arangio-Ruiz, V. 1981. *Istituzioni di diritto romano*. Napels: Jovene: 309 et seq.

[23]C. Spicq, 1931. 490.

clearly seen in the commentary on the Law of Moses written by Philo of Alexandria during the early decades of the Roman Empire.[24] Indeed, it was because the depositor continued to be the owner of the item that the item had to be returned intact and with the interest accrued during the period of deposit, otherwise it was as if it had been withheld by the depositary. Whoever decided to entrust an item as a deposit had to remedy, on his part, the damage caused by the item to the individual who took it into custody. In any case, the agreement between the parties presumed that the item to be returned could not be replaced by one of an equivalent value or by a sum of money. In its canonical form, the depositor expected the depositary to return the individual item and not the *tantundem*. This is why the most specific variant of the institution, the so-called irregular deposit that refers to replaceable items, is worthy of attention. In this case, the depositary can use the object and is not obliged to return it in the specific form in which he receives it as a deposit, but to return one of the same kind with the addition of payment of interest. When studying Greek and Egyptian papyri, Arangio-Ruiz[25] noted that in the practice of business in the ancient world, the term παραθήκε ο παρακαθήκε frequently referred to the transfer of sums of money to someone who then had the option of returning the amount in question, using other money. Roman legal culture also seems to adopt this extension of the deposit, in addition to return of the deposit in its specific form. A jurist from the first century AD, Alfenus, already acknowledged that deposits followed the same rules as loans for which either the same item or an equivalent value could be returned. In the first case, the lender or depositor continues to be the owner of the item, while in the second case his position is that of a creditor vis-à-vis the borrower or the depositary:

> rerum locatarum duo genera esse, ut aut idem redderetur (sicuti cum vestimenta fulloni curanda locarentur) aut eiusdem generis redderetur (veluti cum argentum pusulatum fabro daretur, ut vasa fierent, aut aurum, ut anuli): ex superiore causa rem domini manere, ex posteriore in creditum iri. Idem iuris esse in deposito (*D.*, 19, 2, 31).

Papinianus, the great jurist who lived between the second and third centuries AD, was to place even greater emphasis on how thin the line was between deposit and loan, when asked to voice his opinion on the case of the consignment of one hundred coins by Titius to Sempronius through his slave acting as a manager (*D.*, 16, 3, 24). As far as he is concerned, it is unquestionable that the matter involves the institution of the deposit even if referring to money, provided it is duly identified in its specific monetary form: *depositi actionem locum habere: quid est enim aliud commendare quam deponere*? And what about the interest accrued? Papinianus specifies that it is not easy to establish it and, if an agreement was drawn up for the return of an equivalent sum and not the same monetary form, then the situation is no longer that of a deposit (*nam si ut tantundem solveretur convenit, egreditur ea res depositi notissimos terminos*). Unless negotiated otherwise, it would, in any case,

[24]Philo of Alexandria, *De specialibus legibus*, IV, 30–36. Cf. also T. Flavius Josephus, *Antiquities of the Jews*, IV, 8. 38, 287.

[25]V. Arangio-Ruiz, 1981. 312.

go against good faith and the deposit's nature if the depositor demanded interest in advance from the party who had done him a favour by taking care of that money (*sed contra bonam fidem et depositi naturam est usuras ab eo desiderare temporis ante moram, qui beneficium in suscipienda pecunia dedit. Si tamen* ab initio *de usuris praestandis convenit, lex contractus servabitur*). The jurists' differing opinions with regard to the case law of deposits, mentioned herein, mark the physiognomy of this institution. An institution which, based on a principle of unavailability of ownership on the part of the depositary, can assume a differing importance depending on whether the item in question is replaceable or, even, the most replaceable of all item, money. At this point, the unavailability of ownership by whoever receives the item and the consequent obligation to return it in its specific form seem to weaken in the case of the irregular deposit given that the depositary also becomes the owner of the item upon using it (as in the case of a loan), and consequently is only obliged to return the *tantundem*. When applied to the context of the *Pastoral Epistles*, an institution with such ambivalent legal characteristics must necessarily adapt itself to the theological and ministerial needs expressed by these documents. This means it must be stripped of any possible misunderstandings regarding the nature of the deposit, with only its «regular» form being admitted. If Timothy is appointed to safeguard the deposit of the faith, in other words the evangelical teaching which he must account for when called upon to do so by the depositor (Christ and, through him, Paul), and if proof of the diffusion of that content to other men worthy of faith and able to spread it further is included in the act of return («and the things you have heard me say in the presence of many witnesses entrust [26] to reliable people who will also be qualified to teach others», 2 *Tm* 2,2), the result is a complex device. Said device combines the administrative need—the depositary is the custodian and not the owner of the item —with a diffusive tendency—the transmission and hence the permanent succession in the task of protecting the intangibility, but also the inappropriability of the faith. Protestant exegesis most likely has good reasons for questioning the equation of deposit with tradition (παράδοσις), and for limiting the former to what the individual Christian, as such, has received without implying the tricky issue of succession.[27] However, herein we have only to consider the deposit's operating and functional characteristics: an inheritance that does not tolerate appropriation and only asks to be protected. The history of tradition springs from this gesture of

[26]The verb used is παράθου, the middle aorist imperative of παρατίθημι, "entrust the deposit". C. Spicq, 1969. 738.

[27]Cf. Dibelius, M. 1955. *Die Pastoralbriefe*. Tübingen Mohr: 69-70. Indeed, it is clear that, equated with tradition, the deposit appears as a restriction that prevents Christians from free use of the revealed word: the freedom of Christianity from the law, which Luther rediscovers in Paul, was to find an awkward conditioning in another law, that of the deposit whose cautious, if not conservative vocation, would be definitively sealed by placement with tradition and apostolic succession. It is no coincidence that in the encyclical *Pascendi* dated 1907 where Pius X was to condemn modernism, the reference to deposit of faith as a safe port of sound doctrine, features as a emblem right from the start of the document.

handing over which implies a protective attitude in the recipient. That is why the metamorphosis of a faith into *Ekklésia*, a process that in itself is not at all necessary, was performed under the aegis of the administrative procedure. The deposit appeared as the normative archetype for conceiving the birth and functioning of an administrative institution on a global scale. However, it is clear that in light of these characteristics, the positions of the Roman jurists of the early centuries of the Empire regarding the deposit's changeable nature do not seem to be confirmed in theological use. In other words there are not many margins for manoeuvre regarding the admissibility of an «irregular» deposit within Christianity of origins, and, probably, also in the following one. Indeed, if the «administrative» procedure marks the depositary's practice, the *systemic* function performed by the deposit, which serves to outline a symbolic area of safety, must not be overlooked. The deposit is also the container which protects a fairly volatile content, the oral teachings (*didaskalia*) that Timothy heard from Paul, and the latter from those who learnt them directly from Christ: «because I know whom I have believed, and am convinced that he is able to guard what I have entrusted to him until that day. What you heard from me, keep as the pattern of sound teaching, with faith and love in Christ Jesus. Guard the good deposit that was entrusted to you—guard it with the help of the Holy Spirit who lives in us» (2 *Tm* 1,12–14). But the deposit is not just a synonym of the *didaskalia*, just as it does not even specify its meaning. The deposit is the institutional form of teaching, it is the way for contributing to the possibility that *didaskalia* becomes a shared heritage to be managed within society. If the Paul of the *Pastoral Epistles* feels the need to turn to the «deposit» to name *didaskalia*, it is because the naked doctrine in itself is fragile and must be given a form which lends it a new social status. The sound constitution of the word of Christ must be preserved within a container that renders it immune to the vicissitudes of history.[28] In this sense, the deposit is the external reflection of *didaskalia*, its content that can be enforced against third parties, to put it in Legalese. Even if absorbed by the metaphorical register, the deposit's armour is still the official expedient for certifying the discourse of the truth the world over. Even before being set down in writing, this oral teaching, also transmitted in the word of the gospels, is set down in the place of that material intangibility which, like a second nature, establishes it in the form of the deposit and thus hands it over to history. The deposit form is the principle which governs the correct meaning of the word of Christ and the law of its circulation within society. This asset must be diffused, but this is the reason why it can deteriorate unless carefully stored within an apparatus whose durability and integrity are easily recognisable by all people. In order for *didaskalia* to be able to be diffused, it must firstly be placed within a symbolic container that qualifies and houses it at the same time. In the antignostic treaty *Against heresies* which was written in second century A.D., Irenaeus of Lyon pictures this container as a

[28]As regards the relationship between *didaskalia* and *paratheke*, see the observations by Iovino, P. 1998. Il deposito della fede e la sana dottrina. In *Il deposito della fede. Timoteo e Tito*, ed. G. De Virgilio. Bologna: Edizioni Dehoniane: 168–169.

precious deposit in an excellent vessel, which causes the vessel itself containing it to renew its youth also (*depositum jevenescens*) (III, 24.1). A negotiation instrument and protected dwelling space, the concept of deposit asserts itself with a unique pragmatic ambivalence. A concise term which defines both a practical administrative obligation and the place where the object held in custody is kept. The deposit does not refer solely to the passing of custody of an item from the owner to a trustworthy person. The deposit is the procedure and space thanks to which and where the word of Christ draws all that semantic potential which marks out the correct meaning. It is only in this way that "fruitful" word generates wealth, because it is included within a perimeter of safety which is also the deepest region, principle and source on which a human community is built.[29] All the paradoxicality of a principle that lives through transmission and external contagion can be grasped from here. A principle which, at the same time, must balance said openness with an unavailability clause which the deposit, as a legal instrument and symbolic place, signifies. So, the use of the deposit is fuelled by this disjunctive accessible-unavailable coupling which lies at the base of all "common" experiences.

8.5 Administrating the Immaterial

We find ourselves facing a series of problems which need to be examined as a result of this brief excursus on the deposit as an archetype of the administrative rationality that emerged where law and theology intersect.

The deposit of a material asset, as in the law of the Old Testament and in Greek and Roman law, becomes the deposit of an intangible asset, faith, in the *Pastoral Epistles*. Said shift is not at all insignificant since it calls for a reflection on the meaning of holding in custody and managing something that lacks physical consistency, even if its purpose is defined forever by the evangelical revelation. The deposit of an idea needs to be made safe until this incorporeal asset re-materialises in *parousia*, until it offers itself once more to the perceivable apprehension of "sight" and "voice", thus taking on a physical statute. It is difficult to imagine that the entrustment of an idea to be conserved and managed is similar to the entrustment of any item or sum of money. Nevertheless, we cannot help but wonder if this idea "deposited" forever in the evangelical message, is unable to produce fruit, how could a plant or a capital with interest do so. The role of the depositary is called into

[29]Something very similar is described by a study by Yan Thomas on the original function of the *ius pontificale* in Rome, and specifically on its being stuck, so to speak, at the root of the city, hidden but at the same time ready to be transmitted. In this regard, Thomas cites the passage by Titus Livius recalling that civil law had been deposited in the depths of the popes' sanctuary (*civile ius, repositum in penetralibus pontificum*, T. Livio, 9, 46, 5). Cf. Thomas, Y. 2011. Idées romaines sur l'origine et la tranmission du droit. In *Les opérations du droit*, eds. M-A. Hermitte, and P. Napoli. Paris: Seuil-Gallimard, Hautes Etudes: 74.

question here since the specific services asked of a manager of an intangible asset are qualitatively different than those offered by the depositary of physical assets. There is a shift in the asset's administrative and protective function when it is an idea rather than a material object, starting from the way in which its "worth" is calculated. At the same time, however, there is a close analogy between the manager of an intangible deposit, such as Timothy, and the guardian of the estate of a pupil. Both of them do not manage a single item, but a collection of items and juridical relations, because both the deposit and the estate form a group on their own, not just the simple sum of their parts. We have two containers-concepts which their respective managers are called upon to look after. Every "item" of the estate or teaching must be attributed to the collective grouping it is a functional part of.

The above considerations attempt to explicate the concerns that accompanied the commentators of these letters throughout the following centuries. To conclude, we will limit ourselves to recalling two extremely substantial reflections. The first is that of a monk, Vincent de Lerins, who lived in Southern Gaul during the first half of the fifth century. He offered the most complete interpretation of the deposit as an administrative institution in his fierce defence of the Catholic church against the danger of heresy. The author asks "Quid est depositum?" in his *Commonitorium* (I, XXII). The reply seems to be that of a jurist given the technical precision and level of practical specification that corresponds to each syntagm:

> id est, quod tibi creditum est, non quod a te inventum; quod accepisti, non quod excogitasti; rem non ingenii, sed doctrinae, non usurpationis privatae, sed publicae traditionis; rem ad te perductam, non a te prolatam: in qua non auctor debes esse, sed custos; non institutor, sed sectator; non ducens, sed sequens. Depositum, inquit, custodi; catholicae fidei talentum inviolatum illibatumque conserva. Quod tibi creditum, hoc penes te maneat, hoc a te tradatur. Aurum accepisti, aurum redde: nolo mihi pro aliis alia subjicias: nolo pro auro aut impudenter plumbum aut fraudulenter aeramenta supponas: nolo auri speciem, sed naturam plane.

It is impossible for us to look at every phrase, but it is clear that in citing the "regular" deposit as the only admissible and valid form (*aurum accepisti, aurum redde…*), the monk exalts the administrative attitude as the only way of maintaining a relationship with faith. Parties to a negotiation which asks them to look after an intangible asset which they did not create, but which they are only conscientious followers of, Christians justify themselves throughout the world with their administrative "professionalism" which clashes with any form of appropriation. The danger of heresy lies in considering the deposited item as a replaceable asset and hence in allowing the item to be returned to the depositor in a generic manner. As if anyone whatsoever were able to stand as a judge of the value of what has been entrusted to him, calculating and manipulating said value through substitute accounting. If the deposit presumes an economy, the latter is not an economy of exchange, but of managerial effectiveness, of governance.[30]

[30]By other means, the idea developed by G. Agamben of an *oikonomia* as a government practise is confirmed. Cf. Agamben, G. 2007. *The Kingdom and the Glory: For a Theological Genealogy of Economy and Government*. Stanford: Stanford University Press.

Thomas Aquinas represents another decisive moment in the history of exegesis of the deposit. Thomas has no doubts when recalling the punishment that awaits those who hide talents: not only must the deposit be conserved, but also increased (*Depositum hominis est omne bonum, quod habet quilibet, quod sibi commissum est a Deo, ut conservet et multiplicet*),[31] both in a qualitative and quantitative manner, making the essence of the plant bear fruit and ensuring its widest diffusion. From Thomas' viewpoint, the deposit becomes dynamic, it is transformed into a real practice which in the ecclesiastical office finds its most complete meaning in the concept of "care": *Et specialiter praelati habent depositum, scilicet curam proximorum et fidelium (ibid.)*. Management of the deposit is a task that awaits all Christians, but when said task involves a ministerial rank, then the entrusted item coincides with exercise of the pastoral power which is the exclusive prerogative of the ecclesia. Care of the deposit and the deposit as pastoral care: a juridical and theological device closes in on itself, celebrating the administrative practice as the supreme redeeming reason.

8.6 In God We Trust

By now I have reconstructed the juridical and theological roots and evolutions of the deposit. To conclude, I would like to draw some remarks, which, as such, could be useful to foster a research perspective that should nevertheless undergo logic and textual checks. In particular, I refer to the hypothesis I have mentioned in the beginning and that I am going to develop in this final paragraph: the possibility of reading the word 'trust' in the identitarian motto "in God we trust" in relation with the co-presence of trust and faith in the deposit.

The deposit entails both faith and trust. The merging in the same institution of a form of contract and of a space of security can be explained, thus, in light of the peculiar combination that deposit produces between faith as a religious value delivered to someone and good faith as a spiritual characteristic—a requisite—of the receiving of the deposit. Christian faith without the Roman *bona fides* is precarious: guarantees are necessary for the administration of the entrusted credo. It is also necessary to select the people to entrust, that is to say the people that deserve to be trusted for a good conservation of the religious truth. The most important thing for Christendom—as specified in 2 Tim 2,2 where the depositary of faith is trustworthy because he has faith ("what you have heard from me, in front of many witnesses, entrust it to trustworthy men"), is to dilute the "laic" good faith in the profession of religious faith testified by the tutor of the deposited good. This way the criterion of the *bona fides* is absorbed by the principle of the revealed truth: the perfect equivalence between *fides* and *pistis* is thus determined, and so the perfect

[31] Super I *Tm.*, 6, l. 4. Cf. Aquinas, 1902. 227 et seq. See above the idea of *depositum juvenescens* conceived by Irenaeus of Lyon.

equivalence between the depositary and the good Christian. The last solution of this interconnection between juridical rationality and theological rationality translates into a contractual axiom: it is more likely that those who respect their debits fund their existential ethics on the Christian ethics. Because of this guarantee (of this "safety"), those people receive more credit and are considered more trustworthy in the commercial transactions. Even if I cannot go in depth into the historical fortune that this ethical rule has gained in the commercial relations, I think it is important to remember that Max Weber during his trip in the United States in 1904 found that this rule was very important for the protestant and baptist Churches of New England, whose members tended to lend money only to those who showed solid Christian sentiments and values ("*ihnen und nur ihnen Kredit und ihr Geld ins Depot geben*", underlines Weber) and thus for this reasons were trusted to be more inclined towards rectitude (*honesty is the best policy*).[32] The deposit defines a scheme of social interaction capable of satisfying equally the need for juridical circulation of a patrimonial value (material or ideal) and the orthodoxy of the truth of the faith.

From a juridical point of view, in the way the deposit functioned there were many analogies with what would have later become the *trust*. It is hard to conceive the trust as one single model of contract: it differs from the deposit for one essential characteristic: where the depositary does not become the owner of the goods deposited, the *trustee* is instead an administrator to whom the *settlor* has transferred also the property of the goods, even if this condition does not give him title to destroy the goods (*salva substantia rerum*).

Apart from this relevant difference, the two juridical instruments share a common logic: to protect a heritage by respecting the purpose and the destination decided by the original owner.

What counts is to preserve in the duration the entity of the good by protecting it from the personal events and from the behaviours of the depositary/*trustee* that cannot change its purpose. Every instrumental use of the good has to be intrinsic to the obligation of the destination and thus to its specific administrative rationality, but a use functional to the interests of the administrator is not admissible. From this derives the analogy with the *fideicommissum*, that compresses the ownerless freedom and preserves the heritage in respect to the destination decided by the testament. All these are juridical mechanisms aimed at limiting the subjective willingness of the owners (under various titles) of the goods (depositary, *trustee*, heir) because a priority is given to the superior utility embodied in the goods themselves and in their substantial inalterability. The legal protection granted to them, both in the faith deposit and in the trust and in the *fideicommissum*, implies a human beneficiary, a presence expressely foreseen in the structure of these juridical instruments; in the deposit, instead, the legal protection is related to the correct fulfillment of the obligation of each depositary: by administrating diligently what he

[32]Weber, M. 1920–21. Die protestantischen Sekten und der Geist des Kapitalismus (1906). In *Gesammelte Aufsätze zur Religionssoziologie*. Tübingen Mohr.

has received, each one concurs in the realization of a highest good, the salvation of mankind.

Maybe here we can find a possible point of identification between the depositary and the *trustee*: both reproduce the figure of the last will executor, that is to say of a someone that mediates between the will of an absent subject and its realization. The role of the executor excludes the possibility to behave as an owner, because it is not admissible to use the good differently from how it has been established—like in the case of the "conditioned property" typical of the ancient Langobardic institute od the *Treuhand*, an institute compared by Frederick Maitland to the trust.[33]

The implementation of this will has as an object a *res incorporalis* par excellence: the doctrine of a religious faith. By putting together all these aspects a juridical institute based on obligation results: the contract of deposit—with the typical elements *ad rem* of the relationship between administrator and the good to be guarded.

The fiduciary agreement and the power to adminstrate the property are two aspects of a regulatory mechanisms that, just like the trust, shows all its precariousness in the distinction between real rights and obligation rights, "rather potential rubrics than technical terms" as Maitland had it.[34]

Such a hybrid juridical construction should confront a fiduciary resource that the person entrusted does not find in himself, but that he finds in a godly source. Let us remember that in 2 Tm 1, 12, where Paul expresses complete confidence in Christ and in his capacity to keep the custody until the last day of the deposit. Faith needs a warrantor so that all the deposits shall be guarded properly. Philo of Alexandria had revealed that in this lays the core of the agreement between depositor and depositary: the non-fulfillment of the depositary breaks a promise made to a superior "third" that protects and guarantees the agreement.

Christ, thus God, is considered the general tutor of the trust of which every believer is a partial tutor. The deposit, the multiple administration and the unique guarantee are three aspects of a scheme that reproduces the system of the credit.

All these traces lead us to read differently the motto *In God we trust*, that since 1864 appears on American banknotes to indicate the profound religous identity that instituted the people of America. It is not on the level of historical interpretation, but it is in the light of a conceptual genealogy that, in that famous sentence, can be found the functioning of the deposit.

The deposit of the fungible good par excellence finds in every bank the keeper of a faith for whose protection there is a central bank, a center for the emission of that good but also the subject of the attribution of the faith on which all the deposits of a society lay.

Trusting God, the universal guarantor, means to deposit faith in society by counting on the fact that faith will be rewarded in the form of a restitution of the

[33]Maitland, F.W. 2003. *State, Trust, Corporation*, ed. by D. Runciman and M. Ryan, Cambridge University Press: 79.

[34]*Ibid.*, p. 77.

deposited good and in the form of a transmission and of a collective investment. Unlike the theological-political model, it is the deposit, that is to say a juridical construction, that relies in God. This explains what the Supreme Court has decided in terms of constitutional law in 2011: the motto does not violate the first amendment about the separation between state and religion because, as confirmed a decision of the San Francisco Court of Appeals, it is "cerimonial and patriotic and has nothing whatsoever to do with the establishment of religion".[35]

It is likely that the motto nowadays does not testify the religous sentiment of the American people in the same original attitude; nevertheless its intrinsically religious content cannot be denied. We could instead suppose that the motto is preceeded by something which is its unsuspected foundation and that, for another reason, makes *In God we trust* acceptable even to those who are not believers. *Etsi deus non daretur*, the παραθήκε would save us, and James Madison would agree: he used to consider every man first of all as a subject of the Governor of the universe and only after as a member of the civil society. No, *In God we trust* does not sing the praises of a secular religion.

References

Adorno, T.W. 1973. *The Jargon of Autenticity*. Chicago: Northwestern University Press.

Agamben, G. 2007. *The Kingdom and the Glory: For a Theological Genealogy of Economy and Government*. Stanford: Stanford University Press.

Aquinas, T. 1902. *In omnes S. Pauli apostoli epistolas commentaria*. Turin: Marietti.

Arangio-Ruiz, V. 1981. *Istituzioni di diritto romano*. Napels: Jovene.

Burtchaell, J.T. 1992. *From Synagogue to Church. Public Services and Offices in the Earliest Christian Communities*. Cambridge: Cambridge University Press.

Dibelius, M. 1955. *Die Pastoralbriefe*. Tübingen Mohr.

Ehrhardt, A. 1958. Parakatathke. *Zeitschrift der Savigny Stiftung für Rechtsgeschichte (Rom. Abt.)* 75: 32–90.

https://www.treasury.gov/about/education/Pages/in-god-we-trust.aspx

Iovino, P. 1998. Il deposito della fede e la sana dottrina. In *Il deposito della fede. Timoteo e Tito*, ed. G. De Virgilio, 163–175. Bologna: Edizioni Dehoniane.

Maitland, F.W. 2003. *State, Trust, Corporation*. In ed. D. Runciman, and M. Ryan. Cambridge University Press

Marcheselli-Casale, C. 2008 (1995). *Le lettere pastorali*. Bologna: Edizioni Dehoniane.

Médebielle, P. 1930–1934. Dépôt de la foi. In *Dictionnaire de la Bible, suppl. vol. II*, 374–375. Paris Letouzey et Ané.

Newdow v. Lefevre, 10-893.

Penna, R. 2011. *Le prime comunità cristiane. Persone, tempi, luoghi, forme, credenze*. Rome: Carocci.

Philo of Alexandria, De specialibus legibus.

Rordorf, W., and A. Tuilier. 1998. (second edition) *La Doctrine des Douze Apôtres (Didaché)*. Paris: Éditions du Cerf.

Schmitt, C. 1996 (1923). *Roman Catholicism and Political Form*. Westport: Greenwood Press.

[35]See case *Newdow v. Lefevre*, 10–893.

Sohm, R. 1892 (1923). *Kirchenrecht. Band. 1: Die geschichtlichen Grundlagen*. München & Leipzig: Duncker & Humblot.
Spicq, C. 1931. Saint Paul et la loi des dépôts. *Revue biblique* 40, 482 et seq.
Spicq, C. 1969. *Les Épîtres pastorales* (2 vol.). Paris: Gabalda. I.
Stephanus, Thesaurus graecae linguae.
T. Flavius Josephus, Antiquities of the Jews
Thomas, Y. 2011. Idées romaines sur l'origine et la transission du droit. In *Les opérations du droit*, eds. M-A. Hermitte, and P. Napoli. Paris: Seuil-Gallimard, Hautes Etudes.
Towner, PhH. 2006. *The Letters to Timothy and Titus*. Grand Rapids: Eerdmans.
von Harnack, A. 1902. *Die Mission und Ausbreitung des Christentums in den ersten drei Jahrhunderten*. Leipzig.
Weber, M. 1920–21. Die protestantischen Sekten und der Geist des Kapitalismus (1906). In *Gesammelte Aufsätze zur Religionssoziologie*. Tübingen Mohr.

Paolo Napoli is Directeur d'études at the Ecoles des Hautes Etudes en Sciences Sociales of Paris. From October 2008 to September 2016 was the director of the Centre d'étude des normes juridiques "Yan Thomas". After having studied the juridical and political thought of Michel Foucault and the concept of "police" in eighteenth- and nineteenth-century France and Germany, his main field of interest is administrative rationality, with a special attention to genealogical legacy of theology and canon law. The questions of "charisma" and "deposit" are to be the content of his forthcoming publications.

Part IV
Out of Many, One

Chapter 9
Appreciation or Appropriation? An Indigenous Moment in the American Numismatic Narrative (1999–2009)

Sarah Marusek

Abstract American coinage, both circulated as well as commemorative, involves a host of cultural markers that represent the legal iconography of American national identity. The umbrella of American identity is one that covers places and peoples living in the continental United States, arctic and subarctic Alaska, and islands in the Pacific and Caribbean Oceans. As legal iconography, state and territorial American quarters serve as emblems of folk legality in which culture and law constitutively craft one another in ordinary tangible ways. While these quarters depict, and perhaps even celebrate a multicultural polity, the iconographic process of remembering may be more a statement of post-colonial design rather than genuine commemoration of the past and indigenous present of American Indian, Samoan, Native Hawaiian, Native Alaskan, Chamorran, Puerto Rican, and other indigenous peoples under American jurisdiction. These quarters present a theoretical paradox involving the portrayal of images that appear on them. This paradox represents an indigenous moment numismatically framed through non-English phrases and depictions of culture outside the continental forty-eight states. This chapter will examine this paradox as an indigenous moment in the numismatic construction of public memory illustrated by the minting of linguistic variety and cultural imagery on American state and territorial quarters.

This work was first presented at *Interpellations: Law, Literature, and the Humanities Association of Australasia* at Australian National University in Canberra, Australia in December 2013 and later published as Marusek, Sarah. 2015. The Crafting of Law and the Coining of Culture: Legal Semiotic of the American Quarter. *Law, Culture and the Humanities*. (https://doi.org/10.1177/1743872115575139). This present paper/current chapter is an expansion of that original paper with a focus on Indigeneity. Some reprinted portions from the original paper appear in accordance with Springer and Sage publication guidelines.

S. Marusek (✉)
Department of Political Science, University of Hawai'i, Hilo, USA
e-mail: marusek@hawaii.edu

S. Huygebaert et al. (eds.), *Sensing the Nation's Law*, Studies in the History of Law and Justice 13, https://doi.org/10.1007/978-3-319-75497-0_9

9.1 Numismatic Constructions of Community

On the obverse side of American quarters, seen in Fig. 9.1, one can find the image of former President George Washington. As the first American president, Washington is a symbol of patriotism and unity as the enduring tether of national pride to a richly diverse populace in the United States. Similar to other national emblems that appear on other money as well as stamps around the world,[1] George Washington's head is similar in scope to the figurehead of Queen Elizabeth on the British pound, the image of the former first President Syngman Rhee on the South Korean hwan, or the Euro coin with distinct images representing each member state (such as animals, architectural landmarks, artwork, and other national symbols). Images on coins give national attention to historical figures, images, and representation of each particular populace.

On the reverse of American coins, one can find the slogan *E PLURIBUS UNUM*, which in Latin, means "out of one, many". With linguistic roots in Latin, and a multitude of other languages, it is of interest that a specifically non-English phrase marks all U.S. quarters. Despite this aspect of uniformity, however, is the evolving plethora of designs on the reverse side (usually above this Latin inscription). In light of the many intricate images that would assuredly provoke further discussion and analysis, this paper is limited in scope to those quarter designs during the period of 1999–2009.

One thing is certain: irregardless of image or prominence of Latin-inscribed slogans, not all Americans speak English (much less Latin). The reverse sides of American quarters invite closer inspection as the depictions of American life are represented in a variety of ways. One of these ways is linguistically. In the United States, English is neither a legally mandated nor officially declared language. Throughout the United States, a multitude of languages besides English are spoken, including Hawaiian, Samoan, Spanish, Chamorran, Ebonics, Creole, Pidgin, Native American languages, American Sign Language. As Mari Matsuda reminds us "from Africa, from Asia, from Europe, from all ends of the planet, the voices came to us".[2] Beyond the borders of the North American mainland, a variety of languages, accents and dialects reflecting geographic location, historical influence, and cultural identity can be found. In the Pacific and the Caribbean, the United States has five territories (American Samoa, Guam, Northern Mariana Islands, U.S. Virgin Islands, and the Commonwealth of Puerto Rico). Additionally, two American states (Alaska and Hawai'i) are located thousands of miles from the continental forty-eight. For example, the state of Hawai'i is roughly three thousand miles from the California coast and six thousand miles from Washington, D.C. The state of Alaska is over

---

[1]Wagner, Anne, and Malik Bozzo-Rey. 2014. French Commemorative Postage Stamps as a Means of Legal Culture and Memory. In *Law, Culture and Visual Studies*, eds. Anne Wagner, and Richard K. Sherwin, 307–328. New York: Springer.

[2]Matsuda, Mari J. 1991. Voices of America: Accent, Antidiscrimination Law, and a Jurisprudence for the Last Reconstruction. *Yale Law Journal* 100(5): 1329–1407.

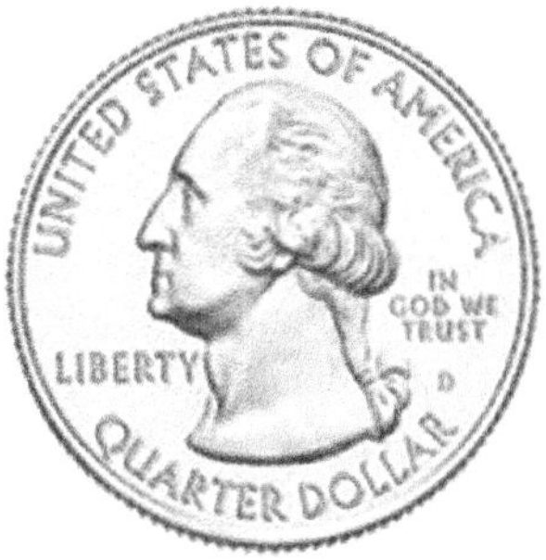

Fig. 9.1 United States Mint, *The American Quarter Dollar (obverse)*, United States Mint: Connecting American Through Coins. D.C. and U.S. Territories Quarters. http://www.usmint.gov/mint_programs/dcandterritories/. Accessed 28 February 2015, Image in the Public Domain

three thousand miles from the nation's capital and Guam, American Samoa, and the Northern Mariana Islands are nearly seventy-five hundred miles away. Puerto Rico and the U.S. Virgin Islands are closer to South America than to the United States. Following these coins' images, the map in Fig. 9.6 illustrates the geographic location of these locations (circled) and their various proximities within the world and the United States mainland.

Wherever the expanse of American jurisdiction may be and whichever languages are included under its umbrella, American currency is used as legal tender. Quarters, a seemingly ordinary form of legal currency, officially, culturally, and numismatically represent the United States. In this way, quarters are symbols of law that perpetuate national meaning through the ordinary appearance of cultural imagery. From 1999 to 2009, American quarter dollar coins were reissued with artistic depictions of each state or territory's unique identity under the *50 States Commemorative Coin Program Act of 1997* [Public Law 105-124-Dec. 1, 1998 (111 Stat. 2534)] and *The District of Columbia and United States Territories Quarters Program under the Consolidated Appropriations Act of 2008* [Public Law 110-161-Dec. 26, 2007 (121 Stat. 1844)]. On one side of these quarters (reverse), each state or territory is represented; on the flip side (obverse), the image of the first American President, George Washington, appears. Each program legislatively encouraged each localized government to submit culture-based designs that characterized the identity of each place. Such cultural-based imagery made cars, trees, Revolutionary War heroes, language, and food emblematic of what represented America.

The aesthetics of these quarters semiotically frame the constitutive relationship between law and culture in three ways. The first way considers the quarter as an emblem of folk legality, where folk legality characterizes the cultural text of law as illustrated through iconic designs on the reverse sides of these coins. The second way concerns the nostalgic jurisprudence of the legal landscape in which colonial beginnings and westward expansion engender a particular commemoration of American historical foundations. The third way examines the legal aesthetic of public memory through the paradoxical representation of indigeneity through indigenous artifacts, cultural practices, histories, and mottos in languages other than English and in places besides the 'lower 48'. This chapter will explore the paradox of "Americanization" found in the visual depictions of indigeneity on state and territorial quarters. On the one hand, these images seem duplicitous, invoking critiques of settler colonialism and cultural tokenism by the United States Mint. On the other hand, these images may herald an indigenous moment in which the illustration of marginalized places and people is a legal statement to recognize and celebrate cultural pluralism. This paradox contributes to the ongoing discussion of public memory in a culturally and linguistically pluralistic community of the United States.

9.2 Coins as Legal Aesthetic and Cultural Text

These coins symbolize a trope of folk legality, in which popular icons of American identity were semiotically constructed as law operationalized through a culture of romanticized national values and sense of community. Folk legality[3] is the cultural approach to law in which legality is exemplified in things typically not associated with formal law yet given legal importance through cultural usage. In this paper, the quarter, and its designs, characterize this concept as objects of a folk legality that is culturally important yet still holds positivist views of law's role in culture. In this way, the quarter signifies law through its perception as a legal token on which the United States insignia can be found. Through the process of quarter design, images of culture are crafted to represent a notion of 'folk' that is, on its surface, non-legal. However, the designs from these two quarters programs represent a "legal semiotic of American identity in which the spatial imaginary of American culture is aligned with the crafting of sanitized legal narratives".[4] Through the designs minted on these quarters, an Americanized sense of public memory is crafted onto these banal objects of everyday transaction. Through tangibility and banality, law and culture intersect through the symbolic characterization of national identity of folk legality. Folk legality is the imagery on these quarters that provides insight into localized expressions about the nation's past and present. These expressions characterize the uniqueness of each state, territory, and district under American jurisdiction and are culturally understood to be rooted in law with legal status loosely attributed to social and historical association.

Whether as states with a particular reputation or as non-states, such as territories and the District of Columbia, the images on these quarters further reveal larger structures of power and jurisdictional assertion in the areas of geographic location, linguistic identity, and place-based cultural affiliation. Through their emblematic

[3]For further discussion of folk legality, please see Sarah Marusek, 2015.
[4]*Ibid.*

representations of cultural identity and public memory, these reissued American quarters numismatically tell the story of American colonial conquest from the late seventeenth century into the present day. This process of Americanization is premised upon the taking of land and the re-creation of what is viewed as native and authentic. Paradoxically, these images infuse (and perhaps infect) the celebration of indigenous plurality with overtones of Americanization. Through the gazes of legal and cultural pluralism, these coins are complicated and even confusing. What can we draw from these images? How do we gain knowledge through these coins and what types of knowledge are we gaining or expected to gain? Who is the 'we' that represents America? Through these coins, we are witness to a process of cultural and legal pluralism that characterizes the numismatic representation and legal semiotic of languages, diverse places, and indigenous cultures through depictions on American coins.

Through their imagery, American quarters materially provide a unique site on which to communicate nationalized culture. One key example of this is the image of the first American president, George Washington, a monarchic figure in American history and national culture, who appears as the head on the obverse side of the quarter. On the state quarters, a variety of other images, ranging from racecars to fruit, appear on the reverse of the coin. On territorial quarters, indigenous symbols and languages are shown. On the District of Columbia, jazz legend Duke Ellington is depicted.

As emblematic productions of folk legality, these coins provide a vantage point of positivist law from which to further consider the constitutive relationship between law, culture, and politics. Imagery on coined money legally characterizes American self-reflexive historical recollection, as is evident in selectively chosen representations of the nation's public memory. For instance, national events involving racial violence, labor strife, and the domestic elimination of native peoples are dimmed against such picturesque images as palm trees, Magnolia blossoms, and sailboats. As a result, such seemingly benign images that appear on coins become visual artifacts of an American past of imperialism and injustice that may be dismissed against the depiction of the bucolic and trivial characterizations of American history that such coinage laws and programs engender and promote. The privileging of a particular sense of American culture is visually constructed on the most banal of national markers such as the coin. In this way, quarters serve as legal semiotic for a version of American identity in which public memory, folk legality and nostalgic jurisprudence shape the legal landscape in which the spatial imaginary of American culture is aligned with the crafting of constructed legal narratives. Those legal narratives are particularly of interest when considering the paradoxical presentation of indigenous territories under American jurisdiction.

The semiotic discourse that appears on the faces of these quarters carries hidden constitutive meaning in how law manipulates culture (and culture manipulates law) through the legal presentation of cultural value. Here, visual meaning is legally crafted at an initial folk level (and later approved by gubernatorial figures) for the purposes of representing an anesthetized and purposeful public memory. Through the images that appear on American quarters in which the national narrative appears as numismatic image design, the socio-legal production of the national story is told.[5] Subsequently, the centrality of visual design as it concerns the legal framing of culture engenders law as "a system of signs which enables the lawyer, the linguist, the reader, and even the viewer to analyze the public space in a semiotic sense".[6] Through the context of the quarter, such imagery serves as the visual medium of state power in which the United States Treasury ultimately exercises the authority to sculpt cultural values and public understandings of American history and identity in places throughout the Pacific and Atlantic Oceans and places in between. Public memory is visually constructed on quarters as material representation of a cultural forum for the process of Americanization and selected portrayals of national consciousness.[7] Using a Peircean semiotic framework, we can view the quarter through a tripartite designation, where the signified is the image on the quarter, the signifier is the quarter itself, and the referent is the reception of that coin.[8] The communicative value of the pictorial data on the quarter suggests that the images presented attribute cultural meaning to a foundation exhibited by law. Insofar as Barthes suggests, "all images are polysemous"[9]; this signifies that the interpretation of the quarter conveys a symbolic message in which normative national images of identity nostalgically foster a utopic image of what America should look like. Indicative of the territorial quarter paradox, Barthes cautions about the "utopian character of denotation," which in this example, serves to transmit understandings of American identity through selected imagery. Through numismatic memorialization, the public understanding of the past and present is presented as idyllic images that represent the officially sanctioned 'code' of what America looks like. While these quarters engage cultural understandings of law and aesthetically provide keen insight into the banal undercurrent of constitutive legal frameworks, the semiotic prioritization of such objects challenges the presumption of meaning found in ordinary, everyday images.[10] This paradox in meaning will be explored further throughout the paper.

---

[5]Seuffert, Nan. 2006. *Jurisprudence of National Identity*. Aldershot: Ashgate.

[6]Wagner, Anne. 2010. French Urban Space Management: A Visual Semiotic Approach Behind Power and Control, *International Journal for the Semiotics of Law*. 24(2): 227.

[7]Page, Max. 2005. Memory Field. *Architecture*. 94(6): 37–45. Dovey, Kim. 1999. *Framing Places: Mediating Power in Built Form*. New York: Routledge.

[8]Jappy, Tony. 2013. *Introduction to Peircean Visual Semiotics*. New York: Bloomsbury.

[9]Barthes, Roland. 1999. Rhetoric of the image. In *Visual Culture: The Reader*, eds. Jessica Evans and Stuart Hall. 37. London: Sage.

[10]Brigham, John. 2009. *Material Law: A Jurisprudence of What's Real*. Philadelphia: Temple University Press.

9.3 State and Territorial Quarters Programs

On 1 December 1997, Public Law 105-124 (111 Stat. 2534) was enacted by the United States Congress with Sections 1–3 known as the "50 States Commemorative Coin Program Act". This law called for the reissuing of quarters over a ten-year period in which each of the 50 United States would be individually commemorated on the reverse side of the quarter. In addition to honoring the federal republic of the United States and modernizing circulating coinage, the purpose of the act was "to promote the diffusion of knowledge among the youth of the United States about the individual States, their history and geography, and the rich diversity of the national heritage" (Sec. 2). Additionally, each quarter would show the date of entry into the union. On 26 December 2007, Public Law 110-161[11] was enacted. Section 622, known as the "Redesign and Issuance of Circulating Quarter Dollar Honoring the District of Columbia and Each of the Territories", declares "the design on the reverse side of each quarter dollar issued during 2009 shall be emblematic of one of the following: District of Columbia, the Commonwealth of Puerto Rico, Guam, American Samoa, the United States Virgin Islands, and the Commonwealth of the Northern Mariana Islands".

Both laws stipulated a design process for the quarters. This process included design review by the Treasury-appointed Citizens Commemorative Coin Advisory Committee following each member's selection to the committee by the appropriate governor or executive officer from each state or territory (and mayor from the District of Columbia) with final approval reserved for Secretary of the U.S. Treasury. In terms of generating the initial designs for the quarter, the vast majority of governors/executive officers solicited artistic entries from their respective jurisdictions, with many schoolchildren participating in the process. Design criteria mandated the "broad appeal to the state's citizens" and the avoidance of "controversial subjects or symbols likely to offend".[12] State landmarks, landscapes, symbols of state resources, state flowers and trees, state icons were encouraged as "suitable subject matter". A variety of images were presented with a select few selected for the final cut. Designs chosen appear on these quarters, which have circulated widely since the beginning of the program in 1997, are gradually replacing earlier quarters. These quarters bear the same obverse image of the first U. S. President George Washington as pre-1999 quarters. According to the Mint's Report, *50 State Quarters Report: 10 Years of Honoring Our Nation's History and Heritage*, an "estimated 3.5 million people participated in the design process for their state quarter either through concept submission or voting".[13]

---

[11]Consolidated Appropriations Act 2008, Division D, Section 622, [H.R. 2764].

[12]*United States Mint 50 State Quarters Report* 1999–2008*: 10 Years of Honoring Our Nation's History and Heritage,* 14. http://www.usmint.gove/downloads/min_programs/50sqreport.pdf; Accessed 26 November 2013.

[13]Ibidem, 15.

Approximately 34.8 billion commemorative quarters honoring the 50 states were produced and after ten years of production, the program is said to have generated $470.1 million in revenue from coin sales and related numismatic products.[14] The original conception for the idea of commemorative state quarters was based upon a similar program instituted by the Royal Canadian Mint in honoring its provinces (US Mint 2008: 4). Interestingly, and perhaps even comically, in the United States, Kermit the Frog served as the "official 'Spokesfrog'" for the 50 State Quarters Program. While this program received much fanfare, including coin collecting programs for children, commemorative collecting books for adults, and popular celebration of the new coins, the District of Columbia and the United States Territories Quarter Program received much less recognition and statistical attention by the U.S. Mint. The contrast between the promotion and reception of these two quarter programs reflects the general absence of attention paid by American culture to the five United States territories, or to the fact that the United States even has such quasi-colonial jurisdictions.

According to the website of the United States Mint entitled "Connecting American through Coins", the mission of the Mint is to produce currency that "connects us with the core values of America" [accessed 2 October 2013; http://www.usmint.gov/about_the_mint/]. These core values semiotically appear as legal aesthetics, or images that are sanctioned by law on the quarters discussed in this paper. Because these image-based values are sources of constructed meaning authored by the U.S. Department of the Treasury under Congressional authority as granted by the U.S. Constitution, coins in this sense, illustrate national identity through imagery. Moreover, these coins communicate a symbolic meaning that is culturally tethered to their design as phenomenologically complex semiotics of law.[15] In this way, the coins symbolize law's meaning in American cultural identity. Similarly, quarters engender territorial jurisdiction as enacted through the visual making of memory; these coins perpetuate a culturally specific architecture that maps the jurisdictional understandings of what it means to be American.[16]

---

[14]Ibidem, 15.

[15]Yanow, Dvora. 2006. How built spaces mean: A semiotics of space. In *Interpretation and Method: Empirical Research Methods and the Interpretive*, eds. Dvora Yanow and Peregrine Schwartz-Shea, 349–66. Turn, Armonk, NY: M.E. Sharpe. Kevelson, Roberta. 1992. Semiotics and the art of 'discovery' in law. In *Law and Aesthetics*, ed. Roberta Kevelson, 245–79. New York: Peter Lang.

[16]Ford, Richard T. 2001. Law's territory (a history of jurisdiction). *Legal Geographies Reader: Law, Power, and Space*, eds. Nicholas Blomley, David Delaney, and Richard T. Ford 200–217. Malden, MA: Blackwell.

9.4 Folk Legality and Nostalgic Jurisprudence

Through the crafting of quarter design, folk legality is the transmittance of law and legality at the cultural level through popular frameworks of how law is made tangible. In this way, law constitutively reacts with surrounding cultural texts to reveal a method of seeing law's response to everyday banality. Folk legality is law that is crafted according to the articulations of that which are stereotypically characterized as core American values. As depicted on these coins, these values translate to eating and driving fast. Additionally, the design process of these images engenders democratic contributions through such images that normatively symbolize American life. Walter Benjamin characterizes this reproduction of culture through art as a phenomenological statement of endurance through space and time and reminds us "by close-ups of the things around us [and] by focusing on hidden details of familiar objects [we can] extend our comprehension of the necessities which rule our lives".[17] Heretier further adds to Benjamin's sentiment by suggesting contemporary legal theory, through a semiotic perspective, cannot be referred solely to the concepts of text and norm, but must take into account the connection between image and law".[18] Hence, quarters serve to remind us of the numismatic connection between image and law that is crafted through the quarters' design process, which carefully omits the recognition of not only key social movements that expanded the rights of citizenship in American culture on the basis of race, ethnic background, disability, and sexual orientation, but historically defining struggles of organized labor against corporate power.

Images of cultural relevance as depicted on a variety of state quarters illustrate the public memory associated with American identity and national sense of community. Through images of animals, eating, leisure activities, and statues, American identity on quarters takes on the quality of everyday familiarity. This presumed sense of familiarity can be characterized as folk legality, or as the variety of ways in which law is translatable through culture. Animal depictions such as the grizzly bear (Alaska), the salmon (Alaska and Washington), the Peregrine Falcon (Idaho), the buffalo (Kansas and North Dakota), and thoroughbred horses (Kentucky) each promote understandings of power and prowess as cultural icons of strength and fortitude. Ironic to note here, is the fact that the buffalo is an appropriated Native American symbol. Eating is a fundamental activity to most cultures, including the United States. Images of corn, cows, cheese wheels, (Wisconsin for these three images), a peach (Georgia), and maple trees (Vermont) are texts of American identity insofar as each conveys a type of food particular to discourse of eating and culture in the United States (i.e. 'she's such a peach!'; 'grilled cheese sandwiches'; 'what could be more American than maple syrup?'). Leisure activities also

[17]Benjamin, Walter. 1999. The work of art in the age of mechanical reproduction. In *Visual Culture: The Reader*, eds. Jessica Evans and Stuart Hall, 78. London: Sage.

[18]Heritier, Paolo. 2014. Law and image: Towards a theory of nomograms. In *Law, Culture and Visual Studies*, eds. Anne Wagner and Richard K. Sherwin, 25. New York: Springer.

represent what can be framed as folk legality, as almost the reification of norms through a status quo of popular activities. Country music (Tennessee), jazz music (District of Columbia and the image of Duke Ellington), nautical activities such as sailing and navigation (Rhode Island, Guam, and Northern Mariana Islands) and fishing (Minnesota and Maine via the lighthouse image), reading (Alabama and the image of Helen Keller and Braille), and driving fast (Indiana and the image of the Indianapolis 500 race car) are other activities constructed as American pastimes. Lastly, popular identities residing in the faces of four U.S. Presidents at Mount Rushmore (South Dakota), President Abraham Lincoln (Illinois), and Lady Liberty at the Statue of Liberty (New York), frame a folk-based understanding of cultural representations of American political history, as told and retold by popular history. Through these iconographic narratives, such semiotics of Americanness connote a framework of law that supports stereotypical notions of American culture and lifestyle through numismatic presentation. The medium for this semiotic logic is connected to a context of folk legality in which people touch and use these objects in their sheer state of banality.

On the 50 State Quarters, the colonial foundations of the United States are represented by trees, ships, and masculine images that signify the nation's founding. Connecticut's quarters depict a white oak, the 'Charter Oak,' as the tree in which the state charter was successfully hidden from the British. The South Carolina quarter depicts the Palmetto Tree from which logs were used to build a small fort that impeded the intruding British fleet. On Virginia's quarter, three large masted ships are pictured in order to represent the early colonization of the New World, as the American colonies are self-referenced. Masculine images appear on the quarters of Delaware, Massachusetts, and New Jersey in which the image is riding on a horse (Delaware) to symbolize a delegate riding to Independence Hall to attend the Continental Congress, holding a gun (Massachusetts) to represent the 'Minutemen' early colonial militia, and riding in a boat (New Jersey) to signify George Washington and members of his colonial army successfully navigating and crossing the Delaware River during the Revolutionary War.

The theme of westward expansion illustrates the land acquisition of the United States on a variety of state quarters. From the mountains to the prairie to the desert, images of exploration, development, and taming represent the plush west from the Atlantic to the Pacific Ocean. The taming of natural resources is shown on the Arkansas quarter in which a lake, mountains, a duck, rice stalks, and a diamond are pictured. Exploration is symbolized in the Grand Canyon (Arizona), the image of Yosemite Valley and explorer John Muir (California), a pioneer wagon (Nebraska), a settler schoolhouse (Nebraska), the image of explorers Lewis and Clark on the Missouri River (Missouri), the joining of east and west coasts via the linking of the Central Pacific and Union Pacific railroads at Promontory Point (Utah), the 'New' associated with the nation's expansion is depicted in the image of the star (Texas), the cowboy riding a bucking bronco (Wyoming), and wild mustangs against the backdrop of the setting sun (Nevada). The acquisition of new landscapes can also be viewed in the image of Crater Lake (Oregon) and the Great Lakes (Michigan). Additionally, the nearly doubling of growth of the national geographic scope of the emerging United States is depicted on the map of the Louisiana Purchase in 1803 (Louisiana). Lastly, the image of the space shuttle (Florida) represents American exploration into space.

The process of westward expansion is a salient theme in the nostalgic jurisprudence of the legal landscape. As an extension of "visual legal commentary",[19] images on quarters communicate a legal framework of cultural iconography that connotes a framework of relevance in the American public memory. Memory and memorialization are what Farid Samir Benevides Vanegas refers to as a "field of symbolic dispute: meanings and interpretations about the past are part of the discussion".[20] As such, the legal landscape detailed on quarters intentionally constructs notions of American expansion and land acquisition that ignore the realities of imperialist conquest, obliteration of native peoples, a history of chattel slavery, and the restrictive framework of citizenship that preferenced wealthy, white men who owned property. Yet such disempowerment continues among native people under United States jurisdiction. As an example, over four million people, many of whom are U.S. military veterans, live in the five territories, but cannot vote for the American president. Furthermore, many territorial residents are considered U.S. Nationals for citizenship purposes but are denied the full range of citizen-based rights.[21]

9.5 Appropriation of Indigeneity

Images on quarters aesthetically frame American identity through the presence as well as absence of indigenous artifacts and mottos in languages other than English. A variety of indigenous visuals appear on state quarters. Native American images are shown, such as the bison skull (Montana), the Zia sun symbol (New Mexico), and the Gaillardia, or Indian Blanket, flower (Oklahoma). Each of these images is intended to represent Native American or indigenous heritage in that state. On the Hawai'i state quarter, shown as Fig. 9.2, King Kamehameha I, former Hawaiian monarch, is depicted. Images of the ava bowl ("tanoa") and ava ceremony whisk and staff are depicted on the American Samoa quarter, seen in Fig. 9.3. On the quarter of the Northern Mariana Islands, architectural remnants of ancient Chamorro structures, a canoe, and the native bird MWAR are shown. On the Guam quarter, a Chamorro boat and latte housing stone are depicted.

The correlation between the limited recognition of Native American tribal heritage, the Native Hawaiian monarchy, overthrown by the U.S. at the end of the

[19]Petroski, Karen. 2014. Visual legal commentary. In *Law, Culture and Visual Studies*, eds. Anne Wagner and Richard K. Sherwin, 672–696. New York: Springer.

[20]Benavides Vanegas, Farid Samir. 2014. Film and the reconstruction of memory. In *Law, Culture and Visual Studies*, eds. Anne Wagner and Richard K. Sherwin, 1000. New York: Springer.

[21]Spiro, Peter J. 2008. *Beyond Citizenship: American Identity After Globalization*. New York: Oxford University Press.

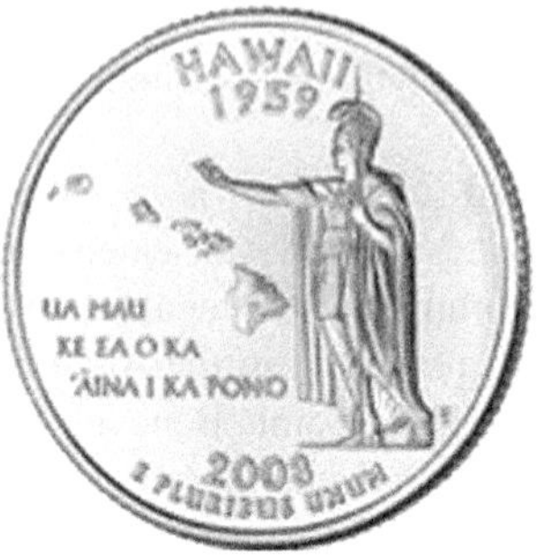

UA MAU KE EA O KA AINA I KA PONO

[Translated in ʻŌlelo Hawaiʻi, "*The life of the land is perpetuated in righteousness*"]

Fig. 9.2 State of Hawaii Quarter *(reverse)*, United States Mint, *The American Quarter Dollar*, United States Mint: Connecting American Through Coins. D.C. and U.S. Territories Quarters. http://www.usmint.gov/mint_programs/dcandterritories/. Accessed 28 February 2015, Image in the Public Domain

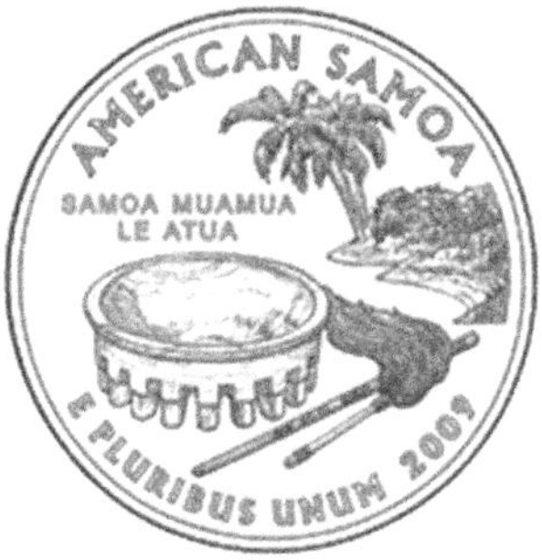

SAMOE MUAMUA LE ATUA

[Translated in Samoan, "*Samoa, God is First*"]

Fig. 9.3 Territory of American Samoa Quarter, United States Mint, *The American Quarter Dollar*, United States Mint: Connecting American Through Coins. D.C. and U.S. Territories Quarters. http://www.usmint.gov/mint_programs/dcandterritories/. Accessed 28 February 2015, Image in the Public Domain

nineteenth century, and the heritage of Pacific Islanders, strikes a paradoxical depiction of indigeneity that whilst acknowledged, is nevertheless contained through quasi-colonial jurisdictions of sovereignty and limitations of agency and political engagement (as shown in the *Insular Cases*[22]). Furthermore, while many Native American elements were considered for state quarter designs, few were

[22]Weiner, Mark S. 2006. *Americans Without Law: The Racial Boundaries of Citizenship*. New York: New York University Press.

included in the final design selection. Examples of these absent Native American images include Mesa Verde National Park with cliff dwellings (Colorado), Chief Little Turtle (Indiana), an American Indian archer (Kansas), Chief Standing Bear (Nebraska), and Native American artifacts and petroglyphs (Nevada). "The Great Land" is on the Alaska coin, a phrase in English that comes from the Aleutian word "Alyeska" (Alaska). In this way, those indigenous elements that do appear seem to be a form of cultural tokenism in which native cultures are continually Americanized through their selective visual markings on quarters. No mention is made of the colonial conquest of the United States, or its history of domination of independent nations and their distinct cultures throughout the Pacific or the continuing harm inflicted upon the Native American nations of the continental United States, much less the countless restrictions on the fundamental identity process of legal tribal recognition.[23] Additionally, the numismatic recognition of indigeneity is aesthetically determined according the fleeting appearance on American money and as Mamdani notes, "The American autobiography is written as the autobiography of the settler. The native has no place in it".[24]

9.6 Appreciation of Indigeneity

Paradoxically, however, it must be noted, as Christine Black, indigenous Australian scholar suggests,[25] that because indigenous elements *are* present at all is a statement of recognition and triumphant expansion of the American cultural umbrella that extends beyond the legal landscape of European-derived Americanism and recognizes existing indigenous cultural distinctions. In her insightful study of the observable as legal phenomenon, legal semiotician Roberta Kevelson characterizes legal aesthetics in many ways, including showing "how encoded values reinforce the actual practice of the laws in isomorphic ways" and captures Habermas's sentiment about similar matters of representation "that take different actual forms and modes of expression".[26] In this way, the moment of American indigeneity is upon us through these quarters, their design, and their circulation. Additionally, the appearance of non-English words and phrases that appear on quarters linguistically challenge the presumption of English-only Americanism. For example, the Hawai'i state motto in Hawaiian reads "UA MAU KE EA O KA AINA I KA PONO" ("The life of the land is perpetuated in righteousness") (Hawaii quarter[27]). Another is the

[23]Cramer, Renee Ann. 2005. *Cash, Color, and Colonialism*. Norman: University of Oklahoma Press.

[24]Mamdani, Mahmood. 2015. Settler Colonialism: Then and Now. *Critical Inquiry* 41(3): 596.

[25]I had the pleasure of talking with Professor Black in Canberra at the Interpellations conference in 2013.

[26]Kevelson. 1992. 3.

[27]As written on quarters in the Americanized writing without the Hawaiian okina (').

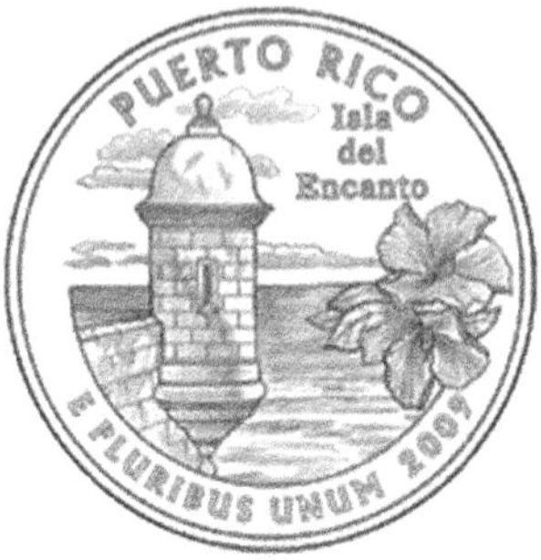

ISLA DEL ENCANTO

[Translated in Spanish, "*Isle of Enchantment*"]

Fig. 9.4 Territory of Puerto Rico Quarter, United States Mint, *The American Quarter Dollar*, United States Mint: Connecting American Through Coins. D.C. and U.S. Territories Quarters. http://www.usmint.gov/mint_programs/dcandterritories/. Accessed 28 February 2015, Image in the Public Domain

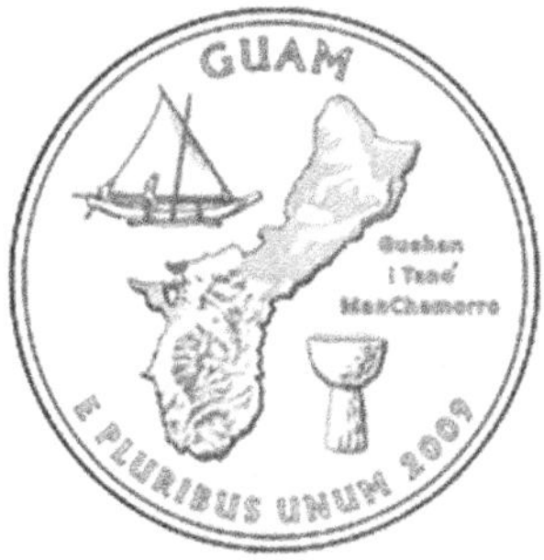

GUAHAN I TANO MANCHAMORRO

[Translated in Chamorran, "*Guam - Land of the Chamorro*"]

Fig. 9.5 Territory of Guam Quarter, United States Mint, *The American Quarter Dollar*, United States Mint: Connecting American Through Coins. D.C. and U.S. Territories Quarters. http://www.usmint.gov/mint_programs/dcandterritories/. Accessed 28 February 2015, Image in the Public Domain

American Samoan territorial motto "SAMOE MUAMUA LE ATUA" ("Samoa, God is First") that appears on the American Samoan quarter. As seen on Figs. 9.4 and 9.5, the Puerto Rico quarter has the Spanish phrase ISLA DEL ENCANTO ("Isle of Enchantment") and on the Guam quarter, the phrase GUAHAN I TANO MANCHAMORRO ("Guam—Land of the Chamorro") can be read.

What is of particular interest here is the history of language-based discrimination that impacted the speaking of these non-English languages. In Hawai'i for example,

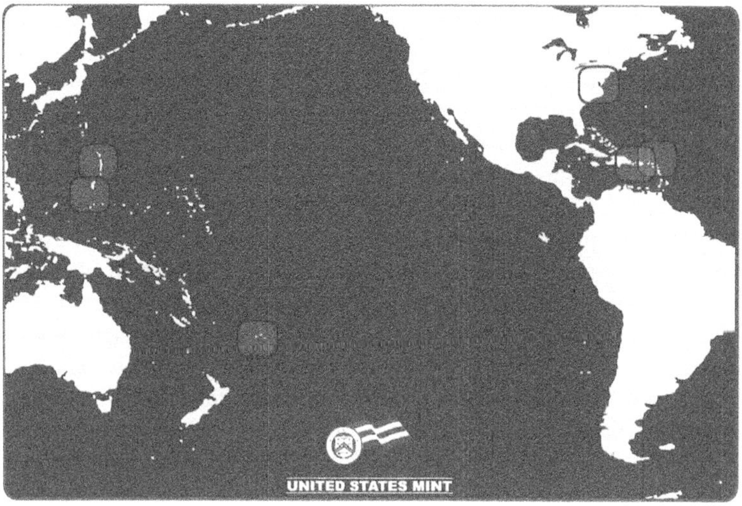

Fig. 9.6 Map of American Territories, United States Mint, *The American Quarter Dollar*, United States Mint: Connecting American Through Coins. D.C. and U.S. Territories Quarters. http://www.usmint.gov/mint_programs/dcandterritories/. Accessed 28 February 2015, Image in the Public Domain

the use of the Hawaiian language, was not allowed in public education until when 1978 when it was officially recognized by the Hawai'i State Constitution as one of two state languages (with English as the other language). In Puerto Rico, people speak Spanish over English as the primary language; however, the First Circuit Court of Appeals that includes Puerto Rico, is a courtroom conducted in English. With so much tension involving language, particularly the usage of Spanish in the southwestern United States, the appearance of non-English languages in former and present territorial areas of the U.S. could perhaps be celebrated, but also problematically be viewed as cultural tokenism (Fig. 9.6).

However, in some places, the speaking of English is itself a form of cultural tokenism. As described by Justin Richland, Hopi courtrooms preference the use of Hopi language and cultural expressions within the Anglo legal adversarial framework. This "pragmatic paradox" as Richland notes, reveals the "ironies of indigeneity that have characterized the anthropology of native cultural politics that now must be seen as shaping the actual iterations of culture difference that constitute the dialectic 'edge' of indigenous sovereignty".[28] The place and usage of the courtroom is the sovereign enactment of redefining who frames the notion of community through legal representation and incorporation of language, place, and position into legal dialogue.

[28]Richland, Justin B. 2007. Pragmatic paradoxes and ironies of indigeneity at the 'edge' of Hopi sovereignty. *American Ethnologist* 34(3): 557.

Hawaiian epistemologist Manulani Aluli Meyer[29] writes in the introduction to her book *Ho'oulu Our Time of Becoming: Hawaiian Epistemology and Early Writings*, "I tell this story to remind myself to not simply 'tolerate diversity'. We should, instead, be fully engaged, changed and humbled by it. We should be directed, enlightened and scolded by it. We should know more of it and critique its influence on our thoughts and actions. And in Hawai'i, the core of this diversity is found in what is Hawaiian". In this way, one way to consider indigeneity is through its connections to place. The recognition of, respect for, and adherence to the traditions and customs that arise from that place engender as well as foster indigenous identities. Perhaps this is the indigenous moment in the United States in which the presence of native peoples, whose population numbers are marginalized and quantitatively decreasing, is in fact increasing in scope and recognition in the popular narrative through practices rooted to place rather than ethnicity. This statement is not meant to diminish the vitality of ethnicity-based identities, but is instead intended to recognize the emphasis on place that may reach out to include those who inhabit such places and celebrate the indigeneity of these places. Hawai'i is one such place. Through the expansion of indigeneity beyond ethnic distinctions to place-based practices, customs, and affiliations that include ethnically non-indigenous participants, indigeneity is enlivened through pluralist participation in the place of Hawai'i. Similarly, the depictions of the five U.S. territories enliven each of these unique places.

At Hawai'i Community College, Dr. Taupōuri Tangarō, Professor and Director of the Hawaiian Lifestyles Program, has initiated an Associate in Applied Science degree in Hula. Tangarō, *kumu hula* (traditional hula teacher), as noted in 2012 interview with *Hana Hou: The Magazine of Hawaiian Airlines*, reminds his students "Do your hula rituals with mindfulness and you enter into communion with your ancestors".[30] Liza Simon, Tangarō's interviewer, further notes "And he clearly doesn't mean only Hawaiian ancestors; students here today represent numerous ethnicities as well as ages and professions".[31] The indigenization of the university that Tangarō teaches and practices is intended to make this place of higher education on Hawai'i Island inviting, receptive, and responsive to people of indigenous as well as non-indigenous descent. This approach has been implemented in the University of Hawai'i Hilo's revised 2009 Strategic Plan to indigenize the university through its programs, curriculum, faculty initiatives, and contributions to the local community. One practical articulation of this recognition of indigeneity at the university is the Uluākea Faculty Cohort, led by Tangarō. In Uluākea, each participant is encouraged to see her/himself as indigenous regardless of ethnic background. For Tangarō, we are all indigenous, insofar as we all have ancestors and places from whence we came and originated from.

---

[29]Meyer, Manulani Aluli. 2004. *Ho'oulu Our Time of Becoming: Hawaiian Epistemology and Early Writings*. Honolulu: 'Ai Pōhaku Press (Native Books), 4.

[30]Simon, Liza. 2012. Hula U. *Hana Hou: The Magazine of Hawaiian Airlines* 15(5).

[31]Ibidem.

According to Douzinas, “the task of legal iconology is to explain how power and normative systems frame what and how we see, to develop a critique of regimes of visuality that will complement the critique of ideology”.[32] If we then look beyond the image on the coins, we can see an ideology of nationalist identity that is legally responsive to the construction of cultural texts as illustrations of a proscribed American identity. Here, the relationship between design and image are linked in such a way as to promote a particular legal aesthetic of cultural normativity. In her study of the legal aesthetics of copyright, Hilde Hein examines the relationship between “law and art [as] vehicles of and contributory to cultural values”.[33] The art on coins is the legal aesthetic of cultural value and American identity. Art is significant on coins as the designs depicted are intentionally and politically chosen to represent a singular national identity. But is it singular? Is it instead pluralist through its linguistic and cultural variety? Similarly, in her article examining accent-based discrimination, Mari J. Matsuda urges us to revisit the ideals of a just society that include a “legal response to a recurring societal conflict over accents” and “asks that law work against subordination and not for it, so that we can walk the streets of our cities freely, without feeling the hate our separations now generate”.[34] With this in mind, the presence of indigenous languages and territorial-based cultural practices is a must for our pluralist vision of the United States to fully include everyone under its umbrella. It is in our public interest to visually establish who we are on the faces of American currency. Community can only benefit from an overt presence that views territory-based linguistic and cultural imagery as culturally sensitive rather than exploitative and/or harmful. Through indigeneity, the “aesthetic, moral, and other interpretive codes that are necessary for communication between cultures in a multi-cultural system”[35] become accessible and celebrated. The process of Americanization is itself indigenized through its numismatic character of a pluralist national identity. The indigeneity of these quarters stands to remind America of what America is all about—inclusion. Through the subtle, yet powerful presence of language and place on these numismatic reminders of cultural identity, nationhood, and public memory, exclusive definitions of a narrowed view of American-ness are defeated through the designs of inclusion.

[32]Douzinas, Costas. 2011. A legal phenomenology of images. In *Law and Art: Justice, Ethics, and Aesthetics*, ed. Oren Ben-Dor, 254. New York: Routledge.

[33]Hein, Hilde. 1997. Legal practice and aesthetic theory: The case of copyright. In *States, Citizens and Questions of Significance*, eds. John Brigham and Roberta Kevelson. New York: Peter Lang.

[34]Matsuda, 1991, 1406.

[35]Maccanell, Dean and Juliet Flower Maccannell. 1982. *The Time of the Sign: A Semiotic Interpretation of Modern Culture*. Bloomington: University of Indiana Press, 70.

9.7 Concluding Remarks

Althusser notes that "ideology has a material existence"[36] and through the quarter, we can see the material manifestation of what it means to be American. We are also reminded of Goodrich's insight into the legal subjectivity of visual texts insofar as "a reading of the legal text which ignores the power of its imagery or the aesthetic of its reception is a reading which is in many senses beside the point in that it ignores precisely that dimension of the test and its effect".[37] Because quarters are so ordinary, they are constantly in the public gaze. Therefore, the social crafting of national identity on the faces of such coins is the construction of meaning according to the particularized presentation of images representing the public interest. In this way, the public's interest is constructed through the design of numismatic imagery out of nostalgic concern for the innocent, if not culturally pleasing reminders of who we are and through romanticized hindsight, where we came from. The quarter is then a built form of public architecture as coins are crafted in ways that reflect as well as constitutively shape the public interest. As Kim Dovey notes, "The public interest does not exist pre-formed but is constructed in the design process".[38] Peter Goodrich echoes this sentiment as perpetuated by the legal framework insofar as "the legal emblem is most simply the legitimate image of law as a mixed knowledge and practice".[39] Lastly, Neil Feigenson speaks of "naïve realism" in terms of the surface impression of the visual image and "visual common sense" that often disregards careful consideration pertaining to the construction of an image.[40] Feigenson cautions against ignoring the "framing" of the image as well as "the prior knowledge and expectations that viewers themselves bring to the viewing" as well as the "overconfidence" and resulting bias of thinking that we know fully what we see and why we see it.[41] Such concern is the foundation for this paper's numismatic examination that frames culture as legal iconography of public memory and national identity. Nostalgic jurisprudence is therefore the notion that through semiotic imagery, a particular picture of identity is sculpted as legal landscape intentional in its communication of meaning through visual cues and absence of others.

The spatial imaginary of the quarter appears as a tangible, portable, and easily recognized material form. As a neologic representation of power, the quarter

---

[36]Althusser, Louis. 1999. Ideology and ideological state apparatuses (Notes towards an investigation). In *Visual Culture: The Reader*, eds. Jessica Evans and Stuart Hall, 318. London: Sage.

[37]Goodrich, Peter. 1992. Specula laws: Image, aesthetic and common law. In *Law and Aesthetics*, ed. Roberta Kevelson, 207. New York: Peter Lang.

[38]Dovey, 1999, 193.

[39]Goodrich, Peter. 1992. Devising law: On the philosophy of legal emblems. In *Law, Culture and Visual Studies*, eds. Anne Wagner and Richard K. Sherwin, 13. New York: Springer.

[40]Feigenson, Neal. 2014. Visual Common Sense. In *Law, Culture and Visual Studies*, eds. Anne Wagner and Richard K. Sherwin, 105–124. New York: Springer.

[41]Feigenson, 2014. 104, 114.

signifies a particular notion of belonging imagined through depictions of the present and omissions of the past. In this way, the space of expression on quarters represents a type of nomospheric technique that manifests a national image of identity that intentionally depicts certain actions, people, and environments while simultaneously forgetting others in a project of constructed identity.[42] As illustrated by the U.S. Mint, the constructed identity of these quarters tethers public memory to legal emblems. As legal emblems, coins are tokens of law that can be picked up, lost, or even, as mentioned earlier, thrown in the fountain for good luck. In this way, the coin serves as a mirror[43] for normative and positivist approaches to an Americanized thinking, living, and remembering. This mirror contributes to Sherwin's work on visual jurisprudence, which reminds us "law lives differently in a visual expressive system than is one exclusively made up of words".[44] Following from Sherwin's insight, the quarter is a site of visual jurisprudence as these two public law coin programs have numismatic craftings that appear and jurisprudentially influence constructions of identity, memory, and cultural value through carefully defined legal imagery.

So, how do quarters constitute us? What do the images on quarters tell us about the relationship between law and culture? How do the legal aesthetics of the quarter coin inform a jurisprudential inquiry into how law works in the everyday? Easily trivialized, the quarter is a coin of cultural medium and national identity and public memory. The quarter is a durable and numismatically legitimized emblem of a ubiquitous democratic iconography of a colonial past and continuing post-colonial presence. The quarter visually communicates the relentlessly figurative nature of legal meaning amidst the jurisprudential backdrop of individualized, local mythology in a self-sustained national identity. Through the two public laws described in this paper, legal images carved onto the medium of the coin celebrate, yet regulate creativity, indigeneity, and public memory. Through the innocuity of images portrayed on coins and the notion that law necessarily has a public character,[45] law acts as a filter in political discourse, constitutive engagements, and socio-legal normative frameworks that sculpt who we are as Americans and seek to engender the implications of Americanization for the wide variety of people and places under such labeling.

---

[42]Delaney, David. 2010. *The Spatial, the Legal and the Pragmatics of World-Making: Nomospheric Investigations*. New York: Routledge.

[43]Dokoupilova, Despina. 2013. Creating Legal Subjectivity through Language and the Uses of the Legal Emblem: Children of Law and the Parenthood of the State. *International Journal for the Semiotics of Law* 26(2): 315–339.

[44]Sherwin, Richard K. 2011. *Visualizing Law in the Age of the Digital Baroque: Arabesques and Entanglements*. New York: Routledge, 18.

[45]Walker, Neil. 2012. On the Necessarily Public Character of Law. In *The Public in Law: Representations of the Political in Legal Discourse*. Editors: Claudio Michelon, Gregor Clunie, Christopher McCorkindale, and Haris Psarras. Burlington: Ashgate, 9.

References

Althusser, Louis. 1999. Ideology and ideological state apparatuses (Notes towards an investigation). In *Visual Culture: The Reader*, ed. Jessica Evans, and Stuart Hall. London: Sage.

Benavides, Vanegas, and Farid Samir. 2014. Film and the reconstruction of memory. In *Law, Culture and Visual Studies*, ed. Anne Wagner, and Richard K. Sherwin, 993–1010. New York: Springer.

Benjamin, Walter. 1999. The work of art in the age of mechanical reproduction. In *Visual Culture: The Reader*, eds. Jessica Evans, and Stuart Hall, 78. London: Sage.

Brigham, John. 2009. *Material Law: A Jurisprudence of What's Real*. Philadelphia: Temple University Press.

Consolidated Appropriations Act 2008, Division D, Section 622, [H.R. 2764]

Cramer, Renee Ann. 2005. *Cash, Color, and Colonialism*. Norman: University of Oklahoma Press.

Delaney, David. 2010. *The Spatial, the Legal and the Pragmatics of World-Making: Nomospheric Investigations*. New York: Routledge.

Dokoupilova, Despina. 2013. Creating legal subjectivity through language and the uses of the legal emblem: Children of law and the parenthood of the state. *International Journal for the Semiotics of Law* 26 (2): 315–339.

Douzinas, Costas. 2011. A legal phenomenology of images. In *Law and Art: Justice, Ethics, and Aesthetics*, ed. Oren Ben-Dor, 254. New York: Routledge.

Dovey, Kim. 1999. *Framing Places: Mediating Power in Built Form*. New York: Routledge.

Feigenson, Neal. 2014. Visual common sense. In *Law, Culture and Visual Studies*, ed. Anne Wagner, and Richard K. Sherwin, 105–124. New York: Springer.

Ford, Richard T. 2001. Law's territory (a history of jurisdiction). In *Legal Geographies Reader: Law, Power, and Space*, eds. Nicholas Blomley, David Delaney, and Richard T. Ford, 200–217. Malden, MA: Blackwell.

Goodrich, Peter. 1992. Specula laws: Image, aesthetic and common law. In *Law and Aesthetics*, ed. Roberta Kevelson. New York: Peter Lang

Hein, Hilde. 1997. Legal practice and aesthetic theory: the case of copyright. In *States, Citizens and Questions of Significance*, ed. John Brigham, and Roberta Kevelson. New York: Peter Lang.

Heritier, Paolo. 2014. Law and image: Towards a theory of nomograms. In *Law, Culture and Visual Studies*, eds. Anne Wagner, and Richard K. Sherwin, 25. New York: Springer.

Jappy, Tony. 2013. *Introduction to Peircean Visual Semiotics*. New York: Bloomsbury.

Kevelson, Roberta. 1992. Semiotics and the art of 'discovery' in law. In *Law and Aesthetics*, ed. Roberta Kevelson, 245–279. New York: Peter Lang.

Maccanell, Dean, and Juliet Flower Maccannell. 1982. *The Time of the Sign: A Semiotic Interpretation of Modern Culture*. Bloomington: University of Indiana Press.

Mamdani, Mahmood. 2015. Settler colonialism: then and now. *Critical Inquiry* 41 (3): 596–614.

Marusek, Sarah. 2015. The crafting of law and the coining of culture: legal semiotic of the American quarter. In *Law, Culture and the Humanities*.

Matsuda, Mari J. 1991. Voices of America: accent, antidiscrimination law, and a jurisprudence for the last reconstruction. *Yale Law Journal* 100 (5): 1329–1407.

Meyer, Manulani Aluli. 2004. *Ho'oulu Our Time of Becoming: Hawaiian Epistemology and Early Writings*. Honolulu: 'Ai Pōhaku Press (Native Books)

Page, Max. 2005. Memory field. *Architecture* 94 (6): 37–45.

Petroski, Karen. 2014. Visual legal commentary. In *Law, Culture and Visual Studies*, ed. Anne Wagner, and Richard K. Sherwin, 672–696. New York: Springer.

Richland, Justin B. 2007. Pragmatic paradoxes and ironies of indigeneity at the 'edge' of Hopi sovereignty. *American Ethnologist* 34 (3): 540–557.

Roland, Barthes. 1999. Rhetoric of the image. In *Visual Culture: The Reader*, eds. Jessica Evans, and Stuart Hall, 37. London: Sage.

Seuffert, Nan. 2006. *Jurisprudence of National Identity*. Aldershot: Ashgate.
Sherwin, Richard K. 2011. *Visualizing Law in the Age of the Digital Baroque: Arabesques and Entanglements*. New York: Routledge.
Simon, Liza. 2012. Hula U. *Hana Hou: The Magazine of Hawaiian Airlines* 15(5).
Spiro, Peter J. 2008. *Beyond Citizenship: American Identity After Globalization*. New York: Oxford University Press.
United States Mint 50 State Quarters Report 1999–2008: *10 Years of Honoring Our Nation's History and Heritage*, 14. http://www.usmint.gove/downloads/min_programs/50sqreport.pdf. Accessed 26 Nov 2013
Wagner, Anne, and Malik Bozzo-Rey. 2014. French commemorative postage stamps as a means of legal culture and memory. In *Law, Culture and Visual Studies*, ed. Anne Wagner, and Richard K. Sherwin, 307–328. New York: Springer.
Wagner, Anne. 2010. French urban space management: a visual semiotic approach behind power and control. *International Journal for the Semiotics of Law* 24 (2): 227–241.
Walker, Neil. 2012. On the necessarily public character of law. In *The Public in Law: Representations of the Political in Legal Discourse*, eds. Claudio Michelon, Gregor Clunie, Christopher McCorkindale, and Haris Psarras. Burlington: Ashgate.
Weiner, Mark S. 2006. *Americans Without Law: The Racial Boundaries of Citizenship*. New York: New York University Press.
Yanow, Dvora. 2006. How built spaces mean: a semiotics of space. In *Interpretation and Method: Empirical Research Methods and the Interpretive*, ed. Dvora Yanow, and Peregrine Schwartz-Shea, 349–366. Turn, Armonk, NY: M.E. Sharpe.

Sarah Marusek Ph.D. (University of Massachusetts Amherst 2008), is an Associate Professor of Public Law in the Department of Political Science at the University of Hawai'i at Hilo. Her research interests focus on sites of constitutive law, legal geography, and legal semiotics that engage legal pluralist frameworks of everyday jurisprudence. She teaches courses in U.S. Constitutional law, legal studies, and legal geography.

Chapter 10
Internormative Gastronomies: Law, Nation and Identity

Richard Mohr and Nadirsyah Hosen

For Roderick Macdonald,
who opened so many doors for us in understanding
legal pluralism and internormativity,
in memoriam.

Abstract Norms applying to food interact with conceptions of nationhood, identity and law. This occurs through gastronomies and ethico-religious standards, recognition and conviviality, and the voice of communities in the sourcing and labelling of their food. Law, nation and identity intersect in the notion of citizenship. The chapter moves from the tight relationships by which persons are constrained within overdetermined categories of state law and national citizenship, to explore the possibilities unleashed by a loosening of the bonds between law, nation and identity. Sections deal in turn with each of these "loosenings", as we prize apart the knots that bind (i) identity and nation, (ii) nation and law, and (iii) law and identity, each in relation to the cultural and legal context of food. With these loosenings, the unified jurisdiction of the nation-state gives way to plural and informal law; a single national identity expands into multiple ethical and ethnic associations; identity is no longer determined by state-centred legal interpellation but allows persons to "inhabit" a range of norms. By expanding the scope for participation and interaction in each of these areas, citizenship finds new networks for expansion, enrichment and reflexivity. The full spectrum of social justice can only be addressed by regimes and networks that ensure fair and adequate distribution of food, that respect the cultural demands as well as the biological needs of communities, and that ensure participation, through choices informed by personally relevant criteria and social and political structures.

R. Mohr (✉)
Social Research Policy & Planning, Sydney, NSW, Australia
e-mail: rmohr@srpp.com.au

N. Hosen
Faculty of Law, Monash University, Clayton, VIC, Australia
e-mail: nadirsyah.hosen@monash.edu

S. Huygebaert et al. (eds.), *Sensing the Nation's Law*, Studies in the History of Law and Justice 13, https://doi.org/10.1007/978-3-319-75497-0_10

10.1 Food and the Polity: Law, Nation and Identity

> "Au lieu de demander comment le droit voit ses sujets, il faut plutôt demander comment les sujets voient le droit".[1] (Instead of asking how law sees its subjects, we need to ask rather, how the subjects see law.)
>
> Rod Macdonald, 1996

Questions of law, identity and nation operate at a high level of abstraction. They are often bound up with the origin myths of a people, as well as an ideological array that legitimizes state law, and justifies obedience to it. To study these questions in any detail requires a descent from those heights to matters that can be observed, or sensed in other ways. We need a subject that we can sink our teeth into. Food, its preparation and regulation, offers a rich field in which to explore these issues. As well as being highly symbolic, of identity and associations, food is also the key link between our bio-social selves and our material environment. It is marked and regulated by numerous criteria derived from ethics, health, culture and religion.

While the term has a broader meaning today, "*gastronomie*" was coined in late eighteenth century France to indicate the *nomos* of eating: the law or codes by which one should eat.[2] The original meaning is still apt, since food continues to be regulated by numerous formal and informal laws, relating to health and purity as well as taste and culture. Gastronomy allows for expression of beliefs, from the spiritual to the corporeal, and operates as a marker of identity. In this chapter we explore the interaction of norms applying to food in relation to the concepts of nations, identity and law, which intersect in the notion of citizenship. We begin by outlining the field of inquiry, and clarifying our concepts and their interactions, before stating the specific terms of this investigation.

- Nations can be understood as an ethnic, linguistic or cultural category, either underlying or cutting across states. The nineteenth century European ideal, influenced by romanticism, historicism and various struggles for self-determination, promoted the nation, as a people or *Volk*, as the natural basis of the state.
- Identity may be based on a range of characteristics, including culture, language, gender, religion, race, ethical or other associations by which we are, or prefer to be recognised, and recognise ourselves.

---

[1]Macdonald, Roderick A. 1996 Les Vieilles Gardes. Hypothèses sur l'emergence des normes, l'internormativité et le désordre à travers une typologie des institutions normatives. In *Le droit soluble. Contributions québécoises à l'étude de l'internormativité*, ed. Jean-Guy Belley. Paris: Librairie générale de droit et de jurisprudence, 152.

[2]Onfray, Michel. 1995. *La raison gourmande*. Paris: Éditions Grasset & Fasquelle, 52ff.

- Law can be associated with a state jurisdiction, but it also grows out of other social milieux or "loci of normative human interaction".[3] The approach taken here is a pluralist one, which sees law as a matrix of intersecting norms: hence, it is internormative.

Now the simplified version of the links between these three concepts is seen in identification with a nation-state, which is itself the source of an exclusive legal regime, or jurisdiction. This is the assumption on which much jurisprudence is based. Individuals owe allegiance to a nation-state, which has a monopoly on violence (regulated by law) within a territory. That relationship of persons to the state is defined as citizenship, which lies at the centre of the relations between law, nation and identity. Regarded by the republican tradition as a status, by reason of inheritance or place (blood or soil, discussed further in the following section), the liberal model conceived citizenship as a contract.[4] The parties to this contract are the state and the individual, and the bond is the law, which is itself based in the nation-state.

Citizenship can be liberated from these overdetermined bonds, both as an empirical fact and as an ethical project. From a single dimension of (static) status or (binding) contract, citizenship can move towards an interactive ideal, by which citizens are enabled to determine both the meaning and the content of that relationship. This "reflexive citizenship" can be developed out of Fraser's theory of justice.[5] In her view, justice has three dimensions: distribution, recognition and representation, which mirror the economic, cultural and political spheres of society respectively.[6]

The significance of each of these dimensions of justice can be clarified in relation to food. Distributive justice requires fair apportionment of resources. The most basic of these are food and shelter, so that fair distribution requires all to receive adequate and equitable nutrition. This demand is well known as the foundation of basic egalitarian economic principles. The second dimension of justice requires that each person is recognised for who they are, both in an individual and a social context. Therefore recognition, by which we mutually regard each other with love, rights or esteem,[7] underlies the conception of identity, not as a marker of difference, but as a way of being in, and being connected to the world. From sharing food as a means of conviviality and connection, to respecting each other's food needs and

---

[3]Macdonald, Roderick A. 1998. Metaphors of Multiplicity: Civil Society, Regimes and Legal Pluralism. *Arizona Journal of International and Comparative Law* 15: 69.

[4]Maine, Henry. 1917. *Ancient Law*. London: J. M. Dent, 100; Feldman, Leonard. 2008. Status Injustice: The role of the state. In *Adding Insult to Injury: Nancy Fraser Debates her Critics*, ed. Kevin Olson, 225–227. London: Verso.

[5]Olson, Kevin. 2008. Participatory Parity and Democratic Justice. In *Adding Insult to Injury: Nancy Fraser Debates her Critics*, ed. Kevin Olson, 266. London: Verso.

[6]Fraser, Nancy. 2008. Reframing Justice in a Globalizing World. In *Adding Insult to Injury: Nancy Fraser Debates her Critics*, ed. Kevin Olson, 277–278. London: Verso.

[7]Honneth, Axel. 1995. *The Struggle for Recognition: The Moral Grammar of Social Conflicts*. Cambridge: Polity Press, 129.

choices, we practice recognition in each culinary encounter. Rawls proposes that our first encounter with injustice ("that's not fair!") is the source of all justice. Here we suggest that the first encounter with misrecognition ("but you *know* I don't eat *that*!") could begin to build respect, by opening the terms of our recognition to negotiation. Many are familiar with the betrayal of hospitality involved in serving our guests something (to them) inedible: meat to vegetarians, gluten to coeliacs, pork to observant Jews or Muslims. This is particularly so if we *should have known*, or have *recognised* that their medical condition, ethical or religious stance prohibited their eating it.

The third dimension of justice, representation, includes all aspects of "having a voice", including participation in public deliberation, particularly in those areas of life that involve the interests or concerns of one's own group. As has already been noted, participatory parity, that all should have an equal voice, is a particularly important component of justice. No society is just unless all, including the marginal and the weak, are involved in the polity. In addition to the expectations, developed above, that all should have their economic, cultural and ethical needs met in regard to the availability and distribution of food, the political dimension requires having a say in how one's food is sourced and identified. The norms relating to food must be relevant to all citizens, and to this end, the processes by which they are developed must be transparent and open to the participation of all.

Some questions of distribution, recognition and representation in food availability and choice have been explored in our earlier work on cultural dimensions of hospitality and conviviality, and on the scientific, ethical and religious foundations of struggles over standards, certification and labelling of food.[8] The empirical foundation of this work draws on those studies of the cultural and normative signifiers of various food outlets on a multicultural main street in an inner neighbourhood of Sydney. In the present chapter we reflect on the results of that work at a higher level of generality, in order to explore new connections between law, nation and identity, that may be compatible with enhanced levels of justice in all its dimensions, and with a pluralist conception of law, including the nomos of food and eating: an internormative gastronomy.

An enriched citizenship deepens the level of participation by all. We have indicated in general terms how decisions about the distribution, consumption and regulation of food relate to the key dimensions of a just citizenship. The choice of food as a field of study allows insights into those decisions which span from the material to the symbolic, and from the personal to the political. In each of the following sections a case study of food—our choices and ingestion of it—contributes to this inquiry into the relationships between law, nation and identity. Food

[8]This paper is the third arising from a study of 117 food outlets on Marrickville Road in Sydney. Readers may refer to the earlier papers for methodological and demographic information on the study and the area involved. Mohr, Richard and Nadirsyah Hosen. 2013. Crossing Over: Hosts, guests and tastes on a Sydney street, *Law Text Culture* 17: 100–128. Mohr, Richard. 2013. Rethinking the Secular: Religion, ethics and science in food regulation. In *Working papers of the Centre for International Governance and Justice*. March: 1–15. Canberra: RegNet, ANU.

is just as physical, and yet just as cultural; just as biological, and yet just as social, as the law and our bodies themselves. We cannot understand the law and its impact unless we consider the physical manifestations and constraints it brings with it. This is why law's violence is such a fundamental issue for social and cultural studies of law. Yet law acts, above all, through ideas, representations and beliefs: the "soft law" of the word is far more pervasive than the "hard law" of the baton and the bailiff, the handcuffs and the perimeter fence.

The plan of this work is to move from the tight relationships by which persons are constrained within overdetermined categories of state law and national citizenship, to explore the possibilities unleashed by a loosening of the bonds between law, nation and identity. In the following sections of this paper, we deal with each of these "loosenings" in turn, as we prize apart the knots that bind identity and nation, nation and law, law and identity. With these loosenings, the unified jurisdiction of the nation-state gives way to plural and informal law; a single national identity expands into multiple ethical and ethnic associations; identity is no longer determined by state-centred legal interpellation constitutive of the person but, as we shall see, allows persons to "inhabit" a range of norms. By expanding the scope for participation and interaction in each of these areas, citizenship finds new networks for expansion, enrichment and reflexivity.

10.2 Loosening I: Identity and Nation

> Today we recognize that people use identities not just to isolate themselves from others, but also to claim relationships. [...] To be a vegetarian, a vegan or a tea-totaller is to claim a particular space more important for many than gender [...].[9]
>
> Rod Macdonald, 2009

The idea of the nation arose in conjunction with ideas of ethnic identity. Classical citizenship was based on *ius sanguinis,* which defined status in terms of one's heritage, and *ius soli,* which referred to one's place of residence.[10] Yet it was only with the rise of the nation-state that the notion of ethnic identity, encompassing a range of cultural, racial and above all linguistic markers, came to be seen as the very foundation of citizenship. This celebration of ethnicity and its natural relationship to nation (which had already become tied to the idea of the state) was associated with the rise of historicism and romanticism.[11] Some two hundred years

[9]Macdonald, Roderick A. 2009. Human Rights and Identity – Human Identities and Rights, *Canadian Issues.* Spring, 63.

[10]Agamben, Giorgio. 1998. *Homo Sacer: Sovereign Power and Bare Life.* Trans. Daniel Heller-Roazen. Stanford: Stanford University Press, 129.

[11]Barnard, F. M. 2003. *Herder on Nationality, Humanity and History.* Montréal: McGill-Queen's University Press, 14; Macdonald, 1998, 74–5.

later, in the multiethnic nations of Canada and Australia, there were simultaneous calls for citizenship itself to be recast as a "multicultural" phenomenon.[12] This has two consequences. First, cultural diversity could coexist with national and legal unity. Second, as the nation is no longer based in ethnicity, now other elements of social life and association could attain primacy as elements of the ethical bond within and between communities. Each of these consequences has resonated in food politics and legal regulation of food: the cultural diversity of the polis can be contested gastronomically; and the legal regime can be expanded to encompass *ethos* as well as *ethnos*, as food choices are made on the basis of a variety of ethical as well as cultural considerations. Here we turn to contests between xenophobic and cosmopolitan approaches to food, before considering the plurality of the ethical and regulatory landscape, as applied to food, in the next section.

Naturally, neither of these developments has proceeded smoothly, nor have they been uniform across nations. Those European and Asian nations traditionally based on the *ethnos*, with one to two hundred years of language and educational policy to cement the place of the dominant, unified ethnicity, have been slower to adopt such policies than postcolonial nations. Even in Canada and Australia policy development ran ahead of social practice, and remains contested. Multiculturalism gains gastronomic expression in the diversity of cuisines available in an Australian or North American city. Culinary diversity is also found in the metropoles of the old empires, where options reflect the former colonies: North African and South East Asian in Paris; Indian, Pakistani and Cantonese in London. Here we draw on findings from Australian research, while noting the political and intellectual parallels with Canada, in particular.

In researching the relationship between food, law and culture on a multicultural main street in Sydney, we were struck by two key descriptions of the food: "fusion" and "authentic". After a glance at their use in regard to food, we will consider the broader implications of these words, and their application to identity. "Fusion" suggests that culinary and other cultural traditions blend together into a new identity: a "melting pot" to use the metaphor once applied to US immigration. "Authenticity" refers to some original or genuine state which has been preserved, or perhaps recreated. It also applies to identity, to suggest that the subject is true to some underlying self.

In this and the following sections, we argue that food choices, central to our self-definition and construction of identity, are made within a rich and varied cultural, legal and ethical framework. Mechanisms of informal as well as formal law establish this framework, including forms of ethical, religious and health certification. Drawing on the work of Roderick Macdonald on legal pluralism,[13] and

---

[12]Castles, Stephen. 1995. *Multicultural Citizenship*. Canberra: Parliamentary Research Service; Kymlicka, Will. 1995. *Multicultural Citizenship: A Liberal Theory of Minority Rights*. Oxford: Clarendon Press.

[13]Macdonald, 1996.

Allison Weir on identities and freedom,[14] we argue that identities can be forged in connections with others and through negotiating and inhabiting a variety of norms, and not simply in submission or resistance to existing power structures and monolithic legal regimes. By loosening these bonds between nation, identity and law, we will show how citizenship can rise above the predetermined expectations of formal state law, to encompass a more expansive and inclusive model.

In Australia's experience of mass migration during the twentieth century, the early decades after the second World War saw discrimination on the basis of culinary traditions, such as the common taunting of immigrant children over their school lunch box.[15] Thereafter, culinary diversity quickly gained acceptance as one of the advantages of multiculturalism. This began at street level, with the popularity of Greek, then Chinese, then Italian, then Lebanese (and so on) restaurants, through the twentieth century. Culinary inclusiveness became official in "Harmony Days", established at the beginning of the twenty-first century, celebrating the cultures, and notably the culinary traditions of the various members of school or work communities. From the early exoticism of the "continental" or "Asian" restaurant, through various fashionable cuisines and celebrated "cosmopolitan" practices (e.g. "café culture"), a variety of culinary traditions have been domesticated through the widespread availability of dietary staples from pizza or pasta to ricepaper rolls and stir-fry, in supermarkets, pubs, clubs and home kitchens across the country.

For all the feel-good inclusiveness of food, it is not isolated from the currents of xenophobia and nationalism. These tensions are seen in approaches to dining and in campaigns for inclusive or exclusive gastronomic choices. Literature from France and England, and media reports from Italy,[16] highlight the tensions between adventurous and conservative diners, neophiles and neophobes,[17] reactionaries and progressives.[18] This is less marked in Australian dining preferences, where a taste for a variety of foods is almost mandatory, given the ubiquity of various "ethnic" cuisines in suburban restaurants, sports club's kitchens and, as mentioned above, supermarket shelves. Progressive and cosmopolitan tastes achieve an almost ideological expression in recent Australian postcolonialism, as in this publication from the (progressive) Marrickville Council, referring to colonial cuisine:

---

[14]Weir, Allison. 2013. *Identities and Freedom: Feminist Theory Between Power and Connection*. Oxford: Oxford University Press.

[15]Yasa, Dilvin. 2017. "'Wogdom', sandwiches and sushi: a story of three lunch boxes". SBS 13 February. http://www.sbs.com.au/food/article/2017/02/13/wogdom-sandwiches-and-sushi-story-three-lunch-boxes Accessed 30 March 2017.

[16]http://www.nytimes.com/2009/03/13/world/europe/13lucca.html?_r=0 published 12 March 2009, http://www.corriere.it/english/09_gennaio_27/kebab_lucca_e6c0ee1c-ec86-11dd-be73-00144f02aabc.shtml published 27 January 2009, both accessed 22 June 2015.

[17]Warde, Alan and Lydia Martens. 2000. *Eating Out: Social Differentiation, Consumption and Pleasure*. Port Chester, NY: Cambridge University Press, 147–151.

[18]Onfray, 1995, 64–65.

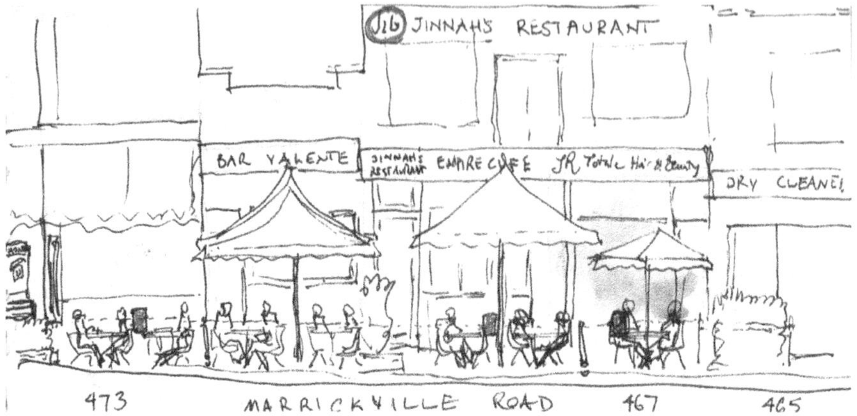

Fig. 10.1 Elevation view of cafés on Marrickville road (pen and ink drawing CC Richard Mohr 2015)

> Despite our climate, most Australians continued to eat a diet that was heavily influenced by British food – and the worst of British food at that. The classic meat and three veg – roasts, potatoes, pumpkin or carrot, and peas – formed the basis of meal after meal, decade after decade after decade.[19]

On this reading, Australia was ripe for decolonisation by the time of its federation in 1901, despite the fact that opposition to Asian immigration was a key motive for casting off British rule. A century later, Marrickville congratulates itself on food as its "most marked characteristic". Residents "can wander from their front door and within a few blocks eat Thai, or Italian, or Greek, or Portuguese, Vietnamese or Brazilian barbecue, Lebanese or Turkish".[20] Food outlets in Marrickville Road, including restaurants, cafes, and fresh food shops (Fig. 10.1), appeal to a wide variety of ethnic groups, social classes and tastes. Our tally found 117 food outlets, of which 62 identified themselves (by signage) with a non Anglo-Australian language or national group, of which there were 17 different cultural identifiers. Ethnicity is one of the key classifiers of food types and preferences. Social class is correlated with preferences for styles of dining, mediated particularly by status or cultural capital, as well as economic standing.[21] Tastes, including taste in food, are moulded by our upbringing and education.

As well as descriptive and ethnic signifiers, several restaurants indicate that their food is "authentic" (e.g. Turkish or Vietnamese), while fewer use the term "fusion".

---

[19]Heath, Elizabeth. 2011. *Eat Streets: A Culinary Adventure through 150 years of Marrickville Council*. Marrickville, NSW: Marrickville Council, 6.

[20]Heath, 2011, 6.

[21]Bourdieu, Pierre. 2010. *Distinction: A Social Critique of the Judgement of Taste*. Trans. Richard Nice. Abingdon, Oxon: Routledge Classics, 173–175; Bennett, Tony, Michael Emmison and John Frow. 1999. *Accounting for Tastes: Australian Everyday Cultures*. Cambridge: Cambridge University Press, 95–96.

The terms "authentic" and "fusion" are used in various social contexts. "Authenticity" is so overused in marketing, particularly in relation to food, that it is in danger of losing all meaning. The Oxford symposium on food and cookery in 2005 saw dozens of papers presented on the theme of "authenticity in the kitchen", with approaches to the topic ranging from the historical to the geographical.[22] Being true to the ingredients was canvassed in both traditional and "molecular" cuisines. Being true to oneself, the individual approach of the chef or family traditions, was another theme, which often cuts across the purity of tradition. Despite these shifting and highly imprecise definitions, authenticity in the sense of personal integrity has a recognisable provenance in philosophy, dating from Socrates' "know thyself",[23] and in literary criticism, in Trilling's influential book on sincerity and authenticity.[24]

"Fusion" is more fashionable than "authenticity". It refers to the blending of various traditions into a new amalgam, so in some ways may be seen as the antithesis of authenticity's pure tradition. In the context of ethnic cuisines, fusion approaches tend to appropriate a variety of cultures to produce something innovative, and perhaps more appropriate or adapted to the new culture of Australia: "il gusto fusion dell'Australia", to quote a 2013 newspaper headline from Italy's *La Repubblica*. In the context of a multicultural community, however, the term has disquieting overtones of the "melting pot" into which all the ethnic groups coming to the United States a century ago were supposed to merge into a new American identity. If authenticity suggests the noble traditions of the old country, fusion hums with the pizzazz of the new: appropriating, assimilating and submerging all other cultural heritages.

How do these two culinary terms map onto identity and personality? "Authenticity" is central to existentialist theories of the self.[25] The modern ideal of authenticity arose with the notion of identity, as a personal way of being. For Taylor, identity "is the background against which our tastes and desires and opinions and aspirations make sense."[26] While the claims to authenticity that light up several ethnic restaurants in Marrickville Road may not be worth the fossil fuels burned in illuminating them, there is a core of meaning relevant to an inquiry into identity.

In our discussions of identity and authenticity, we intend to allow room for personal choice and development. However, we follow Taylor in recognising that identity in the modern world is neither ascribed by authority, nor freely chosen like

---

[22]Hosking, Richard, ed. 2006. *Authenticity in the Kitchen: Proceedings of the Oxford Symposium on Food and Cookery 2005*. Totnes, Devon: Prospect.

[23]Potter, Andrew. 2010. *The Authenticity Hoax: How we get lost finding ourselves*. Melbourne: Scribe.

[24]Taylor, Charles. 1995. *Philosophical Arguments*. Cambridge, MA: Harvard University Press, 227.

[25]Golomb, Jacob. 1995. *In Search of Authenticity: Existentialism from Kierkegaard to Camus*. London: Routledge.

[26]Taylor, 1995. 231.

a buffet dinner. Identity is defined in relation to others and through the various dialogues and codes available to us. If a deterministic Althusserian identity (as discussed below) is in opposition to this ideal, so too is a liberal ideal that allows the unfettered development of personality by an unattached individual. The liberal alternative is characterised by the ideal of negative liberty: each individual is to be free from interference. The result, we suggest, is as vacuous as the image of identity expressed in a beer advertisement that appeared on Marrickville Road during our research, with the message, "Today I'm myself, tomorrow whoever I want."

If identity is to have any content, it is built within a personal narrative of significant others and cultural discourses. Identity is neither an open bar tab, nor a regime imposed by authority. Food choice reflects identity based on cultural, ethical, religious or health criteria. These are intimately bound to self-image and orientation to the world. Food choices tell us who people identify with, their attitudes to care of the self and care for the Other, and their openness to new experiences and other cultures.[27] We discern this as observers, just as the authors of these choices know they are communicating these aspects of their personalities to others.

We have found a broadly inclusive approach, which might be termed "progressive" or "neophile", to gastronomic traditions in urban Marrickville Road, and even in rural and regional Australia. However, frankly xenophobic currents have emerged in Australian food politics since the war on terror and the demonisation of Islam. In 2011, two parliamentary representatives of the ruling Liberal Party warned against allowing halal food to subvert Australian values.[28] Since then there have been concerted campaigns, particularly through social media, against halal food. These have expanded into the mainstream media, and to placing stickers on goods in supermarkets, urging boycotts of manufacturers who display halal certification, including major brands such as Cadburys, Kellogg's and Nestlé.[29] Among the bizarre claims used by such campaigns are suggestions that sales of halal certified produce funds terrorists or that "by having Australians unwittingly eating Halal food we are all one step down the path towards the conversion".[30] In February 2015 more than 20 people in Australia were infected with hepatitis A after eating frozen berries imported from China. Within two weeks of the recall of the products and the extensive media coverage, an email campaign circulated, urging support for a particular Australian manufacturer, on the grounds of health, food security and job

[27]Further to Onfray's (1995) classification of culinary tastes from reactionary to progressive, and Warde and Martens' (2000) "neophobia and neophilia" or conservative and adventurous, discussed above, we have mapped these onto political and social views (Mohr & Hosen, 2013).

[28]Butterly, Nick. 2011. Halal meat converting Aussies: MP, *The West Australian*. 25 November; Lewis, Steve. 2011. Tackle Extreme Islam Before it's too Late, Liberal MPs Warn, *Herald Sun*. 9 February.

[29]Sheehan, Paul. 2013. Halal Easter eggs and cat food: where big money meets religion. *Sydney Morning Herald*. 28 March.

[30]Hansard. Commonwealth of Australia. *Parliamentary Debates*. House of Representatives, 24 November 2011: 13854 (Luke Simpkins MP).

protection. The email closed with the exhortation, in upper case red letters, "Please pass this on to as many people as you can[.] Don't bitch later when all food is halal, imported and expensive [...]."[31]

These campaigns, ranging from the naïve to the manipulative, draw on a suite of concerns, anxieties and political agendas: patriotism, jingoism, fear of pollution, xenophobia. Protecting borders of the nation and the body against foreign elements. Purity demands that the nation and its citizens be protected against surreptitious subversion by unseen forces, from the bacterial to the ideological, in the alarmingly material form of the food we ingest. However, by associating this pollution with Islam, the apparently impersonal rejection of particular foods becomes a means of vilifying and excluding the nation's Muslim citizens and residents. Without expressly requiring Australians to be Christian, un-Muslim, or to hold any other belief or ethnic identification, the very basis of multicultural or inclusive citizenship is undermined for a significant minority.

The simple dichotomy of reactionaries or neophobes, who prefer the food of their home culture, versus progressives or neophiles, who are adventurous and cosmopolitan in their tastes, is too neatly symmetrical to map onto this Australian reality. The dynamics at the level of quotidian food consumption, where a range of exotic foods have been domesticated, plays out in a different register from the shrill xenophobia of the warriors of the right. Yet the paranoia of attempts to exclude and demonise categories of foods (e.g. halal) take advantage of a certain existential anxiety about the purity and compatibility of the material we incorporate. An urge to authenticity—of the self or of the nation—seems to make possible appeals to food security and the gastronomic jingoism that inspires Luke Simpkins to warn, "you cannot purchase the meat for your Aussie barbecue without the influence of this minority religion".[32]

The self-conscious, even manufactured, xenophobia of anti-halal campaigns operate in a more formal register than that of everyday shopping and eating. They infiltrate that quotidian world by placing conspiracy-inspired stickers on goods in supermarkets, and campaigning against halal restaurants through social media.[33] Such campaigns appeal to nationalism by drawing attention to a specific form of food certification. This brings us to the second area of loosening, of knots that tie law to the nation.

---

[31]Personal email correspondence received 28 February 2015.

[32]Hansard, 2011. In a delicious irony of Australian politics, Mr Simpkins lost his parliamentary seat in 2016 to Dr Anne Aly, the first Muslim woman elected to the House of Representatives.

[33]Parkins, B. Restaurant victim of anti-Islamic abuse. *Illawarra Mercury* 13 March 2015. http://www.illawarramercury.com.au/story/2944051/restaurant-victim-of-anti-islamic-abuse/ Accessed 25 April 2015.

10.3 Loosening II: Nation and Law

> Except within the precincts of the legal academy, social diversity and its accompanying multiple loci of normative human interaction are taken as self-evident.[34]
>
> Rod Macdonald, 1998

Food is regulated by numerous formal and informal instruments, from state health requirements to industry and consumer codes and religious certification. The public health measures of the nineteenth century centralised state, which cleaned up cities and regulated the sale of food, assumed that each biological human had similar requirements for safe food. The formal law of the nation-state was the appropriate level of regulation for these universal standards. Law itself took a cultural turn in the late twentieth century, comprehending cultural and racial differences, recognising identity demands, and adapting, in settler societies, to the multicultural realities of the nations of first peoples and diverse immigrants.

In this section we consider the various forms of regulation demanded by consumers and by state, religious and other authorities. The food choices that are available on Marrickville Road, and the norms that govern them, help us to map this diverse regulatory framework. Recognising that law in various guises occupies many diverse niches in the social fabric, we see the guarantees of foods displayed form a network of norms by which consumers can orientate their food choices, according to religious, ethical and health requirements. Consumers choose products labelled "free range" or "fair trade" according to their ethical stance. "Halal" products indicate their appropriateness to Muslim consumers. Various approaches to health include food safety (ensuring food does not cause acute gastro-intestinal illness), nutritional criteria (so the food satisfies our bodily needs without contributing to long-term problems such as heart disease or obesity), or other more personal health concerns such as allergies and fads.

Most of these areas are regulated by voluntary or industry codes (e.g. various certifying authorities for free range or halal products). Suppliers operate in the shadow of the formal law when they limit risk of tort actions with disclaimers about the possible presence of peanuts, or invitations to tell staff of any food allergies. Formal law covers areas of food safety, in the form of regulations imposed or monitored by local or state government: Marrickville Council's Environmental Health Officer or the New South Wales Food Safety Authority. While these authorities can and do prosecute for breach of safety codes, the FSA also uses soft power through a "name and shame" list, published on line and publicised through items in the media.

The common factor in most of these codes is their orientation to advising the consumer, while imposing standards on the food supplier or producer. A wide range of norms is applied to foods, and consumers are guided by those which are the right fit for them. Food choices are made taking into account the norms important to

---

[34]Macdonald, 1998. 69.

particular consumers. These are chosen according to people's priorities for their own health and biological needs, their orientation to the needs of other beings, whether coffee producers or animals, or a spiritual orientation to a world religion. These priorities come to define who we are: our identity is negotiated in the terms of the norms we apply to the food we ingest.

The overlapping regimes regulating food offer a valuable case study in legal pluralism, and its relationship to identity and nation. Just as all citizens belong to the nation, and are bound by its laws, so there is a common denominator, an overarching regime of state law. These codes (in Australia, at Federal and at State level) cover matters of food safety, particularly in relation to infectious diseases and trade practices, including aspects of labelling. They generally operate at a basic level to ensure the people residing and consuming food within a jurisdiction are neither poisoned nor misled.

Even food safety has its own non-state codes, such as the system of Hazard and Critical Control Point (HACCP) quality control and certification. This is a world-wide system for minimising risks from contamination of food, recognised by the World Health Organisation. With its international reach, it offers a means for suppliers and consumers across national borders to understand and have confidence in the chain of food processing and handling. It is also used among domestic suppliers as a form of quality assurance, as seen in Fig. 10.2.

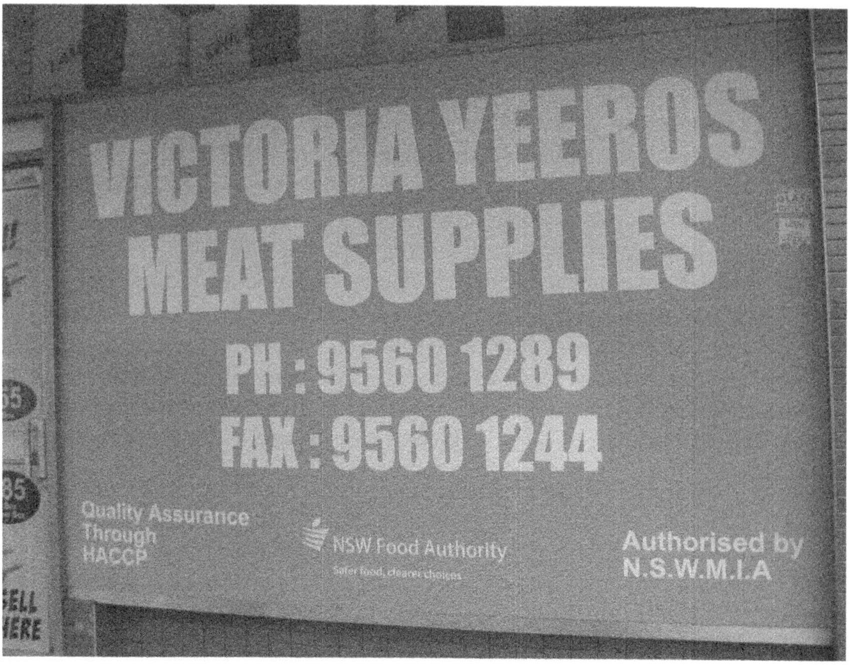

Fig. 10.2 Victoria Yeeros supplies, Victoria road, Marrickville (photograph CC Richard Mohr 2012)

International codes are an important aspect of informal law and legal pluralism. While the informal codes of sub-state communities are widely recognised, they may also be tied in with an international regime. So, for instance, the halal certification by a local Islamic organisation based in an Australian city or state draws on the codes and systems of a world religion for its underlying principles. It must also be recognised within such an international system if it is to have local credibility. Beyond the local level, international trade requires a system of recognition of halal regimes. This intersects with formal state law even in Australia, due to the importance of the international meat trade. The Islamic and governmental organisations are, at the same time, providing some assurance to Australian Muslims that particular certifiers can be trusted to properly impose halal standards. Relationships among different halal certifiers must also be managed at the international level. However, such international halal standards are diverse as they are provided by various halal certifiers. Some of these are officially recognised by the State, as in the case of JAKIM in Malaysia and MUIS in Singapore. There are also non-governmental halal certifiers such as in the case of Indonesia and Australia. This has led to two different international forums: there is a World Halal Council (http://www.worldhalalcouncil.com) and there is also a new forum called World Halal Food Council (http://whfc-halal.com/), and some jockeying for influence among the systems and the *ulama* of different nations.[35] Halal standards assist companies to meet the expectation and requirement of halal certification, particularly for exporting product to other countries. Apart from a religious motive to "standarise" religious requirements, there is also an economic motive driven by a large market. For instance, many Australian halal certifiers tend to follow the Indonesian interpretation of halal requirements due to its big market of 250 million people. The Australian government lists eighteen certifiers on a website administered by the Commonwealth Department of Agriculture, Fisheries and Forestry (DAFF), according to whether they are recognised by particular export markets in Muslim countries.[36]

The links between the codes of a world religion and local communities or various national governments achieve a degree of formality in the case of halal food. Similarly clear and state-recognised standards apply to "organic" or "bio-dynamic" produce. The European Union has guidelines and a logo (a leaf outlined by 12 stars) that must also display "the name or code number of the national certification authority" (e.g. "Agricoltura Italia").[37] Australia follows a similar model in relation to organic produce (for export) as for halal certification:

[35]Hosen, Nadirsyah. 2012. Hilal and Halal: How to Manage Islamic Pluralism in Indonesia? *Asian Journal of Comparative Law*. 7: 1–18.

[36]http://www.daff.gov.au/aqis/export/meat/elmer-3/list-islamic-halal-certification. Accessed 12 February 2013.

[37]http://ec.europa.eu/agriculture/organic/organic-farming/what-is-organic-farming/organic-certification/index_en.htm accessed 22 June 2015.

seven organisations are accredited to provide inspection and certification services.[38] Codes and certification are less formal in the case of other food standards. Vegetarian and vegan labelling is not widely formalised through certifiers, while "free range" standards are notoriously variable and unreliable, certainly in Australia.[39] There is an obvious need for international inspection and recognised standards in the case of "fair trade" claims, where consumers are concerned to protect the interests and well-being of farmers and growers in distant countries. In several of these cases, "fair trade" or "free range" claims may be made by suppliers, retailers or industry bodies (e.g. Starbucks, the Australian Egg Corporation or the dominant Australian supermarkets Coles and Woolworths). The Australian Competition and Consumer Commission (ACCC) took action in the Federal Court of Australia against three poultry suppliers, for misleading and deceptive conduct.[40] The ACCC alleged that phrases such as "free to roam" are misleading and deceptive when chickens "do not, as a practical matter, have substantial space available to roam around freely". The Court found that two of the firms, Baiada and Bartter, and an industry body had made false representations and engaged in misleading and deceptive conduct. However, there is still no formal (national) legal definition of the stocking density at which chickens, eggs or pigs could be claimed to be "free range".

These variously intersecting and independent codes, catering to the demands of a variety of consumers, raise questions of the intersection between decision-making and community membership. There are formal expectations that citizens have a role in national law-making, and procedures exist to ensure their participation. Needless to say, some of these are more successful than others. At the farther end of the spectrum, there are ethical communities of vegans and consumers of animal products who are concerned to protect the welfare of animals. They can make certain demands and assert their market power, but nonetheless they may need formal regimes delivering trustworthy certification. It can be argued that this form of informal law-making can and should be handled within communities. However barriers to widespread acceptance of informal codes are limited by the boundaries and self-definitions of communities, their differing standards and the difficulties of accessing and communicating the necessary expertise, whether ethical, scientific or forensic.

Where the requirements of different communities intersect, or even clash, there exists a difficult area for intercommunal negotiation. Opposition to halal food comes not only from politically motivated xenophobes, but also from animal rights activists. Believing that stunning of animals prior to slaughter is humane, certain organisations and variously motivated campaigns have opposed traditional forms of

---

[38]http://www.dpi.nsw.gov.au/__data/assets/pdf_file/0011/353297/Organic-Standards-and-certification-in-Australia.pdf dated August 2010, accessed 22 June 2015.

[39]Clemons, Rachel. 2012. A Cagey Business. *Choice*, July: 20–22.

[40]Australian Competition and Consumer Commission v Turi Foods Pty Ltd (No 5) [2013] FCA 1109.

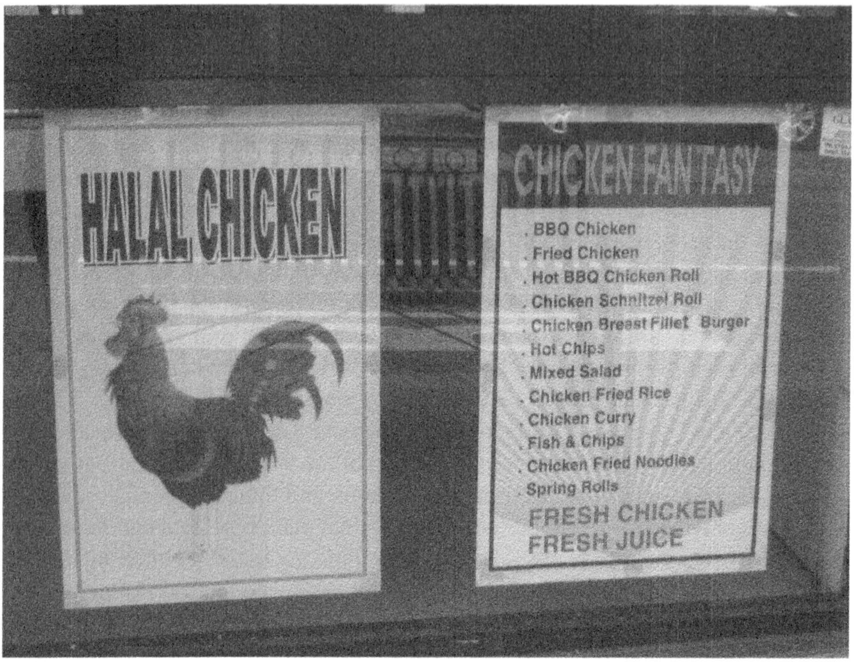

Fig. 10.3 Take away food shop, Marrickville road (photograph CC Richard Mohr 2012)

halal slaughter. Responses to this can be seen coming from both Islamic scholars and particular animal rights activists. Important Islamic *ulama* in both Indonesia (MUI) and Australia (AFIC) accept stunning before slaughter, on both compassionate and religious grounds (modern stunning techniques were not known at the time of the Prophet).[41] Animal rights activists opposing the inhumane export of live animals from Australia have proposed an expanded program of halal slaughter for export of meat from Australia as a means of getting halal products to overseas consumers. It is argued that slaughter under humane and supervised conditions would be preferable to the dangerous overcrowding and uncertain sea journeys involved in the live animal trade.[42] Both these examples, of *ulama* accommodation to contemporary technology, and animal rights organisations accommodating halal requirements, indicate the dynamic nature of informal law, and the potential for its development in practice. This may be particularly flourishing in multicultural societies if diverse ethical communities are able to interact in constructive ways (Fig. 10.3).

[41]Black, Ann, Hossein Esmaeili and Nadirsyah Hosen. 2013. *Modern Perspectives on Islamic Law*. Cheltenham: Edward Elgar, 266–7.

[42]http://animalliberation.org.au/national-rallies-against-live-export/ accessed 16 February 2013.

A legal approach which aims to protect all citizens equally, based on the minimal interference model of negative liberties, may be adequate to the task of protecting the populace from poisoning or deception. However, a richer conception of a polity of diverse citizens can be glimpsed here, in law's wider potential. Where citizens form overlapping and even competing ethical communities, based on religious or cultural orientations and memberships, there is potential for conflict but also for creativity and reconciliation. Informal law, in all its diversity, offers a range of codes and procedures by which communities can orientate themselves and interact with others. Those others may be suppliers or producers of food, formal organisations such as industry or consumer bodies, or parallel ethical communities. This conception of a plural legal nation deepens the notion of multiculturalism, from a simple patchwork of linguistic and cultural communities to encompass the potential of a living, learning and growing body politic.

10.4 Loosening III: Law and Identity

> "Chaque enfant habite un monde qui n'est ni interrompu ni interpellé par les autres."[43]
> (Each child inhabits a world that is neither interrupted nor interpellated by others.)
>
> Rod Macdonald, 1996

Althusser's notion of interpellation defined the law as an organ of state power which constitutes the subject in the name of the law. The primal instance of interpellation is the policeman's shout, "Hey, you there", to which we must respond. Indeed, for Althusser, we *inevitably*, always-already respond to this call: "ideology … transforms the individuals into subjects (it transforms them all)"; when the police hail someone in the street, the right person will turn around ("they hardly ever miss their man").[44] This deterministic structuralism leaves no room for negotiation: the policeman's shout is the legal moment of interpellation that constitutes the subject.

We agree that law has a place in the construction of identity. However, we have two arguments with Althusser. Working from the nature of law and of identity outlined in the previous sections, we reject the reflexive determinacy that sees subjects constructed by a monolithic sovereign law. We have shown that law is diffuse. It is available in a range of forms, moulded to and by differing levels of association, from small enclaves to ethical and cultural communities, and from nations to relations of international trade and world religions. We see identity as an under-determined construct, that may overlap or interact with nationality and other

[43]Macdonald, 1996. 137.

[44]Althusser, Louis. 1994. Ideology and Ideological State Apparatuses (Notes towards an investigation). In *Mapping Ideology*, ed. Slavoj Zizek. 130–31. London: Verso.

forms of belonging. Both law and identity, therefore, are more complex and looser than a determinate bond between the state and the individual.

Foucault, Butler and other subsequent writers have gone beyond Althusser's structural determinism to encompass the possibility of resistance to law or discipline. Foucault has rejected the "mastery or the universality of law", not because law, for him, is plural, but because it is incomplete.[45] It is an almost vestigial remnant of sovereignty in a world ruled by discipline. Neither the law nor the diffuse forms of discipline are determinate in the style of Althusser. The subjects of law, or anyone involved in "power relations can, in their actions, their resistance, their rebellion, escape them, transform them, in a word, cease being submissive".[46] Butler too asserts the possibility of resistance, while concurring with Foucault's image of law as a form of sovereignty. Yet interpellation, the power of naming, persists as an interruption, a challenge and a relation of power.

> It is as if the proper power of the state has been expropriated, delegated to its citizens, and the state then reemerges as a neutral instrument to which we seek recourse to protect us from other citizens, who have become revived emblems of a (lost) sovereign power.[47]

While Butler follows Foucault in looking for law and power outside of the formal and universal word of the sovereign, she maintains the link between power and identity. We may not be defined *by* power, yet we define ourselves *in response to* power. To resist is possible, yet it is still a pushing back, another form of (inter) pellation,[48] exercised against state power: "the very terms of resistance and insurgency are spawned in part by the powers they oppose".[49]

This leads to our second argument against the legal determination of identity through interpellation. Identity is too multifarious, too underdetermined (as already noted) to be constructed from the force of political power, whether that be sovereign and legal or dispersed and disciplinary. Here we challenge the assertion that is it only through relations of power that we construct identities. Identities can be constructed out of a more diverse range of relationships and connections. In response to Althusser's interpellation, and even to Butler's revision that looks beyond the voice of the sovereign power, Weir writes:

> Here again we have lost the possibility of multiple contesting and conflicting relations. For what if the name is called not by a policeman but by a friend or lover? Is the law invoked by the policeman always the source of the name? What if the name was given to us by a parent who loves us, or a community who cares for us?[50]

---

[45]Foucault, Michel. 1991. Governmentality. In *The Foucault Effect: Studies in Governmentality*. eds G. Burchell, C. Gordon and P. Miller, 99. London: Harvester Wheatsheaf.

[46]Foucault, Michel. 2001. *Power*. London: Penguin, 294.

[47]Butler, Judith. 1997. *Excitable Speech: A Politics of the Performative*. New York: Routledge, 82.

[48]Interpellation derives from Latin *interpellere*, to interrupt by speaking, from *pellere*, to push or strike. Morris, William (ed) 1969, *American Heritage Dictionary*. Boston and New York: Houghton Mifflin, 685, 1533.

[49]Butler, 1997. 40.

[50]Weir, 2013. 7.

For Weir, law can contribute to the constitution of an identity of connections. Like Foucault and Butler, she leaves behind universal and sovereign law. However, in place of Foucault's diffuse social power or discipline, she finds an alternative, plural version of law in Mahmood's notion of norms. These surpass fixed and monolithic state law and sovereignty, to furnish a normative plurality that we *inhabit*. Clearly, such a plurality of norms can encompass informal as well as formal law. In constructing an identity in terms of the norms we inhabit, we are in fact negotiating our relationships with the law, understood to encompass a plurality of formal and informal codes. We negotiate the law through our social attachments and relationships.

In concluding this section, we show how our study of food illustrates and elaborates this approach to the relationship between law and identity. We make food choices consistent with the sort of people we imagine ourselves to be, that we aspire to be, or that we have become, through our upbringing and cultural heritage. The food we ingest in infancy nourishes us and creates lasting traces of memory and taste. Only later do we begin to see this food as part of a moral or scientific calculus. With self-consciousness comes the capacity and the need to interrogate our food, to know it, to respond to it in ways beyond the animal urge to satisfy hunger. The tastes we develop in childhood, and throughout our lives, can be justified or questioned, rejected or developed. This discrimination builds on layers of culture, science and ethical deliberation, as well as simple pleasure. In this way, taste encapsulates the passage between knowledge and pleasure: a knowledge that we relish and a pleasure that we understand.[51] In the unconscious development of our tastes in food, we mediate between what we know and what we enjoy. By selecting foods that both delight and that conform to acceptable codes, we match our identity with law. This is not a single law, to which we submit or against which we rebel, the law of a state or exclusive jurisdiction, but a matrix of laws, formal and informal.

Such a matrix of laws provides a scaffolding around which we construct our identity. By matching what we know and believe to what we consume, we are able to bring together our spiritual and physical self: mind and body. Here we arrive at the root form of the word "identity": the consolidation of disparate aspects of self into a whole. Eating alone or in company, with work colleagues or family, taste calls on experience and awareness of various codes, bringing about a reconciliation of being and believing. The norms applicable to food include the formal regulations of health, ethics and religion as well as orientations to culture. We negotiate these norms according to our self-understanding and our associations with others. Those norms derive from various sources outside the self: state, religion or associations of consumers or producers. In this sense they are given and not freely created. Yet due to their diversity they provide a variety of paths that can be negotiated, rather than an interpellation which requires either submission or resistance.

---

[51] Agamben, Giorgio. 2015. *Gusto*. Macerata: Quodlibet, 22.

10.5 Nomos Negotiated

"L'idée du pluralisme évoquée ici est une practique émancipatrice. Le droit vit dans l'âme de tous les membres d'une société."[52] (The idea of pluralism evoked here is an emancipatory practice. The law lives in the soul of all members of a society.)

Rod Macdonald (1996)

To this point we have worked to decouple the deterministic links between identity, law and nation. Decoupling identity from nationality reveals that, even though cultures associated with ethnic or national groups are a significant component of identity, there are other important components. As regards food, we have referred to ethnic cuisines, home cooking and the food of our parents and national heritage as a coherent expression of culture. People orientate themselves to others, and to their cultures, by their attitudes to different cuisines: some pride themselves on their cosmopolitanism, others on their fidelity to a national tradition. Other ways we define ourselves by what we eat include ethical, religious and health concerns.[53] Identity is expressed through a range of associations with the culture of our birth, our links to other cultures, and our attachments to beliefs and like-minded others.

Decoupling law from the nation-state reveals the many layers of legal plurality in relation to food, which may be certified as safe, or ethically or religiously acceptable, by a range of authorities and codes. While some of these are linked to formal state jurisdictions or other institutional entities, others are the preserve of ethical or cultural communities, at smaller or larger scales than nations, from local communities to world-wide movements.

Decoupling identity from state law allows the key concept of citizenship to be reimagined. Loosening the ties that bind citizenship to law, nation and identity, and that bind those social facts to each other, opens up new possibilities. This is not to detract from the rich significance of any of these relationships. Nationality can be a point of social orientation, without being either exclusive or binding. Laws can be enacted and administered at national levels, but also at the levels of both smaller and larger communities. People orientate themselves within this wider landscape of laws according to significant aspects of their identity. In turn, the laws of communities of reference provide a map of associations and principles to guide action.

The liberal image of citizenship as a binding contract, bestowing rights and obligations on individuals, is as inadequate to a participatory ideal as it is to the empirical reality of contemporary societies. Beginning from a fully rounded conception of justice that includes representation and recognition as well as distribution, this study has sought an approach to law and identity that provides room for participation and negotiation. Subjects at the intersection of various normative

[52]Macdonald, 1996. 152.

[53]While health is fundamentally biological and individual, beliefs about health are shared with others and can be included in a conception of a cultural identity.

orders have degrees of choice that are not available if there is a single order, whether that be based on sovereign power, diffused discipline within a unified episteme, or a monolithic juridical order. Within such unified regimes there is, as Butler has it, always the possibility of resistance, not available within Althusser's over-determined schema. Rejecting Althusser's top-down, always-get-their-man approach to the legal constitution of identity, based on monolithic law and structural determinism, we see law as a web of formal and informal norms that people negotiate and inhabit. The two possibilities of pushing against, or being pulled by a unified force allows only a one-dimensional range of options. A pluralist framework opens a vastly increased scope for the orientation of our political identity. Beyond the resistance of a unidirectional force or resistance to it, we can orientate ourselves according to a moral compass of 360°. This compass is calibrated by ethical, spiritual and biological considerations. The material dimension is expressed in food regulation and dietary regimes oriented to health or the environment. Ingesting food has a clear range of physical and biological effects: health and illness, well-being and discomfort, fitness and obesity. The moral and the material overlap in various ontologies of the self. Refusals to eat animals, the fruits of human exploitation, or unsustainable produce are based in a calculus of fairness and purity and a view of our bodies where the ethical is corporeal.

Identities are constructed out of a range of corporeal and cultural elements. Race and gender are well known for the layers of oppression—social, political and personal—that are piled onto dubious distinctions among bodies. They are social categories whose essentialism is founded on the assumed naturalism of the corporeal: sex, skin pigment or facial features. Identities can be negotiated within and among social categories.

Law is one such category. Legal structures frame various definitions of self, including gender, race and nationality. Recognising that these structures are themselves diverse, encompassing informal as well as state law, indicates new pathways for the exploration of identity. Identities are forged from relationships[54] including kinship, love and the ethical, as well as power. Realisation of identity involves recognition of power relations: how we are powerful as well as how we are powerless; our privileges as well as or our abjection; our recognition and our misrecognition. In this we see the beginnings of a reflexive citizenship, negotiated with others, who are both close to us and far away, those whose recognition we share and those whose misrecognition we strive to overcome: the powerless, those less privileged than we are. This realisation is achieved by expanding social circles, reference groups and cultural repertoire.

The various ethnic and ethical relationships that we noted in multicultural Marrickville are a microcosm of a world of mobile populations, ethical contests and widespread communications. Globally, dual citizenship, statelessness and multicultural citizenship are all challenges to the nation-law-identity nexus that we have been unravelling. Locally, we have seen the everyday negotiations involved in

[54]Weir, 2013. 52–3.

selecting and consuming food by reference to cultural or ethnic, ethical, scientific and religious criteria. Rights and binding contracts gain little purchase in explaining this milieu. Tastes extend across flexible ethnic categories, while accommodation and mutual recognition are observed in cases as diverse as the convergence of animal rights and Islamic interests, or the voracious cosmopolitanism of food choices.

Just as tastes can open to other cultures and peoples, norms can promote these levels of interaction, as well as providing guidelines for ethical choices. This network of interlocking codes, both formal and informal, mediates identity through an internormative gastronomy. This is not the anarchy of "gastro-anomie", where the "eating-individuals are abandoned on their own" ("*l'individu-mangeur se trouve livré à lui-même*").[55] Instead it is a framework of interlocking norms, based on the formality of local and state government regulation of planning and food safety. Citizens, producers, restaurateurs and shopkeepers have accommodated within this framework a range of industry, religious and informal codes. This diversity of norms allows consumers to match ethical, spiritual and health requirements with production standards and ingredients.

In conclusion, this framework of internormative gastronomy can be mapped onto Fraser's three dimensions of social justice. The materiality of food as a human need represents distributive justice in areas such as fair access to nutrition and food security. The dimension of recognition requires that the food choices of different cultures and ethical groups should also be respected. This is possible in passive terms, by allowing a range of options and codes to coexist in a multicultural and multi-ethical world. It is expressed positively by the mingling of different groups over food, in convivial and commercial settings: sharing food on "Harmony Days" and in restaurants and shops of various ethnic and ethical persuasions. The dimension of representation suggests, further, that people and groups should have a voice in the standards and codes that apply to the food available to them. Empowerment of consumers is one aspect of this, so that people can be properly informed of their food's nutritional, ethical or spiritual qualities (depending on their own beliefs and relationships). To again shift from a passive or negative mode to an active one, various associations among people can promote institutional responses to food requirements, such as organic food cooperatives or religious organisations which certify food according to mutually accepted standards. Taken together, the full spectrum of social justice can only be covered in regimes and networks that ensure fair and adequate distribution of food, that respect the cultural demands as well as the biological needs of communities, and that ensure participation, through choices informed by personally relevant criteria and social and political structures.

[55]Fischler, Claude. 1979. Gastro-nomie et gastro-anomie: Sagesse du corps et crise bioculturelle de l'alimentation moderne, *Communications* 31: 206.

References

Agamben, Giorgio. 1998. *Homo Sacer: Sovereign Power and Bare Life*, trans. D. Heller-Roazen. Stanford: Stanford University Press

Agamben, Giorgio. 2015. *Gusto*. Macerata: Quodlibet.

Althusser, Louis. 1994. Ideology and ideological state apparatuses (notes towards an investigation). In *Mapping Ideology*, ed. Slavoj Zizek. London: Verso.

Australian Competition and Consumer Commission v Turi Foods Pty Ltd (No 5) [2013] FCA 1109.

Barnard, F.M. 2003. *Herder on Nationality, Humanity and History*. Montréal: McGill-Queen's University Press. 14; Macdonald, 1998.

Bennett, Tony, Michael Emmison, and John Frow. 1999. *Accounting for Tastes: Australian Everyday Cultures*. Cambridge: Cambridge University Press.

Black, Ann, Hossein Esmaeili, and Nadirsyah Hosen. 2013. *Modern Perspectives on Islamic Law*. Cheltenham: Edward Elgar.

Bourdieu, Pierre. 2010. *Distinction: A Social Critique of the Judgement of Taste*, trans. R. Nice. Abingdon, Oxon: Routledge Classics.

Butler, Judith. 1997. *Excitable Speech: A Politics of the Performative*. New York: Routledge.

Butterly, Nick. 2011. Halal meat converting Aussies: MP, *The West Australian*. 25 November.

Castles, Stephen. 1995. *Multicultural Citizenship*. Canberra: Parliamentary Research Service.

Clemons, Rachel. 2012. A Cagey Business. *Choice*, July: 20–22.

Feldman, Leonard. 2008. Status injustice: The role of the state. In *Adding Insult to Injury: Nancy Fraser Debates her Critics*, ed. Kevin Olson, 225–227. London: Verso.

Fischler, Claude. 1979. Gastro-nomie et gastro-anomie: Sagesse du corps et crise bioculturelle de l'alimentation moderne. *Communications* 31(1): 189–210.

Foucault, Michel. 1991. Governmentality. In *The Foucault Effect: Studies in Governmentality*, ed. G. Burchell, C. Gordon, and P. Miller, 87–104. London: Harvester Wheatsheaf.

Foucault, Michel. 2001. *Power*. London: Penguin.

Fraser, Nancy. 2008. Reframing Justice in a Globalizing World. In *Adding Insult to Injury: Nancy Fraser Debates her Critics*, ed. Kevin Olson. London: Verso.

Golomb, Jacob. 1995. *In Search of Authenticity: Existentialism from Kierkegaard to Camus*. London: Routledge.

Hansard. 2011. Commonwealth of Australia. *Parliamentary Debates*. House of Representatives, 24 November 2011: 13854 (Luke Simpkins MP).

Heath, Elizabeth. 2011. *Eat Streets: A Culinary Adventure through 150 years of Marrickville Council*. Marrickville, NSW: Marrickville Council.

Honneth, Axel. 1995. *The Struggle for Recognition: The Moral Grammar of Social Conflicts*. Cambridge: Polity Press.

Hosen, Nadirsyah. 2012. Hilal and halal: How to manage Islamic pluralism in Indonesia? *Asian Journal of Comparative Law*. 7: 1–18.

Hosking, Richard (ed.). 2006. *Authenticity in the Kitchen: Proceedings of the Oxford Symposium on Food and Cookery 2005*. Totnes, Devon: Prospect.

http://animalliberation.org.au/national-rallies-against-live-export/. Accessed 16 February 2013.

http://ec.europa.eu/agriculture/organic/organic-farming/what-is-organic-farming/organic-certification/index_en.htm. Accessed 22 June 2015.

http://www.corriere.it/english/09_gennaio_27/kebab_lucca_e6c0ee1c-ec86-11dd-be73-00144f02aabc.shtml. Published 27 January 2009, accessed 22 June 2015.

http://www.daff.gov.au/aqis/export/meat/elmer-3/list-islamic-halal-certification. Accessed 12 February 2013.

http://www.dpi.nsw.gov.au/__data/assets/pdf_file/0011/353297/Organic-Standards-and-certification-in-Australia.pdf, dated August 2010. Accessed 22 June 2015.

http://www.nytimes.com/2009/03/13/world/europe/13lucca.html?_r=0. Published 12 March 2009, accessed 22 June 2015.

Kymlicka, Will. 1995. *Multicultural Citizenship: A Liberal Theory of Minority Rights*. Oxford: Clarendon Press.

Lewis, Steve. 2011. Tackle Extreme Islam Before it's too Late, Liberal MPs Warn, *Herald Sun*. 9 February.

Macdonald, Roderick A. 1996. Les Vieilles Gardes. Hypothèses sur l'emergence des normes, l'internormativité et le désordre à travers une typologie des institutions normatives. In *Le droit soluble. Contributions québécoises à l'étude de l'internormativité*, ed. J. -G. Belley. Paris: Librairie générale de droit et de jurisprudence

Macdonald, Roderick A. 1998. Metaphors of multiplicity: Civil society, regimes and legal pluralism. *Arizona Journal of International and Comparative Law* 15

Macdonald, Roderick A. 2009. Human rights and identity – Human identities and rights, *Canadian Issues*. Spring

Maine, Henry. 1917. *Ancient Law*. London: J. M. Dent.

Mohr, Richard. 2013. Rethinking the secular: Religion, ethics and science in food regulation. In *Working papers of the Centre for International Governance and Justice*. March: 1–15. Canberra: RegNet, ANU.

Mohr, Richard, and Nadirsyah Hosen. 2013. Crossing over: Hosts, guests and tastes on a Sydney street. *Law Text Culture* 17: 100–128.

Morris, William (ed.). 1969. *American Heritage Dictionary*. Boston and New York: Houghton Mifflin, 685, 1533.

Olson, Kevin. 2008. Participatory parity and democratic justice. In *Adding Insult to Injury: Nancy Fraser Debates her Critics*, ed. Kevin Olson. London: Verso.

Onfray, Michel. 1995. *La raison gourmande*. Paris: Éditions Grasset & Fasquelle.

Parkins, B. 2015. Restaurant victim of anti-Islamic abuse. *Illawarra Mercury* 13 March. http://www.illawarramercury.com.au/story/2944051/restaurant-victim-of-anti-islamic-abuse/. Accessed 25 April 2015

Potter, Andrew. 2010. *The Authenticity Hoax: How we get lost finding ourselves*. Melbourne: Scribe.

Sheehan, Paul. 2013. Halal Easter eggs and cat food: Where big money meets religion. *Sydney Morning Herald*. 28 March.

Taylor, Charles. 1995. *Philosophical Arguments*. Cambridge, MA: Harvard University Press.

Warde, Alan, and Lydia Martens. 2000. *Eating Out: Social Differentiation, Consumption and Pleasure*. Port Chester, NY: Cambridge University Press.

Weir, Allison. 2013. *Identities and Freedom: Feminist Theory Between Power and Connection*. Oxford: Oxford University Press.

Yasa, Dilvin. 2017. "Wogdom", sandwiches and sushi: A story of three lunch boxes. SBS. http://www.sbs.com.au/food/article/2017/02/13/wogdom-sandwiches-and-sushi-story-three-lunch-boxes. Published 13 February 2017, accessed 30 March 2017.

Richard Mohr is a sociologist (Ph.D. *UNSW*) specialising in legal and urban issues. He is director of Social Research, Policy and Planning, incorporated in Australia. He has been manager of a community health service, a consultant on urban planning and social justice issues, and director of the Legal Intersections Research Centre at the University of Wollongong, Australia, where he taught in the Law Faculty. He edited *Law and Religion in Public Life: The Contemporary Debate*, with Nadirsyah Hosen (Routledge, 2013). Many of his articles from socio-legal and semiotic journals are at https://independentresearcher.academia.edu/RichardMohr

Nadirsyah Hosen is a Senior Lecturer at the Faculty of Law, Monash University. Prior to this role, Nadir was an Associate Professor at the School of Law, University of Wollongong. He researches on Indonesian law and Shari'a law, along with the issue of Law and Religion. He is the author and co-editor of numerous books including *Shari'a and Constitutional Reform in Indonesia* (2007); *Islam in Southeast Asia*, 4 volumes, with Joseph Liow (2010); *a Law and Religion in Public Life: The Contemporary Debate*, with Richard Mohr (2013), *Modern Perspectives on Islamic Law*, with Ann Black and Hossein Esmaeili (2015).

Part V
Consensus

Chapter 11
Aesthetic Mediation: Towards Legitimate Power

Angela Condello

> Images apparently occupy a curious position
> somewhere between the statements of language,
> which are intended to convey a meaning,
> and the things of nature,
> to which we only can give a meaning.
> —Gombrich, Ernst, Hans, Jospeh. 1972. *Introduction: Aims and Limits of Iconology*, in *Symbolic Images. Studies in the Art of the Renaissance*, London: Phaidon Press, 2.

Abstract In this chapter I try to explain why the nation, its unity and democratic legitimacy at a certain moment in history had to become visible, tangible, and more generally perceivable. There were indeed paradigmatic moments in which the nation was conceptualized, embodied and given sensory expression and it is to those events that this chapter refers, while trying to link the mediating power of aesthetics, the interrelation between sensible and intellectual knowledge, and the historicity of the single event and its exemplarity.

11.1 Modernity and Mediation: Ontology of the Nation-State

Within that broad and complex order of things which is reality, there are natural objects and social objects. Natural objects exist independently of our will. Social objects are produced by our will, of which they are projections, linguistically constructed. Yet before being constructed, social objects need to be imagined. The nation state is a social object and thus needs to be imagined to be justified and to exist legitimately. This is the first and main reason why, in the present chapter, I argue that the identity of the nation needs to be understood starting from its fictional nature, thus through its intrinsic link with representation. The ontological status of a social object *as* a nation state does not exist in nature but it is created through a

A. Condello (✉)
Department of Law, Roma Tre University and Department of Philosophy,
University of Torino, Rome and Torino, Italy
e-mail: angela.condello@uniroma3.it

S. Huygebaert et al. (eds.), *Sensing the Nation's Law*, Studies in the History of Law and Justice 13, https://doi.org/10.1007/978-3-319-75497-0_11

declaration on which there is agreement.[1] It is because of this origin that the legitimation of a social object such as the nation state across historical periods needs to be based on imagination. In order to resist challenges and changes of institutional forms and balances, e.g. in order to withstand the challenges of revolutionary disorders, national identity needs to be rooted in its rationality and this rationality becomes clearer and effective when made sensible.

The different perspectives collected in this book touch upon diverse moments of such a representational object, national identity, and do so by making reference to: the consensus that validates the representation, the many forms of legality, the diverse bodies of the power, the objects (tangible, visible, generally perceived) that transport and transfer this identity across historical periods.

If one were to find a *fil rouge* connecting all the chapters of this book, it would be the aesthetics of political and juridical power in the modern state. The sensorial nature of the *res publica*, the monumentality of the decisive constitutional moment described by Stefan Huygebaert, the embodiment of a pluralistic identity in one single object like a coin (Marusek) are foundational instances (moments, or single objects) that have the capacity to represent universal concepts such as national identity.

Now, if we want to explain why power needed and needs to be sensed in order to be understood and legitimized, we need to explain how the nation was initially conceptualized. It is only through a critique of the representative medium that a critical perspective on national identity can be elaborated.

Against this background, the present chapter interrogates the foundation of modern national identity starting from its fictional nature. The modern juridical and political order is mainly based on fiction. The conditions of possibility for the existence of law and politics can be realized only through an act of abstraction producing a concept, "state", which can be above conflicts. Only a general idea such as "state" can provide a fertile reaction to the plurality of needs, desires, and identities that characterize modernity: the era of the proliferation of all discourses and forms of production of truth. The transcendence of the ideas of "law" and "state" is not ontologically complete, but it is instead a regulative obligation produced by a collective intentionality and a series of declarations that legitimize the object state *as* state because of its functions and because the sets of conditions that make it a state.

[1]The philosophical possibility of existence of the nation state is essentially connected to its social production through linguistic operations. As John Searle repeatedly underlines in his work, recalling Austin's theory of *speech acts*, when talking about institutions such as the state we are talking about the mode of existence of social objects such as the United States of America, the San Francisco Forty Niners football team, the University of California and the Squaw Valley Property Owners Association, as well as of such large-scale institutions as money or private property. Social facts, social objects, social processes and events, like citizenship, the value of a twenty-dollar bill, etc. - all these are the product of declarations and of an agreement on their status and on their functions. Searle develops these theories in various articles and monographs, among which in particular see Searle, John, Rogers. 1995. *The Construction of Social Reality*. New York: The Free Press and Searle, John, Rogers. 2010. *Making the Social World: The Structure of Human Civilization*. Oxford: Oxford University Press.

I argue that the concept of "state" originated to *stand for* something else: order, governmentality, law, political obligation, population, territory. And it is hard for only one term, "state", [2] to *stand for* many concepts and values. A legal and a political identity such as the state can be realized only through the consciousness of the prior absence of a legal and political identity; following Carl Schmitt, we could say that only the violence negating law and its existence can actually produce law. Political and juridical power in modernity is always the product of a mediation and of a foundational moment. According to the idea of *political theology*,[3] order is never only created by discursive mediations (*logos*) nor through automatisms (*techné*), but it is always the recognition of an origin that can found the power and on which the power can be based. The foundational myth of the creation of the power determines the political and juridical order and therefore the representation of an original constitutive moment, or of a symbolic object that describes the identity of a state nation, making the identity of the state more tangible, understandable and concrete. The artificial creation of the power, nation and law is thus the product of decision and representation. This representation is nothing but a *mediation*[4]: the rational, constructivist and discursive relationship that subjects constitute with objects and with other subjects in order to produce organized orders within which they can recognize themselves and they can constitute a collective identity.

Representations of constitutional assemblies, of national icons and symbols such as the Marianne discussed by Oliver Watts mediate between immanence and transcendence: in modernity, the intertwinement between the two dimensions becomes fictionalized in the figure of the modern sovereign: that is, of the political, juridical *fictio* embodied by the Leviathan. Such a fiction constitutes the rationalistic solution of the modern political paradigm integrating the rational, projectual and ordinative action of the subject that is legitimized reflexively. If it is only through reason that modern sovereignty can be fictionally represented and articulated, the subject and his experience are always at the center of the construction of every theoretical concept such as state, law, power. Rationalistic modern mediation is thus first of all the product of the work of the subject—primarily the representation, production and construction of the rational image of the world seen from the perspective of the subject.

The objectivity of modern (political and juridical) power can only exist inside a rationalist artificial order. In the frame of the modern rationalist order, politics is conceived as the government of social differences which are ontologically articulated according to a fictional and artificial order (produced by rational, free and equal men), the only political paradigm in which human beings can enjoy their rights.

---

[2]Deriving from the Greek *statòs* and the Latin *status*, the terms means the absence of movement: stability and a certain equilibrium.

[3]Schmitt, Carl. 1996 (1927). *The Concept of the Political*, Chicago: Chicago University Press, 19 and following.

[4]From now on when I use the term 'mediation' I refer to this idea of an aesthetic mediation.

From the Hobbesian perspective of the Leviathan, political mediation is central because men are not naturally or immediately social. Men are always *mediately* social and thus aesthetic mediation helps to fix (through a representation) the common belonging to an artificial structure such as the community or, in its institutionalized version, the nation state. Men are born without measures and forms and they need to refer to abstract measures and forms, such as the concept of "state", in order to coexist peacefully.

In each instance the underlying assumption is that sovereignty represents the possibility of being secure, independent, and autonomous. These measures repeat the archaic belief in the possibility of sovereign solitude—the sense that a sovereign subject or people are capable of being and thriving if they are enisled. Political mediation is the core of modern power, a power which is always mediated. Mediation is thus the only possibility for coexistence. The dimension of mediation cannot be but artificial, mainly formal and formalized, and projected through an agreement between conflicting subjects. Sovereignty self-represents itself in the sovereign power: the will for order and peace of each individual becomes a unitarian form that defines the national political identity through the universal system of obligation of the single individuals towards their self-representation.

11.1.1 Representing a Legal and Political Identity

Carl Schmitt's notion of the aesthetic derives from Immanuel Kant and Friedrich Schiller, for whom the experience of the autonomous work of art gives rise to the free play of our faculties: the work of art involves a purposeful purposelessness—or a decisive indecisiveness—that serves to mediate between the physical realm of nature and the moral realm of freedom. For Schmitt, the idea of the aesthetic is part and parcel of a liberal notion of culture, according to which individuals form themselves just as they artificially create the state. Historically, according to Schmitt, the liberal notion of culture has negated the autonomous realm of politics, which does not involve disinterested contemplation or moral self-fashioning but rather existential conflicts between friend and enemy. Schmitt was fascinated with the late sixteenth and early seventeenth centuries as the period in which the modern notion of the state emerged. He associated this emergence with Jean Bodin and Hobbes, but it was particularly the latter who interested him. Hobbes's great insight, according to Schmitt, was that sovereignty is decisionist: the sovereign is the person who decides the exception.[5] Hobbes was thus preliberal in the sense that, within the Hobbesian commonwealth, law is made by the authority, according to the motto

[5]Schmitt, Carl. 1996 (1927). *The Concept of the Political*, Chicago: Chicago University Press, p.34.

"*auctoritas, non veritas facit legem*".[6] The law is a function of authority, rather than of any disinterested notion of truth. But, according to Schmitt, Hobbes was also protoliberal. In asserting the division between public and private, and between sovereignty and individual conscience, Hobbes articulated the bases of the modern liberal state. Hobbes thus stands on the cusp of the modern era, defined both in terms of its break with older theological conceptions of sovereignty and in terms of its anticipation of the mechanisms of representative and liberal democracy.

The centrality of fiction and representation in modernity is very well described by Schmitt when he talks about the irruption and disruption of time in the theatrical piece (*Hamlet or Hecuba*).[7] Sovereignity in modernity is the product of the irruption of time in the discourse, and the irruption is always concretized in the contingency of a single moment. In *Political Theology*, Schmitt presents an understanding of sovereignty according to which all law is *situational* law: it depends on the sovereign's bringing about a normal situation. There is no a priori legal norm, no natural or moral law to which the sovereign refers; rather the sovereign creates the conditions of security in which law can come into being. Because there can be no law regarding exceptions, exceptions have to be decided by the authority that is above the law (or who constitutes the law), and that authority is the sovereign. This sovereign must be absolute—there can be no liberal or constitutional division of powers. Within such an absolutistic equilibrium, a division of powers would merely obscure or repress the question of sovereignty, the question of who decides. Hobbesian decisionism is thus also a personalism—that is, it locates the power of decision in the person of the sovereign.

The modern State is characterized by a circularity between law, politics and the form of power as it is represented to and by the community. Because of this circularity, I argue that aesthetic mediation is the core of the legitimation of modern sovereignty and thus of modern national identity.

The mediation of modern politics is the construction of political unity in the concept of sovereign state: the obligation of the individual towards the community is realized by the form of the law, in whose universality the parts constituting the universality are identified. The modern, unavoidable, transposition of natural rights in the (conventional and artificial) form of the civil rights—the juridification of the political—is the dimension originating in the individual and taking shape in the general idea of sovereign state. In the theoretical structure of modern thinking there is a logical primacy of the political as a universal and transcendent idea of order: modern sovereignty is absolute and can only be understood if represented in its transcendence.

---

[6]"Authority not truth makes the law".

[7]Schmitt, Carl. 2009 (1956). *Hamlet or Hecuba. The Intrusion of the Time into the Play*, Candor: Telos Press.

11.1.2 The Function of the Image in Modernity

Peter Goodrich writes:

> The image is extant in and through the living, through the exemplary ambulant image, but such charismatic personages in their nobility and majesty are but representative, the mere spectacle of the invisible monuments, the unseen causes that exist ineffably and eternally. Honour, and also its attributes, office, rank, lineage and law are greater than the living—they are inheritances, they survive beyond the grave.[8]

In this quote, Goodrich refers to the image in general, which is variously termed a figure, a body, nature or event. The image is to be understood as a glass, a lens onto *anima legis*, the soul of law that only the wise can see and then only in part. The devise, as a figure and as an image, thus represents a structural and necessarily absent order. The image is the visible and inanimate or painted realm, the symbol that forms part of an order of reason and law and of some sort of regulation of human, social and political life. There is an intrinsic normativity in images. We could say that all nature signifies and law is one of the patterns of that signification.

The core issue of modern political reason is in the connection between representation, signification and the fictional nature of power and authority. Is the subject lost and absorbed in the universal idea of power or is there a tension between the individual subject and the form of power? Is the modern form of power only an abstraction or does it is also entail the possibility of the existence of concrete parts beyond the abstraction? The search for concreteness is always related to the search for form. The form representing the power or the authority is a mediation that produces the political in its interconnection of individual and general dimensions: only through fiction can modern sovereignty be conceived.

11.1.3 The Fiction of Modern Sovereignty[9]

The centrality of representation to the modern concept of power is revealed, for instance, by the frontispiece of the *Leviathan* by Thomas Hobbes (1651), seen in Fig. 11.1. The image replaces the entire idea of an intellectual work through the representation of its main themes. Already Vico in the *Scienza Nuova* had devoted more than forty pages to the explanation of the frontispiece as a metaphor of the ideas contained in the book. Iconology and the studies of emblems reveal as well that images and more generally representations of power can give shape and attribute content to the ideas in a text.

---

[8]Goodrich, Peter. 2013. Devising Law. On the Philosophy of Legal Emblems. *New York Law School Law Review* 133 (57): 138–139.

[9]Agamben, Giorgio. 2015. *Stasis. La Guerra Civile Come Paradigma Politico*, Torino: Bollati Boringhieri. Stasis: Civil War as a Political Paradigm. 2015. Edinburgh University Press.

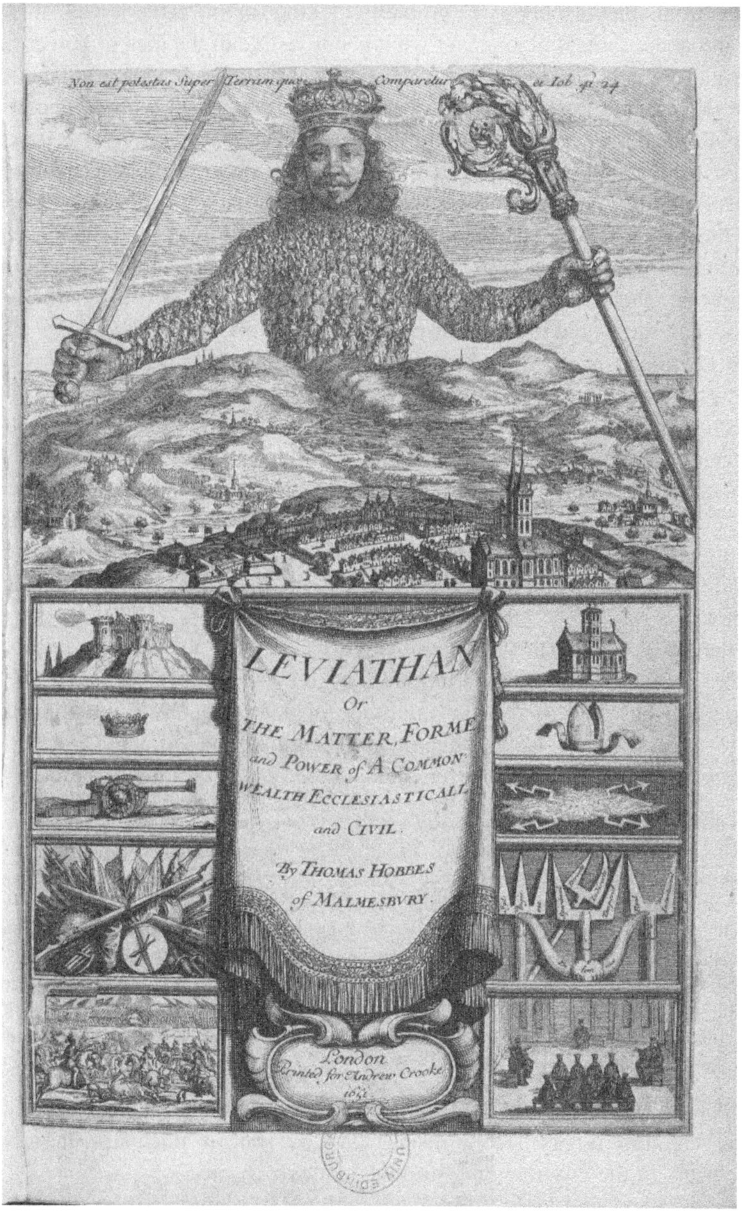

Fig. 11.1 Frontispiece of Thomas Hobbes, *Leviathan or The Matter, Forme and Power of A Common Wealth Ecclesiasticall and Civil*, London, 1651. The University of Edinburgh

In his frontispice, Hobbes was probably looking for an "esoteric veil" that would cover and at the same time uncover what is not visible in the idea of power (an idea that produces both the juridical and the political discourse). A sort of modern *arcanum imperii* that through the figure tells the observer and the reader that sovereignty is a matter of pluralism, multiplication of the subjects involved, connection between secular and sacred power. In the frontispiece of the Leviathan, men look towards the reader/observer, who, suggests Agamben, might be the real sovereign to which the book is dedicated. The Leviathan lives at the doors of the city it is called to govern: the monster is not entirely inside nor entirely outside of the walls of the city: it is part of it, and it is the universal principle that looks over it (the relation between the parts and the whole in modernity is resolved through a fiction).

The Leviathan is an artefact, a machine that moves through complex mechanisms: it is something like an optical device that allows one to build a different perspective on power and its complexity. Optical illusions were widely used in the seventeenth century because they would work well in allowing one to bring a multiplicity into a unity (through an aesthetic mediation based on the use of an image that would symbolically replace the immense number of single instances constituting the universality). The artificial nature of modern sovereignty is thus first and foremost illustrative of, and based on, the mediation between the parts and the whole.

In the body politic, the many converge in the one: this convergence is only possible because of representation and of the perspectival illusion on which modernity is based: how can the multitude of natural bodies populating the city become one entity? It is possible only through fiction. In the *De Cive*, when distinguishing between *populus* (people) and *moltitudo* (multitude), Hobbes writes:

> The people is a unity (*unum quid*), which has one will so that an action can be assigned to it. This cannot apply to the multitude. The people reigns in every state (*populus regnat in omni civitate*): it reigns also in monarchy, for the people wills through the will of one man. The citizens, that is to say the subjects, are the multitude, [...] but the assembly is the people (*curia est populus*). Also in monarchy the subjects are the multitude and, although this is a paradox (*quamquam paradoxum sit*), the king is the people (*rex est populus*). The ignorant and those who do not understand this point speak of the multitude as if it were the people and they therefore say that the commonwealth (*civitas*) revolts against the king, which is impossible [...]. Thus, on the pretext of people, they excite citizens against the city and the multitude against the people.[10]

In representations such as the frontispiece of Hobbes' Leviathan, the body of the Biblical creature is not stable inside the city, but it fluctuates in a sort of "non-place": in the city there are no inhabitants.

The *dissoluta multitudo* (dissolved multitude) represented in the universal political body through a fictional process is similar to the mass of sick people that need to be taken care of in the Bible (book of Isaiah). In the Western philosophical political vocabulary, the terms that refer to a specifically defined group of people

[10]Hobbes, Thomas. 1998 (1642). *De Cive*, Cambridge-New York, Cambridge University Press, 12, 8.

that is named "the people" (*populus*) can also refer to a completely different concept, the unqualified multitude of individuals, since the idea of *populus* itself is based on an original internal divide. On the one hand, it can refer to the *demos* (the people with a coherent identity) and on the other to the *plethos* (the multitude with plural identities which is not qualified). Therefore the very idea of people is directly related to the single individuals that compose the general concept "containing" all of them: the *populus* is the absolutely present that can never be completely present.

11.2 Perceptual Knowledge, Intellectual Knowledge

The formation of an aesthetic consensus is only possible if there is some interconnection between senses (perception) and intellect. And, as a matter of fact, the birth of modern aesthetics corresponds to the beginning of a discourse on such an interconnection. As Baumgarten pointed out already in the eighteenth century, "*Æsthetica est scientia cognitionis sensitivæ*" (aesthetics is the science of perceptual knowledge). The main purpose of modern aesthetics is in fact balancing the perception and the concepts elaborated at an intellectual level. Scientific knowledge and representations (the *aisthetà*) are considered, by the tradition of modern philosophy of aesthetic initiated by Baumgarten, in their more general account—as poles of the opposition with the *noetà*, the conceptual and intellectual forms of knowledge. Perceptual knowledge started to be considered a necessary integration of logic: aesthetics can be considered the science that guides towards a higher level of truth and for this reason perceptual knowledge is the foundation of logical knowledge.

When looking at an image, for instance David's *Tennis Court Oath*, the observing subject is involved also through the emotional and psychical levels of the perceptual experience, levels that interact with the objective and logical level of the information that the observer has of the event represented and of its historical relevance. The perceptual level of knowledge is what Baumgarten names the "*analogon rationis*" (what is analogous to reason and logical knowledge).

Because of the importance attributed to perceptual experience by modern aesthetics, the single elements of the single events become focal. As a matter of fact, in the eighteenth century every representation was a representation of one or more particular men, trees, or elements of reality: figurative representation is thus characterized by determined details capable of recalling the reality of singular elements. All the articulations of the aesthetic phenomena into some form of artistic representation, as the ones considered in this book, are legitimated by their historical materiality and by the concrete occurrence they relate to. The single facts and events, in themselves, have a paradigmatic force.

In this volume, one might say that we do not find "ordinary" representations, but representations that have a specifically symbolic power and that are capable of conveying universal ideas such as state and nation and identity into one image.

11.2.1 Exemplary Representation

The paradigmatic force of single events has an exemplary value. Exemplarity is what makes the single event the paradigmatic event, by linking the concreteness of the specific instance and the universality of the value that is transmitted. To recall the aforementioned example, in the *Tennis Court Oath* many individuals are represented while acting in a *determined* place on a *determined* date. All these determined elements, because of the exemplarity acquired historically by the *Oath*, became symbols of a collective identity being coined, of indeterminacy and chaos translated into the identity of revolutionary France. The exemplarity of the exemplary event is due to the fact that an example is something concrete that performs the functions of something abstract and that does so in a particularly paradigmatic way capable of illustrating—through its *being*—how something *should be*. It is what theoretically could be the "whatever case", but it is capable of producing a discourse that involves the single case and the law, the particular and the general, the accidental and the necessary. A discourse connecting, for instance, the event that took place in the Tennis Court and the concept that the author wanted to represent through that single pivotal event, that in history meant the first time that French citizens formally stood in opposition to Louis XVI.

A good example should have no intrinsic necessity; it must always carry an element of "whateverness" for this randomness to become something authoritative and normative. It happens that a case becomes famous—a *Fall* or an *affaire*. In short, something that exceeds the general level of the abstract norm and that institutes a new one, and is therefore a new normality.

This intrinsic duplicity lying in exemplarity struck Kant to the point that he proposed a terminological distinction between *Beispiel* and *Exempel*.

> Instance [*Beispiel*], a German word, is commonly used as synonymous with 'example' [*Exempel*], but the two words really do not have the same meaning. To take something as an *example* and to bring forward an *instance* to clarify an expression are altogether different concepts. An example is a particular case of a *practical* rule, insofar as this rule represents an action as practicable or impracticable, whereas an *instance* is only a particular (*concretum*), represented in accordance with concepts as contained under a universal (*abstractum*), and is a presentation of a concept merely for theory.[11]

This distinction is rather complicated and not very convincing, showing the transcendental philosopher's unease before the intertwining of empirical and transcendental, concrete and abstract, ordinary and extraordinary, normal and normative characterising the example.

[11]Kant, Immanuel. 1998 (1797). *Groundwork of the Metaphysic of Morals*, Cambridge: Cambridge University Press, Ak VI: 479.

11.2.2 Abstract, Concrete

An exemplary representation must necessarily be an individual case, but precisely because of its individual character it counts as general. An example is abstract in that it is concrete: it is a part, extracted from a series (real or virtual) that, precisely for this extraction, allows for an abstraction—i.e. the transition from the concrete case to the series it refers to. Every time we are faced with a case, if we consider it as an example, we cease to treat it as a simple individual, but seek the series to which it belongs. Let us consider again the *Tennis Court Oath* representing the Oath: because of the exemplarity of the Oath that emerges through the Oath (sketch), as discussed by Mark Antaki and Catherine Le Guerrier's chapter, we do not consider such an event as an ordinary single event. We consider it as the symbol of a new political paradigm. The magic, so to speak, is that nothing outwardly changes in the individual case when, if considered an example, it passes from being concrete to being abstract.

This magic has not gone unnoticed and is at the centre of a dispute between Locke and Berkeley about the general idea. If any experience is always a particular experience, Locke asks, how is it that we can have general ideas, such as the general idea of a triangle? Locke imagines a kind of overlapping: you see an equilateral triangle, then a scalenon, then a rectangle. At the end, the general idea of triangle comes out, namely, a triangle which is "neither Oblique nor Rectangle, neither Equilateral, Equicrural nor Scalenon; but all and none of these at once".[12] Berkeley mocks him: what kind of triangle would that be, one that is large, small, equilateral, scalenon, all of these and none of them? The latter expression ("all and none") is what he finds particularly funny and incongruous, to the point that he quotes Locke's passage in the Introduction to the *Principles of Human Knowledge* (§ 13).

The alternative proposed by Berkeley is called *diagram*: the idea remains particular, but it refers to something general. Berkeley, indeed, is talking about the example. The most remarkable thing is that Berkeley manages to solve a very serious problem (the transition from the concrete to the abstract and vice versa) with great economy. Quite the opposite of Kant who instead, in the *Critique of Pure Reason*, got lost in the grueling problem of schematism, the "hidden art" allowing intellectual concepts to refer to individual cases. This is fine for concepts such as "substance" and "cause" (that become sensitized through the scheme of permanence and succession in time), but doesn't quite work for empirical concepts.

For example, take the schema of the concept of "dog", to which Kant makes a misguided reference in the chapter on schematism: "The concept of a dog signifies a rule according to which my imagination can trace, delineate, or draw a general outline, figure, or shape of a four-footed animal without being restricted to any single and particular shape supplied by experience" (A 141/B 180). What would the scheme of a dog be? What could be the way to construct it so as to recognize the dogs we experience through it? If we chose the feature of "having four feet" as a

[12] Locke, John, *Essay on Human Understanding*, 1689, IV.vii.9.

"construction method" as Kant suggests, I could mistake dogs for any other quadruped, as well as with tables and chairs.

In the *Critique of Judgment* Kant comes out of the impasse. In § 59, he distinguishes pure concepts, which become sensitized through schemes, and empirical concepts, which instead become sensitized through examples: we take a single dog and we generalize, just as with Berkeley's diagram. This is a simple operation, we do it every day, and yet it involves a very sophisticated form of abstraction, a complicated triangulation: we take a member of a series, and then we employ it as a norm (i.e. we grant it a normative function) to recognize similar cases.

11.2.3 Particular, General

An examplary representation, if it be such, must not only prove to be exemplary but also indicate, at the same time, an ought, an end, even an unattainable peak: in short, something that is anything *but* ordinary. There is a very complex logic at work here, where the alternative between *being* and *ought* exists in one exemplary case.

Let us think of the semantics of *model*. In David's painting, we are in front of a model of an oath. It is nothing more than an event, an oath. Unlike the sample, the model has two peculiarities. First, it cannot be a fragment ("a sample of oath", etc.), but claims to be the reproduction of something existing, perhaps aimed at the manufacture of something (for example, there used to be models of clothes, back when people sewed them themselves). Secondly, following the logic of exemplary examples, the model as a typical example can become an ideal, a purpose, a goal, a standard.

This circumstance is particularly evident in that very peculiar example we call *masterpiece*. What is a masterpiece? In craft schools of the past, the masterpiece was the work that the student had to realize to demonstrate some competence. One can therefore believe that most of the time they were quite ordinary works, that is, anything but masterpieces in the current sense of the term. Masterpieces are so called because they are placed at the beginning of a chain of imitations, and maybe invent a whole genre. In liberal arts, synonymous of 'masterpiece' is 'classic': there are various criteria according to which a piece of art can be considered a classic. On the one hand, the *objective value* of an artefact; on the other hand, tradition. A classic is what is beautiful unquestionably, something which is so beautiful that nobody would state it is not beautiful. On the value of a classic there is a collective agreement: historically it is has been defined as a classic, as a fundamental reference of beauty inside a determined cultural community.

The implicit assumption of these imitations is that they will never become masterpieces, and that, if it did, they would cease to belong to the previous series, giving rise to a new one. The opposite of the masterpiece, perhaps a failed masterpiece—a bit like the defeated general, Crassus or Charles of Austria—is the *type*, a minor result of the logic of exemplarity. The type has a unique characteristic: that of being something empirical that has a transcendental value.

Types are for instance the images reproduced on the American coins: a typical kind of tree, a typical animal. The exemplarity of the type is very different from the exemplarity of the *Tennis Court Oath* or of the constitutional moments described by Stefan Huygebaert. Now it is quite obvious that the particular has a different status from the universal. What counts for "exemplary" in these two cases is not directly related to the traits of the individual characters or places or spaces represented: what really counts is the *mythos*, that is to say the story, the sequence of events, what Aristotle in the *Nicomachean Ethics* defined as *mimesis praxeos* (the mimesis of action).

The concrete elements (the character, the individual story) *transcend* their contingency and they acquire a universal meaning. Let us think to the classics of world literature: they intend to be exemplary and their exemplarity is mainly related to their capacity to "be re-used", that is to say to the capacity to count and to be valid also in later contexts. So, if a narrative can be valid beyond the context in which it was produced, it's not because of the answers it gives, but because of the questions it asks and because of how it is accepted in a specific concept: an exemplary representation concerns conflicts that transcend the specificity of the singular contexts and that are recurrent. The *Tennis Court Oath* in its specificity became the symbol of the will to fashion a new collective identity in opposition to a precedent order: it became a *canon*. Interestingly, the semantics of the Greek word (κανών) would originally refer to a straight pole used to measure lenghts or distances. In musical theory, κανών refers historically to a monotonous instrument used in order to measure the mathematical relationships corresponding to the intervals between different volumes. In architecture theory, κανών would guarantee precision in measurements and through the architectural use the word became a synonym for the research of accuracy in every aspect of life. For instance, when Policletus became a model for other artists, the Doryphoros was called κανών by his successors because it was the perfect exemplification of the aesthetic doctrine of their leader. All these meanings were transferred in Christian literature until the Middle Ages and the Modern Age: the Latin word for κανών is "*regula*" or "*norma*" (rule, norm). The artefact that becomes a canon formulates a stylistic ideal by giving it shape: it is performative, it introduces the model by embodying that very model.

11.2.4 The Historicity of the Representation: The Micro and the Macro Perspective[13]

An exemplary case is a case that can be generalized: an example must necessarily be an individual, but precisely because of this individuality it counts as general.

[13]When Discussing the Two Perspectives on History, I Mainly Refer to Ginzburg, Carlo. 1993. Microhistory: Two or Three Things that I Know About It. *Critical Inquiry* 20 (1):10–35. and to Ginzburg, Carlo, 1980 (1976). *the Cheese and the Worms: The Cosmos of a Sixteenth Century Miller*, Baltimore: the Johns Hopkins University Press.

The exemplary case, as stated before, becomes such by means of the narrative form, which is a necessary mediation between individual traits (a name, a place, a time), and similar traits in other existences (other names, other places, other times) that are recognisable because of the narrative form. The individual narrative *becomes* an *exemplum* yet being a particular narrative.

The singularity represented through the aesthetics of the microhistorical event that becomes paradigmatic recalls the irruption of the single event in history. The performativity of the single event is based on the aesthetics of "the moment", "the detail" capable of replacing a definition. The political theology underlying the single event that stands for the idea of nation, of state, of sovereignty, of constitutional power explains the performativity of the singularity that acquires an exemplary force. Even more than *Leviathan*, Hamlet has a long history as the avatar of modernity, particularly in Germany.

Goethe, G. W. F. Hegel, Schiller, Friedrich Schlegel and August Wilhelm Schlegel all offered interpretations of Hamlet as a symbol of modern self-consciousness divided from itself. Such self-division pointed in two directions. On the one hand, Hamlet represented what Hegel described as the modern subject in his weakness of irresolution, in a condition of doubt and perplexity about the reasons that are to guide decisions. The theological nature of the choice of the event to be represented is based on the fragmentation of modern subjectivity, where the *many* cannot be represented and therefore the single event (or the single fictional person, like the Leviathan) stands instead of the multitude.

The single event and the singularity that can stand for a collective identity are a sort of aesthetic *Jetztzeit*: the actual time, the contemporary, the "here and now" described by Walter Benjamin in his *On the Concept of History*, and referred to by Desmond Manderson in his chapter.[14]

In his *Thesis 3* (*Nothing has to be given as lost to history*) Benjamin states:

> The chronicler, who recounts events without distinguishing between the great and small, thereby accounts for the truth, that nothing which has ever happened is to be given as lost to history. Indeed, the past would fully befall only a resurrected humanity. Said another way: only for a resurrected humanity would its past, in each of its moments, be citable. Each of its lived moments becomes a citation *à l'ordre du jour* [order of the day] – whose day is precisely that of the Last Judgement.

This thesis underlines the centrality of the single event in history that can acquire, according to the perspective, a weight, a relevance it did not have before: "nothing which has ever happened is to be given as lost to history" suggests that

[14]Benjamin, Walter. 2009 (1940). On The Concept of History. Theses on the Philosophy of History, in *CreateSpace Independent Publishing Platform*.

every single event might have the potential to become an exemplary event. It is the modern decision-making process, the performative act of choice of one among the many that transforms a singularity into a "universality" for various reasons. The single event becomes the pivotal event capable of coining a collective identity, the French, the Belgian, the Italian or the American, because of the performative potential of the individual that can stand instead of a universal value. The single image thus becomes paradigmatic: the image of the past is at the core of the reconstruction of the past.

Let us consider Benjamin's *Thesis 5* (*Images of the past. Images are central for the reconstruction of the past*):

> The true picture of the past *whizzes* by. Only as a picture, which flashes its final farewell in the moment of its recognizability, is the past to be held fast. "The truth will not run away from us"—this remark by Gottfried Keller denotes the exact place where historical materialism breaks through historicism's picture of history. For it is an irretrievable picture of the past, which threatens to disappear with every present, which does not recognize itself as meant in it.

The images of the past run away, if not escape; our capacity to grasp their sense depends directly on the use we make of them. The images reproduce a moment that historically acquired a symbolic meaning and that stands for a universal idea. History is not a continuous chain of events but it is constituted by a series of "here and now"(s); in fact, in *thesis 14* (*History is a construction whose place is not homogeneous and empty time, but the time full of actuality*) history is described as a non-homogeneous series made of single instances of here-and-now (the so-called "*Jetztzeit*") that can significant[15]:

> History is the object of a construction whose place is formed not in homogenous and empty time, but in that which is fulfilled by the here-and-now [*Jetztzeit*]. For Robespierre, Roman antiquity was a past charged with the here-and-now, which he exploded out of the continuum of history. The French revolution thought of itself as a latterday Rome. It cited ancient Rome exactly the way fashion cites a past costume. Fashion has an eye for what is up-to-date, wherever it moves in the jungle [Dickicht: maze, thicket] of what was. It is the tiger's leap into that which has gone before. Only it takes place in an arena in which the ruling classes are in control. The same leap into the open sky of history is the dialectical one, as Marx conceptualized the revolution.

Contingency is the grammar of the formation of history, which is a chain of single significative events that occur in the "here and now". The representation connects not only the many identities in one single and more universal identity (the national identity), but it also connects the single events with the more complex chain of events that is history.[16]

---

[15]According to what Stefan Huygebaert writes in his chapter, not only do images re-produce a meaningful moment, but - through the reproduction - they actually "produce" it anew. We did not know the moment *in that way* before that specific reproduction.

[16]In *The Structures of Everyday Life*, Fernand Braudel gives his purpose as introducing everyday life into the domain of history: see Braudel, Fernand. 1981. *The Structures of Everyday Life: Civilization and Capitalism*, New York: Harper and Row.

When writing microhistory, finding relevant traits is a constant struggle for historians and a major problem for the author of a microhistory is selecting a subject suitable for study, the individual or event capable of representing a concept, such as national identity.

Macrohistories require a huge amount of data to cover such a wide scope and a paucity of information in one area can badly damage the overall argument. Historians therefore use the techniques of social science to reach estimates with which they fill the gaps in verifiable data and from which they reach more overarching conclusions. Braudel does not only use such techniques but also explains them at length.[17] Through the examination of the single biographical details, of the single man, the symbol is activated and it is in that symbol that the collective intentionality is performed.

11.2.5 The Eruption of Microhistory

In his famous essay *Clues*,[18] Ginzburg discusses the relevance of details in art history in particular with reference to the birth of an epistemological model for the recognition of art pieces based on signs rather than on general definitions, general principles and general rules. Ginzburg writes about a form of knowledge characterized by the ability to construct an intricated reality (that could not be experienced directly) from experiential data and details. When explaining that all signs are mediations between knowledge and reality, he quotes a renowned art historian, Edgar Wind: “our inadvertent little gestures reveal our character far more authentically than any formal posture that we may formally prepare”.[19] This revelation is possible because every designation (*signatura*) implies the inclusion of both knowledge and discourses on the one hand, and of reality, on the other.[20] This interconnection between thought, knowledge and signs is characterized by the necessity to categorize and control reality in order to govern it. Ginzburg shows how a specific knowledge is produced by signs: a knowledge is “characterized by the ability to construct from apparently insignificant experimental data a complex reality that could not be experienced directly. Also, the data is always arranged by the observer in such a way as to produce a narrative sequence”.[21] To enforce his thesis he refers to the examplary activity of hunting: hunters follow traces (clues) that are, as a matter of fact, signs. Around these signs, they reconstruct possible patterns of knowledge (“*this* could have happened”, “*that* could have happened”).

[17]Braudel, Fernand, 1981, *ibidem*.

[18]Ginzburg, Carlo. 1989 (1986). Clues. Roots of an Evidential Paradigm. In *Clues, Myths, and the Historical Method*. Baltimore: Johns Hopkins University Press.

[19]Wind, Edgar. 1985. *Art and Anarchy*. Noyes: Northwestern University Press, 38.

[20]Ginzburg, *ibidem*, 101 and following.

[21]Ginzburg, *ibidem*, 103.

Most likely, Ginzburg suggests, the idea of narration may have originated in a hunting society because of the need of relating the experience of deciphering tracks with real events. Signs have been central to human knowledge because they are the traces that represent synthetically an event or a series of events by "bearing" a meaning, a meaning that is attributed to them because of the necessity of understanding and explaining them. According to this idea, the hunter would have been the first to narrate a story because he alone was able to read, in the silence, in the nearly imperceptible tracks left by his prey, a coherent sequence of events.

Ginzburg's theory of the *signatura rerum* that constituted ordinary language is that every scientific paradigm based on signs (language, law) originates from a necessity to fix meanings inside an order: the history of concepts is the history of words and meaning is the product of necessity.[22]

11.3 Conclusion. Grasping, Representing and Extending the Decisive Moment

The exemplary artefact has the capacity to constitute an identity because in the representation, the relationship between reality and fiction makes it possible to conventionally institutionalize a shared message in the sign (the micro-historical event). The visual representation, be it a painting, a sculpture, a building, a motto, or a tag on a wall, "collects" more than one signification and shares it continuously. Through the mediation of the artefact, the nation, its unity and its identity become perceivable. Having rejected the possibility of a politics based on a single theory that captures the truth of all social events, modernity turns towards a paradigm based on fiction and on the primacy of representation. Even the political is an instance of the sublime and thus art acquires an entirely different function. The latter is complexly composed of singular events that cannot be represented accurately by any rational theory. Only representation can do justice to single events because every representation reproduces a single instance and is exemplary inasmuch as it remains specific and unique.

The representation of legal and political events that relate to the production of a national identity calls attention to the limits of representation and of its affective force: shapes and colours can act as tensors within the system of signification that the artwork forms. Unlike more rigidly structured objects, artworks more readily release their affective energy into different systems of interpretation, reception and influence. In artistic representation, affects are inscribed on a surface without being strictly controlled by an actively willing and organizing subject.

[22]The connection between meaning and necessity has been a central issue in philosophy of language since the publication of Rudolph Carnap's *Meaning and Necessity: A Study in Semantics and Logic* (University of Chicago Press, 1947). Another fundamental contribution in the field is Kripke's *Naming and Necessity* (Harvard University Press, 1980).

Through representations, various levels of human cognition can be reached. Art can provide knowledge of what it is like to be a certain sort of person, or to be in certain sorts of situations, and what it is like to have certain kinds of emotions or experiences: artistic mediation is capable of educating emotions. If art at least partially constructs culture, we can learn about aspects of a specific culture through its art. And art has even been seen as a source of propositional knowledge of different kinds: artistic expression is a part of life, rather than something through which we learn about life.

Arthur Danto argued that art differs from real things by being embedded in the history and theory of art. What makes the difference between art and reality is the consciousness of the difference between reality and art. On the contrary, the objects that constitute reality outside of the artistic realm are such independently of the historical context and of the artistic discourses. A tree and a chair are not a tree and a chair because they are embedded within the history and theory of trees.

These relationships are explored by David Summers in *Real Metaphor*. Real metaphors are substitutes for real things, as opposed to what Summers calls 'images', for which resemblance is the key to their pictorial content. Substitutes, or real metaphors, create instead "subjunctive spaces", in which desires are fulfilled, created and sustained through their capacity to serve as substitutes. Real metaphors, such as paintings, are themselves real objects, and subjunctive spaces are real spaces, where paintings become substitutes for real things. Paintings become substitutes partly by their ability to transform the spaces in which they exist, by making them into spaces where it is appropriate to do things, and not merely to look and contemplate visual forms. A typical Western attitude since Plato has been to consider images as substitutes for real things: as something that has a "second-class" status. Images are not as real, as true, as powerful as their originals, and so they are condemned as being weak imitations of the real thing, with a correlative tendency to confuse us about the nature of truth and reality. But what this tradition has ignored is that substitutes extend the power of the original: a bust of the emperor in every province, a painting of the Virgin Mary on every altarpiece, portraits of the ancestors in every vestibule, or, as analysed by Anne Wagner in her chapter, a picture of the president in every post office: these imitations produce new spaces of action for the subjects and objects represented. Images are a device for making something present by functioning as a substitute for that thing. No one can be in two places at the same time, but through substitutes, one can transform multiple spaces at the same time as sites for human actions.[23]

Paintings, sculptures, representations, as real metaphors, create subjunctive spaces and reinforce certain habitual modes of acting and thinking. The distance between substitute and substituted object is not the distance between appearance and reality, or between truth and a piece of possible evidence. The distance is between the viewer and objects that relate to our desires, and the desires are

[23]Summers, David. 1991. Real Metaphor. In *Visual Theory: Painting and Interpretation*, eds. Norman Bryson, Michael Ann Holly, and Keith Moxey, 231–259. New York: Harper Collins.

sustained and satisfied by substitutes for those objects, substitutes that take the form of representations of them.

Artefacts like paintings, sculptures, buildings, coins (as, for example, discussed by Sarah Marusek), and monuments (as discussed by Stefania Gialdroni)—but also food (as discussed by Richard Mohr and Nadirsyah Hosen), and even mottos such as "in God we trust" (as discussed by Paolo Napoli) can represent the universality of a historical moment and of abstract concepts such as "state" and national "identity": they "capture" and grasp a passing moment and, through their reproduction, they are capable of extending the characters of the moment also beyond it. For instance, the *Tennis Court* becomes the icon for the formation of an identity from the multitude of classes and social paradigms—against the king. The very word "monument" derives from "*monère*" (to remember, to let someone know) and the termination "*mèntum*" indicates the means through which we remember. Therefore, the monument fixes an instant in its most exemplary form, be it a gesture or a collective action of a group of people (in the Tennis Court, or in the Parliament).

Any artistic representation aimed at fashioning a collective juridical and political identity orients the body politic towards reality and social spaces and, in this way, makes it possible to acknowledge and to classify the world. The *substratum* of the artefacts considered in this volume is what Summers would name "real metaphors": artefacts to which we assign a meaning and that are then displaced to new contexts and asked to stand for a meaning (for instance, the image of the Tennis Court Oath stands for the concept of "French revolutionary identity"). The artistic representations of historical moments, be they figurative or symbolic, *tokens* (the single event, like the Tennis Court Oath or the Belgian constitutional moment) or *types* (the oak or the buffalo in the American coin)—integrate the social and the political differentiations initiated in the ancient world by sacred temples and sites. In modernity, collective identity is represented through the detail and in the details: the nation would not exist nor resist naturally if it wasn't artificially produced and maintained through aesthetic experience.

References

Agamben, Giorgio. 2015. *Stasis. La guerra civile come paradigma politico*. Torino: Bollati Boringhieri.

Baumgarten. 1986. Alexander Gottlieb, *Aesthetica*, 1750.

Benjamin, Walter. 2009 (1940). On the concept of history. Theses on the Philosophy of History, in *CreateSpace Independent Publishing Platform*.

Braudel, Fernand. 1981. *The Structures of Everyday Life: Civilization and Capitalism*. New York: Harper and Row.

Carnap, Rudolph. 1947. *Meaning and Necessity: A Study in Semantics and Logic*. Chicago: University of Chicago Press.

Ginzburg, Carlo. 1980 (1976). *The Cheese and the Worms: The Cosmos of a Sixteenth Century Miller*, Baltimore: The Johns Hopkins University Press.

Ginzburg, Carlo. 1989 (1986). Clues. Roots of an evidential paradigm. In *Clues, Myths, and the Historical Method*. Baltimore: Johns Hopkins University Press.
Ginzburg, Carlo. 1993. Microhistory: Two or three things that i know about it. *Critical Inquiry* 20 (1): 10–35.
Goodrich, Peter. 2013. Devising law. On the philosophy of legal emblems. *New York Law School Law Review* 133 (57): 138–139.
Gombrich, Ernst, and Joseph Hans. 1972. Introduction: Aims and limits of iconology. In *Studies in the Art of the Renaissance*, ed. Symbolic Images. London: Phaidon Press.
Hobbes, Thomas. 1998 (1642). *De Cive*, Cambridge, New York: Cambridge University Press.
Kant, Immanuel. 1998 (1797). *Groundwork of the Metaphysic of Morals*, Cambridge: Cambridge University Press.
Kripke, Saul. 1980. *Naming and Necessity*. Cambridge: Harvard University Press.
Locke, John, 1689, *Essay on Human Understanding*.
Schmitt, Carl. 1996 (1927). *The Concept of the Political*, Chicago: Chicago University Press.
Schmitt, Carl. 2009 (1956). *Hamlet or Ecuba. The Intrusion of the Time into the Play*, Candor: Telos Press.
Searle, John Rogers. 1995. *The Construction of Social Reality*. New York: The Free Press.
Searle, John Rogers. 2010. *Making the Social World: The Structure of Human Civilization*. Oxford: Oxford University Press.
Summers, David. 1991. Real metaphor. In *Visual Theory: Painting and Interpretation*, ed. N. Bryson, M. A. Holly, and K. Moxey, 231–259. New York: Harper Collins.
Wind, Edgar. 1985. *Art and Anarchy*. Noyes: Northwestern University Press.

Angela Condello is Temporary Lecturer at the University of Roma Tre and Fellow Researcher at the University of Torino where she also directs LabOnt Law. She cooperates with the Human Rights Committee of the Italian Senate of the Republic. In 2015 she was Fernand Braudel Fellow (EHESS, CENJ) and in 2014 she was a Fellow at the Käte Hamburger Kolleg "Law as Culture". Until 2016 she was Guest Professor at the Law School of the University of Ghent. She teaches Law and Humanities at Roma Tre. She organizes the International Roundtables for the Semiotics of Law and is in the boards of Law Text Culture, Law & Literature. She is Associate Editor of *Brill Research Perspectives in Art and Law*. She recently received a *Jean Monnet award*.

The manufacturer's authorised representative in the EU is Springer Nature Customer Service Centre GmbH, Europaplatz 3, 69115 Heidelberg, Germany. If you have any concerns regarding our products, please contact ProductSafety@springernature.com

Printed and bound by CPI Group (UK) Ltd, Croydon, CR0 4YY
30/09/2026
02225659-0008